APPLIED STATISTICS

Business and Management Research

Andrew R. Timming

Los Angeles | London | New Delhi
Singapore | Washington DC | Melbourne

For my Dad

Los Angeles | London | New Delhi
Singapore | Washington DC | Melbourne

SAGE Publications Ltd
1 Oliver's Yard
55 City Road
London EC1Y 1SP

SAGE Publications Inc.
2455 Teller Road
Thousand Oaks, California 91320

SAGE Publications India Pvt Ltd
B 1/I 1 Mohan Cooperative Industrial Area
Mathura Road
New Delhi 110 044

SAGE Publications Asia-Pacific Pte Ltd
3 Church Street
#10-04 Samsung Hub
Singapore 049483

Editor: Ruth Stitt
Assistant editor: Jessica Moran
Production editor: Imogen Roome
Copyeditor: QuADS Prepress Pvt. Ltd.
Proofreader: Brian McDowell
Marketing manager: Kimberley Simpson
Cover design: Jennifer Crisp
Typeset by: C&M Digitals (P) Ltd, Chennai, India

Library of Congress Control Number: 2021948596

British Library Cataloguing in Publication data

A catalogue record for this book is available from the British Library.

ISBN 978-1-4739-4744-3
ISBN 978-1-4739-4745-0 (pbk)

CONTENTS

ABOUT THE AUTHOR

Andrew R. Timming is Professor of Human Resource Management and Organizational Psychology at RMIT University, also known as the Royal Melbourne Institute of Technology, in Australia. He holds a Ph.D. degree from the University of Cambridge, England. He is the inaugural Registered Reports Editor at *Human Resource Management Journal*. His previous book, *Human Resource Management and Evolutionary Psychology: Exploring the Biological Foundations of Managing People at Work* was published in 2019. Professor Timming is mainly known for his research on tattoos and is currently researching mental illness in the workplace. When he's not working in the office, he can usually be found working at home.

ACKNOWLEDGEMENTS

No one is born with a built-in knowledge of statistics. We gain that knowledge from others. I want to start by thanking all my math teachers, from elementary school in Wisconsin through to graduate school at Cambridge. Was I the best math student? No. Did I enjoy math as a child? Also no. But I worked hard and persevered in the end. This book is living proof that children who hate math can grow up to love it, as I have in recent years. I thank my family, and especially my wife, for providing me with a supportive and nurturing home environment as I wrote this tome. I hope my children read this book someday when they enter higher education. I'm quite sure the massive royalties I make from this book will be just enough for them to buy the textbook for themselves. Finally, I also want to thank the good folks at Sage for their patience as I completed this book. You'd be shocked at the number of tasks in life that take precedence of writing an applied statistics textbook.

Prof. Andrew R. Timming
Melbourne
August 2021

ONLINE RESOURCES

Visit **https://study.sagepub.com/timming** to access a range of online resources designed to support teaching and aid learning. *Applied Statistics: Business and Management Research* is accompanied by:

For Lecturers

A **Tutor's Guide** containing chapter summaries and ideas for tutorials and seminars.

PowerPoints that can be adapted and edited to suit specific teaching needs.

For Students

WERS Datasets that can be downloaded and used alongside exercises in the book.

PREFACE

So, math isn't really your thing, eh? Well, you're not alone, and you've come to the right place. This non-technical, introductory statistics textbook was designed and written for students and scholars just like you. If you are studying or researching in the following fields (in no particular order of importance), you will benefit from this concise textbook: business administration, management, marketing, human resource management and employment relations, organizational behavior, industrial-organizational psychology, the sociology of work, and industrial engineering, among others. Postgraduate students (including MBAs) are encouraged to read through the whole book, whereas undergraduate students can satisfy their intellectual curiosity by primarily focusing on Parts I, II, and III. Additionally, doctoral students and established academics interested in learning "practical stats" could benefit as well.

This book is organized into four parts. Part I discusses the foundations of quantitative research in business and management studies, broadly conceived. Don't skip this part. It will help you to understand concepts discussed later in this book. Part II looks at the most important statistical tests we use to compare mean scores across different groups or categories. Part III examines two of the most popular non-parametric and correlational tests. In Part IV, we move on to discuss key multivariate methods of data analysis. Please don't panic if you don't understand what the terms "bivariate" and "multivariate" mean. We'll get there soon enough. Trust me, I'm a doctor! By the end of this book, you'll be a statistics pro.

This is what you'll get if you decide to continue reading. For starters, you'll get a concise, practical explanation of how to carry out successful quantitative research in the area of management and organization studies, broadly conceived. There will be some basic mathematics, but these will be explained on a step-by-step, line-by-line basis so you won't get lost. Each chapter is expressly designed and written for the non-mathematician, and practical examples and real data are used to illustrate the methods.

We will be using the United Kingdom's 2011 Workplace Employment Relations Survey (WERS). "Survey" is actually a misnomer. The Workplace Employment Relations "survey" actually consists of four inter-related surveys: a survey of managers, a survey of employees, a survey of employee representatives, and a financial survey. We will be using the survey of managers (where the unit of analysis is the organization) and the survey of employees (where the unit of analysis is the employee) in this book. The WERS data are freely available through the Data Archive (www.data-ar-chive.ac.uk), but I've also made parts of the dataset available on the companion website, located at https://study.sagepub.com/timming.

To analyze these real-world data, we will be using a statistical software package called IBM SPSS. Most universities have a license to use this software. It is one of the most commonly used programs for the analysis of statistical data in the world and a good way to introduce yourself to data science. Best of all, it does all of the maths for you at the click of a button! You only need to know how to interpret the results and have a basic understanding of what's going on when you click "Run."

Once you master the material in this book, you can move on to learn more advanced statistics using languages like R and Python.

Are you ready to learn statistics, then? Okay. Let's do this.

PART I
FOUNDATIONS

You're probably keen to dive right into the statistics, but I urge you to be patient. Just like Luke Skywalker wasn't ready to face Darth Vader until he first learned the ways of the force, you're not ready to start doing stats until you've learned the ways of statistical inference and methodology. So let's start with the basics and then move onto the more complex methods. I think this underscores why you should read this book linearly, from Chapter 1 to Chapter 12, rather than jumping around from chapter to chapter. Each chapter builds on crucial knowledge learned from the previous one. Therefore, you ought not to skip any material.

Part I will focus on building up your knowledge and skills in general research methods, basic statistics, and the IBM SPSS Statistics Software (SPSS®) environment, culminating with a discussion of the principle of statistical inference, which is basically the theory that underlies all of statistics. Take your time and digest these chapters. They will provide you with a broad understanding of the foundations of applied statistics.

Chapter 1 starts with a look at general research methods. It distinguishes between two fundamental epistemologies: qualitative and quantitative research. It then looks at the processes of quantification (i.e., turning ideas and concepts into numbers) and survey design as well as item construction. It then discusses the different types of variables, followed by a brief explanation of reliability, validity, and measurement error. The chapter rounds out with a description of different types of survey administration and sampling.

Chapter 2 is designed to introduce you to the SPSS environment. SPSS is a statistical package that is used to carry out the simple and more advanced statistical tests you will learn throughout this book. It's not the only software out there, but it is fairly user-friendly and a good program to use if you have no previous knowledge of coding or programming. It uses a simple 'point and click' method of data analysis and does most of the heavy lifting for you.

Chapter 3 is where you will find your first statistics concepts and equations. Don't worry. I've written this chapter in accessible language. Moreover, the basic concepts we'll be analyzing in this chapter are probably familiar to you from high school. We will focus primarily on the core summary statistics that are used to describe a variable. These include percentages, frequencies, the mean, median, and standard deviation, among others. We will also look at how we can graphically describe data using helpful visual representations.

Chapter 4 is really the crown jewel of Part I. In this chapter, we'll be learning about the principle of statistical inference. This is the theoretical mechanism that we'll be using throughout the book to generalize the results of our research to a wider population of individuals or organizations. We can make this 'quantum leap' from our sample to the population because of certain assumptions we make about how representative our sample data are compared with population-level data.

If you feel up to the task, keep reading. Chapter 1 is a thrilling tale of introductory statistics. It's a real page turner. Trust me.

1

Introduction to Statistics

Social scientists are driven to understand the social world. Business and management researchers are a specific type of social scientist. We are motivated to understand organizations (public, private, and nonprofit), leaders, employees, consumers, markets, and the regulatory environments within which firms operate. To understand these phenomena, we ask research questions. These are the *anchor* of all social research. Good research questions are worded in the simplest language possible, and ideally, they ask something that we don't already fully understand. Why would you want to ask a question whose answer is already clear? If your research questions do not meet these criteria, then you need to go back to the drawing board.

Here are just a few examples of the types of questions that applied statisticians in the area of business and management, broadly defined, might ask:

- What are the effects of tattoos and piercings on job applicants' chances of success in a job interview (Timming et al., 2017)?
- To what extent does adding scent and music to a retail environment influence consumers' choices and behaviors (Mattila and Wirtz, 2001)?
- What is the impact of acquisitions and takeovers on firm performance (Dickerson et al., 1997)?
- How does host-country mentoring influence the socialization of expatriate employees (Feldman and Bolino, 1999)?
- What is the effect of internationalization and foreign direct investment on the performance of small- and medium-sized enterprises (SME; Lu and Beamish, 2001)?
- Are longer commutes to work associated with higher wages and, if so, why (French et al., 2020)?

Think about it for just a moment or two. What kinds of research questions are you interested in asking? And, crucially, how exactly would you go about answering those questions?

Quantitative Research Versus Qualitative Research

It would be a gross oversimplification to assume that all research questions can be answered in one of two ways. But, then again, this book aims to simplify some extraordinarily complex methods, so let's just go ahead with that oversimplification! Some research questions can be answered best using qualitative methods. Some research questions can be answered best using quantitative methods. In fact, some, if not most, research questions can be answered best using 'triangulation' (Jick, 1979) – that is, a strategic combination of qualitative and quantitative methods. For an example of triangulation, see Timming (2017a).

Qualitative research involves data collection primarily through interviewing or textual analysis. This method often involves having a conversation with respondents and treating whatever they say to you as data. Because qualitative research entails dialogue and narrative, it is usually most suitable for understanding meaning, contexts, and processes. For examples of qualitative research, see Timming (2010b) and Timming (2015).

Quantitative research, on the other hand, involves data collection primarily through survey or experimental methods. This might mean designing a questionnaire that measures numerically the concepts you're interested in studying. By quantifying your ideas, you are then able to understand how, and in what way, they relate to one another. Quantitative research is usually most suitable for understanding the interrelationships between a set of social constructs. An example of quantitative research is Budd et al. (2018).

Table 1.1 highlights the key differences between these two approaches.

This book focuses only on the quantitative side of research, but not because I think qualitative research is any less worthy of attention. Qualitative research is certainly much better than quantitative research at understanding *why* respondents think the way they think. Quantitative research is certainly much better than qualitative research at testing whether our ideas about the social world are generalizable to the wider population. Whatever the merits of qualitative research – and there are many – they will not be discussed further in this book. If you are interested, an in-depth comparison of qualitative and quantitative methods can be found in Bryman (2012).

Table 1.1 Quantitative versus qualitative research

Quantitative research	Qualitative research
Good at testing theories	Good at building theories
Data are numbers	Data are words
Data analysis involves math	Data analysis involves categorizing themes
Positivist philosophy	Interpretivist philosophy
Generally 'big' samples	Generally 'small' samples
Good at generalizing results	Weak generalizability due to small sample
Requires random samples	Non-random samples are the norm
Data generally collected via surveys	Data generally collected via interviews
Hard to establish causality	Better at understanding causal processes
Focus on variables	Focus on meaning and context
More objective	More subjective
Is *X* associated with *Y*?	What do you mean by *X*?

The Quantitative Research Process

The quantitative research process begins with a set of ideas on how we think the social world is organized. These ideas come together coherently in the form of what we call a theory. Often embedded within the theory is a set of hypotheses that we want to test. Let's explore this process a bit.

A *theory* can be defined, simply, as a set of expectations that we hold about the way something works. It is our way of explaining and understanding the world around us. We all theorize our way through life every day. For example, you might be thinking, 'What would happen if I threw this book at my boring professor?' That would be your research question. Then you articulate your expectations of what might happen if you actually chucked the book at me: 'If I threw this book at my professor, he (or she) would probably expel me from the class and possibly even from the university'. If you were feeling especially brave, you could even test that theory by actually throwing the book, just to see what happens (please don't . . . you may damage the book). But this kind of haphazard theorizing that we all do on a daily basis is very different from scientific theorizing.

Good scientific theories have some common characteristics. First, they are grounded in the extant literature. You can't just casually develop a scientific theory off the top of your head. Instead, you need to read extensively and become aware of what others have said about the relationships that you intend to analyse. Second, good theories are often broken down into hypotheses. A *hypothesis* can be described most accurately as an educated guess based on limited evidence. Whereas the theory represents a 'big picture' system, hypotheses are a breakdown of the individual components of that system. Box 1.1 illustrates how hypotheses are related to theories.

————————————— **Box 1.1: Theory Versus Hypotheses** —————————————

Management research is awash with theories: theories of motivation, theories of consumer behavior, theories of impression management, theories of discrimination, theories of firm internationalization, theories of creativity and innovation, and so on. Let's take a look at one commonly used framework in the field of management: the theory of rational choice (Coleman, 1994).

Rational choice theory posits that all human decision-making is driven by self-interest. This is a widely held assumption in microeconomics, and it applies equally to the study of organizations. Rational choice scholars, for example, might assume that employees decide to quit their jobs only when something better comes along, or that managers will always hire the most qualified applicant for the job.

Whereas the theory we use provides the 'big picture' rationale, hypotheses help us to zero in on specific manifestations of the broader theory. Let's take a look at an example. To test rational choice theory, we might ask whether hiring managers really always hire the most qualified applicant for the job. What if some other factor, for example, a job applicant's attractiveness, interfered with rational choice? We could test this belief with the following hypothesis:

More qualified job candidates who are less attractive score lower on hireability ratings than less qualified job candidates who are more attractive.

To test this hypothesis, we could design an experiment where hiring managers are shown photographs of more attractive and less attractive job candidates with varying degrees of qualifications and asked

(Continued)

to rate them on a scale of 1 to 10, where 1 = *low hireability* and 10 = *high hireability*. If the results of our experiment demonstrate that more highly qualified, but less attractive candidates are rated lower on hireability than the less qualified but more attractive candidates, then this finding would be a fairly strong condemnation of rational choice theory. We could then explain the result, perhaps, by drawing from an alternative theory, for example, evolutionary psychology (Timming, 2019).

Once we have our theory and hypotheses articulated, we need to test them in order to determine whether, or to what extent, they are empirically supported. To test our theory and hypotheses, we must first turn our ideas into numbers. This process, referred to broadly as the quantitative research process, is outlined in Figure 1.1.

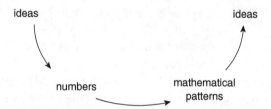

Figure 1.1 The quantitative research process

All quantitative research follows this basic model. We start off with our ideas about the way in which the world works. These ideas are conveyed through our hypotheses. For example, let's say we want to test the idea that trade union members are more satisfied with their jobs than non–trade union members. We might begin by looking at the relevant literature and proposing a theory about the benefits of union membership to employees. On the basis of this theory, we might then hypothesize that trade union members report higher job satisfaction than non–trade union members. So far, these are just our ideas. To test these ideas, we need to convert them into numbers.

Quantification is the process by which we turn our ideas into numbers. To quantify our ideas, we need to somehow measure them numerically. Let's take job satisfaction (Spector, 1997) as an example. Job satisfaction is a pretty abstract concept, if you think about it. We can't touch it and we can't see it. But we can measure it by asking some employees to self-rate how satisfied they are with their jobs. For instance, we might ask 100 employees, 'On a scale of 1 to 7, where 1 = *extremely dissatisfied* and 7 = *extremely satisfied*, how satisfied are you with your job?'

1 2 3 4 5 6 7

There is always more than one way to quantify a concept or an idea. For example, we could also ask, 'Please indicate how much you agree or disagree with the statement, I am satisfied with my job':

Strongly agree

Agree

Neither agree nor disagree

Disagree

Strongly disagree

In the first example, job satisfaction is already quantified when a respondent selects a number from 1 to 7. In the second example, where the response categories are in the form of hierarchical words (strongly agree, agree, neither agree nor disagree, disagree, strongly disagree), we still have to code those response categories in order to turn our ideas into numbers. *Coding* means assigning numbers to narrative response categories. For example, we could code all 'strongly agree' responses as 5, all 'agree' responses as 4, all 'neither agree nor disagree' responses as 3, all 'disagree' responses as 2, and all 'strongly disagree' responses as 1.

So far, so good. We have turned our idea, job satisfaction, into numbers. But how do we quantify and code our other concept: trade union membership?

We could measure trade union membership by asking the same 100 employees the following simple question: 'Are you a member of a trade union?'

Yes

No

We can quantify this concept by applying a simple code to our Yes/No response categories. For example, we could code all 'yes' responses as 1 and all 'no' responses as 0. In fact, we could use any two random numbers to code this concept. We could say that *Yes* = 1 and *No* = 2, or vice versa. Or we could say that *Yes* = 27 and *No* = 28 (although that would be kind of weird and arbitrary). Generally speaking, when there are only two response categories associated with a concept, social scientists usually code them as '0' and '1', where 0 corresponds to 'no' or 'absent' and 1 corresponds to 'yes' or 'present'.

Now that we have converted our ideas (trade union membership and job satisfaction) into numbers, the next step in the quantitative research process is to look for mathematical patterns in those numbers. Luckily, you don't have to do any real math to find these patterns in the data. Most of the mathematics underlying the statistical tests described in this book are quite complicated when there are 100 (or more) respondents. We use computer programs to do the math for us. These programs, like IBM SPSS Statistics Software (SPSS), the one used in this book, use built-in equations to 'crunch' the data, so you don't have to do it yourself. They produce 'output' that tells us the results of the statistical tests we told them to compute. The thing about these computer programs is that, unlike you, they are really not smart enough to know what 'job satisfaction' or 'trade union membership' mean. But they do know what numbers mean. For example, to test our hypothesis that trade union members report higher job satisfaction than non–trade union members, the software will break the respondents into two groups: trade union members (the group coded '1') and non–trade union members (the group coded '0'). Then, it will calculate average scores on the Job Satisfaction Scale (say, where 1 = *extremely unsatisfied* and 7 = *extremely satisfied*) for each group. Let's assume that the average score for trade union members is 4.27 and the average score for non–trade union members is 4.68. The software will then tell us whether or not this difference in mean scores (0.41, or 4.68 – 4.27) is large enough to generalize beyond the sample of 100 respondents.

Finally, the last step in the quantitative research process is to extrapolate from the results of the mathematical analysis back into your original ideas. If trade union members score an average of 4.27 on the seven-point Job Satisfaction Scale, non–trade union members score an average of 4.68

on the seven-point Job Satisfaction Scale, and the statistical software tells us that this difference of 0.41 is 'significant', then we would reject our hypothesis and conclude, against our initial expectations, that, in fact, trade union members report significantly *lower* job satisfaction than non–trade union members (Bryson et al., 2004). By disconfirming your original hypothesis, you would then move on to build a more advanced theoretical model to explain the result.

For example, you could look at the relationship between trade union membership and pay, and then look at the relationship between pay and job satisfaction. Maybe it's not union membership per se but rather the higher pay associated with union membership that increases job satisfaction. Or maybe you could look at the relationship between trade union membership and awareness of inequality to explain the lower levels of job satisfaction among trade union members. In other words, although trade union membership might increase pay (and thus increase job satisfaction), maybe it also increases awareness of inequality, which simultaneously decreases job satisfaction. To test these alternative explanations, you would need to quantify both 'pay' and 'awareness of inequality' to add to your more complex statistical model. Let's look at how we can measure these two constructs, among others, using an important tool that social scientists use to turn their ideas into numbers: the *survey*, also known as the *questionnaire*.

Survey Design

Management researchers sometimes use already existing secondary data. Other times, they will collect their own primary data. *Secondary data* refer to data that someone else has already collected and deposited for purposes of sharing. The main advantage of using secondary data sources is that you don't have to spend your own time or resources to collect the data since the dataset already exists in a ready-to-analyse format. The main disadvantage is that you don't have any control over what items are asked in the questionnaire and how they are measured. *Primary data* refer to data that you collect on your own. This means that you can design your own survey tailored to your needs, but you also have to commit time and resources to data collection. Whether you use secondary data or collect your own primary data, you should be familiar with the basic principles of survey design.

A *questionnaire* is a survey instrument that researchers use to collect data. Although it could be used to collect qualitative data, it's most typically used to collect quantitative data. You've probably filled out a few questionnaires. Companies use them to evaluate a product or a service. Governments use them to collect information about the labor market or the economy. News media and think tanks use them to track public opinion. Social scientists use them to turn their ideas about how the world works into numbers, so that they can test their theories and hypotheses.

Each question, item, or statement in a questionnaire measures what social scientists call a variable. A *variable* can be defined as any construct that, well, varies. The objective of most quantitative research is to understand the nature of the relationship between variables. *Trade union membership* is a variable. Respondents can be either members of a union, or not. *Job satisfaction* is a variable. Respondents can report higher or lower levels of satisfaction. *Gender* is a variable. Respondents can be male or female. *Age* is a variable. Respondents can be older or younger. *Pay*, or income, is a variable. Respondents can receive higher or lower salaries or wages. *Awareness of inequality* is a variable. Respondents can be either more or less aware of inequality. Table 1.2 reports some of the most commonly used variables in business and management research. How would you measure these variables in a survey? Can you think of any other important organizational variables not on this list?

It is important to distinguish clearly between a variable and its corresponding response categories. Male and female are not variables, but gender is. Male and female are the response categories associated with gender. Strongly agree, agree, disagree, and strongly disagree are not variables. They are response categories, typically for an attitudinal variable like job satisfaction or organizational commitment. A variable is a construct that varies, whereas *response categories* are the possible

Table 1.2 Common variables in management research

Job satisfaction
Organizational commitment
Individual or team productivity
Organizational or unit performance
Profitability
Trade union membership
Organizational size
Quality of work-life balance
Working hours per week
Pay
Intention to quit
Degree of employee participation
Years of education
Expenditure on training
Trust in management
Industry or sector
Nonprofit or for-profit
Number of industrial accidents
Number of employee grievances
Percentage of pay that is merit based
Recruitment expenditure
Presence (or not) of human resource function
Age of the organization
Number of domestic subsidiaries
Number of international subsidiaries
Total debt
Total market capitalization

responses that we use to measure a variable. *Coding*, referred to above, is what we do when we assign a unique number to each response category (e.g., 0 = *no* and 1 = *yes*).

It is also important to distinguish between variables measured across different units of analysis. The *unit of analysis* refers to the level at which the data are collected. Look again at the list of variables in Table 1.2. Some of these variables are measured at the level of the organization (e.g., organizational size, number of subsidiaries, and total debt), and others are measured at the level of the individual employee (e.g., pay, working hours per week, and trust in management). Business and management researchers most frequently design surveys to collect data on organizations and employees. That's why, throughout this book, we will be using two datasets from the Workplace Employment Relations Survey (WERS): a survey of managers, where the unit of analysis is the organization, and a survey of employees, where the unit of analysis is the individual employee.

Nominal, Ordinal, and Scale Variables

There are, broadly speaking, three types of variables in social science research: (1) nominal variables, (2) ordinal variables, and (3) scale variables. Being able to distinguish between these three types of variables is extremely important because all the statistical methods you will learn in this textbook only work with specific combinations of these variables. Therefore, knowing exactly which method to use depends on first knowing what types of variables you have in your dataset. Depending on how they've been measured, you might not be able to use some of the statistical tests.

The first type of variable is commonly referred to as *nominal*. Nominal variables have response categories that have no intrinsic numerical values and are nonhierarchical (in the sense that one category is not 'more' or 'less' than another). What does this mean? Let's look at a few examples. Gender is a nominal variable. The response categories are (typically) male and female. One is not 'more' or 'less' than the other. They cannot be rank-ordered. Men and women are simply different. Trade union membership is also a nominal variable. You either are a union member or you're not. No matter what your union status is, one is not 'more' or 'less' than the other. They're simply different. Anytime a survey asks a question where the answer is either 'yes' or 'no', such an item is always, by definition, a nominal variable. For example, 'Do you intend to quit your job in the next 12 months?' may be answered with a 'yes' or a 'no'. Either way, the responses are nonhierarchical. They're just qualitatively different.

Nominal variables can have two categories, as is the case with the above examples, or more than two categories. When nominal variables have only two categories, they are referred to as *dummy variables*, *binary variables*, or *dichotomous variables*. But sometimes nominal variables have more than two categories. For example, race is often a multicategory nominal variable. A respondent can select, for example, white, black, East Asian, South Asian, mixed race, and so on. Again, these categories are simply different. One is not 'more' or 'less' than another, and they have no intrinsic numerical value. Marital status can also be measured as a multicategory nominal variable. Its response categories might include the following: married, single, divorced, or widowed. Again, one response is not 'more' or 'less' than another. They're simply different. Favorite color is another example of a multicategory nominal variable. Maybe you like green. Maybe you like blue, or red, or purple. These responses are simply different and cannot be rank-ordered, one on top of the other.

The one thing that all nominal variables share in common is that the researcher must *code* them. Remember that coding implies turning qualitative response categories into numbers because SPSS is too stupid to know what words mean. In the case of gender, male and female have no intrinsic numerical value, so the researcher must assign some arbitrary numbers to them: typically 'male' = 0 and 'female' = 1, or vice versa. With a 'yes' or 'no' question, you could code all 'yes' responses as 1 and all 'no' responses as 0, or vice versa. The same principle applies to multicategory nominal variables. For example, let's say you were interested in studying religion in the United States. You could code the responses as follows: 'atheist/ agnostic' = 0, 'Protestant' = 1, 'Catholic' = 2, 'Jewish' = 3, 'Muslim' = 4, 'Hindu' = 5, 'Buddhist' = 6, and 'Other religion' = 7. The reason we have to code nominal variables is that, if you recall from above, words or ideas cannot be analysed mathematically. They must first be turned into numbers through the process of quantification.

The second type of variable is commonly referred to as *ordinal*. An ordinal variable, like a nominal variable, is not intrinsically numerical. In other words, its response categories are not natural numbers, but rather qualitative words that need to be coded. But unlike nominal variables, though, the response categories are hierarchical, meaning that one category represents 'more' or 'less' of that variable. In other words, they can be rank-ordered from most to least, or highest to lowest.

Almost all attitudinal variables are ordinal. Anytime you see a variable with response categories such as 'strongly agree', 'agree', 'disagree', or 'strongly disagree', or 'very interested', 'quite interested', 'somewhat interested', or 'not at all interested', the variable is ordinal. These categories can be stacked up, one on top of the other. We know, for example, that 'strongly agree' implies more agreement than 'agree' or 'disagree'. We also know that 'somewhat interested' implies less interest than 'very interested'. We can't rightly say that 'strongly agree' implies exactly twice as much agreement as 'agree', but we are confident that the former implies more agreement than the latter.

These response categories, as is the case with nominal variables, must also be coded. We can't look for mathematical patterns with only these words, but if we turn the words into numbers, then we can. We could use arbitrary numbers to code these types of variables, but a good rule of thumb with ordinal variables is to code the higher response categories with the higher numbers and the lower response categories with the lower numbers. For example, let's say we asked our subjects to respond to the following statement: 'I am satisfied with my job'. The response categories might then be 'strongly agree', 'agree', 'neither agree nor disagree', 'disagree', or 'strongly disagree'. You should code these categories like this: 'strongly agree' = 5, 'agree' = 4, 'neither agree nor disagree' = 3, 'disagree' = 2, and 'strongly disagree' = 1. You'll notice that more agreement corresponds to the highest number in the scale (i.e., 5), and less agreement corresponds to the lowest number in the scale (i.e., 1). We typically code ordinal variables in this way because, once we start looking for mathematical patterns using statistical tests, it will make the interpretations of the results much more intuitive and easier to understand. For example, if we were to code 'strongly agree' as 1 and 'strongly disagree' as 5, then, confusingly, the higher number will actually mean less agreement, and vice versa. This is not very intuitive when it comes to interpretation.

Ordinal variables often employ a *Likert scale* to measure a construct. A Likert scale allows the respondent to self-rate where they stand on the variable. Let's see how this works with a variable that seeks to measure respondents' degree of awareness of inequality in the workplace. There are different ways to measure such a variable. We could, for example, ask respondents to rate how much they agree or disagree with the following statement: 'I am aware of inequality in the workplace'. But on this occasion, let's measure awareness of inequality like this.

To what extent are you aware of inequality in the workplace? Are you

Very aware

Quite aware

Somewhat aware

Not at all aware

Let's then code the responses, such that 'very aware' = 4, 'quite aware' = 3, 'somewhat aware' = 2, and 'not at all aware' = 1. We have now successfully quantified a variable that we could call awareness of inequality. Including this variable in our model might then help us better understand the complex relationship between trade union membership and job satisfaction, as discussed above.

The third and final type of variable is commonly referred to as *scale*. A scale variable is, like an ordinal variable, hierarchical. But, unlike nominal and ordinal variables, the scale variable does not need to be coded. A classic example of a scale variable is age. A respondent might be 27 years old. Or maybe 42 years old. Or maybe 63 years old. These responses are meaningful and self-evident in and of themselves. We don't need to code them by saying that a score of 27 means 27 years, a score of 42 means 42 years, and a score of 63 means 63 years, and so on. Unlike ordinal variables, we know with scale variables that the response has intrinsic numerical meaning. We also know that a response of 40 is exactly twice as much as a response of 20.

Pay is another example of a scale variable. We could ask respondents, 'What is your annual salary before taxes?' One respondent might report £53,000. Another might report £32,000. Another might report £2,000,000. We don't need to code any of these numbers. They are meaningful in and of themselves.

Now that we have measured pay, we can insert it into our model of the relationship between trade union membership and job satisfaction. We might find, for example, that trade union membership is associated with higher pay, but also with higher awareness of inequality, and that the relative impact of awareness of inequality on job satisfaction is stronger than the relative impact of pay on job satisfaction. Figure 1.2 illustrates what this theoretical model might look like.

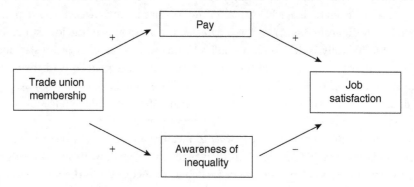

Figure 1.2 The effect of trade union membership on job satisfaction

Sometimes the distinction between ordinal and scale variables is blurry. For example, if we asked respondents to rate how satisfied they are with their jobs on a scale of 1 to 10, where 1 = *very dissatisfied* and 10 = *very satisfied*, this variable would clearly be ordinal. But what if we decided to measure job satisfaction on a scale of 1 to 100, where 1 = *very dissatisfied* and 100 = *very satisfied*? The larger the range of responses, the more an ordinal variable begins to imitate a scale variable.

Another point worth making about scale variables is that we can always later turn them into ordinal or nominal variables, but we can't do it the other way around. For example, if we have continuous age data for a set of individuals, we could always combine responses into ordinal categories like this: '18–25 years' = 1, '26–35 years' = 2, '36–45 years' = 3, and so on. Thus, respondents would need to be coded according to the age range in which they fall. Another option would be to use the median score in order to create a two-category nominal variable, where 'young' = 0 and 'old' = 1. The process of combining responses into different categories, or reordering them, is referred to as *recoding*.

In summary, there are three types of variables: nominal, ordinal, and scale. Nominal variables are nonhierarchical and require coding. Ordinal variables are hierarchical and also require coding. Scale variables are hierarchical and do not require coding. It is essential that you are able to distinguish between these three types of variables because statistical tests are generally designed to work only with specific combinations of these three types of variables.

Independent and Dependent Variables

The terms *nominal*, *ordinal*, and *scale* refer to the ways in which variables are measured. Another way of thinking about variables is to identify how they fit within your theory or hypotheses. Most theories in business and management research seek to explain how variables influence each other. You're assuming that one variable (or set of variables) impacts on another variable (or set of variables). Ideally, you are seeking to establish input-and-output relationships between two variables, X and Y, where X is referred to as the *independent variable* (aka the predictor variable or exogenous variable) and Y is referred to as the *dependent variable* (aka the outcome variable or the endogenous variable).

The independent variable, denoted X, is commonly said to represent the 'cause', and the dependent variable, denoted Y, is commonly said to represent the 'effect'. In other words, when we test our hypotheses, we are usually assuming implicitly that X causes, influences, or impacts on Y in some way. For example, we might theorize that there is a relationship between race and job satisfaction. A testable hypothesis associated with this theory might be the following: white employees are more satisfied with their jobs than nonwhite employees. In this case, race serves as the independent variable, and job satisfaction serves as the dependent variable. We are implicitly assuming that race affects job satisfaction. In this example, we know that race must be the independent variable and job satisfaction must be the dependent variable because it's impossible for the reverse to be true. That is to say, job satisfaction cannot influence race! In other examples, the distinction is not so clear. Take the relationship between human resource (HR) management practices and firm performance (Guest, 2011). We might hypothesize that HR practices increase productivity, but we could equally hypothesize that, as firms grow and become more productive, they then go on to establish formal HR practices. Essentially, it boils down to a question of which came first: the chicken or the egg? That's where good, old-fashioned theory comes into play.

But before we get carried away attempting definitively to establish and explain cause-and-effect relationships between independent and dependent variables, one very important caveat deserves mention. It is so important, in fact, that I'm putting it in italics: *quantitative social scientists can try to explain cause-and-effect relationships, but they cannot ever prove cause-and-effect relationships*. Let's take another example to see why this is the case.

You might hypothesize that the more hours of on-the-job training an employee receives, the more productive he or she becomes. You could test this hypothesis out by asking a sample of employees how many hours of training they've received in the past 12 months and comparing those numbers with their quantitative performance appraisal scores. After crunching the numbers, let's say you find that training is positively associated with productivity and thus conclude that it was the training that caused the increase in productivity. But how do you really know it was the training, and not some other factor, that resulted in the increased productivity? What if the increased productivity was actually an artifact of the new performance appraisal system, a new profit-sharing program, or some other change? By only measuring training hours, you fail to take account of all the possible 'causes' of increased productivity. This is often referred to as the unavoidable problem of *statistical under-control*. You cannot possibly measure all the possible causes of an outcome. Therefore, you cannot reasonably conclude that your independent variable definitively 'causes' your dependent variable. As a result, you cannot ever conclude that X causes Y in any academic writing. You can say that X is positively (or negatively) associated with Y. You can say that X is positively (or negatively) correlated with Y. But you cannot say that X causes Y without getting yourself into trouble. After all, it may not be X causing Y, but rather Z, a variable that you have not measured in your survey.

Reliability, Validity, and Measurement Error

When measuring a set of variables, we want to ensure that all our items reflect the underlying construct as accurately as possible. With some variables, accuracy is not a significant problem. For example, data on gender are usually fairly precise. Aside from respondents accidentally ticking the wrong box, for the most part, our measurement of gender is without serious errors. But other variables are not so easy to measure. Let's take organizational commitment as an example, measured as follows:

How committed are you to your organization?

Extremely committed (coded as 5)

Very committed (coded as 4)

Somewhat committed (coded as 3)

A little committed (coded as 2)

Not at all committed (coded as 1)

Every respondent is going to have a slightly different perception of the difference, for example, between 'somewhat committed' and 'a little committed'. Because of this difference in perception, some subjects will inflate their level of commitment, while others will underreport their level of commitment. Fortunately, these two types of error will generally cancel each other out, so, in aggregate, we can assume that we have a useable survey item measuring organizational commitment. Another concern is that an employee can have a high level of organizational commitment on one day and then the following day, a lower level of organizational commitment, depending on his or her experiences in the workplace or even mood.

Let's take a look at a few other examples of measurement error. Even variables such as race, which one might reasonably assume is a stable feature, are not always reported accurately. A mixed-race respondent might report himself or herself as 'white' on one day and the very next day as 'black'. How about number of children, a variable that might interest researchers of work–life balance? Again, at first glance, this would seem a fairly stable variable. But one day a respondent might report two children and the very next day she might report having six. It is, of course, possible that the respondent had quadruplets in the meantime, but perhaps more likely that she is confused about whether to include her four stepchildren.

Data entry errors are another importance source of inaccuracy. Do not be surprised, for example, to find out that a respondent reports his age as 147 years! Such a mistake is often the result of a careless data inputting error. For example, the real age might be 47 years.

To ensure the accuracy of our variables, ideally, we want all measures to be reliable and valid. *Reliability* refers to the consistency, or replicability, of a variable. If we can reproduce the same (or at least roughly similar) results with the same survey instrument across different samples, then our variables are said to be reliable. *Validity* refers to the question of whether we're measuring what we say we're measuring. For example, does a high score in a performance appraisal really measure performance, or does it more accurately measure one's social skills and/or likeability?

The reliability of a variable (or set of variables) can be evaluated in three ways. First, you can administer your survey instrument across two different samples and compare the measurements for consistency. This is often referred to as the *test-retest method*. Second, you can randomly split your sample into two groups to look for internal consistency. Statisticians refer to this as the *split-halves method*. Finally, in the event that you have multiple items that purport to measure the same underlying construct, you can generate a statistic called *Cronbach's alpha* to assess reliability. This statistic is always a score between 0 and 1, where 0 means total unreliability and 1 means total reliability. Most social scientists use 0.700 as a cutoff, so any Cronbach's alpha score below this threshold suggests unreliability in your measures.

It should be noted that reliability does not necessarily imply that your variables are accurately measured. Imagine that you step on a scale and it tells you that you weigh 5 kg less than you really weigh (that's my kind of scale!). You then step on it a second and third time, and once again the scale indicates that you are 5 kg under your actual weight. This scale is highly reliable, but obviously not valid (Boo!).

An accurate measure requires both reliability and validity. Although there are some statistical tests, such as exploratory and confirmatory factor analyses (Chapter 11), that can shine (some) light on whether two variables (or sets of variables) are similar or different from one another, validity is still largely a nonstatistical concept. To evaluate validity, you need to apply some combination of common sense and good theoretical scrutiny. Let's say you are interested in studying the relationship between religiosity and productivity, and you hypothesize that religious employees are more productive than nonreligious employees. To measure religiosity, you ask,

How many weeks in an average year do you attend church? (scale variable)

This is likely an invalid measurement of religiosity for a number of reasons. For starters, the word 'church' appears to exclude everyone outside of the Christian faith. But assuming that you were only interested in whether Christians were more productive than non-Christians, this is still a pretty questionable measurement of religiosity. Many Christians may consider themselves highly religious, but do not attend church services regularly. In short, this item does not measure what you think it's measuring. To really 'tap' religiosity, you may need to develop several indicators of the underlying construct and combine them into a single composite variable.

In summary, if you want to maximize the validity and reliability of your variables, and minimize both measurement error and bias, there are a few dos and don'ts of questionnaire design. Let's take a look at them briefly. You may first want to spend some time evaluating how well the items in the WERS datasets conform to the following principles.

How to Design Items in a Questionnaire (and How Not to)

The statistical tests you will learn in this book are meaningless if the questionnaire you use has not been designed properly. Let's take a look at some 'best practices' and at some common mistakes that researchers make when constructing their own survey instrument. More information on how to design items in a survey can be found in Sudman and Bradburn (1982). For now, here are 10 basic principles that you should follow when designing a questionnaire.

Principle 1: Surveys Should Be Theory Driven

A common mistake in survey design is to ask a series of poorly conceived questions that you *think* might be interesting. Questionnaire design should never be a casual undertaking. It takes time and, on occasion, a lot of money to do it right. Furthermore, you frequently only get one shot at it, so make it count.

Let's say that you're interested in researching quantitatively the effects of employee participation in managerial decision-making. The first thing you should do is to look at the previous literature to find out how others before you have measured employee participation. How exactly did they operationalize the construct? Did they use a single item or multiple items to measure employee participation? What kinds of scales and coding did they use to quantify the construct? The second crucial step is to gain an understanding of the key effects. Maybe you think employee participation in decision-making positively impacts variables such as job satisfaction, organizational commitment, and trust in management (Timming, 2012). Maybe you think it also positively impacts profitability or firm performance (Appelbaum et al., 2000). You cannot construct a comprehensive survey instrument unless you first become familiar with the literature and relevant theory. If you neglect to measure a key variable in your questionnaire, the integrity of your research is compromised. So always construct your questionnaire in the light of previous work on the constructs you wish to research and ensure that your research design is underpinned by extant theory.

Principle 2: The Layout Should Be Clear, Not Cluttered

The layout, usability, and overall 'aesthetics' of your survey instrument are extremely important. Appearance matters. A good survey instrument should be inviting, especially in light of the fact that filling out a questionnaire is always a time burden for the respondent. The instrument should be clear in its layout and uncluttered. It should be symmetrical, as much as possible, and the response categories should be neatly aligned and far enough apart, so that they are not confusing to the respondent.

Principle 3: Strike a Balance With the Length of the Instrument

The optimal length of a survey is always difficult to judge. Ultimately, it boils down to the question of balance. As researchers, we want to collect as much data as possible, but we are always constrained by the attention span of the respondents. If your survey is too long, then it is likely that you will suffer from serious attrition and a low response rate. That is, many of your respondents may just quit mid-survey because, let's face it, they've got much better things to do than to fill out your questionnaire. Excessively long surveys almost always lead to a small sample in the absence of significant compensation or other incentives. On the other hand, if your survey is too short, then you are not likely to be able to measure all the relevant variables pertaining to your research question(s).

So where is the equilibrium in terms of survey length? The optimal length seems to be rapidly changing, and in a direction that is unfavorable to social scientists. Decades ago, it seemed as if people were more likely to take the time to fill out surveys. Today, many people suffer from 'survey fatigue'. Companies ask us to fill out surveys about our customer service experience. Marketing firms ask us to fill out surveys about products. And so when social scientists then ask us to share our views, many potential respondents are quick to decline, especially if the instrument demands a lot of their precious time. For this reason, you should limit your instrument to no more than around 15 minutes, maximum, to complete. A survey that takes less than five minutes or so to complete is likely to get a much higher response rate.

Principle 4: Items Should Be Short and Simple

This is, without a doubt, the most important piece of advice for anyone designing a survey. Keep it simple. Keep it very simple. When designing a survey item, always remember the *principle of parsimony*: the simplest, clearest measurement is always best. This means that you should use as few words as possible to measure a variable and also dispense with those 'big' and 'fancy' words that academics so often use.

Let's take an example. Suppose you want to measure a concept such as propensity to take risks. There are any number of ways that this abstract construct could be measured. For example: I am more than willing to sacrifice short-term stability in order to secure longer-term benefits for the sake of my personal and professional development.

Strongly agree (coded as 5)

Agree (coded as 4)

Neither agree nor disagree (coded as 3)

Disagree (coded as 2)

Strongly disagree (coded as 1)

Sure, you could measure risk-taking propensity in this way, but, really, why be so cryptic and verbose? Why use words that, while perhaps sounding fancy and properly 'academic', can be hard to decipher for your average Joe or Jane? What exactly do you mean by 'short-term stability' or 'longer-term benefits'? And what's all this talk about 'personal and professional development'?

Instead, you should go for a simpler, more direct measure of the construct. For example, why not ask the respondent how much she agrees or disagrees with the following statement: I am a risk-taker.

Strongly agree (coded as 5)

Agree (coded as 4)

Neither agree nor disagree (coded as 3)

Disagree (coded as 2)

Strongly disagree (coded as 1)

The best survey items are the ones that can be read and understood quickly and easily. Plus, shorter survey items will save you time, and possibly money.

Principle 5: Avoid Leading Questions

How we ask a question can potentially 'steer' respondents to answer in a way that is favorable to our interests or expectations. By asking so-called 'leading' questions, the objective and scientific nature of our research is compromised. As a general rule of thumb, it is always best to measure constructs without your own personal values or expectations interfering. You may hope, for whatever reason, to uncover a particular finding, but you cannot let that hope influence how you design your instrument.

Sometimes the distinction between a value-laden item and objective item is explicit. For example, 'Are you satisfied with the new performance appraisal system?' is very different from, 'You're not *really* satisfied with the new performance appraisal system, are you?' Both items ask the same question, but in ways that will elicit very different answers. Other times, the distinction is subtler. For example, 'Do you agree that the new health and safety policy will reduce accidents?' is slightly different from, 'Will the new health and safety policy reduce accidents?' By adding an affirmative word in the first item (do you 'agree'), you are perhaps subtly leading respondents toward a more affirmative response. So be careful with your language and make sure that you're not trying to influence responses.

Principle 6: Response Categories Should Be Exhaustive and Mutually Exclusive

Response categories that are not exhaustive and mutually exclusive almost always result in both invalid and unreliable measures. *Exhaustive* refers to measures where all possible responses are offered to the respondent. *Mutually exclusive* refers to items where the response categories are qualitatively different from one another and do not overlap.

Let's look at an example of an item where the response categories are not exhaustive. Say that you are interested in studying the effects of different forms of commuting on employee productivity. You measure variation in commuting with the following item: How do you get to work on most days?

Drive myself (coded as 1)

Carpool (coded as 2)

Bus (coded as 3)

Train (coded as 4)

Walk (coded as 5)

The problem with this measurement should be immediately apparent. Not all the possible answers are represented here. For example, if a respondent bicycles or jogs to work, then he or she has no valid response. When developing response categories, you must ensure that all the possible alternatives are listed. To accommodate responses that are not easy to envisage (hey, someone with a cooler job than I have might rock climb to work), you could add a final, open-ended category such as 'Other: please indicate'. Note that the use of *open-ended* items in questionnaires requires *post hoc* coding.

Now let's look at an example of a measurement where the response categories are not mutually exclusive. Imagine if you asked the question about commuting, but with the following response categories: How do you get to work on most days?

Drive myself (coded as 1)

Carpool (coded as 2)

Public transportation (coded as 3)

Bus (coded as 4)

Train (coded as 5)

Walk (coded as 6)

Cycle (coded as 7)

The problem here is that the response categories clearly overlap. If the respondent takes the train or bus, he or she could potentially also select 'Public transportation', leading to confusion and unreliability. A good measurement has a set of response categories that are qualitatively different from one another and do not overlap.

Principle 7: Respondents Should Be Qualified to Answer the Questions

You may be very interested in researching whether Albanian nonprofit organizations take corporate social responsibility seriously. This is a legitimate research question, and no one has the right to say otherwise. But if you choose to explore this topic, you may want to think twice about your sample. Most average Albanians might be hard pressed to form an opinion on this topic, let alone a bunch of undergraduate students studying at an American university. In short, make sure that your respondents are qualified to have an opinion on your research topic; otherwise, the data you collect will be as good as useless.

Principle 8: Items Must Not Be 'Double-Barreled'

Another source of measurement error is when a single item in a questionnaire actually asks two or more questions. In such cases, it is never clear how the respondent should reply since he or she might agree with one part of the question but not with the other part.

An excellent example of this type of error in the 2004 WERS of Employees is highlighted in Timming (2009). On a five-point scale, please rate how good managers are at allowing employees or employee representatives to influence final decisions:

Very good (coded as 5)

Good (coded as 4)

Neither good nor poor (coded as 3)

Poor (coded as 2)

Very poor (coded as 1)

This item is *double-barreled* in the sense that it's asking the respondent two questions within one. What if, for example, managers are very good at allowing employee representatives to influence final decisions, but very poor at allowing employees to influence final decisions? By asking potentially two questions within one item, you are introducing measurement error into your survey instrument. So always make sure that you are asking one question per item.

Principle 9: Complex Constructs Require Multiple Items

Some of the variables we measure are fairly simple and can easily be captured in a single item. Gender, age, and salary, for example, are pretty straightforward and are frequently measured with just one item each. Other variables, however, are more complicated and may require more than one item to really 'tap' the multiple dimensions that underlie a single construct.

Take job satisfaction as an example. We could measure it with just a single item by asking how satisfied the respondent is at his or her job. But job satisfaction is a complex and multidimensional construct that may require multiple items. For example, you may want to measure a respondent's level of satisfaction with training, pay, job security, and their ability to influence decisions, among other factors. Taken together, these related variables can perhaps more closely and validly approximate the wider concept of job satisfaction than a single item could on its own.

When we use multiple items to measure a construct, we have two options. First, we can create a *composite variable* that is a series of interrelated variables that are added together to make a new one. In effect, to create a composite variable, you simply sum the variables together or create one 'average' variable. The second option is to create a *latent variable*. A latent variable is an unobserved variable that we cannot directly measure, but we assume that it exists based on the presence of a series of interrelated observed variables. We will discuss latent variables in Chapters 11 and 12, where we will learn about factor analyses and structural equation modeling.

Principle 10: Survey Instruments Should Always Be Piloted

The final point worth making about questionnaire design is that all questionnaires should be piloted. A *pilot study* is a very small-scale test of your survey. Once you have the instrument designed, you can administer it to a small, nonrandomly drawn group of 'practice' respondents. These can be friends or colleagues, for example. Once you have piloted the questionnaire, you can ask the respondents for feedback that can then be used to improve the design of the items. Piloting is an important investment that can help prevent future problems, thus saving you time and money in the long term.

Survey Administration

So, you know how to design an effective questionnaire. That's great. Now, what are you supposed to do with it? Questionnaires, however well designed, don't just go filling themselves out. You've got to decide on a method of survey administration.

Survey administration refers to the various methods that researchers use to distribute a questionnaire to a sample of respondents. There are four basic ways of administering a questionnaire: (1) face-to-face, (2) telephone, (3) via post, and (4) online. Each of these alternatives entails some costs and benefits. Which one you ultimately choose depends on several factors, but the most important ones include how much time and money you have at your disposal. Of course, if you, like me, have no money and no time, then you can always forget about collecting data (it's hard work!) and use a good secondary dataset such as the WERS instead.

Table 1.3 summarizes the key advantages and disadvantages of each of the four main methods of survey administration. These days, fewer researchers employ telephone and postal administration. Telephone survey administration is falling out of style mainly because, increasingly, fewer and

Table 1.3 Methods of survey administration, advantages and disadvantages

Methods	Advantages	Disadvantages
Face-to-face	Highest-quality data	Very expensive
	Highest response rate	Very time-consuming
	Good for long surveys	Bad for controversial topics
	Can use visual prompts	Difficult with dispersed sample
Telephone	Very high-quality data	Fewer people have landlines
	Cheaper than face-to-face	Bad for long surveys
	Most quickly produced data	Cannot use visual prompts
Postal	Fairly inexpensive	Very low response rate
	Dispersion of sample irrelevant	Can take a long time
	Can use visual prompts	Bad for long surveys
Online	Free (or cheap)	Biased samples
	No manual data inputting	Low response rates
	Can use visual and audio prompts	Bad for long surveys

fewer people have landlines, and researchers are generally prohibited from using mobile phones to contact potential respondents. Postal administration is decreasing primarily because it has similar disadvantages to online administration, but with greater costs. So the future of survey administration is primarily a choice between online and face-to-face distribution.

As a general rule of thumb, if you have sufficient time and resources, then, by all means, administer your questionnaire face-to-face. Face-to-face administration almost always produces the highest-quality data and the highest response rates. Respondents are much more likely to complete a questionnaire if approached personally, and they're more likely to spend time thinking about their responses, too. But this method can be very expensive, especially if your sample is widely dispersed geographically. If, for example, you're researching consumer preferences in Australian households, face-to-face administration is simply not feasible without a large team of data collectors and some deep pockets. If, on the other hand, your sample is a group of employees located in a single worksite, face-to-face administration becomes much more manageable. A key disadvantage of face-to-face administration, though, is that it does not often work well when researching controversial topics such as, for example, sexual harassment or bullying in the workplace (Timming et al., 2019). Increasingly, researchers are turning to online surveys as a means of data collection.

Online administration involves no (or low) cost to the researcher. Furthermore, data are instantly uploaded into a spreadsheet, so that no extra time is required for data inputting. The use of a computer or smartphone also allows for the questionnaire to contain audio and visual components, as highlighted in Box 1.2. There are, however, several drawbacks to using online surveys. For starters, they tend to have very low response rates because it is so easy for respondents to quit mid-survey if it's taking too much of their time. That's why online surveys tend to be shorter. Another problem with online surveys is that they tend to produce biased samples. At a minimum, they exclude members of a population without access to the internet and those who are not so computer literate, such as some elderly people.

─────────────── **Box 1.2: Using Online Surveys** ───────────────

Online surveys have some very clear advantages over traditional, paper-based ones. Because they are completely digitized, they save money on printing costs. Also, the data can be uploaded instantly onto a spreadsheet for analysis. With paper-based surveys, each response needs to be inputted one by one. Another key advantage is that the costs of administration are slim to nothing. Programs such as Survey Monkey are free to use. Many universities subscribe to Qualtrics, another easy-to-use online survey tool. But one of the most exciting and innovative aspects of online surveys is that you can incorporate visual and audio elements into the instrument.

Let's say you're interested in researching the effects of foreign accents on job applicant employability. You hypothesize that foreign-sounding job applicants making an initial telephone interview will be disadvantaged in the labor market. Using a paper-based questionnaire, you could ask respondents (in this case, hiring managers) to imagine how they would rate foreign accents, but this is a risky and haphazard approach. With online surveys, you could build audio files into the questionnaire, so that all respondents are introduced to the same stimulus. You could then easily unpack the effect of different accents on employability ratings. To see this kind of research in action, refer to Timming (2017b).

For the purposes of this book, you only need to be vaguely familiar with the different methods of survey administration. Fortunately, the data that we'll be using in the following chapters have already been collected through the WERS 2011. If you are interested in learning more about methods of survey administration, Dillman et al. (2014) is an excellent reference.

Sampling

Finally, having designed your survey and chosen a method of survey administration, you might be wondering how you should go about selecting subjects for inclusion in your sample. *Sampling* refers to the process of selecting a group of respondents for analysis. We generally analyse samples, rather than populations, because it's cheaper. A *population* refers to the target group that you intend to study (e.g., Americans, service sector employees, steelworkers, British multinational companies, and potential customers), whereas a *sample* refers to the subset, or portion, of that population that we actually study statistically. We will examine the difference between a sample and a population in greater depth in Chapter 4. For now, I just want to give a brief overview of the different methods of sampling at your disposal. For a more extensive review of sampling, see Thompson (2012).

Table 1.4 describes the different methods of sampling at your disposal. Samples can be categorized as either randomly or nonrandomly drawn. A *random sample* implies that all members of a population have an equal probability of selection into the sample. In other words, no one person (or organization) has any better chance of being included in the sample than any other person (or organization). Random samples are, therefore, composed purely by chance alone. A *nonrandom sample*, on the other hand, implies that no random process has been put in place to select respondents. For example, if you were to stand on the street and 'randomly' asked people to fill out your survey, this would not be a random sample because there may be certain types of individuals that you would be more (or less) likely to approach (like that guy with the spider web tattoo on his face). For this reason, nonrandom samples are always more biased than random samples. *Sampling bias* refers to the over- or underrepresentation of certain types of respondents, often as a result of the personal views or inclinations of the researcher. As will be discussed further in Chapter 4, random samples are always superior to nonrandom samples because the former are much more likely to be representative of the population than the latter, thus allowing for improved capacity for generalizing from the sample to the population.

Fortunately, you don't need to sweat over sampling in this book either because we're using secondary data. In Chapter 2, you will familiarize yourself with the 2011 WERS, which, as noted above, actually consists of four datasets, two of which have been selected for analysis in this book. Both samples, the survey of managers and the survey of employees, have been drawn randomly, so we can be confident that the statistical tests that we perform here are generalizable to the wider population of organizations and employees in Great Britain.

Table 1.4 Methods of sampling

Random sampling

Simple random sampling involves numbering all respondents in a population and then using a random number generator to select respondents for inclusion in the sample.

Random digit dialing involves using a computer to randomly generate telephone numbers.

Systematic random sampling involves numbering all respondents in a population and then selecting every *k*th case, where *k* is the size of the population divided by the desired size of the sample. For example, if you want to select 100 people from a population of 1000, you will select every 10th person on the list.

Stratified random sampling involves drawing a random sample using one of the above methods, but by dividing the sample into groups (e.g., white and black respondents) and perhaps over- or underrepresented respondents within those groups.

Multistage area probability sampling involves random sampling across levels or stages. For example, you might start by taking a random sample of postcodes, followed by a random sample of households within those postcodes, followed by a random sample of persons within those households.

Nonrandom sampling

Purposive sampling involves intentionally targeting a niche demographic of respondents. For example, if you're interested in studying LGBT (lesbian, gay, bisexual, and transgender) employees, purposive sampling would involve data collection from only members of that particular community.

Snowball sampling involves finding one respondent and then asking him or her to refer you to another respondent, who in turn is asked to refer you to another respondent, and so on.

Quota sampling involves using nonrandom sampling to produce a sample that 'looks like' the population. For example, if you know the demographics of the population you wish to study (e.g., an organization that is 50% female, 75% white and 25% nonwhite, 15% managers and 85% employees), you can compose a nonrandom sample that attempts to reproduce these demographics.

What Have You Learned?

This chapter has examined the quantitative research process, including: variable measurement, coding, survey design, item construction, survey administration, and sampling. We looked closely at quantification, the process by which we turn our ideas into numbers, and at the types of variables that we use to measure constructs: nominal, ordinal, and scale. We also distinguished between so-called independent and dependent variables. We then discussed the importance of using valid and reliable measurements as well as outlined common sources of error in measuring variables. We then looked at a list of 'best practices' that can ensure a well-designed survey instrument. Finally, the chapter was drawn to a close with a discussion of survey administration and sampling.

By now, you should have a 'big picture' understanding of how variables are measured and operationalized in business and management research. In Chapter 2, you will become familiar with the datasets we'll use throughout this book and the software that we'll use to analyse those datasets.

Further Reading

Babbie, E. R. (2020). *The practice of social research*. Cengage Learning.

Bryman, A. (2012). *Social research methods*. Oxford University Press.

Fink, A. (2003). *How to design survey studies*. Sage.

Henry, G. T. (1990). *Practical sampling* (Vol. 21). Sage.

Krosnick, J. A. (2018). Questionnaire design. In D. L. Vannette & J. A. Krosnick (Eds.), *The Palgrave handbook of survey research* (pp. 439–455). Palgrave Macmillan.

Stern, M. J., Bilgen, I., & Dillman, D. A. (2014). The state of survey methodology: Challenges, dilemmas, and new frontiers in the era of the tailored design. *Field Methods, 26*(3), 284–301.

In-Class Discussion Questions
---

1. Why would a researcher choose to employ quantitative methods over qualitative methods, and vice versa? What are the advantages and disadvantages of each epistemological approach? Is one method 'better' than the other? Why or why not?
2. Pick 10 variables that are *not* listed in Table 1.2 and quantify them. Select a mixture of nominal, ordinal, and scale variables that you intend to measure and place them in a questionnaire.
3. What is the main difference between an independent variable and a dependent variable? Articulate five research questions, and for each one, identify the independent and dependent variable and specify how you would measure each one.
4. Summarize the 'best practices' and 'worst practices' of survey design.
5. How should a researcher choose a method for administering a questionnaire? Is one method of survey administration better than another? Why or why not?
6. Why are randomly drawn samples generally considered to be better than non-randomly drawn samples? In what circumstances might a non-randomly drawn sample be preferable?

2

Exploring IBM SPSS

Welcome to the wonderful world of IBM SPSS Statistics Software (let's just go with SPSS for short, shall we?). In this chapter, you'll get to know the software that we'll be using in order to carry out the statistical tests illustrated throughout the rest of this book. Although it might seem a bit daunting at first to learn a new interface, you will, I'm sure, come to appreciate this software package, if not only based on the fact that it will save you an enormous amount of time by 'doing the math' for you (yay!). In fact, the two datasets that we'll be using in this book are so immensely large that it could take you days or weeks or even months to calculate, by hand, a simple mean, or average, score. With the help of this dynamic computer software, much more complicated statistics than that which could possibly be computed by hand are generated literally at the click of a mouse.

SPSS stands for Statistical Package for the Social Sciences. At the time of this book's publication, SPSS is currently on version 28. If you have a slightly older (or perhaps newer) version of the software on your computer, fear not. IBM's periodic updates rarely make any major interface changes to the extent that you wouldn't be able to follow the basic procedures outlined in this book. If you are a university student – as most readers of this textbook will be – it is highly likely that your institution has a premium subscription allowing you to use SPSS. The reason I've chosen to use SPSS in this textbook is that it is very easy to use and ideally suited for an applied statistics student. There are, of course, other packages that could have been used, including Excel, Stata, R, and Jamovi, among others. I would urge you to explore these other interfaces.

In addition to demonstrating the SPSS user interface to you, this chapter will also introduce you briefly to the most recent (2011) edition of the WERS, which contains the real-world data used throughout the remainder of this book. WERS is a comprehensive survey of both organizations and their employees across the United Kingdom, and it is widely used by leading business and management scholars in their research. Best of all, the datasets are free to access, and the relevant chapter-by-chapter files are included on the Companion Website.

Before I introduce you to the SPSS user interface environment, let's take a very brief moment to get to know the WERS series.

The Workplace Employment Relation Surveys: A Brief History

WERS is arguably the largest and most extensive source of organizational- and employee-level statistical data in the entire world. Although it is a British dataset, this textbook is nevertheless relevant to students and scholars from across the globe, but especially to those living and studying in similar 'liberal-market economies' (Hall and Soskice, 2001) such as the United States and Canada, Australia and New Zealand, and Ireland.

The roots of WERS 2011 can ultimately be traced back to what was once known as the Workplace Industrial Relations Survey of 1980 (Daniel and Millward, 1983). This was the first ever attempt to collect national-level data on Britain's workplaces. The Workplace Industrial Relations Survey was carried out again in 1984 (Millward and Stevens, 1986) and then in 1990 (Millward et al., 1992), at which time the focus shifted away from *industrial* relations and toward *employment* relations. The study was first administered as the WERS in 1998 (Cully et al., 1999), followed by later iterations in 2004 (Kersley et al., 2006) and, most recently, in 2011 (van Wanrooy et al., 2013). This book uses the WERS 2011 data only, although it should be noted that, should you be so inclined, you could easily link up with previous iterations of the questionnaire in order to conduct longitudinal analyses. *Longitudinal* research refers to statistical analyses that involve data points that stretch across time, whereas *cross-sectional* research involves analyses carried out at a single point in time. The examples in this textbook are cross-sectional inasmuch as they draw exclusively from the WERS 2011 data.

A thorough explanation of the WERS 2011 methodology, survey instruments, and first findings, for those who are interested, can be found at www.wers2011.info. Feel free to explore this website a bit before proceeding further.

In short, the WERS 2011 data were collected between March 2011 and June 2012. The Workplace Employment Relations 'Survey' is actually something of a misnomer. In fact, WERS is a compilation of datasets from separate, but related, survey instruments that were administered simultaneously to separate random samples of managers, workers' representatives, and individual employees based in British workplaces. This textbook uses two of the WERS datasets for most of its examples and empirical illustrations: the management dataset (where the unit of analysis is the organization) and the employee dataset (where the unit of analysis is the individual employee). A *unit of analysis*, as noted in Chapter 1, can be defined in relation to the level (individual or collective) at which an instrument is administered. It should be noted that, although the management questionnaire was administered to managers, the unit of analysis is, in fact, the organization, not the individual manager (because the managers ultimately provided data not about themselves, but rather about their organizations).

In total, the data were collected from 2680 organizations across the United Kingdom, all of which have more than five employees each (therefore, very small firms are excluded from this sample). A senior manager from each of these organizations was asked a series of questions about management policy and practices. These data are contained in the WERS of organizations. The survey instrument that was used to collect the data from these 2680 organizations is very long (involving hundreds of variables). It can be accessed at www.wers2011.info.

Within these 2680 organizations, a separate survey instrument was administered to a random sample of employees. In organizations with 25 or fewer employees, the entire workforce was asked to fill out the survey. For larger organizations, 25 employees were randomly sampled and asked to complete the instrument. In total, 21,981 employees from across these 2680 organizations filled out the WERS of employees. The questionnaire used to collect these data can be found in Appendix A.

In summary, this textbook uses two separate, but inter-related, datasets to illustrate its methods. Both datasets are summarized briefly in Box 2.1. The survey of organizations consists of organizational-level data from 2680 workplaces across the United Kingdom. The survey of employees consists of individual-level data from 21,981 respondents who were randomly selected from those 2680 organizations. The studies were carried out at different levels of analysis and with different foci. Taken together, they are both representative of British workplaces and employees, generally speaking.

Box 2.1: Summary of the Survey of Organizations and Survey of Employees

Survey of Organizations

- Data were collected in the United Kingdom in 2011–2012.
- It provides organizational data from across Great Britain.
- Data consist of a sample of 2680 workplaces.
- Only organizations for more than five employees were included in the sample.
- Agriculture, forestry, fishing, mining, and quarrying workplaces were excluded.
- Sample is representative of 750,000 workplaces and 23.3 million employees.
- Face-to-face interviews were conducted with a senior manager.
- Average length of each interview was 90 minutes.
- Response rate was 46.3%.

Survey of Employees

- Data were collected in the United Kingdom in 2011–2012.
- It provides individual-level data from Britain's employees.
- Respondents were all employees of the 2680 workplaces in the survey of organizations.
- In smaller workplaces with fewer than 25 employees, all workers were given the survey instrument.
- In workplaces with more than 25 employees, a random sample of 25 workers was drawn.
- Response rate was 54.3%.

Let's take a little peek at the WERS 2011 survey of employees by way of familiarizing ourselves with the SPSS environment. Before you move onto the next section, have a look at the survey of employees in Appendix A. Perhaps you could ask someone you know to fill it out, or go ahead and try to fill it out yourself.

Getting Started: Opening Data With SPSS

When you open up SPSS on your machine, you may see the window depicted in Figure 2.1 pop up. I say you 'may' see this window because if you look at the bottom left-hand corner of the box, you'll see an option stating, 'Don't show this dialog in the future'. If someone has previously ticked this box on your computer, then it will not appear (obviously!). But this would be no great loss since the window in Figure 2.1 really adds no value whatsoever to the program. So, if it does appear, just tick the little 'X' box on the top right-hand corner to close it.

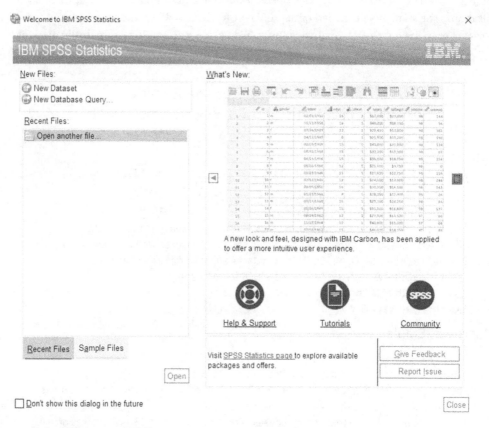

Figure 2.1 Welcome to SPSS

Reprint courtesy of IBM Corporation ©

You will then notice that the spreadsheet depicted in Figure 2.2 opens. This is called the SPSS *Data Editor*, which is the interface, or spreadsheet, where you can now add, remove, and/or edit data. Right now, you'll notice that all the cells in the spreadsheet are empty. That's because we've not entered, or opened, any data. Box 2.2 describes, just in case you're interested, how to enter data from a survey instrument into the data editor. Fortunately, the WERS data that we'll be using in this book have already been collected and entered into a spreadsheet, so we just need to open the file.

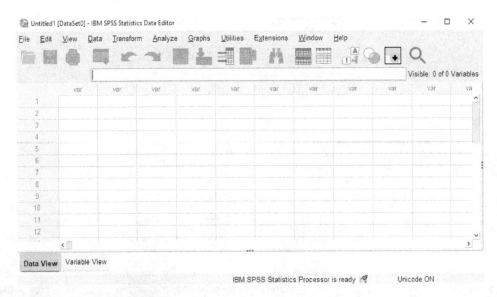

Figure 2.2 The SPSS data editor

Reprint courtesy of IBM Corporation ©

Box 2.2: Data Entry Into SPSS

Entering data into SPSS is as easy as 1, 2, 3 (literally). But there is one very important point you must first bear in mind. Always enter numbers, not words. If SPSS were a person, he or she would be a genius at math, but a dunce at literacy. For example, SPSS, sadly, doesn't understand the words 'male' or 'female', but if you code those words such that 1 = *male* and 2 = *female*, you can enter a series of 1s and 2s instead of male and female. Similarly, SPSS doesn't understand words such as 'strongly disagree', 'disagree', 'agree', and 'strongly agree', but if you code those responses such that 1 = *strongly disagree*, 2 = *disagree*, 3 = *agree*, and 4 = *strongly agree*, you can enter a series of 1s, 2s, 3s, and 4s instead of the words.

Let's say we asked eight workers their gender and how much they agreed with the statement, 'I am the hardest worker in my organization'. Here are the data:

Employee	Gender	"I am the hardest worker in my organization"
1. Andy	Male (coded 1)	Strongly disagree (coded 1)
2. Justin	Male (coded 1)	Agree (coded 3)
3. Josh	Male (coded 1)	Agree (coded 3)
4. Jackson	Male (coded 1)	Strongly agree (coded 4)
5. Meghan	Female (coded 2)	Disagree (coded 2)
6. Cherie	Female (coded 2)	Disagree (coded 2)
7. Diana	Female (coded 2)	Agree (coded 3)
8. Sarah	Female (coded 2)	Agree (coded 3)

(Continued)

If you enter these data into SPSS, it should look like this:

	VAR0000 1	VAR0000 2
1	1.00	1.00
2	1.00	3.00
3	1.00	3.00
4	1.00	4.00
5	2.00	2.00
6	2.00	2.00
7	2.00	3.00
8	2.00	3.00

Note that the names of the respondents are not listed here, only the number of respondents (see the first column in both tables). Usually, research is cofidential and/or anonymous, so the names of the respondents are protected data.

Go ahead and type in some new scores on the spreadsheet.

To open the *survey of employees*, you will first need to save the file somewhere on your computer. Go to the Companion Website (https://study.sagepub.com/timming) and, under 'Chapter 2', go ahead and save the file titled 'Chap2data' on your computer. This file contains variables from the *survey of employees* dataset. Once you have it saved somewhere on your computer, return to the SPSS data editor (which you may, at this point, want to maximize on your screen) and then look along the very top of the window. Click on File , Open, and Data…. Find the 'Chap2data' file where you saved it and then open the data.

Boom! You have successfully opened the WERS 2011 *survey of employees*. I'm sure you can hardly contain your excitement, but don't go overboard. We still have a long way to go in this chapter.

Data Editor Versus Output Viewer

The first thing you might notice when you open the data file is that the empty cells in the data editor are suddenly filled with numbers. These numbers represent *data points* – that is, the actual responses for each variable that were asked on the survey instrument. Another thing you might notice is that a second window has also opened up alongside the data editor. This second window is called the output viewer, depicted in Figure 2.3.

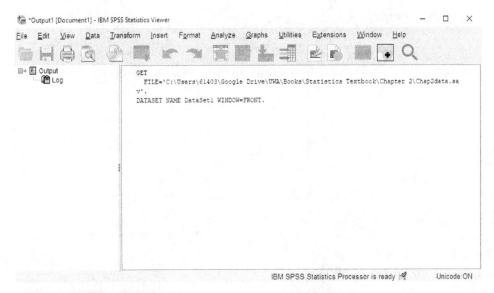

Figure 2.3 SPSS output window

Reprint courtesy of IBM Corporation ©

The *output viewer* window is where you can find the 'results' of all the things you tell SPSS to do. Right now, it's mostly just a white background with a few words along the top. Those words tell you what dataset you've just opened and the directory from which it was opened. Once you start asking SPSS to do things, the results of those procedures will appear on this output window. For example, when you ask SPSS to examine a variable or carry out a statistical test, the output from those requests will appear here. Throughout this book, we will refer to this window as SPSS *output*.

For now, just minimize (but do not close) the output window. This leaves you with a clear view of the SPSS data editor, which you should now maximize if you haven't already.

Data View Versus Variable View

There are two ways of looking at your data within the data editor: the 'Data View' and the 'Variable View'. The data view is illustrated in Figure 2.4, and the variable view is illustrated in Figure 2.5. You'll notice that, in both figures, along the very bottom of the window, just underneath the cells on the left-hand side, are the **Data View** and the **Variable View** options. Go ahead and just toggle them back and forth a few times to see what happens.

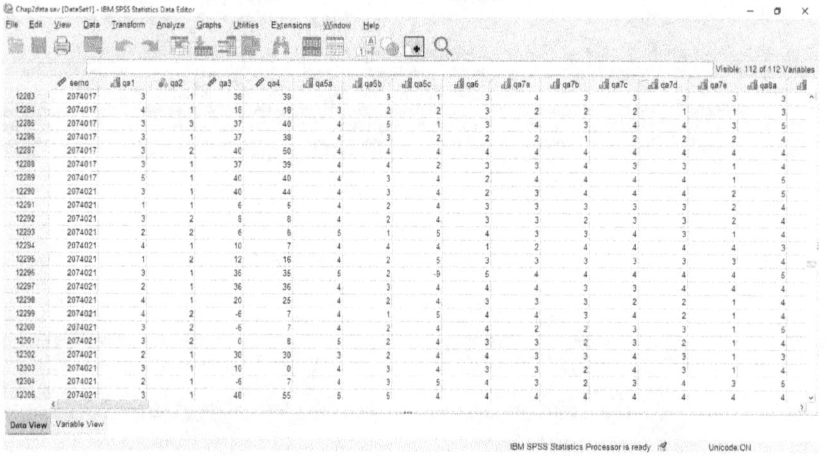

Figure 2.4 Data view in SPSS

Reprint courtesy of IBM Corporation ©

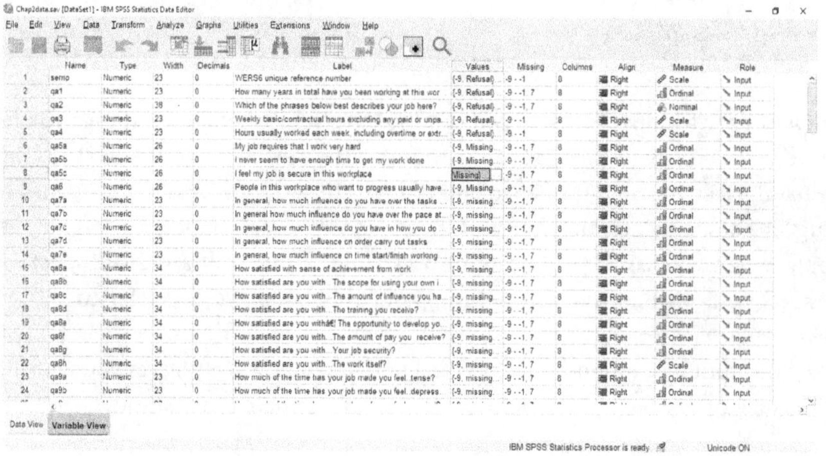

Figure 2.5 Variable view in SPSS

Reprint courtesy of IBM Corporation ©

Data View

In the data view, the rows correspond to individual respondents (in this case, individual employees) who completed the survey instrument and the columns correspond to the variables (items or questions) that were asked of the respondents. The individual cells represent the value for a given respondent on a particular variable.

Note that the rows are labeled by numbers, starting with respondent number 1. If you scroll down the spreadsheet all the way to the bottom, you'll see that there are 21,981 respondents in this dataset. Recall from above that this is the total size of the sample. If you had only administered this survey to 500 employees, then only 500 rows would contain data.

Turning your attention now to the columns, you'll notice that they are labeled with a series of letters and numbers whose meanings are not readily apparent: serno, qa1, qa2, qa3, and so on. The first variable, serno, is a unique identification number for each employee. For the remaining variables, the 'q' stands for 'question' and 'a1' corresponds to question 'A1' on the *survey of employees*, which asks the following question:

> **A1** How many years in total have you been working at this workplace? By workplace we mean the site or location at, or from, which you work.
>
> | Less than 1 year | 1 to less than 2 years | 2 to less than 5 years | 5 to less than 10 years | 10 years or more |
> |---|---|---|---|---|
> | ☐ | ☐ | ☐ | ☐ | ☐ |

In other words, each vertical column in the spreadsheet corresponds to an individual question (or item) that was asked within the instrument, thus constituting a variable.

If, for example, we wanted to find out how respondent 12,287 responded to variable A1, we would start at the column labeled 'qa1' and follow it down 12,287 rows. This particular employee responded '3', which corresponds to '2 to less than 5 years' of total time employed in his or her workplace at the time of the study.

Have a look at some of the other variables for respondent 12,287. How did he or she respond to question 'qd1'?

Variable View

You probably noticed that some very important information is missing from the data view. For example, we don't know what 'qd1' means, and equally important, we don't know whether, or indeed how, that particular variable was even coded. To get this information, and still further details about the variable, select the 'variable view' option, illustrated in Figure 2.5.

When you select *variable view*, suddenly the rows correspond to variables, and the columns correspond to different characteristics, or descriptors, of those variables. So, for example, if you administer a survey instrument with 50 variables in it, then in variable view, there will be 50 rows, each corresponding to one of the variables you asked about. The columns describe each variable in some way or another. Have a scroll down the variable view in the survey of employees. You'll see that there are 151 rows, so you know that there are 151 variables measured in the survey instrument.

Let's take a look at each of these columns. To make changes to them, just click within the relevant cell for each variable.

- *Name:* How you name your variables is entirely up to you. It's an arbitrary choice. You could use a random string of letters or numbers. You could pick a name that reflects the variable: for example, 'whpw' for 'working hours per week'. There are a few restrictions, though. The name cannot have a space and cannot use certain characters such as '&', '!', and '?'. If you try to use one of these restricted characters, SPSS will warn you that the name 'contains an illegal character'. I suspect that 'illegal' might well be a slight exaggeration though, but I have not yet conferred with my attorney on the matter.

- *Type:* This is a relatively unimportant column. By default, the type of variable is set at 'numeric', meaning that the responses are in the form of numbers. It would be unusual to use any other type of variable, so you can just leave this column alone for now.
- *Width:* This column will allow you to widen the number of digits you need to report a score. By default, variables in SPSS are numeric with up to eight digits. If, for example, you need to enter a very large number, you will need to widen this value by clicking within the cell and moving the arrow upward.
- *Decimals:* You can use this column to adjust the number of decimal points you need to add to each variable. Some variables, such as number of co-workers, don't need any decimals, in which case you can leave the setting at zero. If you find that you have 7.6 co-workers in your sample, then you should probably call the paramedics.
- *Label:* This is a very important category. In these cells, you can write out the full variable question, item, or statement, so that you know exactly what is being measured. To do so, you'll need to expand the cell. Do this by hovering the mouse on the line dividing the words 'Label' and 'Values'. Then click and hold while moving the whole line to the right. Notice, for example, that variable qa5c has the label, 'I feel my job is secure in this workplace', and that variable qe2 has the label, 'Age'. Without the correct labels, we would have no way of knowing what qa5c or qe2 mean. Spend some time scrolling up and down the variable view looking at the different labels. Then see how they correspond to the survey of employees located in Appendix A.
- *Values:* This column is equally important. From the 'Labels' column, we already know *what* variables were measured, but we still don't know exactly *how* they were measured and, where applicable, coded. Click in the 'Values' cell to ascertain this information. For example, start with variable qa5c, labeled, 'I feel my job is secure in this workplace'. We obviously know that this is a measure of job security, but we still don't know how this variable was measured. Click in 'Values', and you get the window depicted in Figure 2.6. Here you can see that 1 = *strongly disagree*, 2 = *disagree*, 3 = *neither agree nor disagree*, 4 = *agree*, and 5 = *strongly agree*. Now click on the 'Values' cell for variable qe2, labeled 'Age'. Here, you'll see that age (in years) was measured as an ordinal variable, where 1 = *16-17*, 2 = *18-19*, 3 = *20-21*, 4 = *22-29*, 5 = *30-39*, 6 = *40-49*, 7 = *50-59*, 8 = *60-64*, and 9 = *65 and above*. Whenever you open a dataset, the first thing you should do is to look at the label and values for the variables you intend to use in your statistical analyses.

Figure 2.6 Value labels in SPSS

Reprint courtesy of IBM Corporation ©

- *Missing:* When looking at the values for age, you probably noticed some weird looking numbers. For example, a 97 corresponds to 'multicoded' (which means that a confused respondent must have ticked two or more age ranges on the instrument), and then there are a series of negative numbers that correspond to a set of invalid responses (for various reasons, including refusal or simply not knowing how to respond). SPSS isn't smart enough to know on its own that these are invalid responses, so you need to tell it *not* to factor these numbers into its calculations. You can do this in the 'Missing' column. When you click on the cell, you'll see that you have the option of ticking 'No missing values', giving up to three 'Discrete missing values', or using a range of missing values plus one discrete missing value. Failing to specify missing values means that SPSS will include 97 and the negative numbers into its analyses. If your results suggest, for example, that one of your respondents is –9 years old, this can be explained either by your failure to tell SPSS that these values are 'missing' or by a severe disruption to the space-time continuum. Either way, your statistics aren't very convincing. A good rule of thumb with missing values is to always pick numeric values that cannot possibly be valid responses. For this reason, negative numbers are popular choices for missing values.
- *Columns:* This column is similar to 'Width'. 'Columns' simply refers to the number of viewable digits, whereas 'Width' puts a real restriction on how many digits you can enter. If 'Width' is set at 20, but 'Columns' is only set at 8, then you will only be able to see 8 of the 20 digits.
- *Align:* Alignment can be set at 'left', 'right', or 'center'. This is merely a matter of preference and has no bearing on the statistical analysis.
- *Measures:* Use this column to label each variable as either nominal, ordinal, or scale, as discussed in Chapter 1. Be sure to take the time to do this because there are some functions in SPSS that will only work with properly labeled variables.
- *Role:* You can pretty much just ignore this final column. The 'Role' function facilitates automatic analyses that let SPSS select the variables for you. This is never a good idea since, as established above, SPSS isn't very smart.

Well, there you have it. You are now an expert on Data View and Variable View. Let's now take a quick look at the main toolbar functions available on SPSS.

Toolbar Functions

Figure 2.7 illustrates the various functions available to you in the SPSS toolbar. When viewing any SPSS window, the toolbar is located horizontally along the very top of the screen. A simple breakdown of each function is described below.

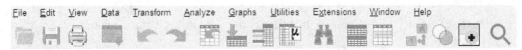

Figure 2.7 SPSS toolbar options

Reprint courtesy of IBM Corporation ©

- *File:* The file menu is pretty standard. You can use it to save or print files and output. You can use it to open data into a spreadsheet or output that has been previously saved. Finally, you can use this function to open a new spreadsheet.

- *Edit:* Here you can cut, copy, and paste either individual data points in each cell or even clear entire rows or columns. For example, in the data view, move the mouse directly over variable qa4 ('Hours usually worked each week, including overtime and extra hours'). Click once and you will notice the entire column is highlighted in gray. Go to Edit and then Copy. Move the mouse all the way to the right to the first empty column you find (labeled 'var'), click it once, and then go to Edit and Paste. You have just copied and pasted the working hours per week variable, which is, by default, labeled VAR00001. Note that if you now enter Variable View and scroll to the bottom of the list, you will see the newly pasted variable now labeled VAR00001. You can change it to 'whpw' (or whatever). If you wanted to clear that variable, you could right click on that row while still in Variable View and select 'Clear'. The Edit function is also useful if you need to Undo an error, 'Go to a case', or 'Go to a variable'.

- *View:* There is no real reason for you to use this menu, but it gives you various options on how to view the data. You can pretty much just ignore it.

- *Data:* The most common reason for using the data menu is to split your dataset or to select only certain cases for your analysis. For example, let's assume you're only interested in analysing the female respondents in the survey of employees. By clicking Data and Select Cases, you can tell SPSS that you only want to select cases 'if' gender = 2 (remembering that gender is coded 1 = *male* and 2 = *female* in the survey of employees). Box 2.3 explains how to carry out this function using SPSS.

Box 2.3: How to Select Cases in SPSS

If you want to analyse only female respondents, you first need to remind yourself of how that variable was measured. Do this by going to the Variable View and scrolling down to your gender variable (qe1). After clicking on the Values box, you will see that 1 = *male* and 2 = *female*.

Now go to Data and Select Cases. Tick 'If condition is satisfied' and then click on 'If'. Scroll down the list on your left until you find 'Gender [qe1]'. Highlight it and move it to the right. Next click on the '=' sign in the little calculator in the middle of the window. Because you only want to select females, and females are coded 2, enter a '2' after the equals sign. So, your equation should look like this:

qe1 = 2

Click Continue and then OK.

If you return to the Data Editor and go to Data View, you will see that about half of the respondents are crossed out. Those are all the men. Any analysis that you carry out under this condition will include only data from female respondents.

To return to the full sample, go back to Data, Select Cases, and then tick 'All cases'. Click 'OK'. If you return to the data editor, you will now see that none of the respondents is crossed out and you can use the full sample again.

- *Transform:* This is where you go when you want to compute a new variable or to recode an existing variable. Both functions are explained in detail later in this chapter, so I won't say anything more about transforming data just now.

- *Analyse:* This is where all the action happens in SPSS. Each statistical test that you'll learn in this book is 'homed' in this menu. There are so many different functions here that I can't even begin to cover them all. So let's go through the ones that are covered in the remaining chapters.

- *Descriptive Statistics:* Before carrying out any of the statistical tests covered in this book, it's always a good idea first to familiarize yourself with the data and to really get a feel for your variables. To this end, you can request Descriptive Statistics in this menu. Commonly requested output includes the mean, standard deviation, skewness, and kurtosis statistics as well as frequency distributions and various graphical representations of the data. All these will be explained in detail in the next chapter.

- *Compare Means:* This is where you go when you want to compare whether two (or more) mean scores are significantly different from one another. For example, do men, on average, make more money than women in Great Britain? Do employees who have already read this book score more highly on their performance appraisals than before they read this book (in this case, you would be comparing performance appraisal scores before and after reading this textbook)? When you are comparing two categories (e.g., men vs. women, white vs. nonwhite, part-time vs. full-time, etc.), you would use the *t*-test, which is described in Chapter 5. When you are comparing three or more categories (e.g., multiple races or ethnicities, nationalities, subsidiaries, units, or departments, etc.), you would use the analysis of variance (ANOVA) test described in Chapter 6. In either of these tests, your independent variable is nominal, and your dependent variable is either ordinal or scale.

- *Correlate:* It should not be surprising to learn that this is where you go when you want to see how two variables correlate with one another. For example, is age positively correlated with income? Is income positively correlated with working hours per week? Is the number of children that a respondent cares for negatively correlated to productivity? In general, both the independent and dependent variables in a bivariate correlation should be ordinal or scale (but it is possible to cheat by using a two-category nominal variable as the independent variable, as will be explained later). The most common correlational test is Pearson's *r*, described in Chapter 8.

- *Regression:* Regression is the foundation of most statistical procedures (Allison, 1999), and it is here that you can find its most common forms. Regression can be bivariate (how does *X* relate to *Y*?) or multivariate (how do *X* and *Z*, among other independent variables, relate to *Y*?). The regression menu branches out into two methods that we will cover in this book. Linear regression uses independent variables ($X_1, X_2 \ldots X_i$) to predict a single ordinal or scale level dependent variable (*Y*). Binary logistic regression uses independent variables ($X_1, X_2 \ldots X_i$) to predict a single dichotomous (two-category) dependent variable (*Y*). Linear regression is explained in Chapters 8 and 9, and binary logistic regression is explained in Chapter 10.

- *Dimension Reduction:* This menu gives you access to factor analysis, which is not exactly a statistical test per se, but rather a way of identifying whether a set of variables can be accurately described by wider factors. For example, if you have 10 variables and you think five measure dimensions of job satisfaction and the other five measure dimensions of organizational commitment, you can run a factor analysis to see if there is any evidence of these two wider factors. This statistical method is described in Chapter 11 of this book.

- *Scale:* This function does not correspond to a particular chapter. You'll recall from Chapter 1 that the reliability of a set of inter-related indicators can be evaluated using Cronbach's alpha (denoted α). You can generate alpha by using this menu, as described in Box 2.4.

Box 2.4: Calculating Cronbach's Alpha in SPSS

Recall from Chapter 1 that a good variable was described as valid, reliable, and accurate. Reliability was defined in terms of the replicability of a variable – that is, can we get (roughly) the same results with an item over and over again.

There is no way, statistically speaking, to evaluate the reliability of a single variable, but when there are multiple variables, each of which relates to one another and 'taps' a wider dimension, we can use Cronbach's alpha to assess reliability. Alpha is always a number between 0 and 1. Generally speaking, statisticians agree that an alpha level of greater than 0.700 suggests an acceptable level of reliability.

Let's ask SPSS to generate an alpha statistic for the five variables in the survey of employees that measure job influence:

A7	**In general, how much influence do you have over the following?**				
					Don't
	A lot	**Some**	**A little**	**None**	**know**
The tasks you do in your job	☐	☐	☐	☐	☐
The pace at which you work	☐	☐	☐	☐	☐
How you do your work	☐	☐	☐	☐	☐
The order in which you carry out tasks	☐	☐	☐	☐	☐
The time you start or finish your working day	☐	☐	☐	☐	☐

Tick one box in each row

Go to 'Analyze', 'Scale', and then 'Reliability Analysis'. Scroll down the list on the left-hand side, select these five variables (qa7a, qa7b, qa7c, qa7d, qa7e) and move them to the right. Click 'OK'.

In the SPSS output, you'll see a box labeled 'Reliability Statistics'.

Reliability Statistics

Cronbach's Alpha	N of Items
.825	5

The alpha level here is 0.825, which suggests an acceptable degree of reliability among these five items measuring job influence.

- *Nonparametric Tests:* Finally, this is where you go when you want to conduct statistical tests of association and when all your variables are nominal (or ordinal with just a few categories). There are multiple nonparametric tests (e.g., Mann–Whitney and Kruskal-Wallis), but we will focus on the chi-square test, which is examined in Chapter 7.
- *Direct Marketing:* This function is not relevant to the WERS datasets, so it is not covered in detail in this book. It is supposedly used by businesses to improve marketing decision-making and customer analysis.
- *Graphs:* Sometimes a picture is worth a thousand words. This is especially true when it comes to data science. This menu gives you access to the SPSS Chart Builder, which creates graphical representations of our data at the click of a mouse. We'll explore the Chart Builder a bit in the next chapter.
- *Utilities:* If you want a quick overview of the variables in your dataset, you can go to Utilities and then Variables. But, then again, you can also access this same information by just clicking into the Variable View. Another useful feature in the Utilities menu is Data File Comments, where you can write up notes about your data and methods.
- *Add-ons:* SPSS is an extremely comprehensive and versatile program, but there are some tests that it simply cannot do. This is where you can access add-on programs that supplement the basic SPSS tests. One add-on is a program called AMOS, which allows us to carry out structural equation modelling (Bollen, 1989). We will learn how to use AMOS in Chapter 12 of this book.
- *Window:* This function allows you to switch from window to window (e.g., from the spreadsheet to the output). But it is easier to do this by pointing and clicking on a PC or by swiping all three fingers up on a Mac mouse pad, so I do not advise using the SPSS Window menu.
- *Help:* I must admit to having made great use of the SPSS Help function back in my days as a student. It can really get you out of a pickle, if you know what I mean. But now that you have this awesome textbook at your disposal, my guess is that you won't need to use this menu. But I won't be offended if you do.

In summary, this is a very general overview of the SPSS toolbar located along the top of your screen. Before moving on to the next section, why not take 15 minutes or so now to further explore this toolbar and the icons below it? Experiment a bit by clicking on some of the functions that were not described above, just to see what happens. Type 'correlation' into the Help function and see what pops up.

Recoding Variables

One of the drawbacks of using secondary data (e.g., WERS) is that you have no control over how the variables were initially measured. Fortunately, there are still ways of modifying how the variables are coded to suit your needs. In Chapter 1, we briefly discussed the concept of recoding. I will now walk you through the recoding process in this section.

We recode variables for various reasons. Maybe the original coding scheme is counter-intuitive or maybe it just doesn't work well with the method you've decided to use. Whatever the reason, recoding is an important skill for any researcher to master. It is often the first thing we do prior to data analysis. Let's look at two examples using the survey of employees.

Recoding Trade Union Membership

Take a look at item D1 in the survey of employees. This item measures trade union membership using three response categories:

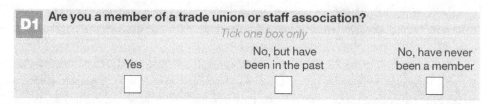

We can see above that there are three response categories, but we still do not know how the variable was coded. To ascertain this information, first go to the Variable View and scroll down to row 59. If you expand the Label section, you'll see, 'Are you a member of a trade union or staff association?' The next column immediately to the right gives the numerical codes that we're looking for. Click that box and you'll see the window depicted in Figure 2.8 open. Scroll through the list and you'll see that the categories labeled between –9 to –1, and 7, are various types of missing data (these should be identified as Missing in the next column over in Variable View). The valid response categories are 1 = *yes*, 2 = *no, but have been in the past*, and 3 = *no, have never been a member*. In other words, there are three valid responses to this variable, coded as 1, 2, and 3.

Figure 2.8 Value labels in SPSS

Reprint courtesy of IBM Corporation ©

You may be perfectly happy to use this variable as it was originally measured, but what if you were only interested in a binary 'yes' or 'no' response to the question? Maybe whether a respondent had been a trade union member in the past is irrelevant to you. To change this variable from a three-category nominal variable to a two-category nominal variable (where 1 = *yes* and 2 = *no*), you're going to have to combine the last two responses into one overarching 'no' category.

To do this, go to Transform along the top of the toolbar in the Data Editor. You'll notice that there are two recode options available in SPSS: Recode into Same Variables... and Recode into Different Variables.... Warning: Do not ever use the Recode into Same Variables option. By recoding into the same variable, you are essentially overwriting the original variable, leaving no trace of it in the dataset. By recoding into different variables, you're creating a whole new (recoded) variable but still keeping the original variable in the dataset for your records. It's always a good idea to leave a visible trail of what you've done, so always use Recode into Different Variables as a default option. When you click on it, you'll see the window depicted in Figure 2.9 open.

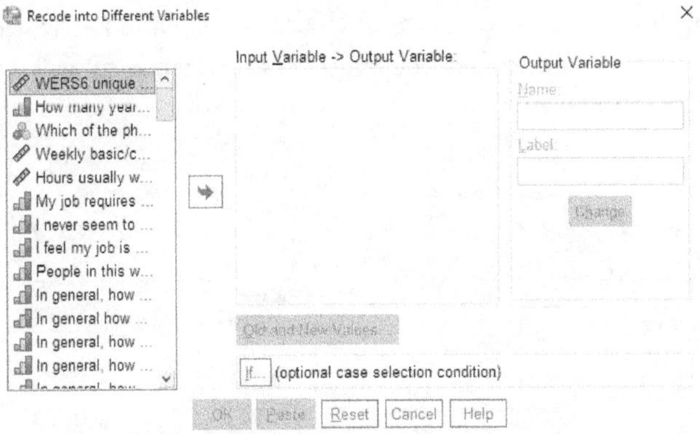

Figure 2.9 Recode into different variables in SPSS

Reprint courtesy of IBM Corporation ©

The first thing you need to do now is to scroll down the list of variables in the left-hand column until you find your trade union variable (qd1). With so many variables, it can be a pain in the you-know-what to find the right one. A good hint is that if you begin to type in the label (e.g., 'Are you a member . . . '), you will automatically go to the variable. To verify that you are at the right one, just hover the mouse over the variable for a few seconds and the full label will expand. When you've found the variable labeled, 'Are you a member of a trade union or staff association? [qd1]', click it and you'll see that it's now highlighted. If you click the ➡ just to the right of that list, you'll notice that the variable qd1 has moved into the box to the right, depicted in Figure 2.10. We now need to create our new output (recoded) variable.

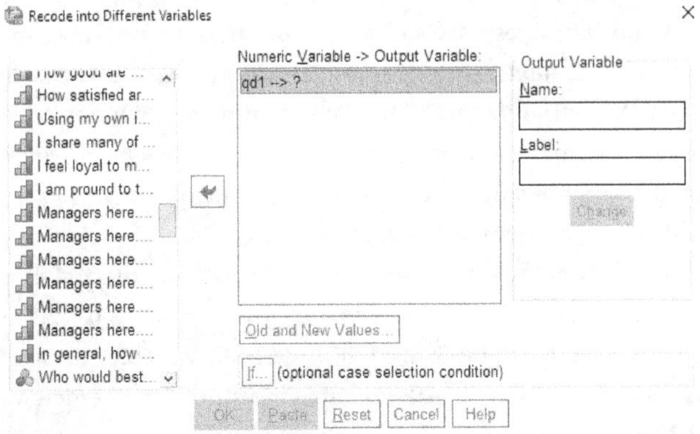

Figure 2.10 Recode into different variables in SPSS, with qd1 as the input

Reprint courtesy of IBM Corporation ©

To the right of the middle box in Figure 2.10, you'll see another box labeled Output Variable. You can name this new variable anything you want, but let's call it 'reqd1'. Type that next to Name. Next to Label, type in 'Recoded Trade Union Membership' to remind yourself that the variable you're creating is a recoded version of the original variable. Click Change and you'll see a new output variable in the middle box: reqd1. But we still haven't recoded the variable yet because we've not told SPSS exactly how we want it recoded. Now click on Old and New Values... and a new window will open up, depicted in Figure 2.11. You'll notice that the left side of this new window is called Old Value and the right side New Value.

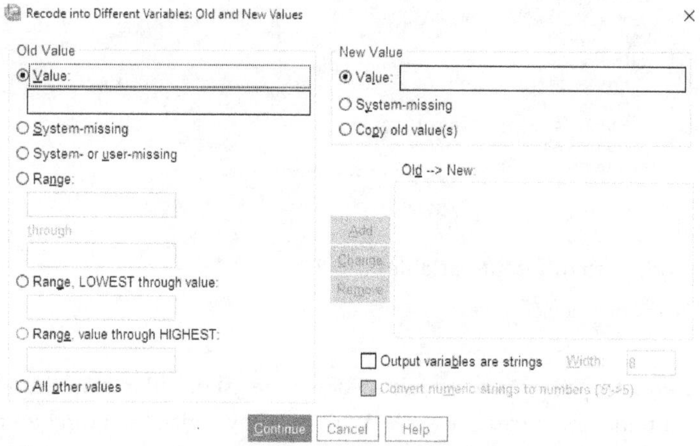

Figure 2.11 Recode into different variables, old and new values

Reprint courtesy of IBM Corporation ©

Let's think about the old and new values for a second. The old values were 1 = *yes*, 2 = *no, but have been in the past*, and 3 = *no, have never been a member*. We want our new values to be, let's say, 1 = *yes* and 2 = *no*. In other words, we want an old value of '1' to remain a new value of '1' (since 'yes' stays the same in both variables) and old values of '2' and '3' to be a single new value of just '2' (which means we're combining both 'no' responses into one overarching 'no' category).

Under Old Value, type in '1' next to ⦿ Value: and then under New Value again type in '1' next to ⦿ Value:. Then click Add. Note that if you fail to click on Add, you will not be able to continue with the recode, so it's very important to remember to click Add after every instruction. You'll see in the box below New Value that an old value of 1 is still a new value of 1 (e.g., 1 → 1). That is to say, 'yes' in the old variable is still 'yes' in the new variable we're creating.

Now under Old Value, click on ⦿ Range: and type '2' through '3' into the spaces. Then move over to New Value and type '2'. Click Add again, and you'll now see that '2 thru 3 → 2'. In other words, you're telling SPSS that what used to be '2' and '3' in the old variable is now just a '2' in the new variable. Alternatively stated, all 2s in the old variable are still 2s in the new variable, but all 3s in the old variable have been converted into 2s in the new variable.

You've now recoded the valid cases (1s, 2s, and 3s), but you still have to do something about those missing values, which, if you recall, were coded between –9 and –1, as well as 7. Let's combine all these different missing data categories into one number, let's say, –9. We can do this because it's not really that important why data are invalid, just that they are invalid. To do this, under Old value, click ◉ All other values at the bottom of the list. Under New Value, type in '–9' next to Value (or you could click 'system-missing', but humor me for now!). The Old → New part of the recode window should now look like the box depicted in Figure 2.12.

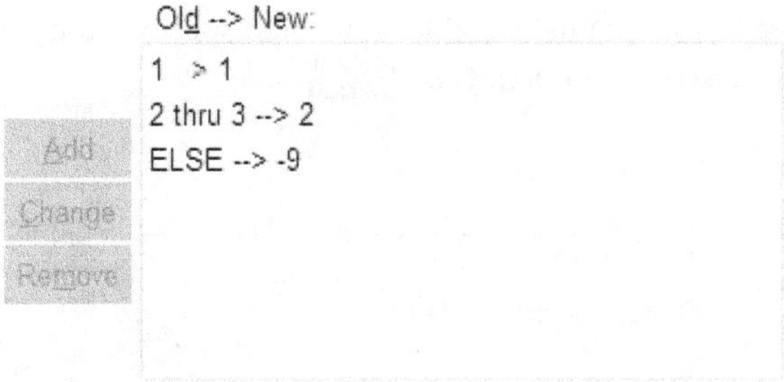

Old --> New:
1 --> 1
2 thru 3 --> 2
ELSE --> -9
Add
Change
Remove

Figure 2.12 Old and new values

Reprint courtesy of IBM Corporation ©

Now click Continue and then OK.

An SPSS output file has just opened up, and on it, you'll see the syntax for the recode function you've just carried out (more on syntax below). Minimize the output window and then scroll to the very bottom of your Variable View. There you'll see the new, recoded trade union membership variable you've just created: reqd1.

Before you can do anything with this newly recoded variable, you must remember to carry out two very important steps. First, click the Values box, which is the column immediately to the right of the new Label. At present, the box should say 'None', since you haven't assigned any values. You need to document for your own benefit exactly how you recoded this variable. When you click just to the right of None, the Values Label window depicted in Figure 12.13 opens. Type '1' next to Value, 'yes' next to Label, and then click Add. Then type '2' next to Value, 'no' next to Label, and then click Add. Finally, type '–9' next to Value, 'missing' next to Label, and then click Add. Then click OK. You've just told SPSS what the numbers 1, 2, and –9 mean.

Value Labels
Value Labels
Value:
Label:
Spelling...
Add
Change
Remove
OK
Cancel
Help

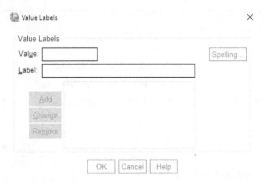

Figure 2.13 Value labels in SPSS

Reprint courtesy of IBM Corporation ©

The second step you need to remember is to tell SPSS that those –9 values are not valid and should therefore be recognized as missing. If you fail to tell SPSS that those –9s are missing values, it will include those numbers in the statistical tests, thus yielding invalid results. To identify missing values, click the Missing box, which is immediately to the right of the Values box you've just been working on in the Variable View. The missing values window depicted in Figure 12.14 opens. Click on ⊙ Discrete missing values and type '–9' into one of the boxes. If you have different types of missing data, as was the case in the original variable, you could specify a range of missing values (e.g., –9 through –1 and 7 as a discrete number). Click OK .

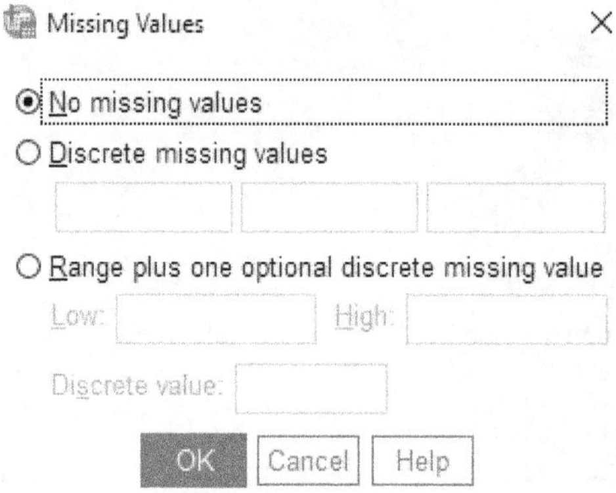

Figure 2.14 Missing values in SPSS

Reprint courtesy of IBM Corporation ©

Boom! You've just recoded your first of many variables on SPSS. You've taken a three-category nominal variable and turned it into a two-category (binary) nominal variable. Go back to Data View. Your new variable will be at the far right of the spreadsheet. Scroll horizontally back and forth to make sure that all 1s in the original variable (qd1) are still 1s in the new variable (reqd1) and that all 2s and 3s in the original variable (qd1) are now 2s in the new variable (reqd1). Nice work!

Recoding Pay Satisfaction

Let's try one more recode before we move on, this time without the graphics to help you. Go to Variable View and scroll down to variable 'qa8f', labeled 'How satisfied are you with . . . the amount of pay you receive'.

To see how this variable was coded, click on the Values box to the right of the label. If you scroll through the list, you will see, once again, a bunch of negative numbers, and 7, coded as various forms of missing data. You'll also see the valid response categories coded as such:

1 = *very satisfied*

2 = *satisfied*

3 = *neither satisfied nor dissatisfied*

4 = *dissatisfied*

5 = *very dissatisfied*

This makes no sense. Under this counterintuitive coding scheme, the *largest* number (5) implies *less* satisfaction and the *smallest* number (1) implies *more* satisfaction. This might not seem like such a big deal to you now, but when you start doing correlational analyses in Chapter 8, you'll want your variables coded more intuitively. Ideally, you want the *largest* number to imply *more* satisfaction and the *smallest* number to imply *less* satisfaction. Think for a moment or two about how we can do that through recoding.

If we were to perfectly invert the Likert scale in our recode, we could make the pay satisfaction variable more intuitively coded. This would mean that all 1s become 5s, all 2s become 4s, 3s remain the same, 4s become 2s and 5s become 1s, as illustrated below:

Original code	Recode
1 = *very satisfied*	5 = *very dissatisfied*
2 = *satisfied*	4 = *dissatisfied*
3 = *neither satisfied nor dissatisfied*	3 = *neither satisfied nor dissatisfied*
4 = *dissatisfied*	2 = *satisfied*
5 = *very dissatisfied*	1 = *very satisfied*

To effect this recode, go to Transform and then Recode into Different Variables… . Scroll down the list on the left-hand side and highlight the pay satisfaction variable (qa8f). Use → to move it to the right. Under the Output Variable box, name it 'reqa8f' and label it 'Recoded how satisfied are you with your pay?'. Click Change .

Click Old and New Values… . An old value of '1' becomes a new value of '5' (click Add). An old value of '2' becomes a new value of '4' (click Add). An old value of '3' remains a new value of '3' (click Add). An old value of '4' becomes a new value of '2' (click Add). An old value of '5' becomes a new value of '1' (click Add). Then, to deal with missing values, under Old Value, select ◉ All other values and under New Value type '–9' and click Add again. Then click Continue and OK .

You've just created your new pay satisfaction variable by perfectly inverting the response categories. But remember that you're not done yet. Scroll to the bottom of Variable View. Go into the Values box and enter your new codes: 1 = *very dissatisfied*; 2 = *dissatisfied*; 3 = *neither satisfied nor dissatisfied*; 4 = *satisfied*; 5 = *very satisfied*; and –9 = *missing*. Then move to the right and click into the Missing box and identify –9 as a discrete missing value to SPSS.

You're a recoding pro now! Fortunately for you, I've already recoded the variables that we'll be using throughout the remaining chapters of this book. But recoding is still an important skill to learn if you want to be an independent researcher someday.

Transforming Data

In addition to recoding, we can also use SPSS to transform variables by, for example, adding several of them together or applying a mathematical operation to each value or response. Let's take a brief look at how we can transform our variables, starting with the procedures for creating a composite. A *composite variable* is a single measure that is composed by adding multiple variables together. For example, look at the following five variables that were used to measure various dimensions of job influence in the survey of employees:

A7 **In general, how much influence do you have over the following?**

Tick one box in each row

	A lot	Some	A little	None	Don't know
The tasks you do in your job	☐	☐	☐	☐	☐
The pace at which you work	☐	☐	☐	☐	☐
How you do your work	☐	☐	☐	☐	☐
The order in which you carry out tasks	☐	☐	☐	☐	☐
The time you start or finish your working day	☐	☐	☐	☐	☐

Here are five separate variables, each of which 'taps' an underlying dimension of job influence. You could just analyse each variable individually, but what if you wanted to create one overall job influence variable that incorporated each dimension? We can create this new composite variable using the Transform function in SPSS.

Note that, to save you time, I've gone ahead and already recoded these five items, such that they are now intuitively coded: 1 = *none*; 2 = *a little*; 3 = *some*; 4 = *a lot*; and –9 = *missing*. The lower score corresponds to less influence, and the higher score means more influence.

To create our new composite variable, go to Transform in the toolbar and then click on ▦ Compute Variable... . The window depicted in Figure 2.15 then opens. Under Target Variable, type 'jobinfl', the name of your new composite variable. Then scroll down the list of variables until you find the first job influence variable (i.e., 'In general, how much influence do you have over the tasks you do [qa7a]'). Click on that variable and then move it to the right using ⇥ . Then in the little calculator in the middle of the window, click the '+' sign. Now move back to the list on the left, highlight the second job influence variable ('In general, how much influence do you have over the pace at which you work [qa7b]'), and move it to the right. Again, click the '+' sign. Repeat these procedures until you have added all five job influence variables.

Figure 2.15 Compute variable function in SPSS

Reprint courtesy of IBM Corporation ©

You could just go ahead and create your new job influence composite variable based on this equation, but then you would lose the original four-point scale (1 = *none*; 2 = *a little*; 3 = *some*; and 4 = *a lot*). If you want to maintain the original four-point scale, you can simply divide all your variables by five (because there are five variables in the new composite variable) by adding a couple of parentheses and a division function. So, your final equation should look like this when typed into Figure 12.15:

(qa7a + qa7b + qa7c + qa7d + qa7e)/5

Click ⬛ OK , return to the Variable View, and then scroll to the very bottom of the list. There you will see your new composite job influence variable, labeled 'jobinfl'. You will need to add some new text under the Label column to remind yourself of what this variable is. Write: 'Job influence composite variable'. You'll also need to remember to click on the Values box and enter the following codes: 1 = *none*; 2 = *a little*; 3 = *some*; 4 = *a lot*; and –9 = *missing*. Finally, don't forget to go into the Missing box and identify –9 as a missing value, so that all those –9s won't be factored into any statistical analyses when using this new composite variable.

You've just created your first composite variable. Good job, soldier!

Let's transform one more variable, just for fun (what???). This time, instead of creating a new composite variable, we're going to apply a mathematical transformation to all of the values in a single variable. Why would we do such a wild thing? I'll explain more in Chapters 3 and 4. For now, let's learn how to use SPSS to square every value in our recoded pay satisfaction variable. Recall that there are five valid responses to this variable, so our transformations should look like this:

Any response of 1 (very dissatisfied) becomes	$1^2 \rightarrow 1$
Any response of 2 (dissatisfied) becomes	$2^2 \rightarrow 4$
Any response of 3 (neither satisfied nor dissatisfied) becomes	$3^2 \rightarrow 9$
Any response of 4 (satisfied) becomes	$4^2 \rightarrow 16$
Any response of 5 (very satisfied) becomes	$5^2 \rightarrow 25$

In other words, after carrying out this simple mathematical transformation, all 1s will still be 1s in the new variable, all 2s will now be 4s, all 3s will be 9s, all 4s will be 16s and all 5s will be 25s.

Go to Transform and then ▦ Compute Variable…. If your equation from the previous exercise is still there, just click Reset in the bottom left-hand side of the window. Name your new target variable 'paysatsq'. Scroll down the list until you find your recoded pay satisfaction variable (reqa8f); highlight it and move it to the right (hint: instead of using the ➜ , you can also double click the variable to move it). To square the values in this variable, click the ** button in the little calculator, and then click or type '2' next to it. Your equation should look like this: reqa8f ** 2. Click ⬛ OK and then scroll down to the bottom of the Variable View. Remember to enter a new Label such as 'Pay satisfaction squared' for the new values (1 = *very dissatisfied*, 4 = *dissatisfied*, 9 = *neither satisfied nor dissatisfied*, 16 = *satisfied*, and 25 = *very satisfied*). Finally, don't forget to identify all –9s as missing values in the next column over.

Now go back to the Data View and scroll to the right to find your newly transformed variable. Go back and forth between the old pay satisfaction variable and the new pay satisfaction variable to make sure that all 1s are still 1, all 2s are now 4s, all 3s are now 9s, all 4s are now 16s, and all 5s are now 25s.

I'm sure at this point you're starting to understand what I said earlier about how great it is that SPSS does the maths for us. Can you imagine how long it would take to square almost 22,000 responses to this variable? Oi!

Syntax

There are two ways to get things done on SPSS. First, you can use the point-and-click graphical interface. This is the approach I take in this textbook. Truth be told, it takes longer to get things done using point-and-click, but it is easier than the alternative. The other option is to use *syntax*, a coding language that can be used to carry out functions in SPSS. If you want to learn SPSS code, don't let me stop you. As I said, using syntax is more efficient than using the graphical user interface. Having said that, if you are interested in coding, I would advise you to use R instead. R is an open source statistical package, meaning you don't have to pay to use it. But it only works if you know how to code. There is no easy point-and-click way of doing stats in R.

If you want to learn SPSS syntax, there is an easy method. Every time we carry out a function in this book, you'll notice that the output window creates the corresponding code. For example, when we created the composite job influence variable above, the following code appeared in the output window:

```
COMPUTE jobinfl=(qa7a + qa7b + qa7c + qa7d + qa7e)/5.
EXECUTE.
```

This code tells SPSS to use the Compute function to add the five job influence variables together, divide those scores by 5, and call the newly created composite 'jobinfl'. But don't worry if you're not into coding. This book uses the graphical interface because it is easier for a beginner.

What Have You Learned?

Well, well, well, look at you. Aren't you an SPSS connoisseur? You know everything there is to know about the SPSS environment (sort of!), and now you're ready to start crunching some numbers. This chapter has introduced you to the WERS datasets that we'll be using in this book and taught you all about the SPSS user interface. You know the difference between Data View and Variable View and how to label variables, code values, and identify missing data. You are an expert on navigating the SPSS toolbar, and you know how to recode and transform variables. Look out world! In the next chapter, you'll learn all about basic descriptive statistics and graphical representations of data. Are you ready? Let's go.

Further Reading

Field, A. (2018). *Discovering statistics using IBM SPSS*. Sage.

George, D., & Mallery, P. (2019). *IBM SPSS statistics 26 step by step: A simple guide and reference*. Routledge.

Leech, N. L., Barrett, K. C., & Morgan, G. A. (2014). *IBM SPSS for intermediate statistics: Use and interpretation*. Routledge.

Pallant, J. (2020). *SPSS survival manual: A step by step guide to data analysis using IBM SPSS*. Routledge.

van Wanrooy, B., Bewley, H., Bryson, A., Forth, J., Freeth, S., Stokes, L., & Wood, S. (2013). *Employment relations in the shadow of recession*. Palgrave Macmillan.

Wagner, W. E., III. (2019). *Using IBM SPSS statistics for research methods and social science statistics*. Sage.

In-Class Discussion Questions

1. What is the difference between Data View and Variable View in SPSS? How are the rows and columns defined differently in each view?
2. How can you recode a variable in SPSS? Why would you recode a variable? What is the difference between recoding into the same variable and recoding into a different variable? Why are you able to recode a scale variable into an ordinal or nominal variable, but not the other way around? Why is recoding useful for Likert variables where 1 = *strongly agree* and 5 = *strongly disagree*?
3. How and why would you use the Compute variable function in SPSS? How and why would you create a composite variable?
4. Why is it so important to update your variable names, labels, codes, and missing values in SPSS? What happens if you forget to instruct SPSS which codes correspond to missing values?
5. How can you select and deselect cases in SPSS? Why would you ever need to do that?
6. How can you square or take the square root of every value in a variable? How can you take the log of every value in a variable?

3

Descriptive Statistics and Graphical Representations

At this stage, you might be feeling so confident in your dynamite IBM SPSS Statistics Software (SPSS) skills that you're ready to start building complex statistical models and testing hypotheses. Well, hold on there, partner. You've still got quite a lot to learn before you can start analyzing like an applied statistician.

This chapter will introduce you to some foundational descriptive statistics as well as ways of representing variables and data graphically. *Descriptive statistics*, as the name clearly implies, describe and summarize variables one at a time. These are distinct from *bivariate statistics*, which examine the relationship between a single independent variable and a single dependent variable (usually denoted X and Y), and *multivariate statistics*, which analyse the relationships between several independent variables ($X_1, X_2, X_3 \ldots X_i$) and/or several dependent variables ($Y_1, Y_2, Y_3 \ldots Y_i$). Chapters 5, 6, 7, and 8 will look at bivariate statistical tests and Chapters 9, 10, 11, and 12 will look at multivariate statistical tests. The descriptive statistics you will learn about in this chapter will help prepare you for those later chapters, so it's best not to skip ahead.

Data can be described and summarized not only with statistics but also with graphical representations. After you've learned how to generate and understand key descriptive statistics in SPSS, we'll also learn to generate charts to help us visualize those variables. The graphs we'll look at will tell us not only about the shapes of our variables, but also about how they might be related to one another.

In this chapter, we'll be using data from the WERS survey of organizations. Recall that this dataset describes organizations, not individual employees within them. It contains data from 2680 workplaces that were randomly selected for inclusion in the WERS sample. Go to the Companion Website and under Chapter 3 Data, open the dataset that is labeled Chap3data.sav.

Measures of Central Tendency

Each variable (nominal, ordinal, or scale) in a dataset can be summarized using one of three *measures of central tendency*. The three measures of central tendency include the following: (1) the mean,

(2) the median, and (3) the mode. All three measures of central tendency aim to 'reduce' information about a single variable to say something about the overall distribution of scores. Crucially, not all three measures of central tendency are relevant to all types of variables. For example, for ordinal- or scale-level variables, we calculate the mean and median, but for nominal-level variables, we calculate the mode. Therefore, different types of variables call for different types of data reduction. Let's take a brief look at each measure of central tendency, in turn. Some basic mathematical calculations are provided here and throughout the rest of the book. You will be shown, step-by-step, how these are calculated.

The Mean

The mean is by far the most common measure of central tendency, and it is probably one with which you are already familiar. The *mean* can be defined as the arithmetic average of a set of scores. It is thus a statistical reflection of the most typical score in a distribution. The mean is important because it is a single number that summarizes all the other numbers in the distribution, but it is only relevant to ordinal- or scale-level variables. The reason we cannot (or should not) calculate the mean for a nominal-level variable is that any such calculation wouldn't make sense. For example, we can't ask what the average 'gender' or 'race' is. We can't ask what the average 'favorite color' is. Such data would be utterly meaningless. However, we can ask about the average debt, profitability, and marketing expenditure. We can ask for the average years of work experience per job candidate or the average score on performance appraisals. Because these are ordinal- or scale-level variables, the mean score is meaningful to us.

Let's imagine that you are studying the internationalization of SME (Knight and Cavusgil, 2004) in Britain and your sample consists of 250 UK-based firms with fewer than 100 employees each. Your sample size is thus $n = 250$. You ask the managers at each firm what percentage of staff were born outside the United Kingdom. The distribution for this variable will include 250 different numbers (provided that you have no missing values). It is not possible to get a feel for the data by looking at 250 different numbers, but if you take the mean, or average, of these numbers and find that it is 7, then you know something 'typical' about that variable: that is, on average, 7% of employees in the organizations you sampled are foreign born.

Let's take a look at Box 3.1 to learn how to calculate the arithmetic mean.

──────────────── **Box 3.1: Calculating the Mean** ────────────────

The equation for the average might appear a bit intimidating at first glance, but it's actually pretty easy. Here it is:

$$\bar{X} = \frac{\Sigma(X_i)}{n}$$

In this equation, $\bar{X}$ is the mean, $\Sigma(X_i)$ is the summation (i.e., adding up all the values) of all the scores in the distribution, and n is the total number of scores in the distribution. Let's take a simple example.

Assume that you administered a short survey to 10 different SMEs asking managers to report the annual training and development budgets for the previous year. You collect the following data:

Manager 1: £500

Manager 2: £0

Manager 3: £300

Manager 4: £250

Manager 5: £0

Manager 6: £750

Manager 7: £400

Manager 8: £10,000

Manager 9: £600

Manager 10: £500

To calculate $\bar{X}$, the first step is to add up all the scores:

$$500 + 0 + 300 + 250 + 0 + 750 + 400 + 10,000 + 600 + 500 = 13,300$$

Then you take that number and divide it by the number of cases (i.e., managers) in the distribution:

$$13,300/10 = 1330$$

Thus, the mean, or average, annual training and development expenditure per company in our sample is £1330.

Using SPSS to calculate the mean for an ordinal- or scale-level distribution is as easy as pie. Let's say you were interested in calculating the average number of training days per year for employees in the largest occupational group in the survey of organizations. The valid responses for that variable (called 'ctrain') include the following:

$1 = no\ time$

$2 = less\ than\ 1\ day$

$3 = 1\ to\ less\ than\ 2\ days$

$4 = 2\ to\ less\ than\ 5\ days$

$5 = 5\ to\ less\ than\ 10\ days$

$6 = 10\ days\ or\ more$

Note that this is an ordinal variable, not a scale variable. A scale measurement would have simply asked how many days, on average, were spent on training in the past year. But even with this ordinal measure, you could imagine how tedious it would be to calculate the mean by hand. There are more than 2680 cases in the survey of organizations, so that's a lot of calculations if done without the help of computer processing! Luckily, our old friend SPSS will kindly calculate the mean at the click of a few buttons. Let's learn how to do it!

First, go to Variable View and find the variable 'ctrain'. You'll notice that this dataset has a lot of variables. You can find ctrain on row 247 in Variable View. Have a look at the Values box to confirm the above schemata and make sure that the Missing column is complete. You'll see that missing values are specified between a low of –9 and a high of –1, so this takes care of all the missing data. Now, to calculate the mean for ctrain, go to Analyze, Descriptive Statistics, and Descriptives... . The new window in Figure 3.1 appears on your screen. Scroll down the list of variables and click on ctrain, moving it to the right using ➡. There are lots of variables in this list, so here's a hint. You can quickly find a variable by typing in the Label – in this case, just start typing 'Number of training days. . . .' Once you have moved ctrain to the right, click on Options... . For now, leave ☑ Mean ticked, but untick ☐ Std. deviation, ☐ Minimum, and ☐ Maximum. Click Continue and then OK . And, boom! You'll notice that the SPSS output window in Figure 3.2 has opened. Check it out.

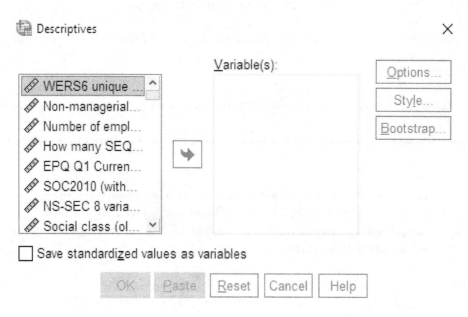

Figure 3.1 Descriptives in SPSS

Reprint courtesy of IBM Corporation ©

➡ **Descriptives**

Descriptive Statistics

	N	Mean
Number of training days experienced staff in largest occ group had in past yr?	2339	4.00
Valid N (listwise)	2339	

Figure 3.2 Descriptive statistics, number of training days

Reprint courtesy of IBM Corporation ©

On the left-hand column of the table, you will see the variable label and 'Valid N'. In the middle column, you'll see that there are 2339 valid cases. 'Hang on', you might be thinking. 'I thought that there were 2680 cases in this dataset!' Well, there are, but not all of the managers provided valid answers to this question. We have missing values that are not calculated into this average: 341 missing values to be exact (2680 – 341 = 2339). Finally, in the right-hand column, we have our mean, 4.00. Remember that this does not mean that, on average, employees in the largest occupational group had four days of training in the last year. If you look at the schemata above, 4 corresponds to '2 to less than 5 days' of training and development. Hence, the average number of days training in the largest occupational group is between two and just under five days.

Now calculate the mean for a few other variables in the survey of organizations. You can pick any variable you want, as long as it's ordinal or scale level. Imagine how long this would take you to do by hand. Are you feeling the love for SPSS just yet?

The Median

Like the mean, the median is only relevant to ordinal- or scale-level variables. It would be wholly meaningless to calculate the median of a nominal variable such as marital status or contract type. The *median* is defined as the exact center in a distribution of scores. Thus, when all the scores are listed out, from the lowest to the highest, the median is the midpoint. A key difference between the mean and the median is that, whereas the mean is affected by extremely high and extremely low scores, the median is not. Take profit as an example. Let's say we asked 10 firms to report their profit margins. Nine of them were SMEs that make hundreds of thousands of dollars in profit, but one of them was Google that makes hundreds of millions of dollars in profit. When calculating the mean,

Google's extremely high profit margin will 'pull' the average score up, leading to a distorted value. However, when calculating a median, Google's extreme score does not affect the midpoint of the distribution, which remains in the hundreds of thousands of dollars. This difference is illustrated in Box 3.2, where you learn how to calculate the median.

─────────────── **Box 3.2: Calculating the Median** ───────────────

There is no real 'equation' as such for calculating the median. Let's use the same data from Box 3.1. Remember that we asked 10 managers to report the annual training and development budget for the previous year. But this time, we'll list out the 10 data points in order, from the lowest training and development budget to the the highest:

Manager 2: £0

Manager 5: £0

Manager 4: £250

Manager 3: £300

Manager 7: £400

Manager 1: £500

Manager 10: £500

Manager 9: £600

Manager 6: £750

Manager 8: £10,000

This is the exact same data from Box 3.1, so we already know that the mean, or average, is £1330. You probably suspected that the reason this number is so high is that it was 'pulled' up by Manager 8, whose firm spent £10,000 on training.

To calculate the median, simply find the middle score. When there is no middle score, as in this distribution, find the two middle scores and then calculate the average. The two middle scores here are Manager 7 (£400) and Manager 1 (£500). So the median in this distribution is (400 + 500)/2 = £450.

Note that the median of £450 is considerably lower than the mean of £1330. This difference is due to the fact that the outlier, Manager 8, exerted influence on the mean, but not on the median.

───

Let's now use SPSS to calculate the median as well as the mean. This time, I'm going to show you a different way compared with how we calculated the mean above. First, let's pick an ordinal- or scale-level variable from the survey of organizations. When looking on the Variable View, scroll down to inuminj (this is on row 793 in the dataset), 'Number of workplace injuries in the last year'. You can see under Values that there is no coding scheme, which suggests that this is a true scale-level variable.

In other words, a response of 8 means that there were eight injuries in the last year, and a response of 1 means that there was only one last year, and so on. You can and should also verify, under the Missing column, that missing values (labeled from –9 to –1) are signaled to SPSS as missing.

To calculate the mean and the median, first go to Analyze, Descriptive Statistics, and Frequencies.... Scroll down to 'Number of workplace injuries in the last year' and move it to the right (Hint: you can find this variable quickly just by typing the label) using ⇥. Now click on Statistics..., and tick ☑ Mean and ☑ Median under Central Tendency. Click Continue. Note that, under the list of variables in the dataset, you'll see that ☑ Display frequency tables is ticked by default. That's fine. Just click OK, and, boom! The SPSS output window in Figure 3.3 opens.

Statistics

Number of workplace injuries in the last year.

N	Valid	443
	Missing	2237
Mean		3.78
Median		1.00

Number of workplace injuries in the last year.

		Frequency	Percent	Valid Percent	Cumulative Percent
Valid	1	230	8.6	51.9	51.9
	2	93	3.5	21.0	72.9
	3	37	1.4	8.4	81.3
	4	22	.8	5.0	86.2
	5	17	.6	3.8	90.1
	6	10	.4	2.3	92.3
	7	4	.1	.9	93.2
	8	4	.1	.9	94.1
	10	13	.5	2.9	97.1
	14	1	.0	.2	97.3
	20	2	.1	.5	97.7
	24	1	.0	.2	98.0
	30	1	.0	.2	98.2
	33	1	.0	.2	98.4
	40	2	.1	.5	98.9
	45	1	.0	.2	99.1
	50	2	.1	.5	99.5
	60	1	.0	.2	99.8
	300	1	.0	.2	100.0
	Total	443	16.5	100.0	
Missing	Don't know	71	2.6		
	Item not applicable	2166	80.8		
	Total	2237	83.5		
Total		2680	100.0		

Figure 3.3 Descriptive statistics and frequencies, number of workplace injuries

The first thing to bear in mind is that these data only include workplaces where at least one accident was reported. Thus, workplaces where there were no accidents at all are excluded. Looking at the first box, you'll see that the valid number of cases is 443. Remember, this is out of 2680 organizations, so this tells us that most managers did not report any accidents, hence the 2237 missing cases. The mean is 3.78, and the median is 1.00. The next box down is the frequency distribution for this variable. A *frequency distribution* is a layout of the total responses for the variable and how they break down in terms of numbers and percentages. Have a look at that second table in Figure 3.3.

Looking at the top line, you can see that 230 organizations reported having '1' accident, constituting 8.6% of the total 2680 cases, but this percentage takes into account the missing data, which includes workplaces with no accidents. The Valid Percent is listed as 51.9%. In other words, of all the organizations that reported an accident, just over half reported only one accident in the last year. This value already explains why the median is 1, because it is the midpoint. Looking further down the table, you can see that several organizations reported up to 300 accidents per year. These large numbers were used in the calculation of the mean, thus 'pulling' up the average score to 3.78.

In short, where the mean is higher than the median, high outliers are pulling the average up. Conversely, where the mean is lower than the median, low outliers are pulling the average down.

The Mode

The *mode* is defined as the most frequently occurring case in a distribution of scores. It is not a terribly helpful measure of central tendency and is typically only used to summarize the 'typical case' for nominal-level variables. For example, when studying occupational groups, the mode will be the group with the highest number of cases.

Let's calculate the mode for the variable kerfis using SPSS. This variable (found on row 977 of Variable View) asks the managers how they measure financial performance. The responses are as follows:

1 = *profit*

2 = *value added*

3 = *sales*

4 = *fees*

5 = *budget*

6 = *costs*

7 = *expenditure*

8 = *stock market indicators* (e.g., share price)

9 = *other* (please specify)

Obviously, in addition to calculating the mode, it would be nonsensical to calculate the mean and median for this variable, but, hey, let's do it anyway just so that you can see that those statistics make no sense.

Go to Analyze, Descriptive Statistics, and ☒ Frequencies... . Start typing 'Measure of financial performance' and then move it to the right using ⇥ . Go into Statistics... and this time tick ☑ Mean,
☑ Median, and ☑ Mode. Now click Continue and then OK . Boom! The results appear in the SPSS
output depicted in Figure 3.4.

Statistics

Measure of financial performance

N	Valid	2626
	Missing	54
Mean		3.22
Median		2.51[a]
Mode		1

a. Calculated from
grouped data.

Measure of financial performance

		Frequency	Percent	Valid Percent	Cumulative Percent
Valid	profit	1083	40.4	41.2	41.2
	value added	235	8.8	8.9	50.2
	sales	207	7.7	7.9	58.1
	fees	34	1.3	1.3	59.4
	budget	699	26.1	26.6	86.0
	costs	156	5.8	5.9	91.9
	expenditure	90	3.4	3.4	95.4
	stock market indicators (e.g. share price)	24	.9	.9	96.3
	other (please specify)	98	3.7	3.7	100.0
	Total	2626	98.0	100.0	
Missing	Refusal	5	.2		
	Don't know	46	1.7		
	Item not applicable	3	.1		
	Total	54	2.0		
Total		2680	100.0		

Figure 3.4 Descriptive statistics and frequencies, measure of financial performance

Reprint courtesy of IBM Corporation ©

Here you can see that there are 2626 valid cases, meaning that there were 54 managers who
did not provide valid responses to this question. The mean is reported as 3.22 and the median as
2.51. Again, neither of these numbers makes any sense. I included these figures to demonstrate the

garbage-in-garbage-out principle in statistics. In short, this means that SPSS will calculate anything you tell it to calculate, even if it makes no sense at all.

Note, however, that the mode of 1 is meaningful. Recall that 1 corresponds to 'profit'. If you look in the frequency distribution in Figure 3.4, 1083 managers reported that they measured financial performance in relation to profit. This corresponds to 41.2 valid percent, which is the highest number by far. The next most frequent way of measuring financial performance was through 'budget', with 26.6 valid percent and then 'value added' with 8.9 valid percent. The least common measure of financial performance was 'stock market indicators', which correspond to only 0.9 valid percent. In other words, just under 1% of the organizations in the sample measured financial performance via the stock market. This should not be surprising, given that only very large firms are listed on the stock exchange.

Measures of Dispersion

So you now know pretty much everything there is to know about measures of central tendency. Nice work, hot shot. Now let's learn about measures of dispersion. Whereas measures of central tendency are focused on the center of a distribution, *measures of dispersion* are focused on the amount of 'spread' across a distribution. In other words, central tendency looks 'inward', whereas dispersion looks 'outward', focusing on the range of scores across a distribution. In fact, the *range* is the first of two measures of dispersion we'll cover in this section. The second is the *standard deviation*. Before we describe these two statistics, it's worth noting at the outset that the range and standard deviation, like the mean and median, are only relevant for ordinal- and scale-level variables. Measures of dispersion are irrelevant for nominal variables.

The Range

The *range* is the simplest measure of the spread across a distribution of score. It is a reflection of the difference between the highest and the lowest scores. Like the median, you simply arrange the scores from the lowest to the highest and then subtract the lowest score from the highest score. The larger the distance between the highest score and the lowest score in a distribution, the larger the range. It's pretty simple.

For example, let's say 10 managers were asked how many full-time employees work in their organizations. They respond, from the lowest to the highest: 12, 25, 40, 45, 170, 350, 500, 1000, 1500, and 2000. To calculate the range, simply take the highest score (i.e., 2000) minus the lowest score (i.e., 12). This gives you a range of 1988.

There is really no point in learning how to use SPSS to calculate the range because, in the broad scheme of things, it's not really that important of a statistic. Moreover, it has one very key limitation when describing the spread of a distribution of scores: it is only based on two numbers, the highest and the lowest. All the numbers in between are not taken into consideration in its calculation.

The Standard Deviation

Because of this limitation of the range, most statisticians, when describing the spread of ordinal or scale (but not nominal) variables will calculate the standard deviation. The *standard deviation* can be defined as the average variability (or spread) of scores in an ordinal- or scale-level distribution. The good thing about the standard deviation, relative to the range, is that it takes into account every single score and its relationship with the arithmetic mean.

There are a few characteristics of the standard deviation that must be kept in mind. First, the standard deviation, like the mean or the median, is a single number that is calculated based on a set of numbers for a given item or question on a survey. Second, as noted above, the standard deviation is only relevant if the item or question is either ordinal or scale. Third, if there is no variability (or spread) in the scores, then the standard deviation will always be zero. For example, if 10 managers were asked what their marketing budget was in the last year, and all 10 answered £12,000, then the standard deviation would be, by definition, zero since none of the scores deviates from the average, which also happens to be £12,000. Fourth, the more variability there is in the scores, the higher the standard deviation, and the less variability there is in the scores, the lower the standard deviation. Thus, variables with scores that extend further from the mean have higher standard deviations than those with scores that are closer to the mean.

Let's explore this fourth characteristic a little further. Imagine that eight managers were asked three questions in a survey. How many working days were lost to strike action last year? What percentage of your employees is unionized? How much did you spend on promotional pens last year? Because eight managers completed the survey, our sample size is $N = 8$. All three questions are true scale-level variables. The results from our hypothetical survey are reported below:

How many working days were lost to strike action last year?

5, 5, 5, 5, 5, 5, 5, 5

What percentage of your employees is unionized?

50, 48, 50, 52, 50, 49, 50, 51

How much did you spend on promotional pens last year?

50, 100, 1000, 500, 2500, 1500, 4500, 5000

Just eyeballing these scores, we know that the standard deviation for strike days is necessarily zero, since there is no variability across the scores. All eight firms reported the same number of working days lost in the last year to strike activity: 5. Looking at the second variable, we can assume that the standard deviation will be pretty low because most of the scores hover around 50%. The highest score is 52% and the lowest 48%, so we can safely assume that there is a lot of *homogeneity* across the scores when it comes to the percentage of employees that are unionized. Homogeneity refers to a high level of uniformity across scores in a distribution. However, when asked to report how much they spent on promotional pens, you can clearly see much more *heterogeneity* in scores, from a low of 50 (pounds or dollars or whatever) to a high of 5000 (pounds or dollars or whatever). Heterogeneity refers to a high degree of diversity, or variation, in scores. Because of this huge variation, we can safely assume that the standard deviation for the last variable will be considerably larger than for the second variable. Let's take a look at how to calculate the standard deviation for all three variables.

Calculating the Standard Deviation

There are many different ways to present a single mathematical formula, but as long as they are algebraically equivalent, you will arrive at the exact same result regardless. Different statistics textbooks use different versions of the standard deviation formula. I have found that Formula 3.1 is best when computing the standard deviation 'by hand', but others might disagree:

Formula 3.1

$$SD = \sqrt{\frac{\sum X_i^2}{N} - \bar{X}^2}$$

Let's break this down so it's less intimidating. First, $\sqrt{}$ means 'take the square root of'. Second, Σ means 'sum up' or 'add up'. Third, X_i^2 means 'all of the scores in the distribution squared'. Fourth, N means 'the total number of cases in the distribution'. Finally, $\bar{X}^2$ means 'the mean, or average, of the distribution squared'. In other words, to calculate the standard deviation for an ordinal- or scale-level variable, X, you take the square root of the summation of each score squared, divided by the total number of cases, minus the mean squared. This may sound a bit complicated, but if you break the process down into steps, it's a lot easier. Let's see how Formula 3.1 works for each of the three variables discussed above.

How Many Working Days Were Lost to Strike Action Last Year?

This one is easy. We already know that the standard deviation must be zero because we can clearly see that there is no variation between each individual score (5, 5, 5, 5, 5, 5, 5, 5) and the mean score (5). But let's just go ahead and calculate it anyway, taking it part by part.

$$\sum X_i^2$$

(1) $(5^2 + 5^2 + 5^2 + 5^2 + 5^2 + 5^2 + 5^2 + 5^2)$

(2) $(25 + 25 + 25 + 25 + 25 + 25 + 25 + 25)$

(3) $= 200$

$$N$$

(1) $= 8$

$\bar{X}^2$

(1) $(5 + 5 + 5 + 5 + 5 + 5 + 5 + 5/8)^2$

(2) $(40/8)^2$

(3) $(5)^2$

(4) $= 25$

So, plugging in the numbers, we get the following:

(1) $SD = \sqrt{\dfrac{200}{8}} - 25$

(2) $SD = \sqrt{25} - 25$

(3) $SD = \sqrt{0}$

(4) $SD = 0$

Thus, as we expected, the standard deviation for this variable is indeed 0, implying that there is no variation between each individual score and the mean score. The distribution is completely homogeneous.

What Percentage of Your Employees Is Unionized?

Okay, now let's try to calculate the standard deviation for this variable. Recall that the eight responses for this question were 50%, 48%, 50%, 52%, 50%, 49%, 50%, and 51%. We can already assume that there is some variation here, so we know that the standard deviation will not equal zero, as it was in the example above. Here we go, nice and slow and easy. Follow each step closely.

ΣX_i^2

(1) $(50^2 + 48^2 + 50^2 + 52^2 + 50^2 + 49^2 + 50^2 + 51^2)$

(2) $(2500 + 2304 + 2500 + 2704 + 2500 + 2401 + 2500 + 2601)$

(3) $= 20{,}010$

N

(1) $= 8$

$\bar{X}^2$

(1) $(50 + 48 + 50 + 52 + 50 + 49 + 50 + 51/8)^2$

(2) $(400/8)^2$

(3) $(50)^2$

(4) $= 2500$

So, once again plugging in the numbers, we get the following:

(1) $SD = \sqrt{\dfrac{20010}{8}} - 2500$

(2) $SD = \sqrt{2501.25} - 2500$

(3) $SD = \sqrt{1.25}$

(4) $SD = 1.12$

Thus, the standard deviation for this variable is 1.12, which is an average measure of the amount of variability in scores relative to the mean.

How Much Did You Spend on Promotional Pens Last Year?

Let's now calculate the standard deviation for our last variable. Just eye-balling the distribution, we can already clearly see that there is much more 'spread' here than for the percentage of unionized employees. Remember that the eight responses for this variable were as follows: 50, 100, 1000, 500, 2500, 1500, 4500, and 5000 (pounds or dollars or whatever). These are some pretty big numbers to calculate by hand, but hang in there:

ΣX_i^2

(1) $(50^2 + 100^2 + 1000^2 + 500^2 + 2500^2 + 1500^2 + 4500^2 + 5000^2)$

(2) $(2500 + 10{,}000 + 1{,}000{,}000 + 250{,}000 + 6{,}250{,}000 + 2{,}250{,}000 + 20{,}250{,}000 + 25{,}000{,}000)$

(3) $= 55{,}012{,}500$

N

(1) $= 8$

$\bar{X}^2$

(1) $(50 + 100 + 1000 + 500 + 2500 + 1500 + 4500 + 5000/8)^2$

(2) $(15,150/8)^2$

(3) $(1893.75)^2$

(4) $= 3,586,289.06$

Finally, plugging in the numbers, we get the following:

(1) $SD = \sqrt{\dfrac{55,012,500}{8}} - 3,586,289.06$

(2) $SD = \sqrt{6,876,562.5} - 3,586,289.06$

(3) $SD = \sqrt{3,290,273.44}$

(4) $SD = 1813.91$

So, as you can see, the standard deviation for the first variable is zero, because there is no variation among the scores. The standard deviation for the second variable is 1.12 because there is a little variation among the scores. And the standard deviation for the last variable is 1813.91 because there is a lot of variation among the scores. The last variable is said to be more heterogeneous than the first two because of the greater diversity in scores.

If you thought that was hard work, I have some good news. Fortunately for us, we never really have to calculate the standard deviation by hand. Why sweat it when SPSS can do it for us? But before you enter the data above into SPSS to double check your long hand math, let me just warn you that SPSS might give you a slightly different number for the standard deviation. The main reason for this slight difference is that SPSS uses a slightly different formula. So don't freak out like I did when I first checked the SPSS results against this formula!

Calculating the Standard Deviation Using SPSS

Calculating the standard deviation using SPSS is easy as pie. In fact, you already know how to do it because it is basically the same procedure that we used above to calculate the mean and median.

Looking at the Variable View, find 'zallemps' (located conveniently on row 6). This variable asks, '[c]urrently how many employees do you have on the payroll at this workplace'. If you go into Values, you'll see that there are no codes here (other than the missing data), so it is a true scale-level variable. In other words, a response of 2457 means that there are 2457 employees on payroll in the organization. Double check the missing box to ensure that all values between –9 and –1 are coded as missing.

To calculate the standard deviation, go to A̲nalyze, D̲escriptive Statistics, and F̲requencies…. Highlight the variable, zallemps (sixth from the top), in the left-hand column and move it to the right using ✦ . Click on Statistics . This time, under Dispersion , tick ☑ Std̲. deviation, ☑ Mi̲nimum, ☑ Ma̲ximum, and ☑ Ra̲nge. While we're at it, let's go ahead and also ask for the ☑ M̲ean and ☑ Me̲dian under Central Tendency. Click Continue and then OK . Boom! The output describing the current number of employees on payroll is depicted in Figure 3.5. Let's take a closer look at this output.

Statistics

EPQ Q1 Currently how many employees do you have on the payroll at this workplace

N	Valid	2680
	Missing	0
Mean		449.30
Median		67.00
Std. Deviation		1213.544
Range		20741
Minimum		5
Maximum		20746

Figure 3.5   Descriptive statistics: How many employees on payroll

Reprint courtesy of IBM Corporation ©

You can see from the first box that there are 2680 valid cases and no missing values. In other words, every manager who completed the survey answered this question on organizational size. You can also see that the average organizational size is 449.30 employees, and the median is 67.00 employees. Recall from the discussion above that a larger mean relative to the median (as in this case) suggests that extremely large organizations are 'pulling' the average up. Indeed, if you look at the bottom of the output box, you'll see that the minimum number of employees in these workplaces is 5 (this was the threshold set by the WERS researchers) and the maximum is a whopping 20,746, which, in part, explains why the mean is so much larger than the median. The standard deviation is reported to be 1213.54 (aren't you glad we didn't have to do this calculation by hand?!?), and the range is 20,741 (which is 20,746 – 5, the maximum minus the minimum values).

So there you have it. Admittedly, the standard deviation is not as easily 'intuitive' as the mean. Most people know that the average represents a central, or typical, case. It is harder to grasp the more abstract concept of dispersion, or spread. But what you really need to take away from this section is that the standard deviation is a number that, in effect, measures how far away each case in a distribution is relative to the mean. The more spread out the scores are relative to the mean, the larger the standard deviation; the closer the scores 'bunch' around the mean, the lower the standard deviation. Where every score is exactly the same, the standard deviation will always be zero.

Frequency Distributions and Histograms

Hopefully you haven't yet closed Figure 3.5, the output for organizational size that we just looked at. If you did, no worries. Just redo the steps above. It'll be good practice. I want to spend a little more time talking about frequency distributions. You should already be familiar with this term – that is, provided that you weren't spacing out while reading earlier parts of this chapter.

Take a look at the second (very long!) table (not reproduced here due to the length). Don't let the size of this table overwhelm you. Let's start with the first column that begins with the word Valid. As you scroll down, you'll see lots of numbers, starting with 5 at the top and ending with 20,746 at the bottom. These are the actual responses from managers to this survey item (i.e., the number of employees in the organization). The next column over is titled Frequency. This column gives the number of managers per response to the question. So, for example, a frequency of 55 means 55 (out of 2680) of the managers reported five employees on payroll. Another 73 (out of 2680) of the managers reported seven employees on payroll. And another 35 (out of 2680) of the managers reported 15 employees on payroll. If you scroll to the very bottom, you'll see that only one (out of 2680) manager reported 20,746 employees on payroll. Go ahead and look at the different organizational sizes and the corresponding number of managers.

The next two columns over, labeled Percent and Valid Percent, are identical for this variable. The reason that they are identical is that there are no missing values for zallemps. That is, all 2680 managers provided valid responses when asked about organizational size. If there were missing values, then the Percent column would give the total out of 2680 responses (including missing values), and the Valid Percent column would only give the total out of the valid responses to the items (thus, excluding missing values). Have a look at the rest of the table and see if you can find out what percentage of organizations report having exactly 100 employees on payroll. If you found 0.3%, then you are correct. This corresponds to 8 organizations. In fact, if you take 8/2680, you get 0.0029, which corresponds to 0.3%. Pretty nifty, eh? Finally, in the last column, you have the Cumulative Percent reported. This starts with the first category of response (5 employees) and simply adds them all up until you get to 100%.

The problem with frequency distributions like this one is that they are sometimes hard to understand and especially to visualize. There are a lot of numbers there, and it's not easy to get a feel for the 'big picture' just by looking at it. Fortunately, we can convert all frequency distributions into visual histograms, and we do this because 'a picture is worth a thousand numbers', as the old saying goes. A *histogram* is defined as a visual representation of a frequency distribution. Let's produce the histogram for this variable using SPSS.

Go to Analyze, Descriptive Statistics, and Frequencies... . The variable should still be listed under the Variable(s): box. Now click on Statistics... and then Continue. You'll see the options you previously ticked are still ticked. This time, I want you to click on Charts... . Now, click next to ⊙ Histograms: and then click Continue and OK . And boom!

The first thing you'll notice is that you've reproduced exactly the same two tables that we were previously looking at (Figure 3.5 and the frequency distribution). But if you scroll to the bottom of the page, you'll see the histogram for this variable. It is depicted in Figure 3.6. Along the X-axis (the horizontal line at the bottom), you'll see the actual responses, from 5 to 20,746 employees. Along the Y-axis (the vertical line on the left-hand side), you'll see the frequency (or number of cases per response). You'll also note that, just to the right of the histogram, the mean, standard deviation, and number of cases are reported. Immediately, you can see a 'bunching' of responses on the lower end of the X-axis. This means that there are a lot of organizations in the WERS dataset with fewer than, say, 200 employees. The larger the organizational size gets, the fewer organizations of that size in the sample. Here you can see, visually, why the mean for this variable (449.30 employees) is so much larger than the median (67.0 employees). The larger organizations, although far fewer in number, are positively impacting on the overall average and pulling it up.

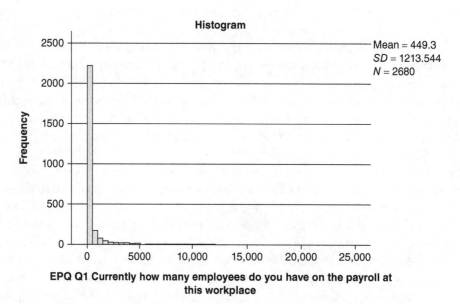

Figure 3.6 Histogram: How many employees on payroll

Reprint courtesy of IBM Corporation ©

The second thing you'll notice is that the histogram is a mirror image of the frequency distribution we examined earlier. Histograms are a visual representation of the frequency distribution. Have a look at both and see how they reflect one another.

What if we removed the influence of the extremely large organizations from the distribution? Let's imagine that we only wanted to look at SMEs with less than, say, 200 employees on payroll. What would the histogram look like then? Let's find out by learning something new in SPSS.

First, go to Data along the top row in SPSS (you can find this at the top of the data editor and the output) and then Select Cases... near the bottom of the list. Click next to ⊙ If condition is satisfied and then click on ⌷ If... ⌷. Find your variable in the left-hand list and move it to the right using ⌷ ➡ ⌷. Then, in the calculator, click the '<' sign and type '200'. So the full equation should look like this: 'zallemps < 200'. Click Continue and then ⌷ OK ⌷. You might not notice that anything has changed in SPSS, but if you go into Data View, you'll see that a number of responses have been 'slashed', like this: ___2___ This slash means that those cases will be omitted from anything you ask SPSS to do from now on. Now, I'd like you to reproduce your histogram by going to Analyze,

Descriptive Statistics , and Frequencies…. If you want, you can double check in Statistics… and Charts…
to make sure everything we requested is still ticked, or you could just trust me and click OK .
And, boom!

Looking at the first box, you'll see that there are now 1872 valid cases, meaning that we removed
808 cases from the sample (2680 – 1872 = 808). These 808 organizations are 'large', defined as having
200 or more employees on payroll. You'll also notice that the new mean (51.67 employees) is much
closer to the new median (32.00 employees). This is because the influence of the very large organizations has been removed for these analyses. The standard deviation is now 49.49, and the range is
194 (i.e., 199 – 5). Now have a look at the frequency distribution below it. Note that it only includes
firms with up to 199 employees on payroll. Then compare it to the new histogram, depicted in Figure
3.7. In effect, what we've done with this new histogram, compared with the one in Figure 3.6, is to
'zoom in' on only the left-hand tail of the distribution. You can see a lot more detail in Figure 3.7.

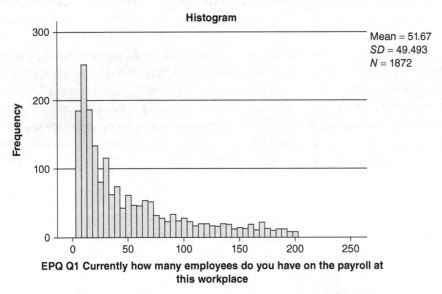

Figure 3.7   Histogram: How many employees on payroll, transformed

Reprint courtesy of IBM Corporation ©

When you are done comparing the two histograms and frequency distributions, don't forget to
go back into Data and Select Cases…. Tick ⦿ All cases and then OK to get back to the full dataset.
If you check in Data View, you'll see that no cases are slashed out anymore. You're back to the full
dataset, including large organizations.

Skewness and Kurtosis

Both skewness and kurtosis are important concepts in statistics. They each say something about
the overall shape of an ordinal- or scale-level distribution of scores. For nominal variables, these
concepts are, again, irrelevant.

In short, *kurtosis* refers to the extent to which a set of scores is clustered close to (vs. far from) the mean. *Skewness* refers to the extent to which a few extreme scores exist at either of the tail ends of the distribution. Let's take a closer look at these concepts, because they are a bit hard to understand without visual aids.

Kurtosis

An ordinal- or scale-level variable is said to suffer from kurtosis if it is excessively 'flat' or excessively 'peaked'. The level of kurtosis is expressed as a single number (much like the mean or the standard deviation). When the kurtosis statistic equals zero, then the distribution does not suffer from kurtosis. When the kurtosis statistic is greater than zero (i.e., when it is a positive number), the distribution is said to be *leptokurtic*. This means that the distribution is excessively 'peaked' (e.g., tall and thin). When the kurtosis statistic is less than zero (i.e., when it is a negative number), the distribution is said to be *platykurtic*. This means that the distribution is excessively 'flat' (e.g., short and wide).

Figures 3.8a and b illustrate the difference between leptokurtosis and platykurtosis, respectively. These are two hypothetical histograms of ordinal- or scale-level variables. The one on the left is leptokurtic, so the kurtosis statistic will necessarily be a positive number. The one on the right is platykurtic, so the kurtosis statistic will necessarily be a negative number. As you can see, the first histogram is very 'peaked', with a lot of cases clustered around the mean and very few outliers in the tails. The second histogram is relatively 'flat', with fewer cases clustered around the mean and more outliers stretching each tail outward, so to speak.

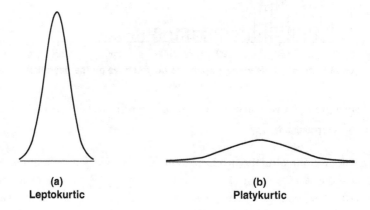

(a)
Leptokurtic

(b)
Platykurtic

Figure 3.8 Leptokurtic (a) and platykurtic (b) distributions

Think for a minute about what you have already learned in relation to the standard deviation. You will recall that the standard deviation is a single number that reflects the amount of 'spread', or variability, in the scores of an ordinal or scale variable. A low standard deviation suggests less spread, while a higher standard deviation suggests more spread. It should be clear to you, at this point, how the standard deviation relates to kurtosis. A smaller standard deviation implies less variability in scores, more clustering around the mean, and thus corresponds to leptokurtosis. A larger standard deviation implies more variability in scores, less clustering around the mean, and thus corresponds to platykurtosis. Alternatively stated, leptokurtic distributions will always have smaller standard deviations than platykurtic distributions.

Skewness

Like kurtosis, skewness presents in one of two ways. An ordinal or scale variable can be positively skewed or negatively skewed. Once again, a single number can describe the level of skewness in a variable. If that number is positive, the distribution is *skewed to the right* or *positively skewed* (meaning that there is a long tail on the right-hand side of the distribution). If that number is negative, the distribution is *skewed to the left* or *negatively skewed* (meaning that there is a long tail on the left-hand side of the distribution). Figures 3.9a and b illustrate positive skew and negative skew. The distribution on the left is positively skewed. Most of the scores are clustered on the left-hand side of the distribution, with a few outliers, or extreme scores, on the right-hand side 'pulling' the tail rightward. The distribution on the right is negatively skewed. Here, you will see that most of the scores are clustered on the right-hand side of the distribution, with a few outliers, or extreme scores, on the left-hand side 'pulling' the tail leftward. The one with positive skew is said to be skewed to the right and the one with negative skew is said to be skewed to the left.

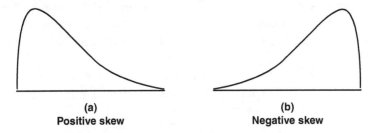

(a)
Positive skew

(b)
Negative skew

Figure 3.9 Positive (a) and negative (b) skewness

Think for a minute about what you already know in relation to the relative location of the mean and the median in an ordinal- or scale-level distribution. It should be obvious at this point how the relative location of the mean and median are related to skewness. In a positively skewed distribution (with a long tail on the right-hand side), the mean will always be higher than the median. This is because the extreme scores on the upper end of the distribution are 'pulling' the average to the right. In fact, looking at Figure 3.6, you can clearly see that this distribution is positively skewed by the very large organizations in the sample. In a negatively skewed distribution (with a long tail on the left-hand side), the mean will always be lower than the median. This is because extreme scores on the lower end of the distribution are 'pulling' the arithmetic average to the left. Thus, in both cases, skewness is caused by extreme scores on either side.

Assessing Kurtosis and Skewness Using SPSS

From the point of view of inferential statistics, kurtosis and skewness are problematic, but you won't find out why this is the case until the next chapter, where we discuss the importance of a 'normal' looking distribution. For now, I want to show you how to use SPSS to evaluate the extent to which a variable's distribution is positively or negatively skewed, or leptokurtic or platykurtic, by generating skewness and kurtosis statistics. It is worth noting that a single distribution can suffer simultaneously from skewness and kurtosis.

Before I show you how to use SPSS to evaluate skewness and kurtosis, I need to clarify one very important point. When using real-world data (as we are in this textbook), it is extremely unlikely, if not statistically impossible, to find variables that have skewness and kurtosis values of zero (thus indicating the total absence of skewness and kurtosis). Every single ordinal- or scale-level variable will suffer from some skewness or kurtosis. The question is: How much is too much? I'll answer this question after I've shown you how to request the statistics in SPSS.

Starting in Variable View, have a look at 'ahowlong' (found on row 123), which asks respondents, 'for how many years has this workplace been in operation?' To request skewness and kurtosis statistics for this variable, first go once again to Analyze, Descriptive Statistics, and Frequencies…. If you have selected any variables, move them back to the left-hand column. Then find 'for how many years has this workplace been in operation'. You can do this quickly just by highlighting the first variable in the list and then start typing in, 'for how many . . .'. Once you've found ahowlong, highlight it and move the variable to the right using ➡. Then go into Statistics…. The Mean, Median, Std. deviation, Range, Minimum, and Maximum should already be ticked, and that's fine. Leave them as they are. But now I want you to tick both ☑ Skewness and ☑ Kurtosis under Distribution. Click Continue. If you want, you can double check, under Charts…, that ◉ Histograms is still ticked. When you are satisfied, click Continue and then OK. Boom! Have a look at the output in Figure 3.10.

Statistics

For how many years has this workplace
been in operation?

N	Valid	2555
	Missing	125
Mean		41.47
Median		25.00
Std. Deviation		59.531
Skewness		6.489
Std. Error of Skewness		.048
Kurtosis		73.739
Std. Error of Kurtosis		.097
Range		997
Minimum		0
Maximum		997
Sum		105968

Figure 3.10 Descriptive statistics: How many years this workplace has been in operation

Reprint courtesy of IBM Corporation ©

Let's take stock of what we now know about this variable. Looking at the first box, we know that there are 125 missing values, meaning that we have full data from 2555 managers. We know that the mean age of these organizations is 41.47 years and the median is 25.00 years. Based on this information alone, we can already assume that the variable suffers from positive skewness. In other words, there are probably a few very old organizations that are 'pulling' the average up. We know that the standard deviation is 59.53, which is an indicator of the amount of spread, or variability, in the scores. Finally, we can also see four extra numbers: the skewness statistic, the standard error of the skewness statistic, the kurtosis statistic, and the standard error of the kurtosis statistic. The skewness statistic is 6.49, suggesting positive skewness (if this number were negative, that would imply negative skewness). The kurtosis statistic is 73.74. Again, the fact that this is a positive number already implies that the distribution is leptokurtic and thus excessively 'peaked'. If you scroll down to the bottom of your SPSS output, you can see that the distribution is indeed skewed to the right and very 'peaked', as our skewness and kurtosis statistics suggest.

Now, to determine whether the skewness and kurtosis levels are excessively problematic, there are a couple of strategies. Some statisticians simply use a cutoff of ±0.700. In other words, if the skewness and kurtosis statistics are greater than 0.700 or less than −0.700, then we can safely assume that the levels are unacceptable and problematic. In both cases, the skewness and kurtosis statistics for organizational age are well beyond these cutoffs. A more accurate way of assessing whether or not skewness and kurtosis are 'significant' problems is to take the skewness statistic (6.49) divided by the standard error of the skewness statistic (0.05) and the kurtosis statistic (73.74) divided by the standard error of the kurtosis statistic (0.10). If the resultant numbers are beyond ±1.96, then we can assume that the distribution suffers from 'significant' skewness and/or kurtosis. Never mind what a standard error of skewness and a standard error of kurtosis mean, and never mind why the cutoff of ±1.96 is used. These questions may be interesting to math nerds (like me!), but for applied statisticians like you, they're not that important. What is important is that you understand the procedure (taking the statistic divided by the standard error of the statistic) and know that any result beyond ±1.96 suggests that you have a variable that suffers from excessive skewness and/or kurtosis. If you carry out these calculations, you will see that both numbers are indeed beyond ±1.96. Thus, this variable is said to be excessively positively skewed and leptokurtic.

Bar Charts and Pie Charts

Histograms are really useful tools for getting the 'big picture' of your data. In fact, you might have noticed that they are not the only visual tools available to you on SPSS. In requesting frequencies, you can also instruct SPSS to provide you with bar charts and/or pie charts. Let's briefly see how this is done, this time using an ordinal variable that is measured using a Likert scale.

Move to the Variable View and scroll down to 'aphras06' (found on row 140), which asks the managers to respond to the following statement: 'Unions help find ways to improve workplace performance'. If you click into the Values box, you will see that the ordinal response categories are as follows: 1 = *strongly disagree*, 2 = *disagree*, 3 = *neither agree nor disagree*, 4 = *agree*, 5 = *strongly agree*; all missing values were coded −9. Double check to make sure that the missing values are recognized by SPSS as missing in the next column over.

Go to A̲nalyze, De̲scriptive Statistics, and F̲requencies…. Find the variable in the left-hand list and move it to the right (hint: to find it quickly, start typing 'Unions help find . . .'. Click on `Statistics…` and tick all the options we have discussed above: Mean, Median, Std. deviation, Minimum, Maximum, Range, Skewness, and Kurtosis. Click `Continue`. Now go click on `Charts…`, make sure to tick ⊙ P̲ie charts, and then go ahead and click `Continue` and `OK`. Boom! Check out the SPSS output in Figure 3.11.

Statistics

Unions help find ways to improve workplace performance.

N	Valid	2650
	Missing	30
Mean		3.05
Median		3.00
Std. Deviation		1.001
Skewness		-.290
Std. Error of Skewness		.048
Kurtosis		-.578
Std. Error of Kurtosis		.095
Range		4
Minimum		1
Maximum		5

Unions help find ways to improve workplace performance.

		Frequency	Percent	Valid Percent	Cumulative Percent
Valid	strongly disagree	197	7.4	7.4	7.4
	disagree	570	21.3	21.5	28.9
	neither agree nor disagree	908	33.9	34.3	63.2
	agree	866	32.3	32.7	95.9
	strongly agree	109	4.1	4.1	100.0
	Total	2650	98.9	100.0	
Missing	missing	30	1.1		
Total		2680	100.0		

Unions help find ways to improve workplace performance.

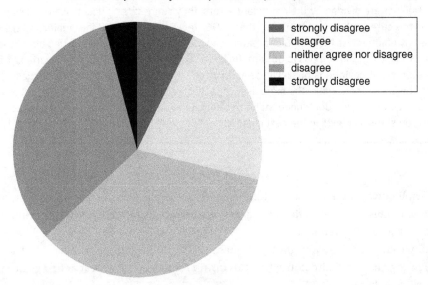

■	strongly disagree
	disagree
	neither agree nor disagree
	disagree
■	strongly disagree

Figure 3.11   Descriptive statistics and frequencies: Unions help improve workplace performance

Reprint courtesy of IBM Corporation ©

First, have a look at the descriptive statistics in the first box. There were 30 missing values for this variable, leaving 2650 valid responses. The mean was 3.05, and the median was 3.00. Note that these two numbers are fairly close to one another, so it is unlikely that skewness will be extreme. The standard deviation is 1.00; the maximum value is 5 (*strongly agree* with the statement), and the minimum value is 1 (*strongly disagree* with the statement). If fact, if you look at the skewness and kurtosis statistics, both are within ±0.700, thus indicating that this distribution does not suffer from skewness or kurtosis, as we suspected. However, if you take the skewness/kurtosis statistics and divide them by their standard errors, these numbers are slightly less than −1.96, indicating skewness and kurtosis problems. If you're wondering why this is the case, check out Box 3.3.

——————— **Box 3.3: Skewness, Kurtosis, and Sample Size** ———————

The absolute skewness and kurtosis statistics in Figure 3.11 suggest a fairly 'normal' looking distribution. Again, a conventional cutoff here is ±0.700. In other words, a statistic greater than 0.700 or less than

(Continued)

−0.700 suggests a problem with skewness or kurtosis. But, as noted above, when these skewness and kurtosis statistics are divided by their standard errors, they suggest 'significant' skewness and kurtosis because, in this case, both numbers are less than −1.96. Recall that the cutoff for 'significant' skewness or kurtosis is any number less than −1.96 or greater than 1.96. You're probably wondering about the reason for this discrepancy. In short, it has to do with the large sample size ($N = 2650$ for this variable). In 'large' samples, even slight deviations of skewness and kurtosis are detected by statistical tests such as this one. Thus, the larger the sample, the more likely it is that we 'overestimate' deviations of skewness and kurtosis. Don't worry if you don't understand this completely. We'll learn more about sample sizes and their effect on statistical tests in the next chapter.

Now scroll down to the bottom and have a look at the pie chart. This is another visual representation of the response categories, and, again, it corresponds to the frequency distribution table immediately above it. Try reproducing the above steps, only this time, in $\boxed{\text{Charts...}}$, tick ⦿ B̲ar charts instead of pie charts. When you run this request, you'll notice that the bar chart, in fact, looks a lot like a histogram. You'll also notice that this distribution does not appear at first glance to suffer from skewness or kurtosis.

What Have You Learned?

So there you have it. Now you know everything there is to know about measures of central tendency, measures of dispersion (spread), frequency distributions, skewness and kurtosis, and graphical representations such as the histogram, pie chart, and bar chart. All these concepts examine characteristics of one variable at a time. Before you do any bivariate or multivariate analyses, it's a good idea to spend some time 'getting to know' your data and variables. You should always request frequency distributions and histograms for every single variable you intend to model: nominal, ordinal, and scale. Have a look at how the responses are distributed and what the distributions look like graphically. Then, only for your ordinal- and scale-level variables, ask for parametric statistics. *Parametric* statistics are those statistics for which the mean and standard deviation are relevant, whereas *nonparametric* statistics are reserved for the analysis of nominal variables where the mean and standard deviation are not at all meaningful statistics. The relevant parametric statistics you should request for ordinal- and scale-level variables include the main ones addressed in this chapter: mean, median, standard deviation, minimum, maximum, range, skewness, and kurtosis. The only nonparametric statistic you really need to look at for nominal variables is the mode.

Okay, at this point you might be thinking, 'Enough of these descriptive statistics! I'm ready to start modeling!' Well, you're not quite there just yet. There are two more concepts that I need to introduce you to before we start crunching numbers: the normal distribution and the principle of statistical inference. These are discussed in the following chapter.

Further Reading

Hanna, D., & Dempster, M. (2013). *Psychology statistics for dummies.* John Wiley.

Hanneman, R. A., Kposowa, A. J., & Riddle, M. D. (2012). *Basic statistics for social research* (Vol. 38). John Wiley.

Healey, J. F. (1999). *Statistics: A tool for social research* (5th ed.). Wadsworth.

Heiman, G. (2013). *Basic statistics for the behavioral sciences.* Cengage Learning.

Holcomb, Z. (2016). *Fundamentals of descriptive statistics.* Routledge.

Lind, D. A., Marchal, W. G., & Wathen, S. A. (2019). *Basic statistics for business and economics.* McGraw-Hill.

In-Class Discussion Questions

1. What are the mean, median, and mode? How are they similar to one another, and how are they different? What types of variables correspond with what types of measures?
2. What is a standard deviation? What is the difference between a measure of central tendency and a measure of dispersion? For what type of variable is the standard deviation irrelevant and why?
3. Calculate the mean, median, and standard deviation for the following variable: commuting time per day in minutes: 35, 25, 15, 60, 80, 45, 40, 30, 5, 50, 25, 30.
4. What are skewness and kurtosis? How are they assessed statistically? How is kurtosis related to the standard deviation?
5. What are frequency distributions and histograms? What is the difference between percent, valid percent, and cumulative percent?
6. How can basic descriptive statistics help improve business decision-making? Give a few examples.

4

The Principle of
Statistical Inference

In Chapter 1, you learned about the different methods of sampling. You might recall that quantitative social scientists use both randomly drawn and nonrandomly drawn samples in their research. Random samples imply that every person (or organization) from the population has an equal chance of being selected for inclusion, whereas nonrandom samples are composed most often out of convenience or to target a very niche group of respondents (e.g., homosexual employees or small- and medium-sized enterprises in the biotechnology sector). Crucially, we learned in Chapter 1 that, *ceteris paribus*, random samples are, generally speaking, superior to nonrandom samples in statistical research because randomly drawn samples are much more likely to be 'representative' of the characteristics of the wider population. In other words, random samples will tend to 'look and behave' a lot like the populations from which they are drawn. The same cannot be said of nonrandom samples.

Ideally, as statisticians, we would like to be able to analyse entire populations, but in practice, this is rarely possible because most populations are simply too large to study without, well, some very deep pockets. Consider, for example, the WERS surveys of organizations and employees used in this book. Because it is not possible, or practicable, to study all organizations in Britain, much less all employees in Britain, the next best thing is that we study a subset of them with the assumption that our statistical analyses of that subset are likely to generalize to the wider population (i.e., all British workplaces or all British workers). *Generalization*, also referred to as *external validity*, refers to the process by which the results of statistical analyses from a sample are estimated to also hold water in the wider population. In other words, if we find a relationship between two variables in the sample, then we can be reasonably sure that the same relationship can also be found in the population.

This chapter is all about the generalization of statistical results from a sample to its population, a process that is ultimately made possible by the principle of statistical inference. The *principle of statistical inference* is the foundation of probability theory and can be defined as the mechanism through which we make a 'quantum leap' from a sample (which is known) to a population (which is unknown). It should not be surprising that we can be much more confident in this 'quantum leap' when our sample is randomly drawn from the population because, in terms of the laws of probability, random samples are much more likely to be representative of the population than nonrandom ones. Note that this does not mean that random samples will always 'look and behave' like the population, but, more often than not, they will generally be an effective conduit for drawing wider inferences or extrapolations. By the same token, we can almost always assume that nonrandom samples do not generalize effectively to wider populations, especially heterogeneous ones. Thus, any attempt to generalize from a nonrandomly drawn sample to its population should be treated with caution. Nonrandomly drawn samples are much more likely to be biased in a way that likely leads to a substantial incongruence between the findings in the sample and the reality of the population.

This chapter is divided into three main sections. In the next section, we describe the significance of the normal curve in quantitative research. After that, we delve into the principle of statistical inference and throw light on the key statistic that data scientists use to generalize from a sample to a population. Finally, we will look at some of the data cleaning procedures we can use in IBM SPSS Statistics Software (SPSS) to prepare for the statistical analyses that will be described in the remaining chapters of this book. Are you ready? Let's get started.

The Normal Curve

In the last chapter, you learned how to calculate the mean, median, and standard deviation for ordinal- and scale-level variables. Recall that the mean is the arithmetic average of a set of scores, the median is the midpoint when those scores are listed out from the lowest to the highest, and the standard deviation is a statistic that says something about how spread out the scores are from the mean. The more spread out the scores, the higher the standard deviation and the 'flatter' the distribution; conversely, the closer the scores hover around the mean, the lower the standard deviation and the more 'peaked' the distribution. When scores are very spread out from the mean, we learned that the distribution suffers from a platykurtic shape; when the scores are highly clustered around the mean, we learned that the distribution suffers from a leptokurtic shape (see Figures 3.9a and b). We also learned that when an ordinal- or scale-level distribution contains just a few scores that are extremely high or extremely low, the distribution is said to suffer from skewness. Extremely high scores lead to positive skewness (where the mean is higher than the median), and extremely low scores lead to negative skewness (where the mean is lower than the median). This difference between the mean and the median is explained by the fact that the extreme scores pull the average up, or down (see Figures 3.10a and b).

You'll notice that I use the word 'suffer' when I talk about skewness and kurtosis. This implies that skewness and kurtosis are to be avoided. You might be wondering, hey, what's so bad about a distribution of scores that are excessively flat (platykurtic) or peaked (leptokurtic), or what's wrong with a distribution of scores that appear to be skewed to the right (positive skewness) or skewed to the left (negative skewness)? The key problem with these abnormally shaped distributions is that they deviate from what statisticians refer to as the normal curve.

The *normal curve*, also referred to as the *bell curve*, is a mathematically defined and naturally occurring distribution that appears bell shaped, as depicted in Figure 4.1. It should be noted that the normal curve is a hypothetical construct, or an ideal type. In practice, no variable in the real world is ever perfectly normally distributed. Let's take a closer look at the two key characteristics of the normal curve.

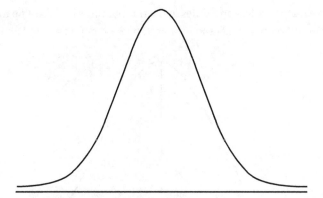

Figure 4.1   The normal curve, also known as the bell curve

In What Way Is a Normal Curve 'Naturally Occurring?'

In short, a normal curve is 'naturally occurring' because it appears to be a universal feature of the social and natural world. Most, though not all, ordinal- and scale-level variables, for whatever reason, tend to be (at least approximately) bell shaped as a matter of course. This means that the lion's share of cases tend to hover around the mean, but a few cases extend much higher and lower than the mean. There seems to be something about the universe in which we live that reproduces this shape, albeit imperfectly, time and time again.

Let's take a look at a few examples of variables that are generally considered by data scientists to be normally distributed. The classic example is the intelligence quotient, or IQ for short. If you gave 100 people an IQ test, most would report an average score of around 100 while a few would report a very high IQ and a few a very low IQ. The higher (and lower) the IQ, the fewer people who report that score. Thus, most people will score around 100 on an IQ test, fewer people will score 120 or 80, and fewer still will score 140 and 60. Height is another example of a variable that generally takes the shape of a normal curve. Most people can be described as average in height, although there are a few people who are very tall (e.g., Shaquille O'Neal) or very short (e.g., my mother-in-law who stands at a towering 4 feet and 10 inches!). As we move toward the extremes of height, we find very few people who are extremely short and extremely tall.

In the field of business analytics, there are numerous variables that also assume a generally normal bell shape. Some organizations, in fact, use a forced distribution for their performance appraisals, whereby most employees are rated average, with a few rated significantly above average and a few significantly below average. Similarly, working hours per week also tends to be a normally distributed variable. Most full-time employees will work around 40 hours per week, but some also work a lot less (my son at his part-time job) and others a lot more (e.g., Elon Musk) than that. What other organizational variables can you think of that might produce a bell-shaped distribution?

In What Way Is a Normal Curve 'Mathematically Defined?'

In addition to being naturally occurring, the normal curve is also mathematically defined. To understand what I mean by mathematically defined, refer to Figure 4.2. It is very important that you understand the basic mathematical properties of the normal curve because all parametric inferential statistics are based on this concept. Let's look at each of the components of Figure 4.2 one by one.

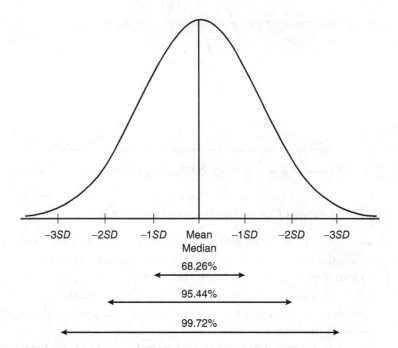

Figure 4.2 The normal curve with mean and three standard deviations

You will first notice that at the very middle of the distribution are the population mean (μ, pronounced mu, like a cow) and the median (*Mdn*). In a perfectly normal distribution, such as this one (bearing in mind, again, that this is an ideal type and that no distribution in real life is ever perfectly normal in shape), the mean and the median are the exact same number. From what you already know about skewness, this implies that the normal distribution is neither positively skewed to the right, nor negatively skewed to the left; it is perfectly symmetrical on each side. In fact, if you calculate the skewness statistic for a normal curve, it will always equal zero. You will also notice that the highest point in the graph is the mean (and the median). This implies that the highest number of scores in the distribution sit at the mean. Scores that are higher or lower than the mean occur less frequently, and scores farthest from the mean (to the right and the left) occur rarely. This is why we call the *Y*-axis of the normal curve the frequency (*f*), because it tells us how many scores within a distribution fall at a particular point. The *X*-axis tells us what each score is, from the lowest (on the left) to the highest (on the right).

You will further notice that to the right and the left of the mean and the median are three standard deviations (*SD*) set out at equal intervals. Recall that 1 *SD* is a measure of the amount of spread in a distribution relative to the mean. Two standard deviations is therefore the standard deviation multiplied by 2 and, similarly, 3 *SD* is the standard deviation multiplied by 3. The three standard deviations to the right of the mean are positive standard deviations (thus corresponding to scores that are 3 *SD* greater than the mean) and the three standard deviations to the left of the mean are negative standard deviations (thus corresponding to scores that are 3 *SD* less than the mean). Just as a normal curve suffers from no skewness, it also suffers from no kurtosis. In other words, if you calculate the kurtosis statistic for a perfectly normal distribution, it will always equal zero.

Now I want you to pay close attention to the space beneath the curve. In a perfectly normal curve like this one, you will always find that 68.26% of all cases in the distribution fit within ±1 *SD* from the mean. You will also always find that 95.44% of all cases in the distribution fit within ±2 *SD* from the mean. Finally, you will always find that 99.72% of all cases in the distribution fit within ±3 *SD* from the mean. In other words, the crucial mathematical properties of the normal curve essentially boil down to the spatial and geographical distribution of cases within it. We can thus infer that extreme cases that are higher than 3 *SD* from the mean and lower than –3 *SD* from the mean account for only 0.28% of all cases in total. In other words, just over one-quarter of 1% of cases in a normal distribution are very very far from the mean, either on the positive side or on the negative side. It should also not surprise you to learn that exactly 50% of the cases fit above the mean and 50% of the cases fit below the mean. How many other ways can you break this space down mathematically? For example, what is the percentage of cases that fit in the space between the mean and 1 *SD*? (*Hint:* Take half of 68.26.)

Remember that Figure 4.2 depicts a purely theoretical model of a normal distribution that only exists in the abstract. Let's see how this model might equally apply to an imperfect real-world variable like working hours per week. Such a variable should be reasonably bell shaped. Imagine that you asked 100 employees how many hours they worked in a typical week. You calculated a mean of 40 (this time, because we're not using population data, but instead we're using sample data, we call the mean $\bar{X}$, pronounced X-bar) median of 41 (*Mdn*), and a standard deviation of 12. This distribution is depicted in Figure 4.3. You can see that the mean and median are pretty close to one another. If the standard deviation equals 12 hours, then 1 *SD* from the mean equals 52 hours (40 + 12) and –1 *SD* from the mean equals 28 hours (40 – 12). In other words, you can conclude that, if this variable were perfectly normally distributed, roughly 68% of the employees work between 28 and 52 hours per week.

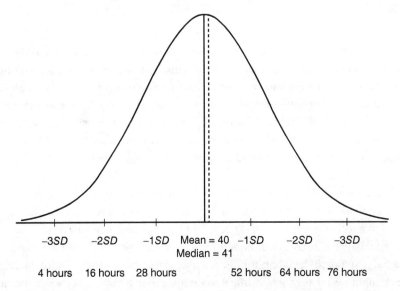

Figure 4.3 Working hours per week, normally distributed

If 1 *SD* equals 12, then 2 *SD* equal 24 (12 × 2). Thus, 2 *SD* to the right of the mean is equivalent to 64 hours per week (40 + 24) and 2 *SD* to the left of the mean is equivalent to 16 hours per week (40 − 24). If we again assume that this distribution is normally distributed, then we can conclude that roughly 95% of employees work between 16 and 64 hours per week.

Finally, if 1 *SD* equals 12, then 3 *SD* equal 36 (12 × 3). This means that 3 *SD* to the right of the mean equals 76 hours per week (40 + 36) and 3 *SD* to the left of the mean equals only 4 hours per week (40 − 36). Again, if we assume that this distribution is a normal curve, then we can conclude that roughly 99% of the employees in our sample work between 4 and 76 hours per week.

This distribution makes sense. We would expect most people to work around 40 hours per week, which is a typical contractual period. A few employees might work slightly more or less than 40 hours per week, and fewer still work as low as 4 hours per week and as high as 76 hours per week. Only a miniscule number of people (like myself) work either less than 4 hours per week or more than 76 hours per week. I'll let you guess which side of the distribution (positive or negative) I'm on.

The *z*-Score and Standardization

Statisticians often use and report two types of statistics simultaneously: raw (aka, unstandardized statistics) and standardized statistics. The distinction between these two is sometimes difficult to grasp, but it is important that you understand the difference because future chapters in this book make reference to both standardized and unstandardized statistics. In short, they both mean the same thing, but are expressed in different ways.

The best way to explain the difference between standardized and unstandardized statistics is through a brief discussion of what are known as *z*-scores. A *z-score* is a conversion of an unstandardized (raw) score into standard deviation units. If this definition isn't clear, don't worry. It will become so after a brief illustration. The *z*-scores are calculated using the following equation:

$$z = \frac{X_i - \bar{X}}{s}$$

where X_i is a raw (unstandardized) score from an ordinal or scale distribution, $\bar{X}$ is the mean score, and s is the standard deviation. Basically, what this equation does is that it takes an original score and converts it into a unit expressed in standard deviations. So a *z*-score of 0 is equivalent to the mean (and median) in a perfectly normal curve. A *z*-score of 1 is equivalent to a raw score that is exactly 1 *SD* to the right of the mean. A *z*-score of −1 is equivalent to a raw score that is exactly 1 *SD* to the left of the mean. A *z*-score of 2 or −2 is equivalent to a raw score that is 2 *SD* above or below the mean, respectively. A *z*-score of 3 or −3 is equivalent to a raw score that is 3 *SD* above or below the mean, respectively, and so on.

Unstandardized scores are simply hard to compare with one another. In one variable the mean might be 40 (say, working hours per week), in another it might be 4 (say, job satisfaction on a scale of 1 to 7), and in another it might be 4000 (say, monthly earnings). But all three of these numbers expressed in standardized *z*-scores will be zero. Similarly, standard deviations are hard to compare across variables. A standard deviation for one variable might be 12 (say, working hours per week), for another it might be 1.2 (say, job satisfaction on a scale of 1 to 7), and for another it might be 773.34 (say, monthly earnings). But expressed in *z*-scores, all three numbers will be 1s.

Thus, every single raw, unstandardized score in a distribution has a corresponding standardized z-score. Using the example above, if we asked 100 employees how many hours they worked a week, we would have 100 raw, unstandardized numbers, most of which, as you already learned, hover around 40 hours per week. We could then take each of these 100 numbers and create 100 z-scores using the equation above. These z-scores, when calculated, are essentially equivalent to the unstandardized scores, but expressed in standard deviations.

Box 4.1 shows you how to calculate z-scores. Check it out, if you dare.

Box 4.1: Calculating z-Scores

Let's use the example of working hours per week, discussed above. Recall that we surveyed 100 employees and asked them how many hours per week they worked. The mean was 40 and the standard deviation was 12.

We already learned that a z-score of 0 is equivalent to the mean. So let's see what happens when we calculate a z-score where X_i is the mean of 40.

1. $z = \dfrac{X_i - \bar{X}}{s}$

2. $z = \dfrac{40 - 40}{12}$

3. $z = \dfrac{0}{12}$

4. $z = 0$

As expected, the mean score of 40 in this distribution is equal to a z-score of 0.

Let's try to calculate the z-score for an unstandardized score of 28 (bearing in mind that this is 1 SD below the mean, or 40 − 12). We know that if a raw score is 1 SD below the mean, then the z-score should be −1.

1. $z = \dfrac{X_i - \bar{X}}{s}$

2. $z = \dfrac{28 - 40}{12}$

3. $z = \dfrac{-12}{12}$

4. $z = -1$

So far, so good, right? Now let's calculate a z-score for an unstandardized score of 76. Remember that 76 hours per week is 3 SD from the mean, so the z-score should be equivalent to 3.

(Continued)

1. $z = \dfrac{X_i - \bar{X}}{s}$

2. $z = \dfrac{76 - 40}{12}$

3. $z = \dfrac{36}{12}$

4. $z = 3$

Nice one, ace! I think you're really getting the hang of this.

Finally, let's pick a random unstandardized score, say, 34 hours per week, and plug it into the formula to calculate the z-score. We know that this number is below the mean of 40 (z-score of 0) but above the standard deviation of 28 (z-score of –1), so the z-score should be somewhere between –1 and 0. Let's find out if this is the case.

1. $z = \dfrac{X_i - \bar{X}}{s}$

2. $z = \dfrac{34 - 40}{12}$

3. $z = \dfrac{-6}{12}$

4. $z = -0.5$

Can you calculate the z-score for a raw score of 63 hours per week? If you can, somebody had better grab a fire extinguisher, because you're on fire!

---

z-Scores are important conceptual tools and they will help you to understand the difference between standardized and unstandardized coefficients in later chapters. But, in practice, z-scores are not often used in applied statistics research. Just in case you were interested, and by way of introducing the WERS of employees dataset, let's spend just a few minutes to figure out how to use SPSS to produce z-scores for every raw, unstandardized value in its working hours per week variable.

Using SPSS to Calculate z-Scores

Go to the Companion Website and open the file 'Chap4data', where you will find the survey of employees' working hours per week variable in the first column of Data View. The working hours per week variable is labeled 'qa4'. Switch over to the Variable View and you will see that the question asked how many hours the respondent usually works each week, including overtime and extra hours. If you go into the Values column, you will see that the only codes are those for missing data (the negative numbers between –9 and –1) and those who work more than 97 hours per week. In other words, we can treat this variable as a scale-level variable, even though it is technically not because it lumps together all values greater than 97 into a score of 97 (but, honestly, who, besides me, works more than 97 hours per week anyway?).

Before we generate the z-scores, let's have a look at the descriptive statistics, frequency distribution, and the histogram for this variable. You should know how to do this already from the previous chapter, but I'll give you a refresher. Go to Analyze, Descriptive Statistics, and Frequencies.... Locate the variable working hours per week in the left-hand column and move it to the right by double clicking the variable. Go into Statistics... and tick ☑ Std. deviation, ☑ Minimum and ☑ Maximum under Dispersion; ☑ Mean and ☑ Median under Central Tendency; and ☑ Skewness and ☑ Kurtosis under Distribution. Click Continue . Then go into Charts... and tick ◉ Histograms along with ☑ Show normal curve on histogram. Now click Continue and then OK .

The output in Figure 4.4 pops up. From the first box labeled Statistics, we can see that there are 21,335 valid responses to this variable and 646 missing cases. The mean is 35.10 and the median is 38.00, suggesting that the distribution is negatively skewed to the left. Indeed, if we take the skewness statistic (–.618) divided by the standard error of skewness (0.017), we get –36.35. Recall that any value that is greater than 1.96 or less than –1.96 implies significant skewness. While we're at it, let's also estimate the level of kurtosis by taking the kurtosis statistic (0.736) divided by the standard error of kurtosis (0.034), resulting in a value of 21.75. Because this value is greater than 1.96, we can assume that this variable suffers from positive kurtosis and is thus likely very 'pointy' relative to the normal curve. Finally, you will note that the standard deviation is 12.93.

Statistics

Hours usually worked each week, including overtime or extra hours

N	Valid	21335
	Missing	646
Mean		35.10
Median		38.00
Std. Deviation		12.927
Skewness		-.618
Std. Error of Skewness		.017
Kurtosis		.736
Std. Error of Kurtosis		.034
Minimum		0
Maximum		97

(Continued)

Figure 4.4 (Continued)

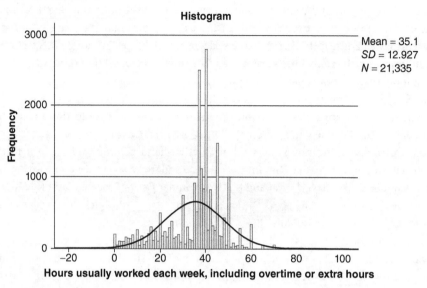

Figure 4.4 Descriptive statistics, working hours per week

Reprint courtesy of IBM Corporation ©

The next box down (not shown in Figure 4.4) shows the frequency distribution, which gives the breakdown of how many participants provided answers for each response. Have a quick look over this box. You'll see that there are 200 employees in our survey who claim to work zero hours per week (sweet job, eh?). At the other extreme, only two employees reported working more than 97 hours per week.

At the bottom of the output, you will see the histogram (shown in Figure 4.4), and as expected, the distribution is 'pointy' and slightly skewed to the left. Although this variable is not a normal curve, you can see that it appears somewhat normal. Most of the cases are clustered around the mean with fewer cases reporting extremely high or low working hours per week. Remember that the normal curve is a hypothetical concept that does not exist in practice.

Now let's see how we can use SPSS to create z-scores for this variable. I mean, come on! We don't want to do those calculations by hand, right? Let's think about what we can expect from this process based on what we already know. For starters, we already know that there are 21,335 valid responses, so there should also be 21,335 z-scores that correspond to each of them. That is, each valid response has its own z-score. We know that the mean is 35.10, so respondents who reported working 35 hours per week should have a z-score that is just ever so slightly below 0. We know that 1 SD is ±12.93 hours, 2 SD are ±25.86 (12.93 × 2), and 3 SD are ±38.79 (12.93 × 3). Thus, looking again at the histogram in Figure 4.4, we can estimate that roughly 68% of cases fall within 22.17 (35.10 − 12.93) and 48.03 (35.10 + 12.93) hours; roughly 95% of cases fall within 9.24 (35.10 − 25.86) and 60.96 (35.10 + 25.86) hours; and roughly 99% of cases fall within −3.69 (or, really, 0, since it's impossible to work negative hours) hours (35.10 − 38.79) and 73.89 (35.10 + 38.79) hours.

Creating z-scores in SPSS is pretty easy. Go to Analyze, Descriptive Statistics, and Descriptives. Find the working hours per week variable in the left-hand column, highlight it, and move it to the right. Just below the left-hand column, you must tick Save standardized values as variables to request z-scores. Then just click OK . In the output window you will see the basic descriptive statistics reported (N, minimum, maximum, mean, and standard deviation), but no z-scores. That's because you have just asked SPSS to create 21,335 new z-scores, one for each raw value. Rather than report these in the output, a new variable has been created, which you can find in the Data View. To the right of working hours per week, you now will see a new variable labeled Zqa4. Here you will find all the z-scores you requested.

Spend some time comparing the raw scores for qa4 and the standardized scores for Zqa4. What is the z-score for those respondents who report working 35 hours per week? Is it close to zero, as we expected? What about the z-scores for those who work 22 and 48 hours? Are the corresponding z-scores similarly close to –1 and 1, respectively?

The Principle of Statistical Inference

Parametric statistical tests use the spatial and geometrical information we just learned about the normal curve to make reasonably accurate inferences from a sample to the population from which it was drawn. The *principle of statistical inference* is the theoretical mechanism that statisticians use to make a 'quantum leap' from the sample that they are analysing to the population that they are interested in drawing conclusions about.

Think about it in these terms. We have perfect information about our sample, but imperfect information about our population. The problem is that, although we know a lot about the sample, we don't really care much about the results of the sample; ultimately, what we really care about is the population from which it is drawn. The sample is just a means that we use in order to make conclusions about the population. But because we don't (usually) have access to the entire population, we can only make estimates about it based on what we know about the sample.

For example, in the WERS of employees, we know a lot about working hours per week for the roughly 21,000 respondents who answered this question. We know that the average working hours per week in our sample is 35.10 hours and that the standard deviation is 12.93 hours. But, for all practical purposes, we don't really care much about these 21,000 respondents, right? What we really care about is the entire population of all British employees and the number of hours that they work per week. We just don't know what the population mean is. We don't know what the population standard deviation is, either. Such census data do not exist. So the next best thing is to make assumptions about the population based on what we know about the sample. Because we assume that the population mean and standard deviation will be similar to the sample mean and standard deviation, and that the frequency distributions will both be normally distributed (on the whole), we can draw conclusions about the population using just the data we have collected about the sample. This is the essence of the principle of statistical inference. We don't know for sure if a relationship between two variables, X and Y, holds water in the wider population, but we can find out if it exists in the sample. If we do find a relationship between X and Y in our sample, the key question then becomes: Is this relationship in the sample strong enough that we can also be reasonably confident that it will be found in the population as well? The stronger the relationship in the sample, the more confidence we can have that it similarly holds water in the population.

This 'quantum leap' that we make from a known sample to an unknown population is made possible by what we call the central limit theorem.

The Central Limit Theorem

Let's review what we have learned so far. We know a lot about the sample. We know its mean, standard deviation, and its shape. But we don't really care about the sample because our objective is to understand the population. Sadly, we don't know a whole lot, if anything, about the population. It has a mean, standard deviation, and shape, but we don't really know what these might look like because we don't have enough time and resources to collect data from the entire population.

To make that 'quantum leap' from the sample to the population, we use a theoretical tool called the *sampling distribution of sample means*. This concept is what allows us to generalize from the sample to the population and it is grounded in the laws of probability. Here's how it works.

Imagine that you are interested in studying organizational commitment in the United States. Your population is all American employees, but you take a random sample of 1000 employees only and ask them to rate their level of organizational commitment on a scale of 1 to 10, where 1 = *not at all committed* and 10 = *completely committed*. The population mean, μ, and population standard deviation, σ, are unknown, but the sample mean ($\bar{X}$) and sample standard deviation (s) are known. Let's assume that, in this sample of 1000 employees, $\bar{X}$ = 5.7 (and s = 2.13). We therefore place this $\bar{X}$ of 5.7 into Figure 4.5. Now let's say you take a second random sample of different American employees, asking the same question, and this time $\bar{X}$ = 6.8 (and s = 2.34). We then place this second $\bar{X}$ on Figure 4.6. Then we take a third random sample of 1000 American employees and find that $\bar{X}$ = 4.1 (and s = 1.86). We place this third $\bar{X}$ onto Figure 4.7. Now imagine that you keep taking thousands upon thousands of different samples from the population and placing them on Figure 4.8, which represents the sampling distribution of sample means. Most $\bar{X}$s will center around the true, but unknown, mean, μ; similarly, most standard deviations will center around the true, but unknown, standard deviation, σ. If we take enough samples over and over again, the sampling distribution of sample means will start to look like a somewhat normal curve. This sampling distribution of sample means, although just a conceptual tool, is what allows us to make that brave 'quantum leap' from the known sample to the unknown population.

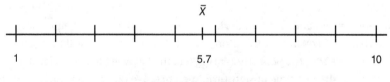

Organizational commitment

Figure 4.5 Sampling distribution of sample means, one sample

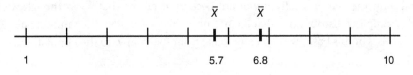

Figure 4.6   Sampling distribution of sample means, two samples

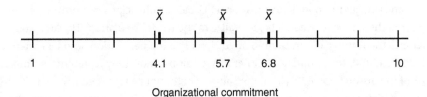

Figure 4.7   Sampling distribution of sample means, three samples

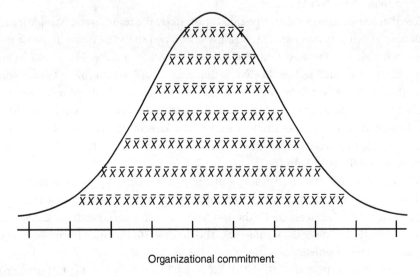

Figure 4.8   Sampling distribution of sample means, many samples

The mechanism that makes this 'quantum leap' possible is referred to as the *central limit theorem*, which states the following:

> If repeated random samples of size *N* are drawn from any population, with an unknown mean of μ (pronounced mu) and a standard deviation of σ (pronounced sigma), then as *N* becomes large, the theoretical sampling distribution of sample means will approach normality, with a mean of μ and a standard deviation of $\sigma/\sqrt{N}$.

The central limit theorem is vitally important because it means that, even though we might be dealing with sampling distributions that are not normally distributed, the sampling distribution of sample means is. On this basis, we can extrapolate from the sample to the population.

The *p*-Value

The sampling distribution of sample means is a purely conceptual (hypothetical) tool. Now let's get back to the real world, shall we? We cannot simply take unlimited repeated samples from a population because that would take too much time and too much money. It might even be more cost-effective to target the entire population just once! Usually, statisticians can only afford to take just one sample and then hope to accurately generalize to the wider population. The key problem here is that sometimes the features of our sample might look like the population, and less often, they will look a bit different from the population. Either way, we don't know how representative our sample is.

Because of the distinct possibility that our sample might not be representative of the population, we always generalize based on probabilities. We can never be 100% certain that our results will hold water in the wider population, but we can estimate the likelihood that they do. The statistic that we use to estimate the likelihood that the results of our sample accurately generalize to the population is called the *p-value*, or probability value.

All inferential statistics use *p*-values to estimate how likely the results of our sample translate into the population. Effectively, every statistical test will give two statistics: one will tell us the known 'result' (e.g., whether, or to what extent, *X* is associated with *Y*) and the second will be an accompanying *p*-value that will tell us how likely it is that result also exists in the unknown population. Remember that, technically, the 'result' of our statistical test was calculated based on the sample statistics, but we don't actually care about the sample. We care about the population. The *p*-value is the mechanism that we use to estimate, based on the laws of probability, whether the result is 'significant' enough to generalize. *Statistical significance* refers to a result that very likely exists in both the sample and the population.

Let's take a look at the statistical features of the *p*-value. First, a *p*-value is always a number between 0 and 1, although, in practice, it will never reach those extremes. As a general rule, the higher the *p*-value (i.e., the closer to 1), the less likely we can generalize from the sample to the population; similarly, the lower the *p*-value (i.e., the closer to 0), the more likely we can generalize from the sample to the population.

Along this continuum (from 0 to 1), statisticians have had to settle on a cutoff point in order to determine what results are 'statistically significant' (and therefore likely hold water in the wider population) and what results are 'statistically insignificant' (and therefore likely do not generalize to the wider population). For whatever reason, the cutoff point is widely recognized to be $p < 0.05$. Thus, *p*-values that are lower than 0.05 point to a statistically significant result, and *p*-values that are 0.05 or greater point to a statistically insignificant, and therefore nongeneralizable, result. It is important to note that, although rare, a *p*-value of exactly 0.05 is still considered statistically insignificant, meaning that the result we found in our sample does not likely generalize to the population.

So what does a *p*-value of 0.05 actually mean? Essentially, a *p*-value is a probability of error, or the probability of making a mistake when generalizing from the sample to the population. Thus, a *p*-value of 0.05 means that there is a 5% chance that the result from the sample does not generalize to the population. Alternatively stated, we are willing to accept that there is a 1 in 20 chance ($1/20 = 0.05$) that the result we found in the sample does not hold water in the wider population. A p-value of, for example, 0.01 means that there is only a 1% chance that the result we found in the sample does not generalize to the population. In other words, we are 99% confident that a statistical result with an accompanying p-value of 0.01 holds water in the wider population. However, a p-value of 0.07 (which is greater than the cutoff point of 0.05) suggests that there is a 7% chance of error in generalizing from the sample to the population, and a p-value of 0.70 (which is much, much greater than the cutoff point of 0.05) implies that there is a 70% chance of error in generalizing from the sample to the population. Now you can see that a higher p-value means that we are less confident in generalizing our result, and a lower p-value means that we are more confident in generalizing our result. Box 4.2 gives some examples of different statistical results and corresponding p-values and provides the correct interpretation of each result.

──────────── **Box 4.2: The Significance of p-Values** ────────────

A p-value will tell you how likely the result of your sample generalizes to the population. If $p < 0.05$, then we have enough confidence in our sample result to say that it very likely generalizes to the population. If $p = 0.05$ or more, then we do not have enough confidence that our sample result generalizes to the population. Don't ask me why we settled on a cutoff of 0.05 to determine statistical significance. It is an arbitrary number. Occasionally, you will see data scientists using a cutoff of $p < 0.01$ or even $p < 0.10$, but the standard is $p < 0.05$, so we'll be using that throughout the book. Let's take a look at a few examples of how p-values work in practice. Let's assume that you found the following results based on your sample.

- Men work more hours per week than women ($p = 0.001$). With this p-value, we are concluding that, in our population, we are 99.9% confident that men work more hours per week than women (alternatively stated, there is a 0.1% chance that we are wrong in generalizing).
- Organizational commitment is positively related to productivity ($p = 0.049$). With this p-value, we are concluding that, in our population, we are 95.1% confident that organizational commitment is positively related to productivity (alternatively stated, there is a 4.9% chance that we are wrong in generalizing).
- Men are more productive than women ($p = 0.963$). With this p-value, we are concluding that there is no relationship between gender and productivity in our population. If we were to assume that men are more productive than women in the population, we could only be 3.7% confident in this claim, or, alternatively stated, there is a 96.3% chance that our generalization is incorrect.
- Commuting time is negatively related to working hours per week ($p = 0.545$). With this p-value, we are concluding that there is no relationship between commuting time and working hours per week in our population. This is because we are only 45.5% confident that this result generalizes or, alternatively stated, there is a 54.5% chance that our generalizations are incorrect.

Looking at the four examples above, the first two are considered statistically significant because the corresponding p-values are < 0.05. As such, the results we found in our sample statistics very likely (with at least 95% confidence) generalize to the population. In the last two examples, the results we found in our sample statistics are statistically insignificant and, therefore, very likely do not generalize because the p-values are greater than 0.05. In other words, we do not have sufficient confidence that our sample results hold water in the population.

You might be wondering how exactly p-values are calculated. The explanation is a bit complicated and, since this is an applied statistics textbook, it is perhaps not necessary to understand the underlying mathematics. Basically, there can be a strong relationship; a weak relationship; or no relationship between two variables, X and Y. The stronger the relationship, the lower the p-value and the higher the likelihood that the result generalizes from the sample to the population. Conversely, the weaker the relationship, the higher the p-value and the lower the likelihood that the result generalizes from the sample to the population. In parametric statistics that assume normally distributed ordinal- or scale-level variables, the p-value is calculated in reference to the test statistics' location on the normal curve. If you don't understand this entirely, fear not, young data scientist. This will become clearer as we start to look at the statistical tests later in this book.

I would like to make one final note about p-values. Even a statistically significant p-value ($p < 0.05$) does not guarantee that the relationship we found in the sample holds water in the population. For example, for a given statistical test, you could find a p-value of 0.0000001, which would mean that there is a 0.00001% chance (0.0000001 × 100) of making an error when generalizing the result to the population. Looking at these odds, it's extremely likely that the results of our analysis of the sample hold water in the population from which it was drawn, but there is still a slight chance that there is something unique about our sample and that it does not represent the population. Indeed, the only way we can be 100% confident that a relationship exists in the population is if we have census data of the entire population. Under such circumstances, inferential statistics are unnecessary and p-values are irrelevant. For a discussion of the pitfalls of using p-values in inferential statistics, see Timming (2010a).

Standard Errors and Confidence Intervals

A *confidence interval* refers to a range of estimated values within which we are reasonably confident that the real value in the population falls. You've likely read about political pollsters who report a 'margin of error' for a candidate's popularity. For example, a pollster might draw a sample of, say, 500 voters and report that a particular candidate has a favorability rating of 63%, with a margin of error of ±3%. Remember that the 63% is a statistic derived from the sample of 500 voters, but we don't really care about those 500 respondents. We ultimately care about all likely voters in the population. Because we cannot be 100% certain that the sample of 500 respondents is perfectly representative of the population, the pollster reports a margin of error of ±3 percentage points. What this means is that the real favorability rating in the population likely falls between 60% (63 − 3) and 66% (63 + 3). This span of 6 percentage points is the confidence interval. The larger the confidence interval, the more confident we can be that the true value in the population falls within it. For example, if the margin of error was ±5%, then the confidence interval would span 58% (63 − 5) to 68% (63 + 5).

Let's consider an example from management. Imagine that you would like to know how likely your employees are to leave your organization over the next 12 months, and whether this level is higher than the national average, lower than the national average, or at the national average. The problem here is that there is no census data on this question. Let's say you've found a nationally representative dataset of 2000 employees who responded to this question: On a scale of 1 to 10, where

1 = *not at all likely* and 10 = *extremely likely*, how likely are you to leave your current job over the next 12 months? Let's say the average is 4.2 on that 10-point scale. We cannot automatically assume that the national average is 4.2, but we could construct a confidence interval at the 95% level (meaning that we are 95% confident that the true value falls within a particular interval, or range). If the margin of error is found to be 1.2 points (again, on that 10-point scale), then we can be 95% confident that, in the population, the true level of intention to leave is between 3.0 (4.2 – 1.2) and 5.4 (4.2 + 1.2). Armed with this information, you can conduct your own employee survey, asking the exact same question, to determine where your workforce sits on the employee turnover continuum.

The standard error is closely related to the idea of confidence interval. The *standard error* can be defined as a measure of the variability of sample means that are repeatedly calculated from the same population. It is, effectively, akin to the standard deviation of the sampling distribution of sample means, as discussed above. But whereas the standard deviation describes the variability of scores within a (known) sample, the standard error is an estimate of the (unknown) population mean across repeatedly drawn samples, as evidenced in the sampling distribution of sample means depicted in Figure 4.8. In short, the standard deviation is a descriptive statistic and the standard error is an inferential statistic.

Sample Size and Statistical Significance

Imagine that you are interested in studying a population consisting of 1,000,000 respondents. Again, you don't have the time and/or the resources to collect census data from all 1,000,000 participants, so you decide to draw a random sample. If you draw a sample of 10 from that 1,000,000, how confident would you be that your sample is representative of the population? Probably not too confident, right? What if you drew a sample of 100? How about 1000? Or 10,000? Or even 100,000? Clearly, the larger your sample, the more confidence you have that it is representative of the population. This trend has important implications for *p*-values and the generalizability of your results.

Larger samples, *ceteris paribus*, have a much greater likelihood of looking like, and behaving like, the wider population. The larger the sample, the closer you get to the population. In similar vein, very small samples are less likely to look and behave like the population because there is a greater probability that they are composed of unique, or atypical, respondents.

Now think for just a moment about how sample size might affect *p*-values and confidence intervals.

If larger samples are more likely to be representative of the population from which they are drawn, then we are less likely to make an error when making that 'quantum leap' from the sample to the population. Because of the improved confidence we have in the representativeness of our sample, *p*-values for large samples are likely to be lower than *p*-values for small samples. Alternatively stated, as sample sizes increase, *p*-values decrease, increasing the chances of a statistically significant finding. Recall that a *p*-value of <0.05 suggests statistical significance.

Similarly, when sample sizes are larger, confidence intervals tend to become smaller, again, because we are much more confident that our sample looks and behaves like the population from which it was drawn. Imagine, for example, that we ask 100 private sector organizations in France how much they spend on marketing per annum and find an average of 8000 Euros with a confidence interval, at the 95% level, of 1000 Euros. Thus, we are 95% confident that the true population average is between

7000 and 9000 Euros. Now, imagine that we ask 1000 organizations from the same population how much they spend on marketing per annum. Again, we find an average of 8000 Euros, but this time the confidence interval is 400 Euros. Because of the increase in sample size, we are now 95% confident that the true mean in the population is between 7600 and 8400 Euros.

Because of the negative relationship between sample size and p-values (i.e., as sample size increases, p-values decrease), researchers must acknowledge the possibility of both Type I and Type II errors, depicted in Figure 4.9.

		Is there a real relationship in the population?	
		Yes	No
Did you find a significant relationship in your sample?	Yes	Correct	Type I error
	No	Type II error	Correct

Figure 4.9 Type I and Type II errors

Type I Error

Type I error, also referred to as *alpha error*, refers to the probability of finding a statistically significant result in your sample when, in fact, there is no relationship in the population. In other words, Type I error means finding a result with a p-value of <0.05 and thus concluding that there is a relationship when, in fact, there is none in the population. Of course, there is always the possibility of Type I error in any inferential statistics given the fact that a p-value cutoff of 0.05 still implies a 5% (or 1 in 20) chance of error. But there are some factors that increase the chances of making a Type I error. Based on what you already know about the relationship between sample size and statistical significance, it should be clear that very large samples could result in Type I errors. If large samples drive p-values down artificially, then it is likely that they may point to statistically significant relationships that do not actually exist in the wider population. How to define 'large' is a bit of a subjective question, although it is possible to do power analysis in order to determine how many respondents, N, are needed in order to uncover an effect. *Power analysis* refers to the statistical evaluation of sample size with the aim of computing the number of cases needed to detect a certain effect. It should be noted that, when using secondary datasets, power analysis is less relevant since the data have already been collected. The WERS of organizations and employees can likely both be considered 'large', so you should be conscious of the possibility of Type I error for all of the statistical tests described in this book.

Beyond sample size, there are some other reasons for Type I errors. Finding a statistically significant relationship that does not exist in the population can be caused by invalid measurements, nonrandomly drawn samples that are not representative of the population, and the possibility of spuriousness. *Spuriousness* refers to a statistical relationship between two variables, X and Y, when in fact the effect in Y is caused by another variable, Z. The possibility of Type I error reinforces the old adage: just because you find a correlation does not mean that you can infer causation.

Type II Error

Type II error, also referred to as *beta error*, refers to the probability of not finding a statistically significant result when, in fact, there is a relationship in the population. Both Type I and Type II errors are equally problematic. Type II error is a concern inasmuch as it means that a real relationship exists in the population, but, for whatever reason, you were unable to find it in your sample. As with Type I error, there are several explanations for Type II error, starting with the possibility that your sample is too small to be able to detect the effect. Again, smaller samples mean larger *p*-values and confidence intervals in the light of the possibility that the sample may not be representative of the populations from which it was drawn. Poor or invalid measurements can also explain Type II error in that it will be difficult to find a relationship if you're not measuring what you think you're measuring. Another reason for Type II error is that you might be looking for the wrong type of relationship. For example, Figure 4.10 shows two types of relationships between *X* and *Y*: a linear relationship and a nonlinear relationship. If you're only looking for one, but not the other, you could end up with Type II error in your model.

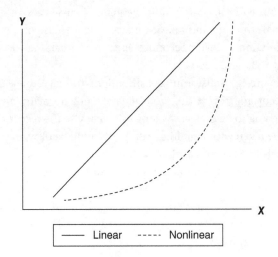

Figure 4.10 Linear versus nonlinear relationships

Normalization Procedures

This chapter has so far provided you with an in-depth treatment of the 'mechanism' that statisticians use to make a 'quantum leap' from our sample to the population. Although a detailed explanation of the mathematics underlying this mechanism is beyond the scope of this applied textbook, it should be clear that generalization from a sample to the population depends on the normality of ordinal and scale variables. We know a lot about the geometric properties of the normal curve, and it is this knowledge that enables us to make accurate inferences about the populations under study.

In practice, however, it should be noted that no variable is ever perfectly normally distributed. There are some variables, like height and IQ, that are mostly normally distributed, but the ideal of the normal curve is just that: an ideal. You learned in the previous chapter that one of the ways in which we evaluate normality is to look at skewness and kurtosis statistics. To reiterate, if you take the skewness or kurtosis statistic divided by the standard error of skewness or standard error of kurtosis statistic, that will give you a number. If that number is greater than 1.96 or less than −1.96, then you conclude that the distribution is not normally distributed. There is, however, a problem with using this procedure on very large datasets (e.g., the WERS used in this book). When the sample size, N, is very large, then even very slight deviations from normality will be detected when taking the skewness or kurtosis statistics divided by their standard errors. In other words, in the WERS datasets, nearly every single ordinal- or scale-level variable will present as suffering from statistically significant skewness or kurtosis, and therefore nonnormality.

Some statisticians obsess over distributional normality. They believe that we cannot accurately generalize from a sample to a population unless the sample distributions are normally distributed. To address or remedy nonnormality, they sometimes employ a series of mathematical data transformations that have the effect of normalizing a nonnormal distribution. Personally, I do not encourage these types of mathematical transformations aimed at normalization. First off, they are largely unnecessary. Because of the central limit theorem, discussed above, even if our sample distributions are nonnormal, we can still make generalizations because of our understanding of the sampling distribution of sample means. Second, these types of data transformations are often not very effective, especially in large datasets.

Rather than mathematically transforming distributions to make them more normal, a better approach is just to accept and report that your data are not normally distributed. After all, no research design is ever going to be perfect. As long as you advise the reader that the results of your statistical tests should be taken with a grain of salt, you should be okay, even when using nonnormally distributed ordinal- or scale-level variables.

Even though we won't be doing any data transformations on the WERS datasets in this book (again, because they would not be effective anyway, given the large size of the samples), I still think it is important to show you how to normalize hypothetical data using SPSS. Not only are these normalization procedures mathematically interesting (nerd alert!), but you may also want to use them someday when using a smaller dataset.

Outlier Analysis, Data Trimming, and Winsorization

Outlier analysis looks for extreme outliers in order to either trim them or winsorize them. *Data trimming* refers to the process of simply cutting extreme values (high or low) out of your dataset. *Winsorizing* refers to the process of changing extreme values to the closest value that is not an outlier.

Extreme outliers are problematic because they can cause skewness by dragging the mean higher (or lower) than the median. Very high outliers cause positive skewness, as depicted in Figure 3.10a and very low outliers cause negative skewness, as depicted in Figure 3.10b.

Let's see how data trimming and winsorization work in practice. Imagine that you've asked 21 employees how many sick days they took in the last year. The data are reported in Box 4.3. Open up a new SPSS file and carefully enter these 21 values into a spreadsheet. If you want, you can go into the Variable View, insert the label for this variable 'How many sick days did you take in the last year?', and change the name of the variable from 'VAR00001' to 'sickd'.

Box 4.3: How Many Sick Days Did You Take in the Last Year?

	VAR00001
1	5.00
2	4.00
3	6.00
4	3.00
5	7.00
6	5.00
7	5.00
8	8.00
9	2.00
10	5.00
11	9.00
12	1.00
13	5.00
14	5.00
15	6.00
16	4.00
17	5.00
18	7.00
19	3.00
20	5.00
21	45.00

Let's first generate some descriptive statistics and frequency distributions for this variable. Go to Analyze, Descriptive Statistics, and Frequencies…. Move the variable to the right-hand column by double clicking it. Now go into Statistics… and tick ☑ Std. deviation, ☑ Mean, ☑ Median, and ☑ Skewness, and then click Continue. Then go into Charts… , tick ⦿ Histograms and then Continue. Click OK. The output is shown in Figure 4.11. You will see a mean of 6.90 and a median of 5.00, both of which suggest positive skewness. If you take the skewness statistic divided by the standard error of skewness (4.25/0.501), you get 8.48, which is clearly higher than 1.96, our cutoff. We therefore conclude that this distribution suffers from excessive skewness.

Statistics

VAR00001

N	Valid	21
	Missing	0
Mean		6.9048
Median		5.0000
Std. Deviation		8.92695
Skewness		4.253
Std. Error of Skewness		.501

VAR00001

		Frequency	Percent	Valid Percent	Cumulative Percent
Valid	1.00	1	4.8	4.8	4.8
	2.00	1	4.8	4.8	9.5
	3.00	2	9.5	9.5	19.0
	4.00	2	9.5	9.5	28.6
	5.00	8	38.1	38.1	66.7
	6.00	2	9.5	9.5	76.2
	7.00	2	9.5	9.5	85.7
	8.00	1	4.8	4.8	90.5
	9.00	1	4.8	4.8	95.2
	45.00	1	4.8	4.8	100.0
	Total	21	100.0	100.0	

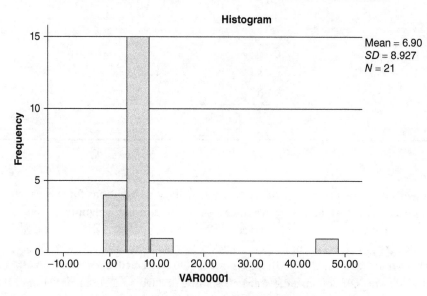

Histogram

Mean = 6.90
SD = 8.927
N = 21

Figure 4.11 Descriptive statistics: How many sick days in the last year

Reprint courtesy of IBM Corporation ©

Just scrolling through the variable in Data View, you will see most respondents took around 5 sick days; however, the last respondent took 45 sick days, which really stands out in the histogram in Figure 4.11. Because this response appears extreme, it is likely to be the key outlier causing the skewness. But, to be certain, we need to set a cutoff, which we can do using z-scores. Let's assume that any value beyond a z-score of 3 is an outlier. Remember that a z-score of more than 3 corresponds to a value that is higher than 3 SD from the mean.

Recall that to calculate z-scores, we go to Analyze, Descriptive Statistics, and Descriptives. Move your variable to the right by double clicking on it and be sure to tick Save standardized values as variables to tell SPSS to produce z-scores for each value. Click OK . Ignore the output and go to Data View instead. You will notice that a new column has been added with a list of the 21 z-scores we requested. Sure enough, the z-score for the respondent who took 45 sick days is 4.27, which is beyond 3, thus pointing to the fact that it is indeed an outlier. Now that we have established this fact, the next question is what to do about it.

We could trim the data by simply deleting case 21 from the dataset. Do this, and then try running the descriptive statistics again to see what the effect is on the mean, median, and skewness statistic. You'll find that the new mean and median are both 5.00, and the skewness statistic is now 0, which is what we were hoping to achieve. The key disadvantage with data trimming is that your N gets reduced, and therefore, you lose some statistical power.

Another thing we could do is to winsorize case 21. This would involve changing that value of 45 to the next highest score, which happens to be 10. Go ahead and type 10 in for case 21. When you change the 45 to a 10, what happens to the mean, median, and skewness statistic? Now you'll find a mean of 5.24 and a median of 5.00. To see whether this winsorized distribution suffers from skewness, just take the skewness statistic (0.314) divided by the standard error of skewness (0.501). The answer is 0.63, which is within ±1.96, thus indicating that the distribution no longer suffers from significant skewness.

Again, in practice, I do not recommend that you carry out any of these procedures because they do alter the data unnecessarily, but you should at least be aware of data trimming and winsorizing because some statisticians use them to normalize nonnormal distributions.

Mathematical Data Transformations

Don't close that dataset just yet, and if you changed case 21 from 45 to 10, you can turn it back to 45 now. Another option for dealing with nonnormality is to employ mathematical transformations that have the effect of normalization. Common mathematical data transformations include taking the log of each value, squaring or cubing each value, or taking the square root or cube root of each value. These procedures have the effect of 'drawing in' extreme values so that they become not-so-extreme. They change every value in the distribution, but maintain the rank-ordering. Let's see how this works in SPSS. We'll do a simple logarithmic transformation, but you can experiment with other types of transformations on your own.

To take the log of all 21 values for this variable, go to Transform and Compute Variable. The window depicted in Figure 4.12 opens. Under Target Variable, type 'sicklog', which gives a name to your new, transformed variable. Now, on the right-hand side of the window, under Function group:

, click Arithmetic. The box below, labeled Functions and Special Variables, will then populate. Double click on Lg10. Doing so, you'll notice that 'LG10(?)' appears at the top under Numeric Expression. Highlight the variable on the left and move it to the right, or simply double click it. The full mathematical expression should be 'LG10(VAR00001)'. Now click OK. You have just instructed SPSS to take the log of every value for this variable.

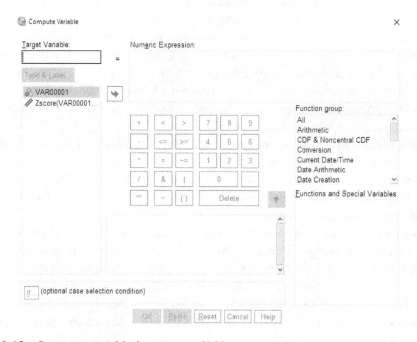

Figure 4.12 Compute variable function in SPSS

Reprint courtesy of IBM Corporation ©

If you go into Data View, you'll see a variable has been created, 'sicklog'. Notice that the log of the old value of 45 is now a new value of 1.65, which is a lot closer to the remaining values in the distribution, all of which have also been transformed logarithmically. But to see if our transformation really worked, we're going to have to generate descriptive statistics for 'sicklog' and then take the skewness statistic divided by the standard error of skewness. If that statistic is within ±1.96, then our transformation was successful and the logged variable is no longer skewed.

Go to Analyze, Descriptive Statistics, and Frequencies…. Move 'sicklog' to the right and go into Statistics…. Tick ☑ Std. deviation, ☑ Mean, ☑ Median, and ☑ Skewness and then click Continue. You can also request ⦿ Histograms under Charts… if you'd like. Click Continue and then OK. Boom! In Figure 4.13, you'll see that the old skewness statistic is 4.25 and the new skewness statistic, after the logarithmic transformation, is 0.872. The standard error, 0.501, is the same between the two variables. If you take 0.872/0.501, you get 1.74. This value is within the range of ±1.96, so we can therefore conclude that our logarithmic transformation was successful and that the variable is no longer significantly skewed.

Statistics

		VAR00001	sicklog
N	Valid	21	21
	Missing	0	0
Mean		6.9048	.7052
Median		5.0000	.6990
Std. Deviation		8.92695	.30298
Skewness		4.253	.872
Std. Error of Skewness		.501	.501

Figure 4.13 Sick days, logarithmic transformation

Reprint courtesy of IBM Corporation ©

Try to carry out another data transformation. To square every value, use '**2' in the arithmetic compute function. What happened to the shape of the distribution and its level of skewness?

What Have You Learned?

Let's recap the main points of this chapter. We first learned that statistical inferences are best calculated when the sample is randomly drawn from the population. Nonrandom samples are rarely 'representative' of the population, so any generalizations made from them will be particularly 'noisy'.

We learned about the spatial and geometrical properties of the normal curve. In a perfectly normal distribution, the mean and the median are identical and the space beneath the curve can be accurately calibrated using standard deviations. The more standard deviations from the mean, the fewer cases in the distribution. We learned that z-scores are standardized expressions of the data and are calculated in reference to standard deviations from the mean.

We learned that we have to analyse samples, but that we don't really care about samples. What we care about is whether the results from our sample generalize to the population. To make this 'quantum leap' from sample to population, we use the central limit theorem. In this context, the sampling distribution of sample means is the mechanism that allows us to make inferences about a population based on sample data.

We learned that at the very heart of inferential statistics is the p-value, and that the cutoff for statistical significance is typically 0.05. In other words, when $p < 0.05$, we can conclude, with 95% confidence, that the results of our sample hold water in the broader population. But we also learned that p-values decrease when the size of the sample gets larger, and vice versa. This is one of the key reasons for Type I error (where we find a relationship in our sample that doesn't exist in the population) and Type II error (where we don't find a relationship in our sample, even though it exists in the population).

Finally, we learned about the procedures that some statisticians use to transform their data in order to make the distributions appear more normal. These normalization procedures, however, are often unhelpful and unnecessary (in my view) when using very large datasets like those used in this textbook.

Okay, hot shot. After four intense chapters that effectively laid the groundwork for inferential statistics, you're finally ready to start running some statistical tests. So, without further ado, let's get to it, starting with the independent samples *t*-test.

Further Reading

Aguinis, H., & Branstetter, S. A. (2007). Teaching the concept of the sampling distribution of the mean. *Journal of Management Education, 31*(4), 467–483.

Cox, D. R. (2006). *Principles of statistical inference*. Cambridge University Press.

Dinov, I. D., Christou, N., & Sanchez, J. (2008). Central limit theorem: New SOCR applet and demonstration activity. *Journal of Statistics Education, 16*(2), 1–15.

Kyburg, H. E., Jr. (2012). *The logical foundations of statistical inference* (Vol. 65). Springer Science & Business Media.

Reid, N., & Cox, D. R. (2015). On some principles of statistical inference. *International Statistical Review, 83*(2), 293–308.

In-Class Discussion Questions

1. Why is it important that your sample is representative of your population? How can you ensure that your sample is representative?
2. What is the normal curve? Why is it an important concept in parametric statistics? Draw a normal curve and label the mean, median, and 3 *SD* above and below the mean. What does the *X*-axis represent? What does the *Y*-axis represent?
3. What is the central limit theorem and how does it enable generalization from the sample to the population?
4. What is the *p*-value? How does it enable generalization from the sample to the population? What are the conventional cutoffs for *p*-values?
5. Why and how would we mathematically transform the values of an ordinal- or scale-level variable? How can we tell if our transformation has been successful?
6. What are Type I and Type II errors? How are they different from one another? What factors can increase or decrease Type I and Type II errors?

PART II
COMPARING MEANS

Welcome to the second part of this applied statistics textbook. You've made it this far, so you must be a patient and diligent student. Congratulations! Now that you have a good foundation in the basics of data science, it's time for you to move on to do your first inferential statistical tests. I'm going to start you off with what are commonly thought to be the easiest of all inferential statistics: the t-test (which you will learn about in Chapter 5) and the analysis of variance (also commonly referred to as the ANOVA) test (which you will learn about in Chapter 6). Both statistical tests are similar in that they are designed to enable a statistician to compare mean scores across groups and determine whether or not they are significantly different from one another. A t-test is used when you wish to compare only two mean scores (e.g., men vs. women or white vs. nonwhite), and an ANOVA is used when you are comparing three or more mean scores with each other. You will almost always find a statistical difference between two or more means within your sample, but remember that you don't care about mean differences within your sample. These are more or less irrelevant. What you care about is whether those mean differences in your sample also exist in the population. The next two chapters will walk you through these types of statistical inferences, and I will show you how to use IBM SPSS Statistics Software (SPSS) to carry out the tests. If you're ready, then turn the page and let's begin with the auspicious independent samples t-test. Ready? Set? Go!

5

The *t*-Test

The independent samples *t*-test (also commonly referred to as just the *t*-test) is one of the most widely used methods of inferential statistics in the social sciences. It is a *parametric* statistical test, which implies that it is based on the concept of the normal distribution, discussed at length in the previous chapter. It is also a bivariate statistical test, which means that it is restricted to analysing the relationship between only two variables at a time, usually denoted X and Y (where X is the independent, or *predictor*, variable and Y is the dependent, or *outcome*, variable). To carry out an independent samples *t*-test, X must always be a two-category nominal variable, and Y must always be an ordinal- or preferably scale-level variable. If your model contains any other configuration of variables, it will be mathematically impossible to carry out this statistical test.

The purpose of the independent samples *t*-test is to determine whether or not there is a significant difference in scores between two groups of respondents within the same sample. For example: do men score differently than women on job satisfaction? Or, if you expected a particular outcome, you could pose this same question with a built-in hypothesis: do men score more highly on job satisfaction than women? In this case, the independent variable is gender, consisting of two groups – men and women – while the dependent variable is job satisfaction, which is likely measured ordinally using some kind of Likert scale (e.g., 1 = *extremely unsatisfied* to 10 = *extremely satisfied*). Note that this test conforms to the requirement of an independent samples *t*-test: the independent variable is a two-category nominal variable, and the dependent variable is either ordinal or scale. To answer this research question, male and female respondents are divided into two groups, and mean scores are calculated for each group. The larger the difference in mean scores, the more likely that the result will be 'statistically significant'. Similarly, the smaller the difference in mean scores, the more likely that we will conclude that there is no significant difference between the two groups in the population. The 'result' of an independent samples *t*-test is the *t-statistic*, defined as a number that reflects the magnitude of the difference in mean scores between the two groups, and a corresponding *p*-value, which tells us whether or not that mean difference can be generalized to the wider population. If the *p*-value of the *t*-statistic is less than 0.05, then we conclude that the mean difference in the sample is indeed significant and, therefore, generalizable to the population. If the *p*-value is 0.05 or greater, then we conclude that the mean difference in the sample is not large enough to warrant generalization to the wider population.

In this chapter, we will first look at how elite applied statisticians like you can use the independent samples *t*-test to answer important research questions in the field of business and management. After that, we will look at the mathematical processes underlying the *t*-test. We will then use the WERS of employees to demonstrate how to carry out the independent samples *t*-test using IBM SPSS Statistics Software (SPSS). Following that, we will briefly look at another type of *t*-test that is based on the concept of repeated measures. Finally, the chapter will conclude with a summary of its key points.

Comparing Two Means in Management Research

The independent samples *t*-test assesses whether or not two groups score, on average, differently across an ordinal- or scale-level variable. The fundamental question is whether one group scores higher (or lower) than the other group. Almost inevitably, within sample data, one group will always score higher than the other. However, you will recall from Chapter 4 that we don't really care about the results of our sample because they could simply be down to random chance. We only care about whether the results of our sample also hold water in the population. Thus, where there is only a very small difference in mean scores in our sample, it is likely that we will not have enough confidence to generalize our result to the population. Similarly, where there is a large magnitude of difference between the two mean scores in our sample, we will be more confident in generalizing that difference to the population. Of course, sample size, as we also learned in Chapter 4, affects generalizability. In larger samples, smaller differences are more likely to be statistically significant. Therefore, it is always wise to be conscious of the possibility of Type I and Type II errors in a *t*-test.

Let's spend some time considering the types of research questions that we can ask and subsequently answer with an independent samples *t*-test. Remember that our research questions must be bivariate and the independent variable, X, must be a nominal two-category variable, while the dependent variable, Y, must be either ordinal or preferably scale in measurement. With these parameters in mind, researchers might ask the following questions:

- *Do trade union members take more sick days than non-trade union members?* The independent variable is trade union membership (yes/no), and the dependent variable is number of sick days per year.
- *Do employees with university degrees score more highly on their performance appraisal than employees without a university degree?* The independent variable is whether or not the respondent has a university degree (yes/no), and the dependent variable is a quantitative measure from a performance appraisal.
- *Do employees with children work fewer hours per week than employees without children?* The independent variable is whether or not an employee has children (yes/no), and the dependent variable is working hours per week.
- *Do white employees report higher levels of trust in management than nonwhite employees?* The independent variable is race (white/nonwhite), and the dependent variable is how much the employee trusts management.
- *Are employees in nonprofit firms more committed to their organization than employees working in for-profit firms?* The independent variable is the type of firm the respondent works in (nonprofit/for-profit), and the dependent variable is a measure of organizational commitment.

- *Do marketing professionals spend more time surfing the world wide web than HR professionals?* The independent variable is type of employee (marketing/HR), and the dependent variable is the number of minutes per week surfing the web.
- *Are atheist employees more sexually active than religious employees* (don't ask me why any statisticians would ever want to ask this question!)? The independent variable in this case is whether or not the respondent is religious (yes/no), and the dependent variable is the number of times the respondent has had sexual intercourse in the past year.
- *Do supervisors report higher levels of workplace stress than nonsupervisory employees?* The independent variable is whether or not the respondent is a supervisor (yes/no), and the dependent variable is some measure of workplace stress.
- *Are men more satisfied in their jobs than women?* The independent variable is gender (male/female), and the dependent variable is job satisfaction.

Let's take a look at how a statistician might answer that last question. Assume that you are a data analytics specialist working at a large multinational corporation with 20,000 employees across Australia. Your population is all 20,000 employees, but because you do not think it is practical to survey the entire workforce, you draw a random sample of 200 employees, half of whom are women.

The first thing you should do is to think about what kind of relationship you expect. Do you think men will be more satisfied, or women? Why? You look at some payroll data and find that the 100 men in your sample earn 18% more than the women (note that this refers to actual differences in pay, not overall satisfaction with one's job, which is our research question). Therefore, you hypothesize that the men may correspondingly report higher levels of job satisfaction than the women.

The survey you administered to your sample of 200 employees asked two questions:

- What is your gender? (male, female)
- How satisfied are you with your job on a scale of 1 to 10, where 1 = *not at all satisfied* and 10 = *completely satisfied*?

Your dependent variable, job satisfaction, is already coded on an ordinal scale of 1 to 10. However, your independent variable, gender, still needs to be quantified, or coded. Remember that SPSS is not smart enough to know what 'male' and 'female' mean, so you must assign numbers to those categories. Typically, when carrying out an independent samples *t*-test, you use 0 and 1 (although, really, any two numbers could be used). So let's code *male* = 0 and *female* = 1, although you could also do it the other way around.

Assume that you've now collected the data and want to begin your analysis. You start by analysing the *pooled sample* ($N = 200$), where men and women are evaluated together as one group. You find that, for the full sample, the mean is 5.6 (remember, where 1 = *not at all satisfied* and 10 = *completely satisfied*), and the standard deviation is 1.2. This job satisfaction variable is depicted in Figure 5.1, where the *X*-axis contains our 1 to 10 Job Satisfaction Scale, and the *Y*-axis reports the frequency for each category.

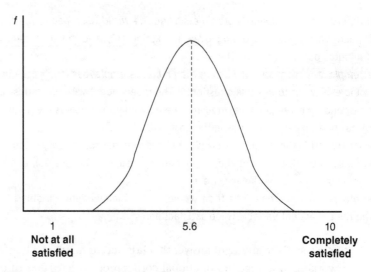

Figure 5.1 Job satisfaction normal distribution

But you're not terribly interested in the overall (pooled) mean. What you're interested in is whether the mean for men is higher than the mean for women, as you initially hypothesized. So now you divide your sample into two groups: male ($N = 100$) and female ($N = 100$) employees. You compute the means and standard deviations for both groups and find that the male employees report an average job satisfaction of 6.2, with a standard deviation of 0.9 and the women report an average job satisfaction of 5.1 with a standard deviation of 1.2. These results are reported graphically in Figure 5.2, where both distributions are superimposed.

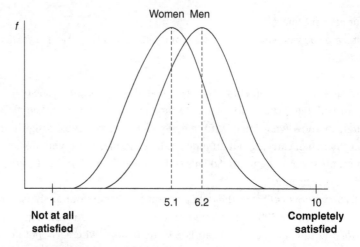

Figure 5.2 Job satisfaction by gender (men vs. women)

So, within our sample of 200 employees, we know that the men score higher on job satisfaction than the women. But, remember, we don't really care about the results of our sample. What we care about is whether this result (i.e., the mean difference between men and women) generalizes to the wider population of 20,000 employees. There is clearly a difference between the two means in our sample (6.2 for men vs. 5.1 for women). The key question, however, is whether the distance between the means (equivalent to 1.1 points on the 10-point Job Satisfaction Scale) is large enough to warrant a 'quantum leap' from the sample to the wider population, such that we can conclude, with a certain degree of confidence (95%, if using a *p*-value cutoff of <0.05), that male employees are more satisfied than female employees in our organization.

To make this quantum leap from the sample to the population, we will need to carry out some mathematical procedures. These are explained in the next section.

The Mathematics Underlying the Independent Samples *t*-Test

The independent samples *t*-test is based on a comparison of mean scores across two groups within a sample. Almost inevitably, when using sample data, one mean score will be higher, and the other will be lower. This could be a result of either systematic differences between the two groups or random differences within the same. Recall that differences in mean scores are, by definition, always restrained to the sample data. The key question is, simply the following: Is the difference between the two means within the sample 'large enough' to justify a generalization of the difference to the population? This is what we really care about.

Before we carry out the mathematical operations of an independent samples *t*-test, let's review the assumptions we must make for the analysis to be valid.

First, the sample we use must be randomly drawn. Recall from the previous chapter that random sampling is required because nonrandom samples are much less likely to 'look like' and 'behave like' the population, making generalization more difficult. Second, the independent variable must be a two-category nominal measure. Third, the two groups must be independent of one another. This means that the selection of a participant into one of the two groups does not affect the probability of the selection of a participant into the other group. Fourth, the dependent variable must be ordinal or preferably scale level in measurement and roughly normally distributed. In other words, the dependent variable must take the shape of a normal distribution, or bell curve, as discussed in Chapter 4. Fifth, you need to achieve *homogeneity of variance*, meaning that the variances (the spread of scores) across the two groups are roughly equal.

In practice, most research will fail to meet all five assumptions. This does not mean that you should simply abandon the research altogether. Should you choose to continue with the research (e.g., by using a nonrandom sample), you would need to acknowledge this shortcoming when reporting your results.

It is also worth noting that an independent samples *t*-test does not require that you draw two separate samples for analysis, although you could do this if you want. You can simply draw one sample, asking participants to assign themselves into one of two groups: for example, males versus females, trade union members versus non–trade union members, white collar workers versus blue collar workers.

There are different variations of the mathematical equation for calculating a t-statistic, but all of them are fairly similar in that they take the difference in mean scores across the two groups divided by an estimate of the standard error. Mathematically, the basic equation for large samples looks like Equation (5.1) below:

$$t = \frac{\bar{X}_1 - \bar{X}_2}{\sqrt{\dfrac{s_1^2}{N_1} + \dfrac{s_2^2}{N_2}}} \tag{5.1}$$

Let's take each component of this equation and break it down to make it simple and (mostly) painless.

Obviously, t is your t-statistic. Remember, the larger your t-statistic, the more likely your sample means will be statistically significantly different, although the key determinant of significance is still the p-value that accompanies the t-statistic. There is no 'cutoff' per se for a t-statistic that will be statistically significant.

$\bar{X}_1$ and $\bar{X}_2$ are, simply, the mean score of Group 1 and the mean score of Group 2. By subtracting the two scores, you will get the magnitude of the difference between the averages. The larger that number, in general, the larger your t-statistic.

S_1^2 and S_2^2 are, respectively, the standard deviations, squared, of Group 1 and Group 2. Remember that the standard deviation is a measure of the amount of spread, or variation, around the mean, where a larger standard deviation means greater spread (and thus a flatter distribution), and a smaller standard deviation means less spread (and thus a more 'peaked' distribution).

N_1 and N_2 correspond to the number of cases within each group. The problem with Equation (5.1) is that it only works when the sample is large and the sample sizes, N_1 and N_2, are equal. Since sample sizes are rarely equal, we simply subtract 1 from each sample size. So, in practice, you should use Equation (5.2) to calculate a t-statistic, rather than Equation (5.1):

$$t = \frac{\bar{X}_1 - \bar{X}_2}{\sqrt{\dfrac{s_1^2}{N_1 - 1} + \dfrac{s_2^2}{N_2 - 1}}} \tag{5.2}$$

As if this isn't complicated enough, a slightly different equation (see Equation 5.3 below) is needed when your sample size is small, say, fewer than 100 cases. This is the equation that one would use if solving for t by hand with a small sample:

$$t = \frac{\bar{X}_1 - \bar{X}_2}{\sqrt{\dfrac{N_1 s_1^2 + N_2 s_2^2}{N_1 + N_2 - 2}} \sqrt{\dfrac{N_1 + N_2}{N_1 N_2}}} \tag{5.3}$$

I know this equation looks daunting and, frankly (let's face it), the world might be slightly better off without it. But let's take a look at how we can use Equation (5.3) to calculate t by hand, just so you know what SPSS is up to when you ask it to do an independent samples *t*-test. We'll take this step-by-step, nice and slow. Take a deep breath . . .

Calculating the *t*-Statistic by Hand

Imagine that you manage a company with 300 employees, and you administer a survey to 12 randomly drawn people: 6 men and 6 women. Ordinarily, this would be much too small a sample to draw valid conclusions, but since we're doing this *t*-test by hand, let's stick with a sample of $N = 12$. You would like to know whether men are more likely to take sick days than women in your organization, so you ask the participants in your sample to record the number of sick days they've taken in the past 12 months. Here are the data:

Participant	Gender (0 = *male*, 1 = *female*)	Sick days
1	0	8
2	0	9
3	0	7
4	0	10
5	0	9
6	0	14
7	1	6
8	1	2
9	1	2
10	1	1
11	1	3
12	1	4

You will note that I coded our nominal, two-category independent variable, gender, such that 0 = *male* and 1 = *female*. This choice was completely arbitrary. I could have just as easily coded it 0 = *female* and 1 = *male*, or 1 = *male* and 2 = *female*, or whatever. Sick days does not need to be coded because it is a scale-level variable. Finally, the first column, 'Participant', isn't a variable, but rather a list of the number of people in our sample ($N = 12$).

Okay, let's tackle Equation (5.3) one step at a time, starting with the average sick days for men ($\bar{X}_1$) and women ($\bar{X}_2$).

$$\bar{X}_1 = (8 + 9 + 7 + 10 + 9 + 14)/6 = (57)/6 = 9.5$$

$$\bar{X}_2 = (6 + 2 + 2 + 1 + 3 + 4)/6 = (18)/6 = 3$$

So we already know that male employees in our sample take an average of 9.5 sick days compared with 3 sick days for female employees. Probably 'man flu', right? But, then again, we don't care much at all about this sample mean difference. What we really care about is whether this difference generalizes to the wider population – in this case, all 300 employees in your organization.

Now we need to calculate the standard deviations for our male and female subsamples and square them. For the standard deviation formula, see page 64.

$$s_1^2 = \sqrt{\frac{8^2 + 9^2 + 7^2 + 10^2 + 9^2 + 14^2}{6} - 9.5^2} = \sqrt{\frac{571}{6} - 90.25} = \sqrt{4.92} = 2.22$$

$$s_2^2 = \sqrt{\frac{6^2 + 2^2 + 2^2 + 1^2 + 3^2 + 4^2}{6} - 3^2} = \sqrt{\frac{70}{6} - 9} = \sqrt{2.67} = 1.63$$

Now that we know $\bar{X}_1 = 9.5$, $\bar{X}_2 = 3$, $s_1^2 = 2.22$, and $s_2^2 = 1.63$, we can easily solve for t using Equation (5.3) by simply plugging in the relevant values, just like this:

$$t = \frac{\bar{X}_1 - \bar{X}_2}{\sqrt{\frac{N_1 s_1^2 + N_2 s_2^2}{N_1 + N_2 - 2}} \sqrt{\frac{N_1 + N_2}{N_1 N_2}}}$$

$$t = \frac{9.5 - 3}{\sqrt{\frac{(6)(2.22) + (6)(1.63)}{6 + 6 - 2}} \sqrt{\frac{6 + 6}{(6)(6)}}}$$

$$t = \frac{6.5}{\sqrt{\frac{13.32 + 9.78}{12 - 2}} \sqrt{\frac{12}{36}}}$$

$$t = \frac{6.5}{\sqrt{\frac{23.10}{10}} \sqrt{\frac{12}{36}}}$$

$$t = \frac{6.5}{\sqrt{2.31} \sqrt{0.33}}$$

$$t = \frac{6.5}{(1.52)(0.57)}$$

$$t = \frac{6.5}{0.87}$$

$$t = 7.47$$

And boom! You've just calculated your first t-statistic by hand. I told you it wasn't so bad.

Now, this number ($t = 7.47$) corresponds to a specific p-value that will tell us whether the difference between the mean scores ($\bar{X}_1 = 9.5$; $\bar{X}_2 = 3.0$) is generalizable to the population (in this case, all 300 employees in the organization). Many statistics textbooks have a bunch of tables in the back that will allow you to figure out what the correct *p*-value is for a given *t* statistic, but these are cumbersome and pretty needless, given that our old friend SPSS will figure out the correct *p*-value for us. Come to think of it, SPSS will also do the above calculations for us as well and in just a fraction of the time that it took us! So, let's just draw this section to a close and learn how to use SPSS to run an independent samples *t*-test.

The Independent Samples *t*-Test Using SPSS

Calculating a *t*-statistic by hand is so passé. I mean, really, who would ever want to do such a crazy thing if there were an easier option? Fortunately for us, there is an easier option, a much easier option. Let's just let our old friend SPSS do the math for us. Why should we do all the hard work when we can fairly simply instruct a computer program to do it for us?

You might recall from Chapter 1 that we were thinking about the effect of trade union membership on job satisfaction. Our reasoning went something like this: we know that trade union members make more money than non–trade union members, and we think that more money should make people happier, so we hypothesize that trade union members (as a group) will have higher levels of job satisfaction than non–trade union members (as a group). If we were writing an essay, we could perhaps present the hypothesis like this:

Hypothesis 1: Trade union members will report higher job satisfaction than non-trade union members.

To test this hypothesis, let's run an independent samples *t*-test on SPSS. First, go into the Companion Website and open up the file named Chap5data.sav. This is a file containing the relevant variables from the WERS of employees.

The first thing we should do is to familiarize ourselves with the relevant variables. This means starting in Variable View and checking out the following: (1) the names of the variables, (2) the labels attached to those variables, and (3) how the variables were coded. You might recall that the original variable measuring trade union membership was a three-category nominal variable:

D1 **Are you a member of a trade union or staff association?**
Tick one box only

Yes	No, but have been in the past	No, have never been a member
☐	☐	☐

You might be thinking, 'Wait a minute! I thought that the independent variable in an independent samples *t*-test had to be nominal with only two categories!' You're right, so this three-category measure won't work. Fortunately, I've gone ahead and recoded this variable for you in the dataset. If you look into the Values tab, you'll see that the recoded variable (labeled 'tradeu') is now coded such that 0 = *Not currently a trade union member* and 1 = *Currently a trade union member*.

Now generate a frequency distribution for this nominal variable by going to Analyze, Descriptive Statistics, and Frequencies. Move 'tradeu' from the left-hand column into the right column by double clicking the variable and click OK. You will see the output in Figure 5.3. As you can see here, we have 21,857 valid cases and 124 missing values. Looking at the frequency table, you can see that 37.2 valid percent of the respondents are currently members of a trade union or staff association and 62.8% are not.

Statistics

Are you a trade unionist

N	Valid	21857
	Missing	124

Are you a trade unionist

		Frequency	Percent	Valid Percent	Cumulative Percent
Valid	not currently a trade union member	13721	62.4	62.8	62.8
	currently a trade union member	8136	37.0	37.2	100.0
	Total	21857	99.4	100.0	
Missing	missing	124	.6		
Total		21981	100.0		

Figure 5.3 Descriptive statistics, trade union

Reprint courtesy of IBM Corporation ©

Now, what about our dependent variable, job satisfaction? As you can see, the survey of employees has eight separate measures of job satisfaction, each of which can be said to 'tap' a unique dimension of the construct. All eight items were measured on a five-point Likert scale, where 1 = *very dissatisfied*, 2 = *dissatisfied*, 3 = *neither satisfied nor dissatisfied*, 4 = *satisfied*, and 5 = *very satisfied*. Any one of these variables could potentially serve as our dependent variable for the *t*-test.

Here is what the eight job satisfaction variables look like in the survey instrument:

AB How satisfied are you with the following aspects of your job?

Tick one box in each row

	Very satisfied	Satisfied	Neither satisfied nor dissatisfied	Dissatisfied	Very dissatisfied	Don't know
The sense of achievement you get from your work	☐	☐	☐	☐	☐	☐
The scope for using your own initiative	☐	☐	☐	☐	☐	☐
The amount of influence you have over your job	☐	☐	☐	☐	☐	☐
The training you receive	☐	☐	☐	☐	☐	☐
The opportunity to develop your skills in your job	☐	☐	☐	☐	☐	☐
The amount of pay you receive	☐	☐	☐	☐	☐	☐
Your job security	☐	☐	☐	☐	☐	☐
The work itself	☐	☐	☐	☐	☐	☐

Rather than looking at only one of these variables, let's create a *composite* job satisfaction variable instead. A composite variable is one that is composed by combining a series of variables together. This means that we need to add up these eight variables to create a new variable that reflects all these dimensions.

To create the new composite variable, go to Iransform and Compute Variable. Under Iarget Variable, simply type jobsat. Use the items in the column on the left and move them, one at a time, to the right-hand box under Numeric Expression:. One way of doing this is by double clicking each variable and using the | sign in the little calculator. But the other way of doing this is by just typing in the correct equation. In this case, you want to type in the following exactly: (qa8a + qa8b + qa8c + qa8d + qa8e + qa8f + qa8g + qa8h)/8. With this operation, you're telling SPSS to add together the scores for all eight job satisfaction variables and then to divide by 8. The reason for dividing by 8 is that there are 8 variables; thus, you can rescale the new composite variable, so that it is still based on the original Likert, where 1 = *very dissatisfied* to 5 = *very satisfied*. The window should look exactly like the one depicted in Figure 5.4. To create your new composite job satisfaction variable, click OK.

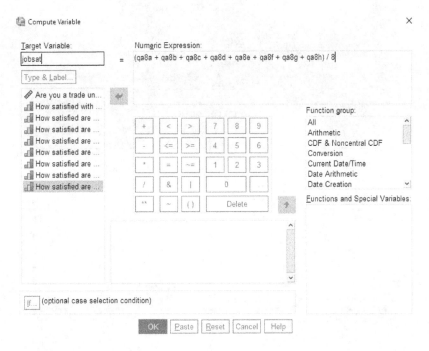

Figure 5.4 Compute variable function in SPSS

Reprint courtesy of IBM Corporation ©

Go into the Variable View and you will see that your new variable, jobsat, has been created. Under 'Label', write 'Job satisfaction composite variable'. Under 'Values', reproduce the original 1 to 5 Likert scale. A quick way to do this is to copy and paste a 'Values' box from one of the eight original job satisfaction variables. Remember also to go into the 'Missing' box and tell SPSS that any value of –9 should be coded as a discrete missing value (click on 'Missing', tick 'Discrete missing values', and type '–9' into the first box and then OK). If you don't do this, SPSS will include all instances of –9 in any statistical calculations.

Before conducting the independent samples *t*-test, first have a look at the descriptive statistics for your newly created job satisfaction composite variable. Go to Analyze, Descriptive Statistics, and Frequencies. Find 'jobsat' in the left-hand column (you may have to scroll down a bit in the column because newly created variables are situated at the very bottom) and move it over to the right by double clicking. Go into Statistics... and tick ☑ Mean, ☑ Median, ☑ Std. deviation, ☑ Skewness, and ☑ Kurtosis, and then click Continue. Now go into Charts... and tick ⦿ Histograms: and ☑ Show normal curve on histogram. Click Continue and then OK. Boom! Have a look at the output in Figure 5.5.

Statistics

Job sat composite

N	Valid	20666
	Missing	1315
Mean		3.5550
Median		3.6250
Std. Deviation		.72121
Skewness		-.511
Std. Error of Skewness		.017
Kurtosis		.319
Std. Error of Kurtosis		.034

Job sat composite

		Frequency	Percent	Valid Percent	Cumulative Percent
Valid	very dissatisfied	36	.2	.2	.2
	1.13	22	.1	.1	.3
	1.25	38	.2	.2	.5
	1.38	43	.2	.2	.7
	1.50	77	.4	.4	1.0
	1.63	73	.3	.4	1.4
	1.75	94	.4	.5	1.9
	1.88	119	.5	.6	2.4
	dissatisfied	168	.8	.8	3.2
	2.13	223	1.0	1.1	4.3
	2.25	299	1.4	1.4	5.8
	2.38	379	1.7	1.8	7.6
	2.50	439	2.0	2.1	9.7
	2.63	501	2.3	2.4	12.2
	2.75	598	2.7	2.9	15.0
	2.88	711	3.2	3.4	18.5
	neither satisfied nor dissatisfied	869	4.0	4.2	22.7
	3.13	1041	4.7	5.0	27.7
	3.25	1066	4.8	5.2	32.9
	3.38	1202	5.5	5.8	38.7
	3.50	1437	6.5	7.0	45.7
	3.63	1546	7.0	7.5	53.1

	3.75	1673	7.6	8.1	61.2
	3.88	1549	7.0	7.5	68.7
	satisfied	1839	8.4	8.9	77.6
	4.13	1027	4.7	5.0	82.6
	4.25	873	4.0	4.2	86.8
	4.38	704	3.2	3.4	90.2
	4.50	568	2.6	2.7	93.0
	4.63	446	2.0	2.2	95.1
	4.75	370	1.7	1.8	96.9
	4.88	285	1.3	1.4	98.3
	very satisfied	351	1.6	1.7	100.0
	Total	20666	94.0	100.0	
Missing	System	1315	6.0		
Total		21981	100.0		

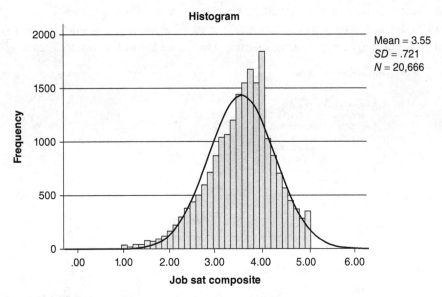

Figure 5.5 Descriptive statistics, job satisfaction composite

Reprint courtesy of IBM Corporation ©

In the first box, you will see that there are 20,666 valid cases and 1315 cases with missing data. The large number of missing cases with respect to the composite variable is explained by the fact that, if any one of the eight original job satisfaction variables has a missing case, then the composite is defined as missing. The mean job satisfaction score for our composite variable is 3.56 (again, on a five-point scale); the standard deviation is 0.72; and the median is 3.63. Looking at the skewness and kurtosis statistics, both are within the ±0.700 range, so we can conclude that the distribution is fairly normal in shape. The next box contains the distribution of scores, followed by the histogram, which, as we expected, appears mostly bell shaped.

At this point, having examined the descriptive statistics and frequency distributions for our independent variable (tradeu) and dependent variable (jobsat), we are now ready to conduct our first ever independent samples *t*-test. First, remember that trade union is coded 0 = *not currently a trade union member* and 1 = *currently a trade union member*, as this detail is important. You will need to remember this coding scheme in order to carry out the test.

To carry out an independent samples *t*-test, go to Analyze, Compare Means, and Independent-Samples T Test. The window depicted in Figure 5.6 will appear. First, in the left-hand column, find your dependent variable, jobsat. It should be the last variable at the bottom of the column. Highlight the variable and use ⬆ to move it to the right under Test Variable(s). Second, find your independent variable, tradeu, and move it to the right under Grouping Variable. Third, click on Define Groups... . You will see a new window pop up, depicted in Figure 5.7. You can see that there are two groups here: 'Group 1' and 'Group 2'. These correspond to the two categories of your independent variable: in this case, 'currently a trade union member' and 'not currently a trade union member'. We need to tell SPSS how we coded these two groups. So, next to 'Group 1', write 0, and next to 'Group 2', write 1. This is letting SPSS know that you have two categories, coded '0' and '1'. Remember that the coding of nominal variables is arbitrary, so if you had coded trade union as 1 = *not currently a trade union member* and 2 = *currently a trade union member*, you would enter 1 next to 'Group 1' and 2 next to 'Group 2'. After assigning 0 to 'Group 1' and 1 to 'Group 2', click Continue.

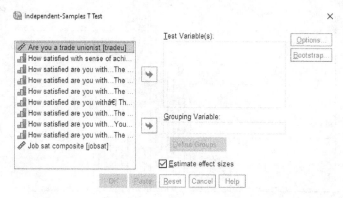

Figure 5.6 Independent samples *t*-test function in SPSS

Reprint courtesy of IBM Corporation ©

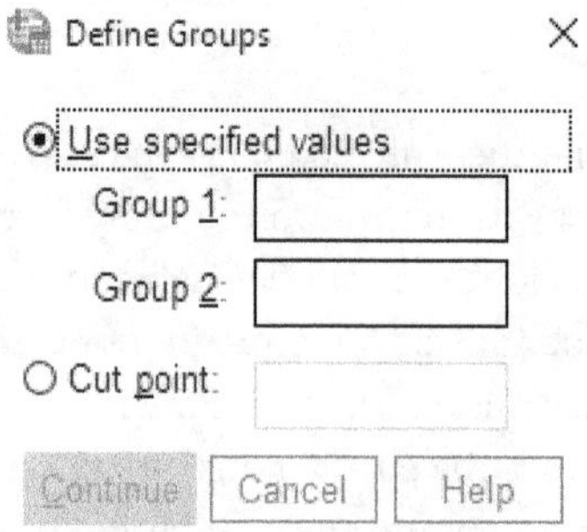

Figure 5.7 Define groups function in SPSS

Reprint courtesy of IBM Corporation ©

When you are ready to carry out your independent samples *t*-test, simply click OK. Boom! The output depicted in Figure 5.8 appears.

Group Statistics

	Are you a trade unionist	N	Mean	Std. Deviation	Std. Error Mean
Job sat composite	not currently a trade union member	12906	3.6068	.70615	.00622
	currently a trade union member	7667	3.4682	.73773	.00843

Independent Samples Test

		Levene's Test for Equality of Variances		t-test for Equality of Means					95% Confidence Interval of the Difference	
		F	Sig.	t	df	Sig. (2-tailed)	Mean Difference	Std. Error Difference	Lower	Upper
Job sat composite	Equal variances assumed	30.792	.000	13.392	20571	.000	.13866	.01035	.11836	.15895
	Equal variances not assumed			13.243	15546.133	.000	.13866	.01047	.11814	.15918

Independent Samples Effect Sizes

		Standardizer[a]	Point Estimate	95% Confidence Interval	
				Lower	Upper
Job sat composite	Cohen's d	.71808	.193	.165	.221
	Hedges' correction	.71811	.193	.165	.221
	Glass's delta	.73773	.188	.160	.216

a. The denominator used in estimating the effect sizes.
Cohen's d uses the pooled standard deviation.
Hedges' correction uses the pooled standard deviation, plus a correction factor.
Glass's delta uses the sample standard deviation of the control group.

Figure 5.8 Independent samples *t*-test output, job satisfaction composite, by trade union

Reprint courtesy of IBM Corporation ©

In the first box, you'll see the group statistics. Here you can find the mean difference in job satisfaction across the two categories. Of the 12,906 respondents who are not trade union members, the average job satisfaction score is 3.61 ($SD = 0.71$). In contrast, the mean for the 7667 trade union members is 3.47 ($SD = 0.74$). But remember that this result is only provisional because it is confined just to our sample, and we don't really care about our sample. What we care about is whether our result generalizes from the sample to the wider population.

The second box in Figure 5.8 speaks to the generalizability of this result. There is a lot going on in this box, so let's take it bit by bit. First, you will notice some statistics under 'Levene's test for equality of variances'. This is not the result of your independent samples *t*-test, but rather a separate statistical test that will tell you whether you have met one of the key assumptions of the *t*-test – for example, that the variances for each group are roughly equal. You'll recall that the variance, like the standard deviation, is a measure of dispersion (or spread) of scores vis-à-vis the mean, where a higher variance implies a greater spread of scores. The *t*-test requires that, for each category (in this case, trade union members vs. non–trade union members), the two distributions appear roughly equally normal, with a similar spread, or distribution, of scores around the mean. You don't need to be concerned about the mathematics underlying Levene's test for equality of variances. Instead, you just need to note whether the *p*-value (denoted 'Sig.' in the table) is statistically significant or not. Using a cutoff of 0.05, it appears that the result of Levene's test is significant because $p = 0.000$ (with a corresponding *F*-score of 30.79). This significant result means that, unfortunately, equal variances cannot be assumed, so you can skip the first row of the table and go straight to the second row. It is worth noting, however, that Levene's test is highly sensitive when the sample size is large, as described in Box 5.1.

Box 5.1: Levene's Test and Sample Size

Levene's test tells you whether the variances across the two groups are roughly equal. If they are not equal, then SPSS will make a correction to the *t*-statistic. Another term for unequal variance across the two distributions is *heterogeneity of variance*. In a similar vein, when two variances are roughly equal, this is referred to as *homogeneity of variance*. Ideally, you will hope that the *p*-value associated with your Levene's test is greater than 0.05, signaling homogeneity of variance (which is a good thing). Under these circumstances, you will use the 'Equal Variances Assumed' *t*-test results.

One problem with Levene's test, however, is that it is extremely sensitive to large sample sizes. When there are thousands of respondents (as with the survey of employees), very slight deviations in variability across the two distributions will drive down the *p*-value, suggesting heterogeneity of variance (which is a bad thing). So don't be surprised if most of the *t*-tests you run using this dataset fail Levene's test. This isn't ideal, but neither is it a serious problem. When Levene's test yields a *p*-value of >0.05, then you simply report the results corresponding to the 'Equal variances not assumed' row in the SPSS output for the independent samples *t*-test.

And finally, we arrive at the moment of truth. Following the 'Equal variances not assumed' row along the bottom of the table, you will see that the *t*-statistic for this statistical test is 13.24. Can you imagine just how long it would take to calculate this statistic by hand? In the next column over can be found the degrees of freedom, denoted '*df*', which is 15,546.13. Degrees of freedom is, for all practical purposes, a nonessential statistic for the applied data scientist. In other words, you don't really have to understand it to interpret a statistical test. However, for those of you out there who simply have to know, *degrees of freedom* can be defined as the number of cases in the sample that are free to vary. Because our Levene's test tells us that equal variances cannot be assumed for job satisfaction scores between the trade union members and non–trade union members, SPSS makes a downward adjustment of degrees of freedom from 21,571 to 15,546.13. Again, the mathematics for this downward adjustment are not important to the applied statistician.

In the next column over, you have the *p*-value of your independent samples *t*-test, denoted 'Sig. (2-tailed)'. This is where you find out whether your mean difference in the sample generalizes to the population. As it turns out, whether equal variances are assumed or not, your *p*-value is still 0.000. In other words, we can now conclude that trade union members report significantly lower levels of job satisfaction compared with non–trade union members. Technically, most statisticians would say that $p < 0.001$, and not $p = 0.000$. The reason why the former is preferred over the latter is that no *p*-value is ever equal to 0. SPSS only estimates the *p*-value to three decimal places, but if you were to calculate to further decimal places, you would eventually find a nonzero digit.

It turns out that, even though trade union members generally make more money than non–trade union members, they are still significantly less satisfied with their jobs. What a bunch of whiners, right?

Moving further to the right across the bottom row of the table gives a few more important tidbits of information. We can see that the mean difference in scores between the two groups is 0.139 ($3.61 - 3.47 = 0.139$). Now, this may not seem like a 'significant' difference, given that job satisfaction was measured on a five-point Likert scale. But that's the beauty of the principle of statistical inference. It doesn't matter how large the difference seems at first glance; what matters is whether the difference is large enough to produce a *p*-value that is <0.05. Even further over, you can see the 95% confidence interval for the mean difference in scores. We would interpret this as follows: we are 95% certain that the true population mean difference between the two groups lies between 0.118 on the lower end and 0.159 on the higher end. Confidence intervals are further described in Box 5.2.

Box 5.2: Confidence Intervals in Inferential Statistics

Confidence intervals are very useful, and they regularly appear by default in SPSS output. Wherever possible, you should report the results of your statistical tests and the corresponding confidence intervals.

You are probably already familiar with confidence intervals because they are widely reported by political scientists in their analyses of electoral data. For example, you may have heard that a politician has a 52% approval rating, ±3%. This statistic of 52% may seem pretty good in that a majority of people in the sample support the politician. However, the ±3% means that the likely support for the politician lies somewhere between 49% ($52 - 3$) and 55% ($52 + 3$). In other words, there is a confidence interval, or range, estimating where the true approval rating falls in the population.

Most confidence intervals are reported at the 95% level. This means that we can be 95% confident that the true value lies between the reported scores. Alternatively stated, we are willing to accept a 5% risk that the true population statistic falls outside of the confidence interval range.

If you look at the SPSS output in Figure 5.8, you can see that the difference between the two mean scores is 0.139, but, remember, this difference is linked to the sample means, whereas we really only care about the population means. At the lower end, we estimate that the difference in population means could be 0.118, and at the higher end, it could also be 0.159. We can be 95% certain that the true population mean falls somewhere between these two scores.

Obviously, the confidence interval is closely related to the sample size. The larger the sample, the smaller the confidence interval. This is because larger samples are closer to the population, and so we are more likely to be accurate in our estimates. In smaller samples, you will find much larger confidence intervals because we are less sure that the true population statistic lies with a smaller range of scores.

Finally, the last box in Figure 5.8, labeled 'Independent Samples Effect Sizes', contains a few statistics that speak to the effect size. (*Note:* if you are using SPSS 26 or lower, you will not see this last table; it is only available on SPSS 27 or higher.) An *effect size* refers to the extent or degree to which your independent variable, *X*, is associated with your dependent variable, *Y*. The effect size is important because it says something about the magnitude of the relationship between *X* and *Y*. The fact that the difference in mean scores was found to be statistically significant already tells us that there is an effect, but the effect size tells us even more about the strength of the effect. In this table, the only effect size you really need to know is Cohen's *d*, the most widely reported effect size in such tests. Because this is an applied statistics text, you don't need to understand the mathematics underlying the calculation of Cohen's *d*. But you should understand how Cohen's *d* is related to effect size. A Cohen's *d* of 0.20 represents a 'small' effect size; a Cohen's *d* of 0.50 represents a 'medium' effect size; a Cohen's *d* of 0.80 represents a large effect size; and a Cohen's *d* of above 1.20 represents a huge effect size. In other words, the larger the value of Cohen's *d*, the greater the effect of *X* on *Y*. In our case, if you look at the last table in Figure 5.8, you will see that Cohen's *d* is 0.193 (found under 'Point Estimates'). Thus, although the effect is large enough to be generalizable to the wider population, it is still, relatively speaking, a fairly small effect size. Alternatively stated, there are many other factors beyond trade union membership that affect job satisfaction.

If you were reporting this result in your independent samples *t*-test, you would write something like this:

> Trade union members report significantly lower levels of job satisfaction than non–trade union members [$t(15,546.13) = 13.24$; $p < 0.001$]. However, the effect size (Cohen's $d = 0.193$) points to a small effect size.

Congratulations, hot shot! You've just carried out your first ever statistical test using SPSS. You initially hypothesized that trade union members would report higher job satisfaction than non–trade union members. But it turns out that the opposite is true. We can conclude, with a *p*-value of <0.001, that trade union members are *less* satisfied than non–trade union members. This *p*-value suggests that we are willing to accept a 0.1% chance ($0.001 \times 100 = 0.1$) of Type I error that our generalization from the sample to the population is incorrect. Alternatively stated, we can be around 99.9% ($100 - 0.1 = 99.9$) confident that trade union members are less satisfied than non–trade union members in the wider population. Having said that, the effect of trade union membership appears to be rather small.

Let's do one more exercise, just to make sure you really understand how to use SPSS to carry out an independent samples *t*-test. You've just done a *t*-test using trade union membership as the independent variable and a composite of job satisfaction as the dependent variable. Recall that your composite was created by adding together eight separate job satisfaction indicators, each of which 'taps' a unique dimension of the construct. How about we now do eight separate independent samples *t*-tests using trade union membership as the independent variable (again) and the eight original job satisfaction indicators as the dependent variables? This may seem like a big undertaking, but it is not going to be as much work as you think because I'm going to show you a nifty shortcut.

We've already looked at the descriptive statistics for trade union membership, so we don't need to do that again. Instead, let's have a quick look at the descriptives for our eight dependent variables.

Go to Analyze, Descriptive Statistics, and Frequencies. Highlight all eight of the job satisfaction variables (qa8a, qa8b, qa8c, qa8d, qa8e, qa8f, qa8g, and qa8h) in the left-hand column and move them to the right (don't forget to remove your composite job satisfaction variable if it's still there). Now go into [Statistics...] and tick ☑ Mean, ☑ Median, ☑ Std. deviation, ☑ Skewness, and ☑ Kurtosis, and then click [Continue]. Next, go into [Charts...] and tick ⊙ Histograms: and ☑ Show normal curve on histogram. Click [Continue] and then [OK]. Boom!

Have a look through the descriptive statistics, reported in Figure 5.9. You'll notice that there is a bit of variation across the eight mean scores, from a low of 3.01 (how satisfied are you with the amount of pay you receive) to a high of 3.89 (how satisfied are you with the scope for using your own initiative). You'll also notice that some of your dependent variables appear to suffer from excessive skewness or kurtosis. One option to correct for this nonnormality is to mathematically transform these variables, as illustrated in Chapter 4. But in the interest of time, we're not going to do that now, but I'd be totally impressed if you did this of your own accord!

Statistics

		How satisfied are you with... The sense of achievement from work	How satisfied are you with... The scope for using your own initiative	How satisfied are you with... The amount of influence you have over job	How satisfied are you with... The training you receive?	How satisfied are you with... The opportunity to develop your skills in your job?	How satisfied are you with... The amount of pay you receive?	How satisfied are you with... Your job security?	How satisfied are you with... The work itself?
N	Valid	21759	21721	21596	21591	21636	21698	21233	21710
	Missing	222	260	385	390	345	283	748	271
Mean		3.86	3.89	3.60	3.41	3.38	3.01	3.41	3.86
Median		4.00	4.00	4.00	4.00	4.00	3.00	4.00	4.00
Std. Deviation		.920	.918	.961	1.075	1.078	1.129	1.073	.885
Skewness		-.968	-.962	-.608	-.514	-.465	-.211	-.603	-.983
Std. Error of Skewness		.017	.017	.017	.017	.017	.017	.017	.017
Kurtosis		1.035	.956	.073	-.386	-.422	-.945	-.290	1.235
Std. Error of Kurtosis		.033	.033	.033	.033	.033	.033	.034	.033

Figure 5.9 Descriptive statistics, individual job satisfaction measures

Reprint courtesy of IBM Corporation ©

Have a brief look at the eight frequency tables and the eight histograms (not depicted in Figure 5.9). They all appear somewhat bell shaped, which is a good thing.

Now let's conduct the eight *t*-tests to see whether trade union members differ from non–trade union members across these eight job satisfaction indicators. Rather than doing these one-by-one, we can instruct SPSS to do them all simultaneously. Let me show you how to do this, saving you from an extra hour of work (you can thank me later)!

Go to Analyze, Compare Means, and Independent-Samples T Test. If 'jobsat' is still listed under Test Variable(s):, highlight it and move it back to the left-hand column. Then highlight all eight of the job satisfaction variables (qa8a, qa8b, qa8c, qa8d, qa8e, qa8f, qa8g, and qa8h) and move them to the right under Test Variable(s):. Your independent variable, tradeu, should still be under Grouping Variable:, along with the correctly defined groups (Group 1 = 0; Group 2 = 1). Click [OK], and boom! Have a look at the output you produced.

There is a lot going on here because the output reports eight separate *t*-tests simultaneously, all of which have the same independent variable (trade union membership), but eight different dependent variables. Starting first with the 'Group Statistics' depicted in Figure 5.10, you'll notice that the mean scores for non–trade union members are higher across all eight tests than the mean scores for trade union members. In other words, it appears, once again, that trade union membership is associated with lower job satisfaction. But these statistics are confined to our sample, and we don't really care about the sample. What we care about is whether these mean differences also generalize to the wider population. To draw these conclusions, take a look at the second table down (not depicted in Figure 5.10).

Group Statistics					
	Are you a trade unionist	N	Mean	Std. Deviation	Std. Error Mean
How satisfied are you with ... The sense of achievement from work	not currently a trade union member	13589	3.89	.898	.008
	currently a trade union member	8066	3.81	.954	.011
How satisfied are you with ... The scope for using your own initiative	not currently a trade union member	13562	3.94	.886	.008
	currently a trade union member	8058	3.79	.963	.011
How satisfied are you with ... The amount of influence you have over job	not currently a trade union member	13490	3.68	.928	.008
	currently a trade union member	8005	3.46	.998	.011
How satisfied are you with ... The training you receive?	not currently a trade union member	13478	3.46	1.064	.009
	currently a trade union member	8013	3.34	1.089	.012
How satisfied are you with ... The opportunity to develop your skills in your job	not currently a trade union member	13501	3.44	1.061	.009
	currently a trade union member	8034	3.27	1.095	.012
How satisfied are you with ... The amount of pay you receive?	not currently a trade union member	13546	3.02	1.127	.010
	currently a trade union member	8051	2.99	1.132	.013
How satisfied are you with...Your job security?	not currently a trade union member	13277	3.50	1.031	.009
	currently a trade union member	7857	3.26	1.124	.013
How satisfied are you with ... The work itself?	not currently a trade union member	13552	3.90	.862	.007
	currently a trade union member	8056	3.80	.918	.010

Figure 5.10 Group statistics, individual job satisfaction measures

Reprint courtesy of IBM Corporation ©

First look at the results of the Levene's test for equality of variances. All p-values (denoted 'Sig.' in the table) are statistically significant except for one test: when the dependent variable is pay satisfaction, $p = 0.108$, which means that equal variances can be assumed for this test. For the other seven tests, equal variances cannot be assumed.

Next, look at the p-values [denoted 'Sig. (2-tailed)'] for the eight t-tests. Using a p-value cutoff of 0.05, all the t-tests point to statistically significant differences. Even the difference in pay satisfaction between trade union members and non–trade union members has a p-value of 0.04. Therefore, we can conclude that trade union members are, across the board, less satisfied on these dimensions of their work than non–trade union members.

With regard to effect sizes, the last table in the output (also not depicted in Figure 5.10) reports small effect sizes of the relationship of our independent variable – trade union membership – on each of our eight dependent variables. If you look at the Cohen's d column, you will see that the smallest effect size (0.028) is for the difference in pay satisfaction, and the largest effect size (0.231) is for the difference in satisfaction over the amount of influence over one's job. Either way, these are considered 'small' effect sizes.

Overall, our initial hypothesis that trade union members are more satisfied than non–trade union members at work was disconfirmed. We were flat out wrong! You might even feel like a bit of a failure. Well, please don't. What we did was good science. We started with a reasonable expectation but found out that our expectation was incorrect. The next step might be to further explore these relationships through multivariate analyses, but let's not get ahead of ourselves. Once you master the bivariate tests described in Part II of this book, you can then move on to the multivariate ones described in Part III.

Why don't you, at this stage, put down this book and use the dataset to carry out some other independent samples t-tests? What if you used gender as your independent variable and the five job influence indicators as your dependent variables? Would you expect men or women to report higher levels of influence in the workplace? Why? What do the results of the independent samples t-tests tell you?

The Paired Samples *t*-Test and Repeated Measures

The independent samples t-test compares two mean scores on one dependent variable across two separate (that is to say, 'independent') groups. This is a useful statistical test, but it is technically constrained to a design that involves a two-category nominal independent variable and an ordinal or scale-level dependent variable. What happens if you encounter a research question involving the comparison of two means that cannot be answered within this design?

For example, let's say that you want to know whether an organizational training intervention is effective (or not) in terms of increasing employee productivity. In this case, your dependent variable is employee productivity, and we'll assume that this is a score from 1 to 10 on each employee's performance appraisal, where 1 = *the lowest category of performer* and 10 = *the highest category of performer*. The research question is, simply, the following: does the training intervention (let's say, an online course on lean production) increase employee productivity?

Now, you could answer this question using an independent samples *t*-test. For example, you could divide your workforce into two groups, one of which takes the online training course and the other doesn't. Thus, your independent variable would be 0 = *not taken the training course* and 1 = *taken the training course*. You could then compare the mean performance appraisal scores across these two groups using the independent samples *t*-test. But there are some problems with this approach. First, you're depriving half of your workforce of a training intervention. This could lead to reduced morale when some employees find out that they're being 'invested in' and others are not. Second, you have no measure of the employees' productivity scores before the training intervention. For these two reasons alone, the independent samples *t*-test is perhaps not appropriate. So what is to be done?

Fortunately, there is another type of *t*-test called the paired sample *t*-test that is designed for this kind of research question. The paired sample *t*-test is based on the concept of repeated measures over time. Whereas the independent samples *t*-test compares two means *cross-sectionally* (i.e., at one point in time), the paired sample *t*-test allows you to compare two means *longitudinally* (i.e., at two points in time). In this case, you could look at the performance appraisal scores of your employees before the intervention (mean at time 1), administer the training program, and then look at the performance appraisal scores of your employees after the intervention (mean at time 2). Thus, instead of comparing mean scores across two groups at one time (as would be the case with the independent samples *t*-test), you're comparing mean scores across one group at two times – hence the term *repeated measures*.

Unfortunately, the WERS datasets are not suitable for repeated measures analyses because the questions were only asked once (at one point in time). You might be thinking, hey, didn't you say in Chapter 1 that there are several WERS datasets that have been compiled over the years? Yes, I did. But these would still not be suitable for a repeated measures analysis because different respondents answered the same question across the different iterations of the survey. To properly use repeated measures such as a paired sample *t*-test, the same respondents must answer the same question at two different points in time.

Even though we can't use WERS data to carry out a paired sample *t*-test, I still want to show you how to carry out this test using SPSS. It's pretty simple to do. We'll use the following hypothetical data. Let's say you randomly selected the performance appraisal scores at Time 1 (T1) of 15 employees. Remember that these are measured on a scale of 1 to 10, where 1 is the lowest performance score and 10 is the highest performance score. You then administered an online training exercise on lean production techniques to your sample. After the intervention, you conducted a second performance appraisal with the same 15 employees using the exact same scale. Here are the data:

Employee	Performance T1	Performance T2
1	5	6
2	7	6
3	5	5
4	4	7
5	5	4
6	8	5
7	3	6
8	7	3

9	5	6
10	9	5
11	7	8
12	5	6
13	4	5
14	2	4
15	4	6

You could open a new SPSS spreadsheet and enter the data listed in the second and third columns. Or, if you're lazy (like me), you could go to the Companion Website and open the file called Chap5paired.sav. The advantage of opening the file from the Companion Website is that I've already entered the data and labeled the variables for you. Performance at Time 1 is labeled 'perform1', and performance at Time 2 is labeled 'perform2'.

Before you carry out a paired sample *t*-test, ask for the descriptive statistics (including the means and standard deviations) for these two variables. If you're really feeling saucy, you could also request the median, skewness, and kurtosis statistics. I could remind you how to do all of this here, but I'm going to assume that you've been paying attention and so are already a pro at generating descriptives. The two key statistics you're interested in comparing are the mean scores for each variable. As you will see, the mean performance score at Time 1 is 5.33, and the mean performance score at Time 2 is 5.47. So, within your sample, there was an increase in performance after the lean production training program was administered. But, remember, we are not concerned about sample statistics, but rather the extent to which these statistics generalize to the wider population.

Carrying out a paired sample *t*-test using SPSS is as easy as apple pie. First, go to Analyze, Compare Means, and Paired-Samples T Test. The window in Figure 5.11 then appears. Move each variable, perform1 and perform2, from the left-hand column to the right. Then click OK. Boom!

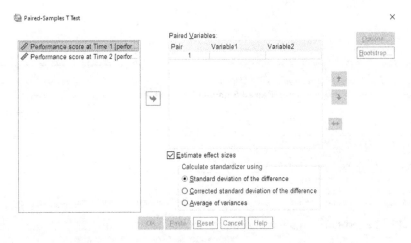

Figure 5.11 Paired samples *t*-test function in SPSS

Reprint courtesy of IBM Corporation ©

Have a look at the output in Figure 5.12. In the first table, you will again see the mean scores for the two variables, where performance at Time 1 averaged 5.33 and performance at Time 2 averaged 5.47. You can skip the second table for now (labeled 'Paired Samples Correlations') and go straight to the third table, where the results of the paired sample t-test are reported. You'll notice that there is no Levene's test in the paired sample output. If you follow the table all the way to the right, you'll see that the p-value, directly under 'Sig. (2-tailed)', is 0.825, with a corresponding t-statistic of −0.225. This p-value is not statistically significant, because it is greater than the 0.05 conventional cutoff. Therefore, we conclude that there is no significant difference in performance before and after the intervention. If you spent big money on that lean production training program, I'd ask for your money back.

Paired Samples Statistics

		Mean	N	Std. Deviation	Std. Error Mean
Pair 1	Performance score at Time 1	5.33	15	1.915	.494
	Performance score at Time 2	5.47	15	1.246	.322

Paired Samples Correlations

		N	Correlation	Sig.
Pair 1	Performance score at Time 1 & Performance score at Time 2	15	-.010	.972

Paired Samples Test

		Paired Differences							
					95% Confidence Interval of the Difference				
		Mean	Std. Deviation	Std. Error Mean	Lower	Upper	t	df	Sig. (2-tailed)
Pair 1	Performance score at Time 1 - Performance score at Time 2	-.133	2.295	.593	-1.404	1.138	-.225	14	.825

Paired Samples Effect Sizes

			Point Estimate	95% Confidence Interval	
		Standardizer[a]		Lower	Upper
Pair 1	Performance score at Time 1 - Performance score at Time 2	Cohen's d	2.295	-.058	-.564	.449
		Hedges' correction	2.359	-.057	-.548	.437

a. The denominator used in estimating the effect sizes.
Cohen's d uses the sample standard deviation of the mean difference.
Hedges' correction uses the sample standard deviation of the mean difference, plus a correction factor.

Figure 5.12 Paired samples t-test output, performance at T1 and T2

Reprint courtesy of IBM Corporation ©

Finally, because the result of this paired samples *t*-test was not statistically significant ($p = 0.825$), you can automatically skip the last table, which reports the Cohen's *d* effect size. Given that the result was insignificant, we can just assume that the effect size is zero in the population.

What Have You Learned?

Well, well, well, look at you now. You're a real *t*-test pro! Let's summarize what you've learned so far in this chapter. An independent samples *t*-test requires one independent variable that must be nominal with two categories and one dependent variable that can be either ordinal or preferably scale. The independent samples *t*-test asks whether there is a significant mean difference between the two groups on the dependent variable. To carry out this test, a *t*-statistic is calculated, along with a corresponding *p*-value. If the *p*-value is <0.05, then we conclude that there is indeed a significant difference in mean scores between the two groups. If $p = 0.05$ or higher, then we conclude that there is no generalizable difference in mean scores between the two groups.

We also looked at the paired sample *t*-test, which compares two mean scores across repeated measures (Time 1 compared with Time 2). Whereas the independent samples *t*-test compares mean scores across two groups, the paired sample *t*-test compares mean scores across the same dependent variable measured at two different points in time. The paired sample *t*-test similarly generates a *t*-statistic and a corresponding *p*-value. Using the same 0.05 cutoff, we can then conclude whether or not the result can be generalized to the wider population.

Now, you might be thinking, 'This is a pretty cool test, but it only works if I'm trying to compare two mean scores at a time. What if you want to compare mean scores across a multicategorical independent variable?' Fortunately, there is a separate, but related, statistical test you can use for just such an occasion. We'll look at it closely in the next chapter.

Further Reading

Bakker, M., & Wicherts, J. M. (2014). Outlier removal, sum scores, and the inflation of the Type I error rate in independent samples *t* tests: The power of alternatives and recommendations. *Psychological Methods, 19*(3), 409-427.

Barnard, G. A. (1984). Comparing the means of two independent samples. *Journal of the Royal Statistical Society: Series C (Applied Statistics), 33*(3), 266-271.

Derrick, B. (2017). How to compare the means of two samples that include paired observations and independent observations: A companion to Derrick, Russ, Toher and White (2017). *Quantitative Methods for Psychology, 13*(2), 120-126.

Rasch, D., Teuscher, F., & Guiard, V. (2007). How robust are tests for two independent samples? *Journal of Statistical Planning and Inference, 137*(8), 2706-2720.

Rietveld, T., & van Hout, R. (2015). The *t* test and beyond: Recommendations for testing the central tendencies of two independent samples in research on speech, language and hearing pathology. *Journal of Communication Disorders, 58*, 158–168.

Rochon, J., Gondan, M., & Kieser, M. (2012). To test or not to test: Preliminary assessment of normality when comparing two independent samples. *BMC Medical Research Methodology, 12*(1), 1–11.

▬▬▬ In-Class Discussion Questions ▬▬▬

1. What types of variables must be used in an independent samples *t*-test? What types of variables must be used in a paired samples *t*-test?
2. What do homogeneity/heterogeneity of variance mean in the context of a *t*-test? Why is homogeneity of variance important?
3. List out five research questions that a management scientist might answer using a *t*-test.
4. Further to question 3, list out the 10 variables that might be used to answer those five research questions. Describe how each one could be measured and, where necessary, coded.
5. How would you report the results of a *t*-test? Which statistics would you include and how would you interpret the results?
6. What are the key differences and similarities between the independent samples *t*-test and the paired samples *t*-test? When would you use one test over the other?

6

Analysis of Variance

Analysis of variance (aka ANOVA) is one of the most widely used statistical tests (and it's also my favorite!). It is particularly popular among psychologists (like me) interested in researching group differences. The logic underlying ANOVA is very similar to that of the t-test. In both cases, the aim of the research is to determine whether or not there are significant differences across groups. However, whereas the t-test is confined to the analysis of only two groups (e.g., men vs. women or white vs. nonwhite) at a time, ANOVA can look simultaneously at differences across multiple (i.e., two or more) groups in a single test. Whereas the t-test calculates a t-statistic that says something about the magnitude of the difference between two mean scores, the ANOVA test calculates a comparable F-statistic that says something about the magnitude of the difference among multiple (i.e., two or more) mean scores at the same time. The larger the F-statistic, the larger the difference in mean scores across the groups of the independent variable. The larger the difference in mean scores across the groups of the independent variable, the lower the p-value associated with the ANOVA test. The lower the p-value, the more generalizable the result from our sample to the population. It's that simple.

Because ANOVA looks at differences between two or more groups, in theory you could also use it instead of a t-test when looking at only two groups. But here we'll be focusing on mean differences across three or more groups. There are many different types, or variations, of the ANOVA test. In this chapter, we'll be concentrating largely on the one-way ANOVA and the repeated measures ANOVA. More complex ANOVA models involving more than just two variables (e.g., analysis of covariance, multivariate ANOVA, and multivariate analysis of covariance) are not covered in this introductory textbook. If you are interested in learning about these advanced ANOVA models, see Tabachnick and Fidell (2019).

The one-way ANOVA test and the independent samples t-test share much in common. Both are bivariate statistical tests with a nominal (i.e., categorical) independent variable and an ordinal or preferably scale-level dependent variable. Both involve comparing means across groups. Both are parametric tests that share the same assumptions regarding normal distributions. Both use Levene's test of equality of variance to ensure that the distributions across the groups have a roughly equal spread of scores around the means. The key difference is that the ANOVA looks at several means at a time, not just two means. But the presence of several means within a single test introduces a new complication in the analysis: a significant *p*-value in an ANOVA test tells us that there are differences somewhere among the means, but it does not specify exactly where those differences exist. Let me give you an example. Imagine you've done an ANOVA test to compare profitability across a set of American companies (Group A), British companies (Group B), and Chinese companies (Group C). The *F*-statistic yields a *p*-value of 0.02. This tells us that Groups A, B, and C differ on profitability, but it doesn't say where exactly the differences are located. Maybe American companies are significantly different from British companies, but not from Chinese companies. Maybe American companies are significantly different from Chinese companies, but not from British companies. To assess these 'pairwise' differences, you also have to ask SPSS to carry out some '*post hoc*' statistical tests that resemble *t*-tests in that they look at differences between only two groups at a time. If you don't quite follow this logic, just sit tight. You will by the end of this chapter.

Before we explore the mathematics underlying the one-way ANOVA, let's take a look at the kinds of research questions that we, as applied statisticians, could answer using this test.

Comparing Three or More Means in Management Research

If you're interested in researching differences across multiple groups, then ANOVA is your test of choice. As I said, you could use it to compare means across two groups, such as disabled versus abled employees, but what if we want to delve down into the finer detail? Let's imagine a workplace with a sizable proportion of disabled employees, some of whom have a physical disability and others have a mental disability. This would result in a three-category nominal variable (physically disabled, mentally disabled, and abled), making it impossible to use within the parameters of an independent samples *t*-test. Say you were interested in looking at perceptions of discrimination in such an organization across those three categories. You asked a sample of 300 employees to respond to the following statement, where 1 = *strongly disagree* and 5 = *strongly agree*:

I have felt discriminated against in this organization.

This is an ordinal level dependent variable in the ANOVA test.

You also asked the respondents to report their disability status, where 1 = *physically disabled*, 2 = *mentally disabled*, and 3 = *abled*. This is your independent variable. Remember that the numbers assigned to the different categories in this variable are arbitrary (in other words, you could have also coded them 0 = *physically disabled*, 1 = *mentally disabled*, and 2 = *abled*).

After collecting the data, you calculate mean scores on perceptions of discrimination across the three groups. You find that the physically disabled employees report a mean of 4.05, mentally disabled employees report a mean of 4.27, and abled employees report a mean of 1.83. These three mean scores seem to suggest a significant difference across the sample groups in relation to perceptions of discrimination, but remember, we don't really care about the sample; we are instead interested in the wider population. An ANOVA test will calculate an *F*-statistic associated with these three mean scores and a corresponding *p*-value. A significant *p*-value (i.e., $p < 0.05$) indicates that there is a generalizable difference somewhere within those three groups, but it doesn't say where exactly. You might assume that there is a significant difference between the two disabled categories vis-à-vis the abled employees, but it's unclear from these statistics whether there might also be a significant difference between physically disabled and mentally disabled employees. To evaluate these 'pairwise' differences, SPSS must be told to produce some '*post hoc*' (i.e., after the fact) statistics comparing all of the different configurations between two groups. That's all there is to the ANOVA test! Pretty simple, eh?

Here are some other types of relevant research questions that a management researcher could answer using a one-way ANOVA test.

- Are employees from a high socioeconomic status more productive than employees from an average and a low socioeconomic status? In this case, your independent variable is socioeconomic status (three categories) and your dependent variable is some standardized employee productivity score.
- Do students from Harvard score higher on a cognitive (e.g., IQ) test than students from Princeton, Yale, and Columbia? In this case, your independent variable is university (four categories) and your dependent variable is a numerical score on the IQ test.
- Are job applicants from France more creative than job applicants from China, Japan, South Korea, and Singapore? In this case, your independent variable is country (five categories) and your dependent variable is a numerical score on some sort of creativity measure.
- Are there significant differences in number of sick days across 10 subsidiaries of the same company? In this case, your independent variable is subsidiary (10 categories) and your dependent variable is the number of sick days taken by employees in the sample subsidiaries.
- Are employees who have read Karl Marx's *Das Kapital* less committed to their organization than employees who have read Frederick Hayek's *The Constitution of Liberty* and employees who have never read either book? In this case, your independent variable is books read (three categories) and your dependent variable is some ordinal measure of organizational commitment.
- Are there significant differences in working hours per week across the 35 member countries of the Organisation for Economic Co-operation and Development (OECD)? In this case, your independent variable is country (at the moment, there are 35 countries in the OECD, so this variable has 35 categories) and your dependent variable is working hours per week.
- Are more grievances filed against public sector organizations, private sector organizations, or nonprofit organizations? In this case, your independent variable is organization type (three categories) and your dependent variable is the number of grievances filed.
- Do married employees report lower work-life balance satisfaction than divorced and single employees? In this case, your independent variable is marital status (three categories) and your dependent variable is some ordinal measure of work-life balance satisfaction.

Let's see how we could approach this last question using the ANOVA test. Imagine that you have collected data from 300 employees on their marital status and work–life balance satisfaction. The independent variable is measured as follows:

Are you married, divorced, or single? (1 = *married*, 2 = *divorced*, and 3 = *single*)

The dependent variable is measured as follows:

Overall, how satisfied are you with your work–life balance on a scale of 1 to 10, where 1 means you are absolutely unsatisfied with your work–life balance and 10 means you are perfectly satisfied with your work–life balance?

Your first step in conducting the ANOVA would be to look at the overall mean score and distribution for your dependent variable, work–life balance satisfaction, across all 300 respondents. The overall distribution is depicted in Figure 6.1.

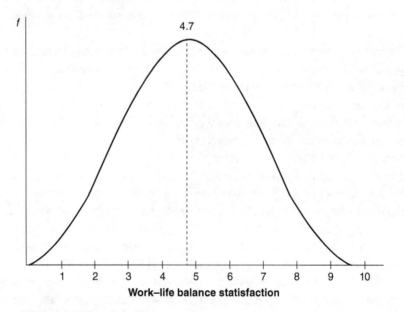

Figure 6.1 Work–life balance satisfaction

As you can see, the distribution appears fairly normal and the mean is 4.7 on the 10-point scale.

Next, you will need to break up your dependent variable into three separate distributions corresponding to the three categories of your independent variable. Imagine that in your sample of 300 respondents, 100 are married, 100 divorced, and 100 are single. These three distributions are depicted in Figure 6.2

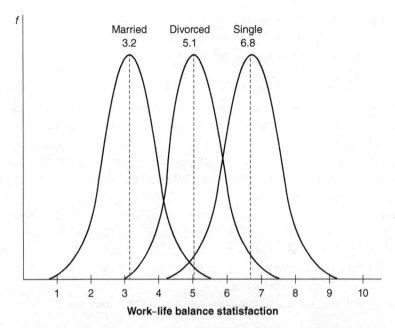

Figure 6.2 Work–life balance satisfaction by married, divorced, and single

As you can see, the mean score for the married respondents is 3.2, the mean score for the divorced respondents is 5.1, and the mean score for the single respondents is 6.8. On the face of it, these seem like significant differences, but remember that they are confined to the sample. Before we can generalize these differences, we need to calculate an F-statistic, which is accompanied by a p-value. If the F-statistic corresponds to a significant p-value ($p < 0.05$), then we would conclude that there is a significant difference somewhere among those three mean scores.

Let's now have a look at how the F-statistic is calculated in a one-way ANOVA test. I promise this won't hurt, much!

The Mathematics Underlying the One-Way Analysis of Variance

Simply put, the computation of the F-statistic is based on a mathematical comparison of differences within categories relative to differences between categories. *Within-category difference* refers to the variation (e.g., variance/standard deviation) within each category of the independent variable. *Between-category difference* refers to the variation in mean scores across the multiple categories of the independent variable. Basically, the larger the differences between the categories, relative to the differences within each category, the larger the F-statistic and, therefore, the lower the p-value and more generalizable the differences.

Within-category differences are also referred to as the *sum of squares within* (SSW). Between-category differences are also referred to as the *sum of squares between* (SSB). Together, the SSW plus the SSB equal what is known as the *sum of squares total* (SST). These are the three basic features of the one-way ANOVA.

In addition to calculating the SSW, SSB and SST, you will also have to calculate the *degrees of freedom within* (dfw) and *degrees of freedom between* (dfb). The dfw is calculated by taking the total number of cases in the sample minus the total number of categories in the independent variable. The dfb is calculated by taking the number of categories in the independent variable minus 1.

Once you have calculated the SSW, SSB, SST, dfw, and dfb, you can then use these statistics to calculate the *mean square within* (msw), which is the SSW divided by dfw, and the *mean square between* (msb), which is the SSB divided by dfb.

Finally, the calculation of the *F-statistic* is a simple ratio that takes the msb divided by the msw.

Okay, armed with this rationale, I think we're ready to work through the basic math and get to know the equations that lead up to the calculation of the *F*-statistic. Looking at the big picture, these calculations can seem at first glance to be rather formidable. That's why we're going to break the computation up into more manageable parts.

Here are the eight steps for calculating a one-way ANOVA by hand:

1. Calculate the SST using Equation (6.1).

$$SST = \Sigma X^2 - N\bar{X}^2 \tag{6.1}$$

where ΣX^2 = the sum of all of the scores squared and $N\bar{X}^2$ = the total number of cases times the mean squared.

2. Calculate the SSB using Equation (6.2).

$$SSB = \Sigma\, N_k\, (\bar{X}_k - \bar{X})^2 \tag{6.2}$$

where $\Sigma\, N_k$ = the sum of the number of cases in a category and $(\bar{X}_k - \bar{X})^2$ = the mean of a category minus the overall mean squared.

3. Calculate the SSW using Equation (6.3).

$$SSW = SST - SSB \tag{6.3}$$

4. Calculate the dfw using Equation (6.4).

$$dfw = N - k \tag{6.4}$$

where N = the total number of cases and k = the total number of categories.

5. Calculate dfb using Equation (6.5).

$$dfb = k - 1 \tag{6.5}$$

where k = the total number of categories.

6. Calculate the msw using Equation (6.6).

$$\text{msw} = \frac{\text{SSW}}{\text{dfw}}$$ (6.6)

7. Calculate the msb using Equation (6.7).

$$\text{msb} = \frac{\text{SSB}}{\text{dfb}}$$ (6.7)

8. Finally, calculate the F-statistic using Equation (6.8).

$$F-\text{statistic} = \frac{\text{msb}}{\text{msw}}$$ (6.8)

Don't get discouraged by the apparent complexity of these calculations. Let's walk through an example using the data in Table 6.1. Bear in mind that the unit of analysis in this example is not the individual, but rather the organization ($N = 18$).

Table 6.1 Yearly staff turnover percent data by ownership structure

Organization	Ownership structure	Yearly staff turnover %
1	Family owned	3
2	Family owned	2
3	Family owned	0
4	Family owned	3
5	Family owned	1
6	Family owned	1
7	Publicly listed	7
8	Publicly listed	7
9	Publicly listed	3
10	Publicly listed	8
11	Publicly listed	6
12	Publicly listed	10
13	Not-for-profit	3
14	Not-for-profit	2
15	Not-for-profit	3
16	Not-for-profit	1
17	Not-for-profit	2
18	Not-for-profit	3

This dataset contains two variables. The independent variable, ownership structure, is a three-category nominal measure, where 1 = *family owned*, 2 = *publicly listed*, and 3 = *not-for-profit*. The dependent variable, yearly staff turnover percent, is a scale variable. The research question for these data might be something like:

Do publicly listed companies have higher yearly staff turnover than family-owned and not-for-profit firms?

Okay, let's calculate the *F*-statistic, starting with the first step. Here we go!

Step 1: Calculate the SST using Equation (6.1)

$$SST = \Sigma X^2 - N\bar{X}^2$$

$$SST = (3^2 + 2^2 + 0^2 + 3^2 + 1^2 + 1^2 + 7^2 + 7^2 + 3^2 + 8^2 + 6^2 + 10^2 + 3^2 + 2^2 + 3^2 + 1^2 + 2^2 + 3^2) - (18 \times 3.61^2)$$

$$SST = (9 + 4 + 0 + 9 + 1 + 1 + 49 + 49 + 9 + 64 + 36 + 100 + 9 + 4 + 9 + 1 + 4 + 9) - (18 \times 13.03)$$

$$SST = (367) - (234.54)$$

SST = 132.46

Step 2: Calculate SSB using Equation (6.2)

$$SSB = \Sigma N_k (\bar{X}_k - \bar{X})^2$$

$$SSB = (6)(1.67 - 3.61)^2 + (6)(6.83 - 3.61)^2 + (6)(2.33 - 3.61)^2$$

$$SSB = (6)(-1.94)^2 + (6)(3.22)^2 + (6)(-1.28)^2$$

$$SSB = (6)(3.76) + (6)(10.37) + (6)(1.64)$$

$$SSB = 22.56 + 62.22 + 9.84$$

SSB = 94.62

Step 3: Calculate the SSW using Equation (6.3)

$$SSW = SST - SSB$$

$$SSW = 132.46 - 94.62$$

SSW = 37.84

Step 4: Calculate the dfw using Equation (6.4)

dfw = $N - k$

dfw = 18 − 3

dfw = 15

Step 5: Calculate the dfb using Equation (6.5)

dfb = $k - 1$

dfb = 3 − 1

dfb = 2

Step 6: Calculate the msw using Equation (6.6)

$$msw = \frac{SSW}{dfw}$$

$$msw = \frac{37.84}{15}$$

msw = 2.52

Step 7: Calculate the msb using Equation (6.7)

$$msb = \frac{SSB}{dfb}$$

$$msb = \frac{94.62}{2}$$

msb = 47.31

Step 8: Calculate the *F*-statistic using Equation (6.8)

$$F = \frac{msb}{msw}$$

$$F = \frac{47.31}{2.52}$$

F = 18.77

There, that wasn't so bad now, was it? You've just calculated your first F-statistic by hand! Awesome work! This F-statistic is, as noted above, a ratio of the amount of variation between categories to the amount of variation within categories. Thus, the higher the F-statistic, the more likely there are significant differences between the three categories, or mean scores.

Each F-statistic is accompanied by a correspondent p-value and, again, if $p < 0.05$, then we conclude that there is a significant difference there somewhere among those three categories. We don't know if family-owned firms are significantly different from publicly listed firm, if publicly listed firms are significantly different from not-for-profit firms, or if family-owned firms are significantly different from not-for-profit firms (more on this later).

You might be wondering how the p-value is calculated for each F-statistic you calculate. Normally, a table of numbers is used to derive the p-value and cutoff, but I say we let SPSS do all the hard work from now on. Enough of this math. Let's now turn to the software.

The Analysis of Variance Using SPSS

In Chapter 5, we used the WERS of employees to illustrate the independent samples t-test. In this chapter, we're going to shift gears and use the survey of organizations. Remember that the unit of analysis in the survey of employees is the individual employee, whereas the unit of analysis in the survey of organizations is the institution, although information about the institution is provided by an individual, typically the HR manager.

Open up the dataset labeled chap6data from the Companion Website. If you scroll up and down in Data View, you'll see that $N = 2680$. In other words, this dataset contains information on 2680 organizations based in the United Kingdom. Now, if you go into Variable View, you'll see the variables we will be using in the ANOVA test. Remember, one-way ANOVA is a bivariate test where the independent variable is a multicategory nominal measure and the dependent variable is either ordinal or scale.

The research question we intend to answer through this test is as follows: Is an organization's ownership structure significantly related to employment relations climate? We will be using two variables in our dataset to answer this question.

The independent variable, owner (labeled 'ownership' in the Variable View), is a nominal variable with four categories: 1 = *private publicly listed*, 2 = *privately owned*, 3 = *trust/charity*, and 4 = *public sector*. In essence, 1 and 2 are private companies, but organizations labeled 1 are listed on the public stock exchange whereas organizations labeled 2 are privately owned; 3 is equivalent to a not-for-profit organization; and 4 consists of local and central government employers.

The dependent variable, rerelated (labeled 'Recoded ER Climate' in Variable View), is a five-category ordinal variable asking the respondent (again, usually the HR manager) to rate the quality of the employment relations between employees and management in each organization. The ratings are as follows: 1 = *very poor*, 2 = *poor*, 3 = *neither poor nor good*, 4 = *good*, and 5 = *very good*. The reason we're using Recoded ER Climate instead of the original variable, mrelate (also found in the dataset, for you to compare the two variables with one another), is that the latter was originally coded such that 1 = *very good* to 5 = *very poor*. I already recoded this variable for you by inverting the scale (e.g., 1 = *very poor* to 5 = *very good*) so that the results we generate are easier to interpret.

Spend a few moments verifying how each of these two variables (owner and rerelate) is coded in the Variable View by clicking into the Values column. In addition, make sure that SPSS has been told that all missing values are coded –9 in the column just to the right of Values. Everything should be in order to proceed.

But before we move forward with the analysis, let's think about what kind of relationship we might find using these data. Basically, we're looking at four different kinds of workplaces: two from the private sector (publicly listed and privately owned), the nonprofit sector, and the public sector. How might the employment relations climate differ across these sectors? One might expect, for example, that the two private sector workplaces may have more antagonistic relations between employees and employers because of the competitive environment and need to turn a profit. By the same token, one might expect nonprofit managers and public sector managers to be more cooperative with employees because of the positive vision and mission of such organizations. With these hypotheses in mind, let's run the ANOVA and find out if we're right.

Remember, the first thing we do before any type of statistical test is to look at the descriptive statistics for our variables in question. Let's look at the independent variable, owner, first. Go to Analyze, Descriptive Statistics, and Frequencies. Find Ownership in the left-hand column and move it to the right-hand column by double clicking it. We don't need to go into Statistics… because this is a nominal variable, so the mean and standard deviation are irrelevant. But let's go into Charts…, tick ⊙ Pie charts, and then click Continue. Now press OK. Boom! The output is depicted in Figure 6.3.

Statistics

Ownership

N	Valid	2280
	Missing	400

Ownership

		Frequency	Percent	Valid Percent	Cumulative Percent
Valid	publicly listed	434	16.2	19.0	19.0
	privately owned	978	36.5	42.9	61.9
	trust/charity	214	8.0	9.4	71.3
	public sector	654	24.4	28.7	100.0
	Total	2280	85.1	100.0	
Missing	missing	400	14.9		
Total		2680	100.0		

(Continued)

Figure 6.3 (Continued)

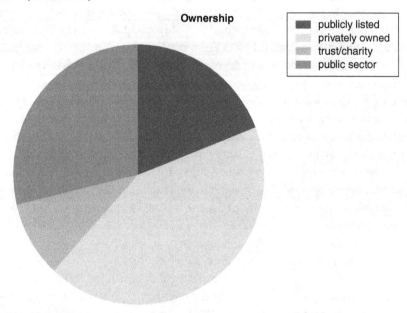

Ownership

- publicly listed
- privately owned
- trust/charity
- public sector

Figure 6.3 Descriptive statistics, ownership

Reprint courtesy of IBM Corporation ©

You'll first notice that there are 2280 valid cases, or organizations, responding to this question. Then you'll see the frequency distribution, where we find that the largest category is privately owned firms (n = 978, or 42.9 valid percent of cases), followed by public sector organizations (n = 654, or 28.7 valid percent of cases), publicly listed private firms (n = 434, or 19.0 valid percent of cases), and, last, charities/trusts (n = 214, or 9.4 valid percent of cases). These percentages are depicted graphically in the pie chart. You may be wondering why there are 400 missing cases. To find out why, read Box 6.1.

Box 6.1: Why Are There 400 Missing Cases in Ownership?

The ownership variable in the SPSS file chap6data.sav is what we call a derived variable. That is to say, you cannot find it in the original WERS dataset. What you can find in the original WERS dataset is a variable that asks respondents (HR managers): What is the formal status of this workplace (or the organization of which it is a part)? The response categories in the original dataset include the following:

−9 = refusal

−8 = don't know

−6 = multicoded

−2 = schedule not applicable

−1 = item not applicable

1 − public limited company

2 = private limited company

3 = company limited by guarantee

4 = partnership

5 = trust/charity

6 = body established by royal charter

7 = cooperative/mutual/friendly society

8 = government owned limited company/nationalized industry

9 = public service agency

10 = other nontrading public corporation

11 = quasi-autonomous national government organization

12 = local/central government

So there are 12 valid types of organizations and five negative numbers for missing or invalid data. I thought it would be difficult for your first ANOVA test to compare 12 categories, so instead, I recoded the original variable so only compare the four major categories: publicly listed, privately owned, trust/charity, and public sector. For the sake of simplicity, I also collapsed all five negative numbers into −9 and labeled that 'missing'.

Now let's have a look at the descriptives for our dependent variable, Recoded ER Climate. Go to Analyze, Descriptive Statistics, and Frequencies. If ownership is listed under the Variables list, you can move it back to the left-hand column using ⬅. Find Recoded ER Climate and move it to the right-hand column by double clicking. Because Recoded ER Climate is an ordinal variable (1 = *very poor*, 2 = *poor*, 3 = *neither poor nor good*, 4 = *good*, and 5 = *very good*), parametric statistics like the mean and standard deviation are meaningful. So this time go into Statistics… and make sure to tick ☑ Mean, ☑ Median, ☑ Std. deviation, ☑ Skewness, and ☑ Kurtosis. Then click Continue. Now go into Charts…, tick ◉ Histograms:, and click Continue. Now click OK. The output is depicted in Figure 6.4.

Statistics

Recoded ER Climate

N	Valid	2672
	Missing	8
Mean		4.26
Median		4.00
Std. Deviation		.683
Skewness		-.785
Std. Error of Skewness		.047
Kurtosis		1.125
Std. Error of Kurtosis		.095

Recoded ER Climate

		Frequency	Percent	Valid Percent	Cumulative Percent
Valid	very poor	4	.1	.1	.1
	poor	42	1.6	1.6	1.7
	neither good nor poor	218	8.1	8.2	9.9
	good	1407	52.5	52.7	62.5
	very good	1001	37.4	37.5	100.0
	Total	2672	99.7	100.0	
Missing	missing	8	.3		
Total		2680	100.0		

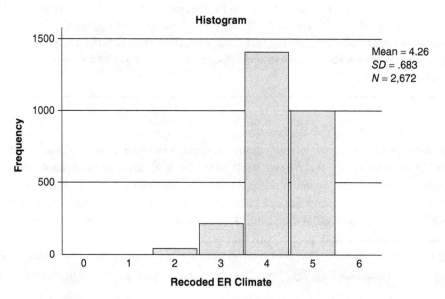

Figure 6.4 Descriptive statistics, recoded employment relations climate

As you can see, we have valid data for 2672 organizations, with only 8 missing. The mean is 4.26 and the standard deviation is 0.68. It should be noted that this mean (relative to the median) suggests a negatively skewed distribution, and this is borne out in the skewness score of –0.785. The distribution also suffers from kurtosis, with a score of 1.13. We could transform this variable, but so as not to create extra work for you (and me!), let's just accept that our analysis violates the assumption of normality.

The frequency distribution and accompanying histogram demonstrate the extent of the nonnormality. Just a handful of workplaces were described as having a 'very poor' employment relations climate ($n = 4$, or 0.1% of the cases) and very few as 'poor' ($n = 42$, or 1.6% of the cases).

Having now gone through the descriptive statistics for our independent and dependent variables, we are ready to carry out the one-way ANOVA test. Are you ready?

To do this, go to Analyze, Compare Means, and One-Way ANOVA. The box in Figure 6.5 should appear. As is normally the case, your test variables are listed in the left-hand box. Just to the right, you'll see the Dependent List: and, below that, a space for one Factor: variable. The Dependent List: is where you place your independent variable, and under Factor: you place your independent variable. So move Recoded ER Climate under Dependent List: and move Ownership under Factor: using ➡. There are a few options to the right that you will not yet be familiar with. For the moment, ignore Contrasts…, Post Hoc…, and Bootstrap…, but go into Options…. When you click on it, the box in Figure 6.6 appears. Be sure to tick ☑ Descriptive, ☑ Homogeneity of variance test, and ☑ Means plot. SPSS does not report descriptive statistics (in this case, the mean Recoded ER Climate scores on the four categories of your independent variable) by default, so you need to instruct it to by ticking ☑ Descriptive here. In addition, unlike with the *t*-test, SPSS does not report Levene's test in a one-way ANOVA by default, so you're requesting the equality of variance test by ticking ☑ Homogeneity of variance test. Finally, the ☑ Means plot is always useful because it reports your results graphically. Click Continue. Before clicking OK, tick ☑ Estimate effect size for overall tests, noting that this option will only be available if you are using SPSS Version 27 or higher.

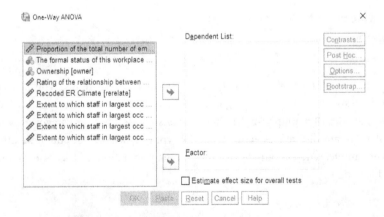

Figure 6.5 One-way ANOVA function in SPSS

Reprint courtesy of IBM Corporation ©

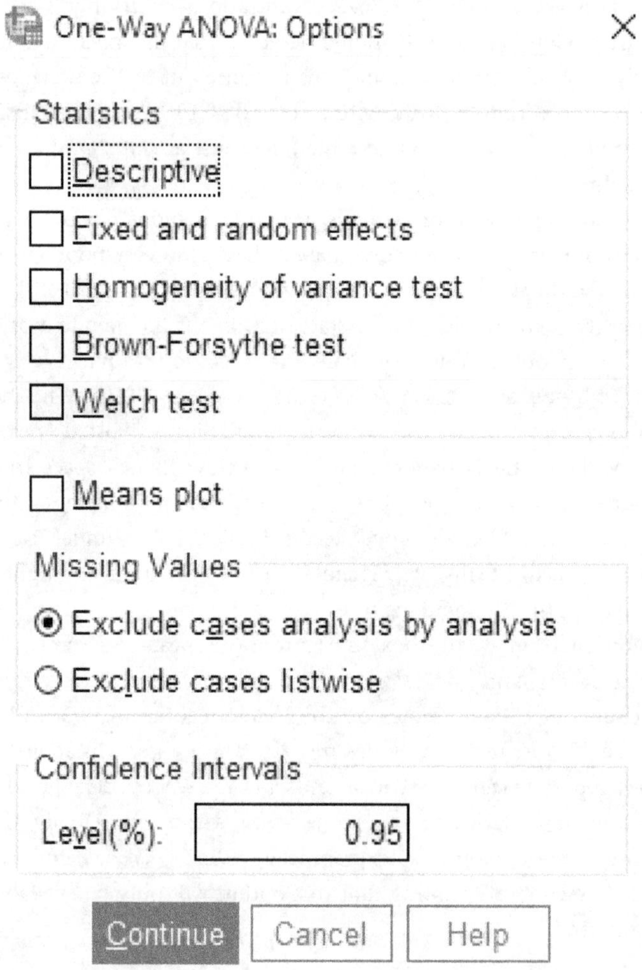

Figure 6.6   One-way ANOVA options in SPSS

Reprint courtesy of IBM Corporation ©

Boom! The results of your one-way ANOVA are reported in Figure 6.7. The first table reports your descriptive statistics. There is a lot going on here, so I urge you to spend a few moments reviewing the statistics. By comparing the mean scores across the four categories, you can obviously see that there are differences across the four types of workplace. But these differences are confined to the sample, whereas our concern is with the population, in this case, all organizations in the United Kingdom.

Descriptives

Recoded ER Climate

	N	Mean	Std. Deviation	Std. Error	95% Confidence Interval for Mean		Minimum	Maximum
					Lower Bound	Upper Bound		
publicly listed	434	4.29	.670	.032	4.23	4.36	1	5
privately owned	977	4.34	.648	.021	4.30	4.38	1	5
trust/charity	214	4.23	.698	.048	4.13	4.32	2	5
public sector	649	4.13	.695	.027	4.08	4.19	2	5
Total	2274	4.26	.676	.014	4.24	4.29	1	5

Tests of Homogeneity of Variances

		Levene Statistic	df1	df2	Sig.
Recoded ER Climate	Based on Mean	2.199	3	2270	.086
	Based on Median	1.396	3	2270	.242
	Based on Median and with adjusted df	1.396	3	2265.835	.242
	Based on trimmed mean	1.666	3	2270	.172

ANOVA

Recoded ER Climate

	Sum of Squares	df	Mean Square	F	Sig.
Between Groups	17.558	3	5.853	13.010	.000
Within Groups	1021.184	2270	.450		
Total	1038.742	2273			

ANOVA Effect Sizes[a]

		Point Estimate	95% Confidence Interval	
			Lower	Upper
Recoded ER Climate	Eta-squared	.017	.007	.028
	Epsilon-squared	.016	.006	.027
	Omega-squared Fixed-effect	.016	.006	.027
	Omega-squared Random-effect	.005	.002	.009

a. Eta-squared and Epsilon-squared are estimated based on the fixed-effect model.

(Continued)

Figure 6.7 (Continued)

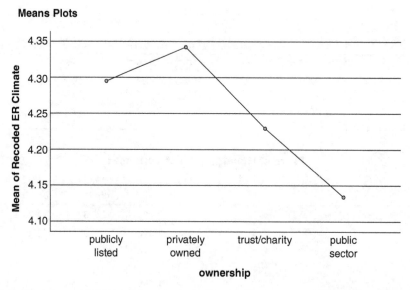

Figure 6.7 One-way ANOVA output, recoded employment relations climate by ownership

Reprint courtesy of IBM Corporation ©

The second table reports the results of Levene's test. Here, the most important statistic is the *p*-value, labeled Sig. in the table. Remember, with Levene's test for equality of variances, we want to find a *p*-value that is >0.05 because such a value suggests that the variances across the categories are indeed roughly equal. In this case, $p = 0.085$ (based on mean), which is good news. We can conclude equality of variance in this ANOVA.

In the third and fourth tables, we have the results of the ANOVA test and effect sizes, respectively. You should see some familiar terms based on the ANOVA math you've done already. The third table in Figure 6.7 reports the 'sum of squares between', 'sum of squares within', and 'sum of squares total'. It reports the degrees of freedom (*df*) and mean squares. As you can see, the *F*-statistic is 13.01, with a corresponding *p*-value of 0.000 (although we would report this as $p < 0.001$). This statistically significant *p*-value tells us that there is a significant difference *somewhere* among those four means, but it doesn't tell us exactly where. The fourth table reports the effect sizes as point estimates. The most commonly used effect size in this table is eta-squared (0.017), which can be interpreted as the amount of variation in our dependent variable (Recoded ER Climate) explained by our independent variable (Ownership). Thus, an eta-squared of 0.017 means that Ownership explains 1.7% of the variation in Recoded ER Climate ($0.017 \times 100 = 1.7$). I'm not sure why SPSS reports eta-squared here in the output, when a far better effect size is partial eta-squared. Luckily, calculating partial eta-squared by hand is pretty easy, as shown in Box 6.2.

Box 6.2: Calculating Partial Eta-Squared for ANOVA

Partial eta-squared is by far a better effect size than eta-squared for ANOVA tests. Yet, for whatever reason, SPSS chooses to report the latter. But never fear! You can calculate partial eta squared easily using the information from our ANOVA test (the third table in Figure 6.7).

To calculate partial eta-squared, simply take the SSB/(SSB + SSW). Looking at the third table in Figure 6.7, we can see that the SSB is 17.56 and the SSW is 1021.18. So we plug in those values to calculate partial eta-squared:

1. 17.56/(17.56 + 1021.18)
2. 17.56/(1038.74)
3. 0.017

You'll note that this is the same value as eta-squared, reported in the fourth table of Figure 6.7. In this case, both values are identical, but occasionally there are differences between eta-squared and partial eta-squared. Where there are differences, it's always better to rely on partial eta-squared because it is an unbiased effect size.

In any event, you could say that an eta-squared or a partial eta-squared of 0.017 is pretty small, because it means that the independent variable only explains 1.7% of the variation in the dependent variable.

At the bottom of Figure 6.7, you can see the mean plot, which quite simply illustrates the differences in mean scores across our four categories graphically. Here, you can see that privately owned companies score the highest on employment relations climate, followed by publicly listed companies, trusts and charities, and public sector organizations.

So it turns out that we were wrong in our hypotheses. Contrary to our expectations, it seems that the two private sector workplaces report better ER climates than the trust/charity and public sectors. But looking at the mean plots, we can only estimate that there are significant differences somewhere among those four categories, but we cannot say exactly where.

You might now be wondering, 'how I can tell if the pairwise differences are significant?' Good question! First, let's list out all of the possible combinations of pairs within these four categories. There is a simple formula that can be used to identify the total number of pairwise combinations across multiple categories, as shown in Box 6.3.

Box 6.3: How Many Pairwise Combinations Are There Within Your Categories?

There is a simple formula you can use to identify the number of pairwise combinations within a set of categories across the independent variable in an ANOVA test:

$k(k-1)/2$

where k is the total number of categories in our independent variable.

(Continued)

In our case, Ownership has four categories: (1) publicly listed, (2) privately owned, (3) trust/charity, and (4) public sector. Therefore, $k = 4$. Plugging this number into the equation, we get:

1. $4(4 - 1)/2$
2. $4(3)/2$
3. $12/2$
4. 6

So where the independent variable has four categories, we have six pairwise comparisons. How many pairwise comparisons would we have if our independent variable had 8 categories (i.e., $k = 8$)?

Based on Box 6.3, we know that there are six pairwise comparisons among our four categories in Ownership. The research questions surrounding the six pairwise comparisons are as follows:

•   Are publicly listed firms different from privately owned ones?
•   Are publicly listed firms different from trusts/charities?
•   Are publicly listed firms different from public sector organizations?
•   Are privately owned firms different from trusts/charities?
•   Are privately owned firms different from public sector organizations?
•   Are trusts/charities different from public sector organizations?

In other words, there are six derivative research questions that cannot be answered by a one-way ANOVA test. So what is to be done?

One option, you might be thinking, is to do six independent samples t-tests to answer these questions. After all, t-tests were designed to answer questions about whether one category differs from another on an ordinal or scale outcome. While this might seem a sensible solution, it would be a mistake (and poor science) to explore pairwise comparisons using a set of t-tests because it would lead to family-wise error. *Family-wise error* can be defined as the increased likelihood of making Type I error (concluding that there is a significant relationship when, in fact, there isn't) across multiple hypothesis tests. It is not necessary that you understand the mathematics underlying family-wise error, but you should understand that if you were to carry out these six t-tests using a standard $p < 0.05$ cutoff, each test has a slightly higher chance of being statistically significant, even though there may be no real relationship. This extra likelihood of a 'false positive' can throw the accuracy of all our statistical inferences into question. So let's not do six t-tests to explore these extra research questions.

Fortunately, there is a way that we can analyse these pairs '*post hoc*' through SPSS. A *post hoc* procedure, in this case, is a supplemental set of tests that already 'correct' for family-wise error by making the relevant adjustments to the p-values. The three most common *post hoc* corrections for a one-way ANOVA are least significant difference (LSD; trust me, it's not as psychedelic as it sounds), Bonferroni, and Tukey. SPSS offers all three and then some. I don't use LSD because it can induce mind-altering madness, but I highly recommend Bonferroni and Tukey corrections. In fact, most of these corrections give essentially the same result.

Let's see how to ask SPSS for these additional *post hoc* tests. We're going to have to run the original one-way ANOVA again. Hopefully, your variables and options will still be populated in SPSS. Go to Analyze, Compare Means, and One-Way ANOVA. Click on Post Hoc..., and the box depicted in Figure 6.8 appears. Tick ☑ Bonferroni, Continue, and OK.

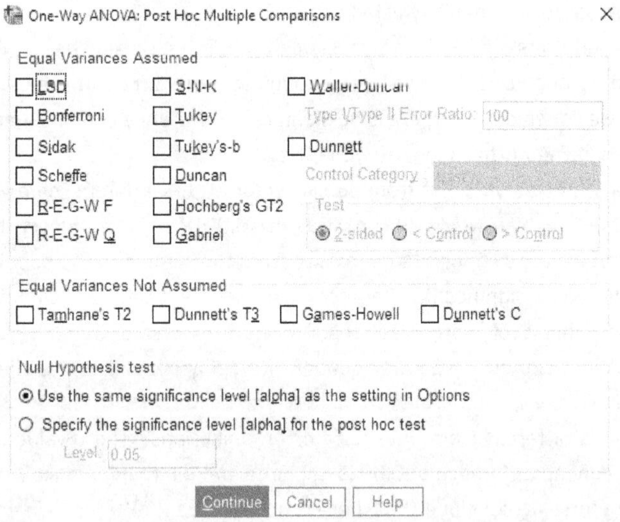

Figure 6.8 One-way ANOVA *post hoc* comparisons function in SPSS

Reprint courtesy of IBM Corporation ©

I have not reproduced the output because you will notice that you've seen most of this output already in Figure 6.7, but there is now one additional box labeled Multiple Comparisons. You can find this new box in Figure 6.9. Here you will see 12 multiple comparisons, although really there are only six that matter because the other six are just repetitions. Using these *post hoc* comparisons, you can answer the six research questions above. The most important column for purposes of interpretation is the one labeled 'Sig.' These *p*-values have already been corrected to avoid potential family-wise Type I error. As always, we use $p < 0.05$ as the cutoff, that is, we will assume that there is a significant pairwise difference only for those pairs whose *p*-value falls below this cutoff. Let's answer each question one at a time:

- Are publicly listed firms different from privately owned ones? The *p*-value here is 1.00, which suggests that the miniscule mean difference of −0.05 is not large enough to generalize from the sample to the population. Therefore, we conclude that there is no significant difference in employment relations climate between publicly listed and privately owned firms.
- Are publicly listed firms different from trusts/charities? The *p*-value here is again 1.00, which suggests that the mean difference of 0.07 is not large enough to generalize from the sample to the population. Therefore, we conclude that there is no significant difference in employment relations climate between publicly listed firms and trusts/charities.

- Are publicly listed firms different from public sector organizations? The p-value here is 0.001, which suggests that the mean difference of 0.16 is indeed large enough to generalize from the sample to the population. Therefore, we conclude that there is a significant difference between publicly listed firms and public sector organizations on employment relations climate. Alternatively stated, we conclude that public sector organizations have a significantly lower quality of employment relations climate compared with publicly listed firms.
- Are privately owned firms different from trusts/charities? The p-value here is 0.115, which suggests that the mean difference of 0.11 is not large enough to generalize from the sample to the population. Therefore, we conclude that there is no significant difference in employment relations climate between privately owned firms and trusts/charities.
- Are privately owned firms different from public sector organizations? The p-value in this pairwise comparison is 0.000 (which we could report as $p < 0.001$), which suggests that the mean difference of 0.21 is indeed large enough to generalize from the sample to the population. Therefore, we conclude that there is a significant difference in employment relations climate between privately owned firms and public sector organizations. Alternatively stated, we conclude that public sector organizations have a significantly lower quality of employment relations climate compared with privately owned firms.
- Are trusts/charities different from public sector organizations? The p-value here is 0.436, which suggests that the mean difference of 0.09 is not large enough to generalize from the sample to the population. Therefore, we conclude that there is no significant difference in employment relations climate between trusts/charities and public sector organizations.

Multiple Comparisons

Dependent Variable: Recoded ER Climate

Bonferroni

(I) Ownership	(J) Ownership	Mean Difference (I-J)	Std. Error	Sig.	95% Confidence Interval Lower Bound	Upper Bound
publicly listed	privately owned	-.047	.039	1.000	-.15	.06
	trust/charity	.066	.056	1.000	-.08	.21
	public sector	.161*	.042	.001	.05	.27
privately owned	publicly listed	.047	.039	1.000	-.06	.15
	trust/charity	.113	.051	.155	-.02	.25
	public sector	.208*	.034	.000	.12	.30
trust/charity	publicly listed	-.066	.056	1.000	-.21	.08
	privately owned	-.113	.051	.155	-.25	.02
	public sector	.095	.053	.436	-.04	.23
public sector	publicly listed	-.161*	.042	.001	-.27	-.05
	privately owned	-.208*	.034	.000	-.30	-.12
	trust/charity	-.095	.053	.436	-.23	.04

*. The mean difference is significant at the 0.05 level.

Figure 6.9 Multiple comparisons output, recoded employment relations climate by ownership

Reprint courtesy of IBM Corporation ©

So what have we learned from this one-way ANOVA and its subsequent *post hoc* tests? Well, we were dead wrong in our hypotheses, and that's okay. There's nothing wrong with being wrong in statistical research. That's how science advances (Popper, 2005). As it turns out, the employment relations climate is much better in publicly listed and privately owned firms compared with the public sector, where it appears that managers and employees simply don't get along all that well.

It's worth noting at this point that an ANOVA test is good at establishing that there are differences between categories, but it can't explain *why* those differences exist. So we know that employment relations in the public sector are pretty bad compared with the private sector, but we don't know why this might be the case. Only further research can answer that 'why' question. Let's take a stab at trying to understand why the public sector has such a negative employment relations climate. Maybe it's because public sector employees have less variety in their work than private sector workers, and as a result of this lack of variety, they are unhappy with their managers.

As it happens, the survey of organizations has another variable, cvariety, that asks the respondent the extent to which employees in the largest occupational group have variety in the work they do. If you check the Variable View, you'll see that the valid ordinal response categories are listed on a scale of 1 to 4, where 1 = *none*, 2 = *a little*, 3 = *some*, and 4 = *a lot*.

First things first. Have a look at the descriptive statistics for just this new dependent variable. Go to Analyze, Descriptive Statistics, and Frequencies. Move cvariety from the left-hand column to the right-hand column by double clicking (note that you may first need to move Recoded ER Climate from the right-hand column back to the left-hand column using ← . Make sure, under Statistics , that the mean and standard deviation, along with skewness and kurtosis statistics, are ticked. Click Continue and OK . The descriptive statistics are reported in Figure 6.10. This is obviously a pretty skewed distribution, but we're going to run the ANOVA test anyway.

Statistics

Extent to which staff in largest occ group
have variety in their work

N	Valid	2674
	Missing	6
Mean		3.31
Median		3.00
Std. Deviation		.762
Skewness		-.847
Std. Error of Skewness		.047
Kurtosis		.035
Std. Error of Kurtosis		.095

(Continued)

Figure 6.10 (Continued)

Extent to which staff in largest occ group have variety in their work

		Frequency	Percent	Valid Percent	Cumulative Percent
Valid	none	50	1.9	1.9	1.9
	a little	338	12.6	12.6	14.5
	some	1013	37.8	37.9	52.4
	a lot	1273	47.5	47.6	100.0
	Total	2674	99.8	100.0	
Missing	Refusal	6	.2		
Total		2680	100.0		

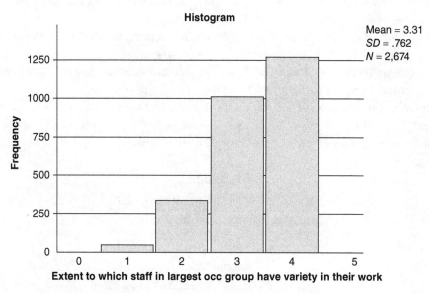

Figure 6.10 Descriptive statistics, extent to which staff have variety in work

Reprint courtesy of IBM Corporation ©

Go to Analyze, Compare Means, and One-Way ANOVA. Move cvariety from left to right under the dependent variables list (note that Ownership should already be listed under Factor: and, again, you may need to remove Recoded ER Climate). Make sure you go into Post Hoc... and ensure that ☑ Bonferroni is ticked. Click Continue. Then go into Options... and make sure ☑ Descriptive, ☑ Homogeneity of variance test, and ☑ Means plot are ticked. If so, click Continue and then OK. The results of the ANOVA test are depicted in Figure 6.11.

Descriptives

Extent to which staff in largest occ group have variety in their work

	N	Mean	Std. Deviation	Std. Error	95% Confidence Interval for Mean		Minimum	Maximum
					Lower Bound	Upper Bound		
publicly listed	434	3.19	.770	.037	3.12	3.26	1	4
privately owned	977	3.25	.771	.025	3.20	3.30	1	4
trust/charity	214	3.41	.737	.050	3.31	3.51	1	4
public sector	650	3.47	.689	.027	3.42	3.53	1	4
Total	2275	3.32	.753	.016	3.29	3.35	1	4

Tests of Homogeneity of Variances

		Levene Statistic	df1	df2	Sig.
Extent to which staff in largest occ group have variety in their work	Based on Mean	1.841	3	2271	.138
	Based on Median	3.010	3	2271	.029
	Based on Median and with adjusted df	3.010	3	2084.734	.029
	Based on trimmed mean	3.418	3	2271	.017

ANOVA

Extent to which staff in largest occ group have variety in their work

	Sum of Squares	df	Mean Square	F	Sig.
Between Groups	29.562	3	9.854	17.748	.000
Within Groups	1260.936	2271	.555		
Total	1290.498	2274			

ANOVA Effect Sizes[a]

		Point Estimate	95% Confidence Interval	
			Lower	Upper
Extent to which staff in largest occ group have variety in their work	Eta-squared	.023	.012	.035
	Epsilon-squared	.022	.010	.034
	Omega-squared Fixed-effect	.022	.010	.034
	Omega-squared Random-effect	.007	.003	.012

a. Eta-squared and Epsilon-squared are estimated based on the fixed-effect model.

(Continued)

Figure 6.11 (Continued)

Post Hoc Tests

Multiple Comparisons

Dependent Variable: Extent to which staff in largest occ group have variety in their work

Bonferroni

(I) Ownership	(J) Ownership	Mean Difference (I-J)	Std. Error	Sig.	95% Confidence Interval	
					Lower Bound	Upper Bound
publicly listed	privately owned	-.060	.043	.987	-.17	.05
	trust/charity	-.222*	.062	.002	-.39	-.06
	public sector	-.285*	.046	.000	-.41	-.16
privately owned	publicly listed	.060	.043	.987	-.05	.17
	trust/charity	-.162*	.056	.023	-.31	-.01
	public sector	-.225*	.038	.000	-.32	-.13
trust/charity	publicly listed	.222*	.062	.002	.06	.39
	privately owned	.162*	.056	.023	.01	.31
	public sector	-.063	.059	1.000	-.22	.09
public sector	publicly listed	.285*	.046	.000	.16	.41
	privately owned	.225*	.038	.000	.13	.32
	trust/charity	.063	.059	1.000	-.09	.22

*. The mean difference is significant at the 0.05 level.

Means Plots

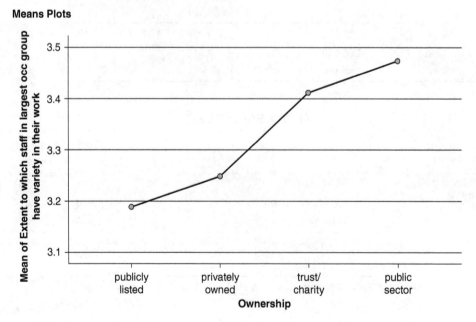

Figure 6.11 One-way ANOVA output, variety in work by ownership

Reprint courtesy of IBM Corporation ©

Spend a few moments reviewing the output and think about what can be concluded from the results of the test.

You'll see from the descriptive statistics that there are differences between the four means, but our concern is, as always, whether these sample differences generalize to the wider population. You'll see from the results of Levene's test, based on mean ($p = 0.138$), that we can assume homogeneity of variance, which is a good thing. You'll see that the ANOVA test resulted in an F-statistic of 17.75 and a p-value of 0.000 (which we would report as $p < 0.001$). So this p-value suggests that there are significant differences *somewhere* among those four mean scores, but it doesn't specify exactly where those differences are.

You'll see from the multiple comparisons that there are a series of statistically significant pairwise *post hoc* tests. Specifically, publicly listed firms are significantly different from trusts/charities ($p = 0.002$) and public sector organizations ($p < 0.000$) and privately owned firms are significantly different from trusts/charities ($p = 0.023$) and public sector organizations ($p < 0.000$).

If you look at the means plot, you'll see that the means are different in the wrong way from what we hypothesized. According to these results, it turns out that employees in the public sector and charities/trusts have more variety in their work than employees in the two private sector types of firms! In other words, the poor employment relations climate (at least in the public sector) apparently cannot be explained by the lack of variety in employees' work.

However, there is one important caveat to this conclusion. Remember that the respondents to the survey of organizations are typically HR managers, and just because HR managers in the public sector report that employees have a lot of variety in their work does not mean that employees in the public sector actually have a lot of variety in their work. Maybe they don't have much variety at all, but we'll never know from these statistics until we actually collect data from employees. In fact, the same argument could hold for our measure of employment relations climate. The ratings are given by management, and their perception of the ER climate may or may not overlap with that of employees.

Repeated Measures Analysis of Variance Using SPSS

A repeated measures ANOVA is similar to a paired sample t-test. Whereas a one-way ANOVA always involves two variables, one a nominal multicategory variable and the other an ordinal or scale-level variable, a repeated measures ANOVA typically involves three or more variables, all ordinal or scale level in measurement. Thus, instead of breaking one ordinal or scale-level dependent variable into independent groups (as in the case in one-way ANOVA), a repeated measures ANOVA makes comparisons across multiple ordinal or scale-level variables answered sequentially (hence the term *repeated measures*).

Unfortunately, the survey of organizations, like the survey of employees, contains no variables that qualify as repeated measures. Therefore, it is impossible to demonstrate this statistical technique using WERS data. But don't fret. I have some data that perfectly fit the bill. Open the file named 'c6repeatedm' from Chapter 6 on the the Companion Website.

Imagine that you are doing some marketing research to find out how the emotional expressions of service sector staff affect consumer spending. Specifically, you wonder whether different emotions expressed by service sector staff are associated with different levels of spending. You hypothesize that service sector staff with a visible smile will result in higher levels of consumption than service sector staff with a neutral expression, and that both the smile and neutral expression will result in higher levels of consumer spending than service sector staff with an angry facial expression.

To test this hypothesis, you take photographs of a young woman with three different facial expressions: smiling, neutral, and angry. These are depicted in Figure 6.12.

Neutral: Happy: Angry:

Figure 6.12   Three emotional states

Let's now say that you showed these three photographs to 185 consumers and asked them to approximate how much they would spend in a retail outlet when being served by these three employees. These data are reported in the repeated measures dataset, c6repeatedm.

All 185 respondents looked at the three photos and indicated how much money (in US dollars) they would spend in each store at which the young woman is assumed to work (hypothetically). Thus, in our repeated measures ANOVA, we have three scale-level variables that report consumer spending across the three emotional expressions.

To find out whether the mean scores are different across these three variables, you will need to run a one-way repeated measures ANOVA. To do this, go to Analyze, Generalized Linear Models, and Repeated Measures. The box depicted in Figure 6.13 appears. The first thing we need to do is to tell SPSS how many repeated measures, or factors, there are in this model. Since we have three photographs, we will tell SPSS we have three factors. Erase 'factor1' and replace it with 'Emotion'. Next to 'Number of levels', write 3, and then click Add . Now click Define and a new box appears, depicted in Figure 6.14.

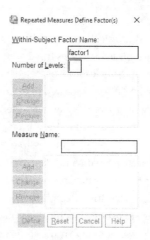

Figure 6.13   Repeated measures ANOVA define factors function in SPSS

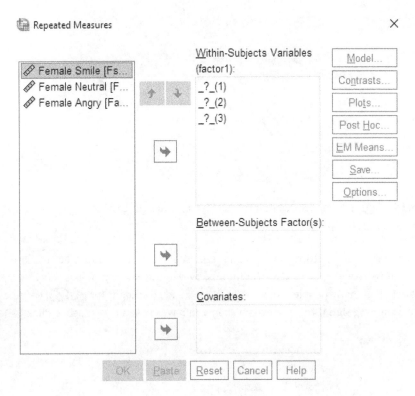

Figure 6.14 Repeated measures ANOVA model build function in SPSS

Reprint courtesy of IBM Corporation ©

In the left-hand column of Figure 6.14, you will see your three variables. In the right-hand column, you will see three factors initially listed as '_?_(1)', '_?_(2)', and '_?_(3)'. You will need to move your variables into the right-hand column, which is labeled 'Within Subjects Variables (Emotions)'. You could move them all at once by highlighting all three, but I want you to move them over one at a time to make sure that they are in the right order. First, highlight Female Neutral and move it to the right using ⟶ . Then highlight Female Smile and move it to the right. Finally, highlight Female Angry and move it to the right. The reason we are running the repeated measures ANOVA test in this order is that we want the neutral face to be our baseline and to see whether there are significant differences vis-à-vis the smiling face and the angry face.

Now click on ⟨Contrasts...⟩ . The box shown in Figure 6.15 appears. Next click on the word Polynomial ∨ , and a list of options will appear in a drop-down menu. Select Simple. Then, next to Reference Category:, tick ⦿ First. Then click ⟨Change⟩. Having done all this, under Factors, you should see Emotions(Simple(first)). The reason we changed the contrasts from Last to First is that we want to make the neutral face (the first variable in the list of three) the reference category. Click ⟨Continue⟩.

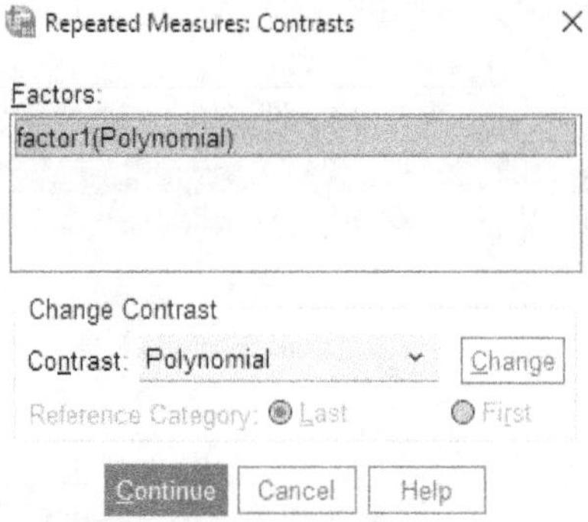

Figure 6.15 Repeated measures ANOVA contrasts function in SPSS

Reprint courtesy of IBM Corporation ©

Now click on [Plots...] to request a visual representation of the repeated measures. The box shown in Figure 6.16 will appear. Move 'Emotions' over to the Horizontal axis using [➡]. Now click [Add]. Beware that many people forget to tick [Add] and go straight for [Continue]. Fortunately, SPSS will put up a warning sign if this happens. When you have clicked [Add], then click [Continue].

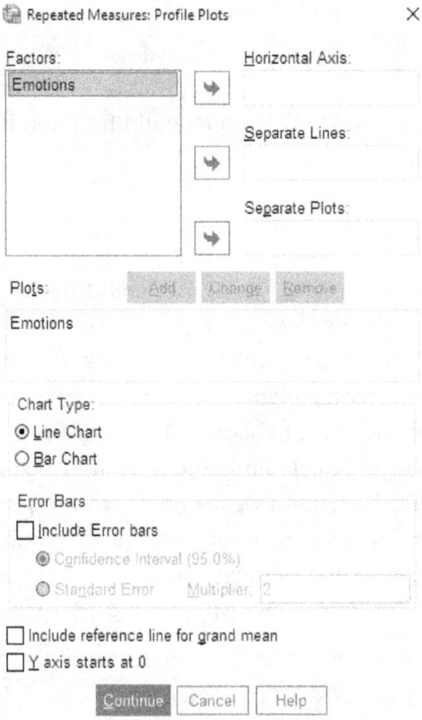

Figure 6.16 Repeated measures profile plots function in SPSS

Reprint courtesy of IBM Corporation ©

Now click on EM Means... and you'll see the box shown in Figure 6.17. Move both '(OVERALL)' and 'Emotions' from the left-hand column to the right-hand column using ⮕. Immediately below the right-hand column, tick ☑ Compare main effects. Then under Confidence interval adjustment, select 'Bonferroni' and then click Continue.

Last, click Options... and tick ☑ Descriptive statistics and ☑ Estimates of effect size, followed by Continue. When you are ready to run your first repeated measures ANOVA, simply click OK.

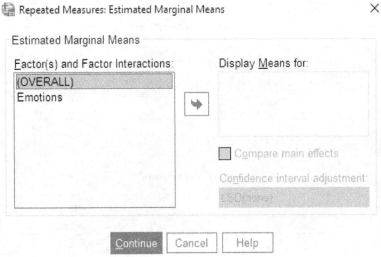

Figure 6.17   Repeated measures ANOVA estimated marginal means function in SPSS

Reprint courtesy of IBM Corporation ©

Boom! Nice work, partner. You did it! Now have a look at the output shown in Figure 6.18. There's a lot going on here, so let's examine it section by section.

Within-Subjects Factors

Measure: MEASURE_1

Emotions	Dependent Variable
1	Fneutral
2	Fsmile
3	Fangry

(Continued)

Figure 6.18 (Continued)

Descriptive Statistics

	Mean	Std. Deviation	N
Female Neutral	10.9027	8.62827	185
Female Smile	21.4000	6.73182	185
Female Angry	4.2595	7.04548	185

Multivariate Tests[a]

Effect		Value	F	Hypothesis df	Error df	Sig.	Partial Eta Squared
Emotions	Pillai's Trace	.798	362.351[b]	2.000	183.000	.000	.798
	Wilks' Lambda	.202	362.351[b]	2.000	183.000	.000	.798
	Hotelling's Trace	3.960	362.351[b]	2.000	183.000	.000	.798
	Roy's Largest Root	3.960	362.351[b]	2.000	183.000	.000	.798

a. Design: Intercept
Within Subjects Design: Emotions

b. Exact statistic

Mauchly's Test of Sphericity[a]

Measure: MEASURE_1

Within Subjects Effect	Mauchly's W	Approx. Chi-Square	df	Sig.	Epsilon[b] Greenhouse-Geisser	Huynh-Feldt	Lower-bound
Emotions	.960	7.435	2	.024	.962	.972	.500

Tests the null hypothesis that the error covariance matrix of the orthonormalized transformed dependent variables is proportional to an identity matrix.

a. Design: Intercept
Within Subjects Design: Emotions

b. May be used to adjust the degrees of freedom for the averaged tests of significance. Corrected tests are displayed in the Tests of Within-Subjects Effects table.

Tests of Within-Subjects Effects

Measure: MEASURE_1

Source		Type III Sum of Squares	df	Mean Square	F	Sig.	Partial Eta Squared
Emotions	Sphericity Assumed	27634.317	2	13817.159	434.702	.000	.703
	Greenhouse-Geisser	27634.317	1.923	14367.303	434.702	.000	.703
	Huynh-Feldt	27634.317	1.943	14220.194	434.702	.000	.703
	Lower-bound	27634.317	1.000	27634.317	434.702	.000	.703
Error(Emotions)	Sphericity Assumed	11697.016	368	31.785			
	Greenhouse-Geisser	11697.016	353.909	33.051			
	Huynh-Feldt	11697.016	357.570	32.713			
	Lower-bound	11697.016	184.000	63.571			

Tests of Within-Subjects Contrasts

Measure: MEASURE_1

Source	Emotions	Type III Sum of Squares	df	Mean Square	F	Sig.	Partial Eta Squared
Emotions	Level 1 vs. Level 3	8164.546	1	8164.546	154.136	.000	.456
	Level 2 vs. Level 3	54352.654	1	54352.654	725.630	.000	.798
Error(Emotions)	Level 1 vs. Level 3	9746.454	184	52.970			
	Level 2 vs. Level 3	13782.346	184	74.904			

Tests of Between-Subjects Effects

Measure: MEASURE_1

Transformed Variable: Average

Source	Type III Sum of Squares	df	Mean Square	F	Sig.	Partial Eta Squared
Intercept	27478.496	1	27478.496	778.924	.000	.809
Error	6491.059	184	35.277			

Estimated Marginal Means

1. Grand Mean

Measure: MEASURE_1

Mean	Std. Error	95% Confidence Interval	
		Lower Bound	Upper Bound
12.187	.437	11.326	13.049

2. Emotions

Estimates

Measure: MEASURE_1

Emotions	Mean	Std. Error	95% Confidence Interval	
			Lower Bound	Upper Bound
1	10.903	.634	9.651	12.154
2	21.400	.495	20.424	22.376
3	4.259	.518	3.237	5.281

Pairwise Comparisons

Measure: MEASURE_1

(I) Emotions	(J) Emotions	Mean Difference (I-J)	Std. Error	Sig.[b]	95% Confidence Interval for Difference[b]	
					Lower Bound	Upper Bound
1	2	-10.497*	.583	.000	-11.905	-9.089
	3	6.643*	.535	.000	5.350	7.936
2	1	10.497*	.583	.000	9.089	11.905
	3	17.141*	.636	.000	15.603	18.678
3	1	-6.643*	.535	.000	-7.936	-5.350
	2	-17.141*	.636	.000	-18.678	-15.603

Based on estimated marginal means

*. The mean difference is significant at the .05 level.

b. Adjustment for multiple comparisons: Bonferroni.

(Continued)

Figure 6.18 (Continued)

Multivariate Tests

	Value	F	Hypothesis df	Error df	Sig.	Partial Eta Squared
Pillai's trace	.798	362.351[a]	2.000	183.000	.000	.798
Wilks' lambda	.202	362.351[a]	2.000	183.000	.000	.798
Hotelling's trace	3.960	362.351[a]	2.000	183.000	.000	.798
Roy's largest root	3.960	362.351[a]	2.000	183.000	.000	.798

Each F tests the multivariate effect of Emotions. These tests are based on the linearly independent pairwise comparisons among the estimated marginal means.

a. Exact statistic

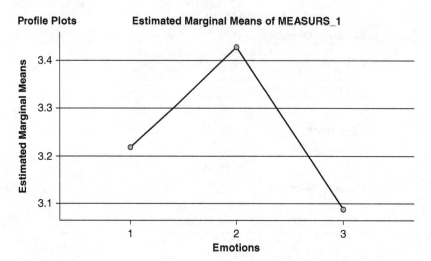

Figure 6.18 Repeated measures ANOVA output, facial emotions

Reprint courtesy of IBM Corporation ©

The first box, Within-Subjects Factors, simply lists out your three variables.

The second box, Descriptive Statistics, reports the means and standard deviations for each variable. So a mean of 10.90 for the neutral face implies that consumers would spend, on average, $10.90 when being served by a frontline employee with a neutral facial expression. The same consumers would spend, on average, $21.40 when being served by the smiling face and only $4.26 when being served by the angry face. These obviously appear like pretty large mean differences, but, again, they are confined to the sample of 185 consumers. We want to know whether these differences generalize to the wider population of American consumers.

You can skip the table called Multivariate Tests. Just trust me on this one. You don't need to know how to interpret this for purposes of applied statistics.

The next table down is called Mauchly's Test of Sphericity. Again, you don't need to know the mathematics underlying Mauchly's test, but you should know that it is very similar to Levene's test for equality of variances. It basically looks at the spread of scores across the three variables in your repeated measures ANOVA. It should be noted that Mauchly's test is only relevant when you have three or more variables; if you are doing a repeated measures ANOVA with only two variables (which is essentially akin to a paired sample t-test), it isn't a relevant statistic. To interpret Mauchly's test, look at the p-value, which in this case is 0.024. If $p < 0.05$, then we can assume that we have violated the assumption of sphericity, which is a bad thing. Because our $p = 0.024$, we cannot assume sphericity and so we need to make some kind of correction in our statistical test to account for this violation. There are two corrections that SPSS provides by default: the Greenhouse–Geisser and the Huynh–Feldt. These are similar to the Bonferroni corrections we carried out in the one-way ANOVA. As a general rule of thumb, if the values of these two statistics reported in this table are greater than 0.75, then we would typically use the Huynh–Feldt correction. In this case, the value of Greenhouse–Geisser is 0.962 and the value of Huynh–Feldt is 0.972, so we're going to use Huynh–Feldt.

In the next table down, labeled Tests of Within-Subjects Effects, we have the global result of our repeated measured ANOVA. You'll see that the statistics are reported twice, once for Emotions and once for Error(Emotions). You can skip the error terms since they are not useful for purposes of applied statistics. Looking at Emotions, you have four choices. Remember that we cannot choose the first option, Sphericity Assumed, because we violated that assumption, as suggested by the Mauchly's test. We agreed to make a Huynh–Feldt correction, so you can follow that row across to interpret the results. The key statistics are the F-statistic, p-value, and Partial Eta Squared. In this case, the F-statistic is 434.70 and the corresponding p-value is 0.000 (which we would report as $p < 0.001$). This p-value tells us that there is a significant difference *somewhere* among those three means, but it doesn't say exactly where. The Partial Eta Squared of 0.703 gives an indication of the strength of the relationships among these variables. We would interpret this by saying that roughly 70% of consumer decision-making can be explained by the variations in facial expressions (meaning that we still haven't accounted for the other 30% in our model). This is a very high Partial Eta Squared.

The next table down, Tests of Within-Subjects Contrasts, compares your baseline (neutral) face with the two emotional expressions. You'll see that these are expressed in terms of Level 1, Level 2, and Level 3. To remind yourself of which level corresponds to which emotion, you can look at the first box. Level 1 is the neutral face, Level 2 is the smiling face, and Level 3 is the angry face. The first row in this table compares Level 1 (neutral) with Level 3 (angry). The F-statistic is 154.14 and the p-value is 0.000 (i.e., $p < 0.001$), indicating that there is a significant pairwise difference in consumer spending between the two facial expressions. The second row compares Level 2 (smile) with Level 3 (angry). The F-statistic here is 725.63 and the p-value is 0.000 (i.e., $p < 0.001$), again indicating that there is a significant pairwise difference in consumer spending between these two facial expressions.

You can skip the box labeled Tests of Between-Subjects Effects as it is not relevant to our exclusively within-subjects analysis.

The next set of boxes report the estimated marginal means. First you'll see the grand mean across all three variables, which is 12.19 (corresponding to an average spend of $12.19). Then you'll see the means for each of the three variables (these have already been reported above in the Descriptive Statistics). After that, you'll see the Bonferroni corrected pairwise comparisons that specify where, exactly, the bivariate differences are among the three categories. If you look at the column labeled Sig., you'll see that all p-values are reported as 0.000 (i.e., $p < 0.001$), meaning that all bivariate combinations are statistically significantly different: a smile results in significantly higher consumer spending vis-à-vis the neutral face, an angry face results in significantly lower consumer spending vis-à-vis the neutral face, and the smile results in significantly higher consumer spending vis-à-vis the angry face.

You can again skip the table called Multivariate Tests and finish up the analysis by having a look at the mean plot at the bottom of the output in Figure 6.18. This mean plot visually confirms our results.

So what can we conclude from this basic marketing research? It would appear that service with a smile (Pugh, 2001) is important when it comes to revenue generation. To maximize consumer spending, all customer-facing staff should be trained in the appropriate emotional expression and to avoid neutral and especially angry faces when dealing with customers.

What Have You Learned?

Take a moment to look at yourself in the mirror. That person staring back at you is a real star. You now know how to carry out bivariate ANOVA tests in two different forms. The one-way ANOVA compares a set of mean scores across multiple categories of the independent variable, whereas the repeated measures ANOVA compares a set of mean scores across multiple variables measured sequentially. Both tests essentially tell us whether the mean scores we are comparing are significantly different from one another and, if so, where they are different.

You learned about the types of research questions that lend themselves to the ANOVA test and then worked through the mathematics of a simple example on how to calculate an F-statistic. After that, you learned how SPSS can make your life a lot easier by doing the one-way ANOVA test for you. It calculates the F-statistic, and corresponding p-value, for you and it also can provide *post hoc* pairwise comparison statistics so you can explore the different variations of bivariate relationships within the wider multicategory ANOVA.

Then you learned about repeated measures ANOVA and how SPSS can do this test for you with a simple click of a mouse. The repeated measures ANOVA similarly reports differences in mean scores, but instead of across categories (as in the one-way ANOVA), they are reported across sequentially measured variables. It similarly reports an F-statistic and a corresponding p-value that tells you whether there is a significant difference *somewhere* across the variables, and it also provides pairwise comparisons so you can explore those bivariate differences.

By now you must be having so much fun with these ANOVA tests that you're probably bursting with joy. Well, take some time to calm yourself down because the fun is only getting started. Now we're going to have a look at some nonparametric bivariate tests.

▬▬▬▬▬ Further Reading ▬▬▬▬▬

Cardinal, R. N., & Aitken, M. R. (2013). *ANOVA for the behavioral sciences researcher*. Psychology Press.

Cortina, J. M., & Nouri, H. (2000). *Effect size for ANOVA designs* (No. 129). Sage.

Girden, E. R. (1992). *ANOVA: Repeated measures* (No. 84). Sage.

Miller, R. G., Jr. (1997). *Beyond ANOVA: Basics of applied statistics*. Chapman & Hall/CRC Press.

Rutherford, A. (2001). *Introducing ANOVA and ANCOVA: A GLM approach*. Sage.

Timming, A. R. (2019). *Human resource management and evolutionary psychology: Exploring the biological foundations of managing people at work*. Edward Elgar.

In-Class Discussion Questions

1. What are the key differences and similarities between a one-way ANOVA and a repeated measures ANOVA? Describe the types of variables you can use with each statistical test.
2. What are *post hoc* analyses in the context of ANOVA? Why is it inadvisable to carry out an ANOVA test and not follow up with *post hoc* analyses?
3. List out five research questions that a management scientist might answer using an ANOVA test.
4. Further to Question 3, list out the 10 variables that might be used to answer those five research questions. Describe how each one could be measured and, where necessary, coded.
5. What is Levene's test for equality of variance? Why do we usually ask for Levene's test when carrying out an ANOVA? How should we interpret the results of a Levene's test?
6. How would you report the results of an ANOVA test? Which statistics would you include and how would you interpret the results?

PART III
NONPARAMETRIC AND CORRELATIONAL RELATIONSHIPS

You're half-way through this book. Don't give up just yet! The best is yet to come. Now that you're an ace at carrying out t-tests and ANOVAs, you can move on to another set of commonly used bivariate statistical tests: the chi-square (pronounced 'kai'-square) test, simple regression, and Pearson's r correlation coefficient test. Like the t-test and ANOVA, these new statistical tests also involve a single independent variable and a single dependent variable (hence the descriptor, *bi*variate). But they involve different configurations of variables, as you'll soon discover over the next two chapters. In Chapter 7, we'll take a close look at the chi-square test. This is one of the most commonly used statistical tests and it's quite versatile. It is known as a nonparametric test, which means that it does not take account of mean scores and presupposes distributional normality. For this reason, chi-square is useful when both of your variables are nominal or categorical in nature. We will return to the chi-square test later in Chapters 11 and 12 of this textbook because it is foundational to the assessment of model fit in confirmatory factor analyses and structural equation models (also referred to as analysis of covariance structures). After looking at the chi-square test, we'll move on to Chapter 8, where we'll learn about simple regression and Pearson's r correlation coefficient. These are two variations of pretty much the same statistical test. Simple regression reports an unstandardized weight to describe the relationship between X and Y, whereas Pearson's r reports a standardized weight to describe the exact same relationship. We would typically use simple regression if we are interested in predicting Y given a value of X. If we were instead just interested in understanding how strongly X is related to Y, we would use Pearson's r correlation coefficient. Okay, without further ado, let's get to it!

7

Chi-Square

So far, we've looked in depth at the independent samples *t*-test, the paired sample *t*-test, the one-way ANOVA, and the one-way repeated measures ANOVA. You've probably detected a common thread across these statistical tests. In each case, you're comparing mean scores, either across categories (in the cases of the independent samples *t*-test and one-way ANOVA) or across repeated variables (in the cases of the paired sample *t*-test and repeated measures ANOVA). Because of this focus on mean scores, all four of these tests are *parametric* in nature. This means that they are based on the shape of a normal distribution, as discussed in Chapters 3 and 4. Recall that normal distributions are roughly bell shaped (hence, the bell curve) with a known mean and standard deviations. In light of the fact that these are parametric tests, they are technically only for use when the dependent variable is normally distributed, or at least somewhat normally distributed.

You might be wondering, what if I have two variables of interest, and neither is parametric and/or normally distributed? In other words, what am I supposed to do if I'm interested in investigating the relationship between two nominal-level variables? For example, imagine that you are interested in finding out whether there is a relationship between gender and whether or not an employee has received a promotion in the last year. Like the *t*-test and ANOVA, this is a bivariate test. The independent variable is gender and the dependent variable is whether or not the employee has been promoted in the last year. But unlike the *t*-test and ANOVA, there is no ordinal- or scale-level variable on which to compare mean scores. When there are only two categories in a variable, the average score (i.e., the mean), although it can technically be calculated, is meaningless. With these two variables, it would be impossible to carry out a *t*-test or an ANOVA because the dependent variable, by definition, is not normally distributed, that is, it is not bell shaped (since it is impossible to produce a bell curve with only two categories).

Fortunately, there are some *nonparametric* statistical tests that are designed to answer exactly these types of research questions. A nonparametric test makes no *a priori* assumptions whatsoever about the shapes of the distributions of either variable. Furthermore, they are quite versatile as statistical tests. The example I gave above is a 2 × 2 test: Gender (male vs. female) × Whether or not the employee has been promoted in the last year (yes vs. no). But nonparametric tests are also capable of analysing bivariate relationships with even more categories, for example, 2 × 3 (Whether or not the respondent is a trade union member × Contract type measured as full-time, part-time, or temporary); 3 × 3 (Religion measured as Christian, Muslim, or Jewish × Contract type measured as full-time, part-time, or temporary); or 4 × 3 (Race measured as black, white, East Asian, or South Asian × Performance tier measured as high performance, average performance, and low performance); and so on.

In this chapter, we're going to look at some popular nonparametric tests at your disposal, focusing primarily on the formidable chi-square test. Now, just so you don't embarrass yourself in front of anyone, 'chi' is pronounced 'Ky', as in Kylo Ren. Legend has it that Kylo Ren's parents named him so in honor of the chi-square test. No, I'm just kidding . . . or am I?

As usual, first we'll look at the types of research questions that can be answered using nonparametric tests. After that, we'll look at the mathematics underlying the chi-square test. Then I'll show you how to carry out a chi-square test on IBM SPSS Statistics Software (SPSS) using real data from the survey of organizations. Finally, we'll look briefly at another nonparametric test, the Mann–Whitney U test.

Are you up to the challenge?

Well, of course you are! Let's do it, young Jedi.

Comparing Categorical Variables in Management Research

As demonstrated in the last two chapters, there are many circumstances in the workplace where researchers are interested in whether one group of individuals (or organizations) scores, on average, higher or lower than another. But management researchers may also be interested in nonhierarchical questions, too. Nonparametric statistical tests allow us to answer these types of nonhierarchical questions.

The most common nonparametric method is the chi-square test. To qualify for a chi-square test, both variables, X and Y, must be categorical. Alternatively stated, neither of the variables can be continuous or scale level. For example, a variable like age could not be used in a chi-square test if it were measured continuously. However, if you measured age, for example, across two categories (old vs. young) or three (old, middle age, young), then it would be appropriate. As a general rule, if both variables are nominal in measurement (i.e., nonhierarchical), then they are appropriate for a chi-square test. In certain circumstances, it may also be possible to compare ordinal variables in a chi-square test, but there may be a more appropriate method like the Mann–Whitney U test, discussed below, or even the t-test or the ANOVA.

Let's consider an example of a simple 2 × 2 chi-square test that a management researcher like you might well conduct.

Imagine you've collected some data from 100 employees working in the same company. You would like to know if employee gender is related to whether or not they feel 'listened to' by their managers. In this case, the research question might be something like this: Do male employees feel like their managers listen to them more than female employees? You might hypothesize that male employees will feel more listened to or, alternatively stated, that women will feel more ignored by their managers.

You administer the survey and ask two questions in the instrument:

What is your gender? (0 = *male*, 1 = *female*)

Do you feel that your manager listens to you? (0 = *no*, 1 = *yes*)

Let's assume you stratified your sample, so that half are men ($n = 50$) and the other half are women ($n = 50$). The tabulated results are presented in Table 7.1.

Looking at these frequencies, it would appear that, as expected, a greater proportion of men feel 'listened to' at work (76%, or 38/50) than women (62%, or 31/50). But the key question, as always, is, do these results generalize from our sample to the population? Can we make that quantum leap? Whereas the *t*-test is based on a *t*-statistic and ANOVA is based on an *F*-statistic, the chi-square test is based on . . . wait for it . . . a chi-square statistic. If the chi-square statistic for these data has an associated *p*-value of < 0.05, then we would conclude that gender and whether or not an employee feels listened to at work are dependent, that is to say, there is a significant relationship between the two variables. Similarly, if our chi-square statistic tells us that $p > 0.05$, then we would conclude that there is no relationship between gender and whether or not an employee feels listened to at work, implying that the difference in the sample (76% vs. 62%) is down to random chance and therefore cannot and should not generalize to the population. As it happens, in fact, the *p*-value associated with these data is $p = 0.130$, implying that this result does not generalize to the population. In other words, there is no statistically significant difference between men and women in terms of whether they feel 'listened to' by managers (at least, based on these hypothetical data).

Drawing from relevant examples in the fields of management and marketing, let's take a look at some additional research questions that could be answered using a chi-square test.

- Are employees with postgraduate degrees more likely to report having discretion over their work than employees without postgraduate degrees? In this case, the independent variable is level of education (0 = *no postgraduate degree*, 1 = *postgraduate degree*) and the dependent variable is whether or not employees report having discretion over the work they do (0 = *no*, 1 = *yes*).
- Are left-handed employees more likely to meet performance benchmarks than right-handed employees? In this case, the independent variable is hand dominance (0 = *right-handed*, 1 = *left-handed*) and the dependent variable is whether the employee has met performance benchmarks in the last year (0 = *no*, 1 = *yes*).
- Are businesses with formal HR departments more likely to be publicly listed than businesses without formal HR departments? In this case, the independent variable is whether the organization has a formal HR department (0 = *no*, 1 = *yes*) and the dependent variable is whether the organization is publicly listed on a stock exchange (0 = *no*, 1 = *yes*).

Table 7.1 Cross-tabulation, listened to by gender

	Listened to	Not listened to
Male employee	38	12
Female employee	31	19

- Are black employees more likely to perceive that they have been discriminated against at work than East Asian and South Asian employees? In this case, the independent variable is race (0 = *black*, 1 = *East Asian*, and 2 = South Asian) and the dependent variable is whether the employee perceives that he or she has been discriminated against in the workplace (0 = *no*, 1 = *yes*).
- Are LGBTQ (lesbian, gay, bisexual, transgender, and queer) employees more likely than heterosexual employees to make a complaint of sexual harassment at work. In this case, the independent variable is sexual orientations (0 = *heterosexual*, 1 = *LGBTQ*) and the dependent variable is whether or not the employee has filed a sexual harassment complaint.
- Are female consumers more likely to make a purchase when entering a shop than male consumers. In this case, the independent variable is gender (0 = *male*, 1 = *female*) and the dependent variable is whether or not the consumer made a purchase when entering a shop (0 = *no*, 1 = *yes*).
- Are graduates from Cambridge University more likely to be employed than graduates from Oxford University? (But isn't the answer to this question obvious!). In this case, the independent variable is alma mater (0 = *Oxford*, 1 = *Cambridge*) and the dependent variable is whether or not the respondent is employed (0 = *no*, 1 = *yes*).
- Are tall male employees more likely to hold managerial roles than short male employees? In this case, the independent variable is height (0 = *short*, 1 = *tall*). (One way to create such a variable would be to measure the height of your respondents on continuous scale, and then to use the median to divide the sample into two groups: short and tall.) The dependent variable is whether or not the respondent holds a managerial position (0 = *no*, 1 = *yes*).
- Are employees whose favorite color is red more likely to engage in an office romance than employees whose favorite colors are blue and green? In this case, the independent variable is favorite color (0 = *red*, 1 = *blue*, 2 = *green*) and the dependent variable is whether or not the employee has engaged in an office romance (0 = *no*, 1 = *yes*).
- Are disabled employees with a mental illness likely to miss greater than two weeks of work per year than disabled employees with a physical illness? In this case, the independent variable is primary type of disability (0 = *physical*, 1 = *mental*) and the dependent variable is whether or not the respondent has missed more than two weeks of work in the last year (0 = *no*, 1 = *yes*).

Let's explore this last question a bit more and see how we could use a chi-square test to answer it. The first thing you'll notice about this research question is that it is confined to a very specific population of employees: those who are already disabled in some way. In other words, when collecting your data, you will need to sample from this specific population because nondisabled employees, who are the vast majority of the workforce, are not relevant to the research question.

Imagine that you've managed to get a sample of disabled employees (*N* = 87) to complete a survey instrument with these two questions:

1. Is your disability primarily physical or mental? (0 = *physical*, 1 = *mental*)
2. Have you missed more than two weeks of work in the last year? (0 = *no*, 1 = *yes*)

Let's say you have 32 respondents reporting a mental disability and 55 respondents reporting a physical disability. You compile the data into a cross-tabulation, as shown in Table 7.2.

Table 7.2 Cross-tabulation, missed work by disability type

	Missed > 2 weeks of work	Not missed > 2 weeks of work
Physical disability	25	30
Mental disability	22	10

Looking at these absolute frequencies, it's hard to determine whether physically disabled employees are more likely to have missed more than two weeks of work compared with mentally disabled employees. The reason it is difficult to draw conclusions here is that, unlike in Table 7.1, there is an unequal number of respondents with physical and mental disabilities, making it more difficult to assess the relationship.

If we were to carry out a chi-square test on these data, we would need to (1) calculate the chi-square statistic and corresponding p-value and (2) convert the absolute numbers in Table 7.2 into proportions, or percentages. With regard to (1), the chi-square statistic is, in fact, 4.42 and the corresponding p-value is 0.036 (don't worry about how I calculated these statistics; you'll soon know how). This tells us that the two variables are dependent and statistically significantly related to one another. With regard to (2), have a look at Table 7.3, where the absolute numbers from Table 7.2 have been converted into percentages.

When the data are expressed in percentages, instead of absolute terms, it appears that mentally disabled employees are more likely to have missed greater than two weeks of work per annum compared with physically disabled employees. Indeed, the p-value of 0.036 suggests that we are able to generalize these results from the sample to the population. Thus, we would conclude (if these were real data) that employees with mental disabilities are significantly more likely to have missed greater than two weeks of work compared with employees with physical disabilities.

Now that you have a general understanding of what kinds of research questions a chi-square test can answer, let's delve into the mathematics underlying the test. Don't worry. This won't hurt . . . much.

Table 7.3 Cross-tabulation, missed work by disability type with percentages

	Missed > 2 weeks of work	Not missed > 2 weeks of work
Physical disability	25/55 = 45% (n = 55)	30/55 = 55% (n = 55)
Mental disability	22/32 = 69% (n = 32)	10/32 = 31% (n = 32)

The Mathematics Underlying the Chi-Square Test

To calculate a chi-square statistic, you must first present your data in what is known as a cross-tabulation. A *cross-tabulation* is a bivariate table looking at the intersection of categories across the two (typically nominal) variables.

A cross-tabulation always consists of four elements: the columns, the rows, the cells, and the marginals. Technically, you can list the independent variable in the column and dependent variable in the rows, but I tend to prefer to list the independent variable in the rows and the dependent variable in the columns. A cross-tabulation for a simple 2 × 2 chi-square test is depicted in Table 7.4.

Table 7.4 Model for calculation of 2 × 2 chi-square

		Dependent variable		
		Category A	Category B	
Independent variable	Category A	Cell AA	Cell AB	AA + AB marginal
	Category B	Cell BA	Cell BB	BA + BB marginal
	AA + BA marginal		AB + BB marginal	Total marginal

The four cells contain the absolute count, or *observed frequencies*, for each combination of scores. The marginals are calculated by adding up the observed frequencies, either horizontally or vertically. You'll notice that, in a 2 × 2 chi-square test such as this one, there are four intersectional marginals and one total marginal. The *total marginal* will always add up to the total number of cases in your sample.

The utility of a 2 × 2 chi-square test is best understood and illustrated with a practical example. Imagine that you were interested in the question of whether employees without young children are more likely to meet their key performance indicators (KPIs) than employees with young children. You hypothesize that employees with young children are less committed to work and more sleep deprived vis-à-vis employees without young children.

You administer a questionnaire to a random sample of employees (*N* = 278). The survey instrument contains these two items:

1. Do you have children younger than five years old living at home? (0 = *no*, 1 = *yes*)
2. Did you meet your KPIs last year? (0 = *no*, 1 = *yes*)

Using Table 7.4 as a template, you can compile the results into the cross-tabulation shown in Table 7.5.

There are four cells in this table. Of the 278 respondents, 75 have young children and met their KPIs, 24 have young children and did not meet their KPIs, 122 do not have young children and met their KPIs, and 57 do not have young children and did not meet their KPIs.

Spend a few moments adding up the numbers vertically and horizontally to make sure your marginals and marginal total are correct.

Table 7.5 Cross-tabulation, met key performance indicators last year by having young children

		Met KPIs last year?		
		Yes	No	
Have young children?	Yes	75	24	*n* = 99
	No	122	57	*n* = 179
		n = 197	*n* = 81	*N* = 278

Source: KPI = key performance indicators.

Now, let's see how we can use these data to calculate the chi-square statistic, shall we? The chi-square formula is reported in Equation (7.1):

$$\text{Chi-square} = \Sigma \frac{(f_0 - f_e)^2}{f_e} \qquad (7.1)$$

In this formula,

f_0 = the actual frequencies, or scores, observed in each cell

and

f_e = the frequencies, or scores, that would be expected in each cell if the two variables were independent (i.e., not related to one another).

Now, f_0 is easy to identify. These are the actual scores in the bivariate table. In this case, the observed frequencies are 75, 24, 122, and 57.

But the calculation of f_e requires a bit more effort, as shown in Equation (7.2):

$$f_e = \frac{\text{Row marginal} \times \text{Column marginal}}{N} \qquad (7.2)$$

In other words, the expected frequency for a given cell is calculated by taking the total row marginal multiplied by the total column marginal and dividing that by the total number of cases in the sample.

Okay, let's do the math using the data in Table 7.5. We'll take it nice and easy, step by step.

We already have the four observed frequencies: 75 (top-left of table), 24 (top-right of table), 122 (bottom-left of table), and 57 (bottom-right of table). But we still need to calculate the expected frequencies. We'll follow the same order.

First, the expected frequency for the top-left of the table is the row marginal (99) × the column marginal (197) divided by the total number of cases (278). Thus,

$$f_e = \frac{99 \times 197}{278} = 70.15.$$

Second, the expected frequency for the bottom-left of the table is the row marginal (179) × the column marginal (197) divided by the total number of cases (278). Thus,

$$f_e = \frac{179 \times 197}{278} = 126.85$$

Third, the expected frequency for the top-right of the table is the row marginal (99) × the column marginal (81) divided by the total number of cases (278). Thus,

$$f_e = \frac{99 \times 81}{278} = 28.85$$

Last, the expected frequency for the bottom-right of the table is the row marginal (179) × the column marginal (81) divided by the total number of cases (278). Thus,

$$f_e \frac{179 \times 81}{278} = 52.15$$

So our four expected frequencies are 70.15 (top-left), 126.85 (bottom-left), 28.85 (top-right), and 52.15 (bottom-right). These numbers, coupled with the observed frequencies that are already in the table, are enough to calculate the chi-square statistic. It's just a matter of plugging them into Equation (7.1). Let's do it.

$$\text{Chi-square} = \Sigma \frac{(f_o - f_e)^2}{f_c}$$

$$\text{Chi-square} = \frac{(75 - 70.15)^2}{70.15} + \frac{(122 - 126.85)^2}{126.85} + \frac{(24 - 28.85)^2}{28.85} + \frac{(57 - 52.15)^2}{52.15}$$

$$\text{Chi-square} = \frac{(4.85)^2}{70.15} + \frac{(-4.85)^2}{126.85} + \frac{(-4.85)^2}{28.85} + \frac{(4.85)^2}{52.15}$$

$$\text{Chi-square} = \frac{23.52}{70.15} + \frac{23.52}{126.85} + \frac{23.52}{28.85} + \frac{23.52}{52.15}$$

$$\text{Chi-square} = 0.34 + 0.19 + 0.82 + 0.45$$

$$\text{Chi-square} = 1.80$$

Boom! You just calculated your first chi-square statistic by hand! That wasn't so hard now, was it? This chi-square statistic, however, is not enough on its own to determine whether or not you can generalize your result from the sample to the population. Just like with the t-statistic and the F-statistic, the chi-square statistic corresponds to a particular p-value, and it's this p-value that will speak to the generalizability of the result. I could show you how to find the p-value using a chi-square table, but why not just let SPSS do the work for us? In this case, we can conclude that the chi-square statistics of 1.80 corresponds to a p-value of 0.18 (i.e., $p >$ the 0.05 cutoff). Thus, we conclude that there is no relationship between whether an employee has children and whether he or she has met his or her KPIs in the last year. The two variables are thus independent of one another.

   One of the difficulties of the chi-square test is that it can be difficult to interpret the raw (observed) numbers in the contingency table. One thing that researchers often do is to convert those raw numbers into percentages. This standardization often gives us more insight into the data. Even though this particular result was not found to be statistically significant, let's convert Table 7.5 from raw numbers to percentages. To do this, simply take the observed number in each row divided by the total number for the row. So 75/99 = 0.76, or *76%*; 24/99 = 0.24, or *24%*; 122/179 = 0.68, or *68%*; and 57/179 = 0.32, or *32%*. These percentages suggest that employees with young children are more likely to have met their KPIs in the last year compared with those without young children, but, again, this difference isn't large enough to generalize from the sample to the population. You can see the calculations in Table 7.6.

Table 7.6 Cross-tabulation, met key performance indicators last year by have young children with percentages

		Met KPIs last year?		
		Yes	**No**	
Have young children?	Yes	75.8%	24.2%	*n* = 99
	No	68.2%	31.8%	*n* = 179
		n = 197	*n* = 81	*N* = 278

Source: KPI = key performance indicators.

This was a simple chi-square test, in which both variables have only two categories. Chi-square can also be calculated when one or both variables have more than two categories. I think it makes sense to do one more test by hand, but this time using a 3 × 2 design.

Imagine that you're interested in finding out whether employees who regularly read books are more productive than employees who do not regularly read books. You hypothesize that regular reading signals a commitment to learning, and that this type of personality will tend to be more productive in the workplace.

You administer a questionnaire to 872 employees, all of whom were randomly drawn. The item you used to measure your independent variable is,

Do you read for at least one hour per day? (0 = *no*, 1 = *yes*)

For your dependent variable, productivity, you have a couple of options. First, you could ask the respondents to self-rate their productivity. This is generally inadvisable because self-ratings are often inflated and can result in *common method variance*. Common method variance refers to a type of measurement bias where subjective data for the independent variable and dependent variable are collected from the same person. To prevent common method variance, you ask the line managers of all 872 employees to rate them on productivity using the following item:

How would you rate [respondent's] productivity? (1 = *less productive than average*, 2 = *average productivity*, and 3 = *more productive than average*).

You have now collected all the data, and they are reported in the cross-tabulation depicted in Table 7.7.

Table 7.7 Cross-tabulation, productivity by reading per day

		Productivity?			
		High	**Average**	**Low**	
Read > 1 hour per day	Yes	127	158	63	*n* = 348
	No	164	152	208	*n* = 524
		n = 291	*n* = 310	*n* = 271	*N* = 872

This is an example of a 2 × 3 chi-square test. In this case, the independent variable, Read, has two categories (yes/no) and the dependent variable, Productivity, has three categories (high, average, low). If you're wondering why we are using chi-square with these variables instead of ANOVA, check out Box 7.1.

Box 7.1: Chi-Square Versus ANOVA and *t*-Test

Sometimes it is not clear why we use some statistical tests as opposed to others. For example, we already learned that we can use either a *t*-test or an ANOVA if your independent variable is nominal with two categories and our dependent variable is ordinal or scale in measurement. Either test will work under that constraint. In looking at the relationship between Read (yes, no) and Productivity (low, average, high), you might be wondering why we can't just use ANOVA or a *t*-test. The independent variable, Read, is a two-category nominal variable. The dependent variable, Productivity, is ordinal. But with only three categories, we don't typically have a normal distribution (e.g., bell curve), as is an assumption of both the *t*-test and ANOVA. What's great about a chi-square test is that it is nonparametric, meaning that we do not need to assume that the shapes and the distributions are normal. So, in theory, though you could run this statistical test using ANOVA or *t*-test, it makes more sense to use chi-square here.

The first thing you want to do with Table 7.7 is to check that your marginals are correct. You'll see that the six cells properly add up vertically and horizontally to 872. Already we know from these data that a majority of respondents ($n = 524$) do not read more than one hour per day. Looking at the observed frequencies in the six cells, it would appear that there are more high performers that do not read more than one hour a day ($n = 165$) compared with high performers who do read more than one hour a day ($n = 127$), but these absolute numbers are difficult to compare because there are, overall, more participants who do not read more than one hour per day than participants who do read more than one hour per day. The numbers allocated to the 'average' productivity category are roughly similar ($n = 158$ vs. $n = 152$). However, it would appear that there are far more low productivity participants who do not read more than one hour per day ($n = 208$) compared with low productivity participants who do read more than one hour per day ($n = 63$). Let's test whether or not there is a significant relationship between our two variables by calculating the chi-square statistic for this 2 × 3 design.

First, we need to calculate the expected frequencies for each cell in the cross-tabulation. We do this using Equation (7.2).

The expected frequency for the top-left cell (i.e., those 127 respondents who read more than one hour per day and are classified as highly productive) is calculated by taking the Row marginal (348) × the Column marginal (291) divided by the Total number of cases (872). Thus,

$$f_e = \frac{348 \times 291}{872} = 116.13$$

The expected frequency for the top-middle cell (i.e., those 158 respondents who read more than one hour per day and are classified as average in productivity) is calculated by taking the Row marginal (348) × the Column marginal (310) divided by the Total number of cases (872). Thus,

$$f_e = \frac{348 \times 310}{872} = 123.72$$

The expected frequency for the top-right cell (i.e., those 63 respondents who read more than one hour per day and are classified as low in productivity) is calculated by taking the Row marginal (348) × the Column marginal (271) divided by the Total number of cases (872). Thus,

$$f_e = \frac{348 \times 271}{872} = 108.15$$

The expected frequency for the bottom-left cell (i.e., those 164 respondents who did not read more than one hour per day and are classified as highly productive) is calculated by taking the Row marginal (524) × the Column marginal (291) divided by the Total number of cases (872). Thus,

$$f_e = \frac{524 \times 291}{872} = 174.87$$

The expected frequency for the bottom-middle cell (i.e., those 152 respondents who did not read more than one hour per day and are classified as average in productivity) is calculated by taking the Row marginal (524) × the Column marginal (310) divided by the Total number of cases (872). Thus,

$$f_e = \frac{524 \times 310}{872} = 186.28$$

Finally, the expected frequency for the bottom-right cell (i.e., those 208 respondents who did not read more than one hour per day and are classified as low in productivity) is calculated by taking the Row marginal (524) × the Column marginal (271) divided by the Total number of cases (872). Thus,

$$f_e = \frac{524 \times 271}{872} = 162.85$$

Now that we have calculated all six of the expected frequencies, we simply plug those numbers into the chi-square formula listed in Equation (7.1):

$$\text{Chi-square} = \Sigma \frac{(f_o - f_e)^2}{f_e}$$

$$\text{Chi-square} = \frac{(127-116.13)^2}{116.13} + \frac{(158-123.72)^2}{123.72} + \frac{(63-108.15)^2}{108.15} + \frac{(164-174.87)^2}{174.87} +$$
$$\frac{(152-186.28)^2}{186.28} + \frac{(208-162.85)^2}{162.85}$$

$$\text{Chi-square} = \frac{(10.87)^2}{116.13} + \frac{(34.28)^2}{123.72} + \frac{(-45.15)^2}{108.15} + \frac{(-10.87)^2}{174.87} + \frac{(-34.28)^2}{186.28} + \frac{(45.15)^2}{162.85}$$

$$\text{Chi-square} = \frac{118.16}{116.13} + \frac{1175.12}{123.72} + \frac{2038.52}{108.15} + \frac{118.16}{174.87} + \frac{1175.12}{186.28} + \frac{2038.52}{162.85}$$

$$\text{Chi-square} = 1.02 + 9.50 + 18.85 + 0.68 + 6.31 + 12.52$$

$$\text{Chi-square} = 48.88$$

Nice one, partner! You just calculated your second chi-square statistic by hand. What can I say? I'm impressed with your perseverance.

Obviously, a chi-square statistic of 48.88 is much larger than the previous one we calculated (which was only 1.80). This difference suggests that there is a much stronger relationship in our second chi-square test compared with our first chi-square test. But again, the question now becomes: Is it strong enough to generalize from the sample to the population? To answer this, we need to find the correct p-value associated with this chi-square statistic. SPSS will calculate this for you. For now, you'll just have to trust me that the p-value associated with a chi-square statistic of 48.88 is < 0.001. In other words, we are extremely confident that this relationship generalizes to the population. That is, whether an employee is a regular reader is strongly related to whether he or she is classified by managers as a high performer, an average performer, or a low performer.

To better understand the data, we will again convert the absolute (raw) frequencies into percentages. The reason we do this is that absolute numbers are hard to compare, but when expressed in percentages, they become relative.

To convert to percentages, we simply take the three numbers in each row and divide by the total for that row. When we do this, we get Table 7.8.

Having now converted the absolute frequencies into percentages, the nature of the relationship between the independent variable and dependent variable is now clearer to us. The biggest differences appear to be in the average and low-performing employees. Frequent readers are much more likely to be rated average and high by their supervisors, whereas infrequent readers are much more likely to be rated low performers. This is exactly what we expected, and so our hypothesis is confirmed.

Okay, I think you've now had enough math for the time being. Let's see how we can use SPSS to carry out the chi-square test for us.

Table 7.8 Cross-tabulation, productivity by reading per day with percentages

		Productivity?		
		High	Average	Low
Read > 1 hour per day	Yes	36.5%	45.4%	18.1%	$n = 348$
	No	31.3%	29.0%	39.7%	$n = 524$
		$n = 291$	$n = 310$	$n = 271$	$N = 872$

The Chi-Square Test Using SPSS

We're going to use data from the survey of organizations again. Go to the Companion Website and open up the file named chap7data. You'll see that there are a few variables in this spreadsheet. First things first, go to Variable View and have a look at how each one was measured.

The first variable in the list, bstrateg, is going to serve as our independent variable in these chi-square tests. The variable asks, simply, whether or not this workplace is covered by a formal strategic plan. The response categories for this variable are 'yes' or 'no'. Remember that both variables in a chi-square test must be categorical (e.g., nominal or ordinal). As a binary variable, this one obviously fits the bill, and therefore is appropriate for use in a chi-square test.

Before we carry out the chi-square statistical test, let's request frequencies for our independent variable just to get a feel for it. Go to Analyze, Descriptive Statistics, and Frequencies…. The box in Figure 7.1 will appear. Find your variable, bstrateg, and move it to the right-hand column by double clicking it. Because this is not an ordinal or scale variable, we do not need to request any parametric statistics like the mean, median, or standard deviation. So just go into Charts and select ⊙ Pie charts, then click Continue and OK. The output is depicted in Figure 7.2.

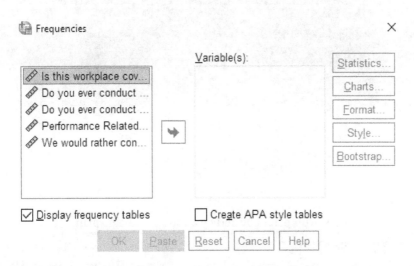

Figure 7.1 Frequencies function in SPSS

Reprint courtesy of IBM Corporation ©

Statistics

Is this workplace covered by a formal strategic plan?

N	Valid	2673
	Missing	7

(Continued)

Figure 7.2 (Continued)

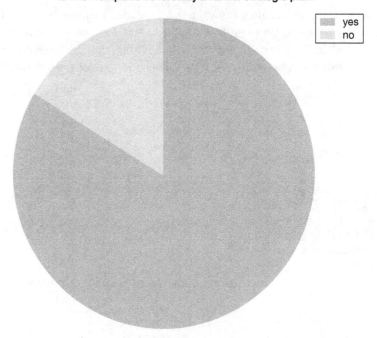

Is this workplace covered by a formal strategic plan?

		Frequency	Percent	Valid Percent	Cumulative Percent
Valid	yes	2239	83.5	83.8	83.8
	no	434	16.2	16.2	100.0
	Total	2673	99.7	100.0	
Missing	Don't know	7	.3		
Total		2680	100.0		

Is this workplace covered by a formal strategic plan?

yes
no

Figure 7.2 Frequencies, workplace covered by a formal strategic plan

Reprint courtesy of IBM Corporation ©

As you can see, there are 2673 organizations that responded to this item, with only seven missing values. The frequency distribution, followed by the pie chart, suggests that the vast majority of organizations, 83.8%, report that they have a formal strategic plan in place.

Now let's have a think about potential dependent variables for this chi-square test. We should expect to see fairly strong differences between organizations that have a formal strategic plan in place and those that don't, right? One potential question we could test is whether the more 'strategic' organizations employ different employee selection and assessment procedures compared with the 'nonstrategic' organizations. We might hypothesize, for example, that organizations that put time and effort into developing a strategic plan are also more likely to put time and effort into formal selection and assessment procedures. This makes sense.

To this end, one dependent variable that we could use to test this hypothesis is catestw1, which asked the respondents if they ever conduct any type of personality or attitude test. The response categories for this variable are as follows: 1 = *yes*, for managerial positions, 2 = *yes*, for nonmanagerial positions, and 3 = *no*, no tests conducted. This nominal variable with three categories is appropriate for use in a 2 × 3 chi-square test.

Let's quickly generate the frequencies for this variable by going to Analyze, Descriptive Statistics, and Frequencies.... Move our variable, catestw1, to the right by double clicking and make sure that you request the pie chart again in Charts.... When you are all set, click OK and you will see the output depicted in Figure 7.3.

Statistics

Do you ever conduct any type of
personality or attitude test?

N	Valid	2658
	Missing	22

Do you ever conduct any type of personality or attitude test?

		Frequency	Percent	Valid Percent	Cumulative Percent
Valid	managerial	953	35.6	35.9	35.9
	non-managerial	83	3.1	3.1	39.0
	no tests conducted	1622	60.5	61.0	100.0
	Total	2658	99.2	100.0	
Missing	Don't know	6	.2		
	Item not applicable	16	.6		
	Total	22	.8		
Total		2680	100.0		

Do you ever conduct any type of personality or attitude test?

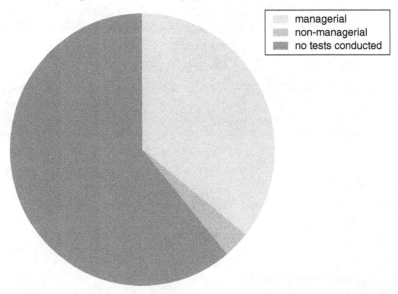

Figure 7.3 Frequencies, ever conduct personality or attitude test

You will see that there are 2658 valid responses to this variable and 22 that are missing. In total, 35.9% of organizations report using these tests for managerial positions, only 3.1% for nonmanagerial positions, and 61.0% report using no personality or attitude tests on their workforce.

Now, let's conduct the chi-square test and find out whether these two variables are significantly related (or 'dependent') and, if so, how.

First, go to Analyze, Descriptive Statistics, and Crosstabs…. The window depicted in Figure 7.4 will appear. Now move your independent variable (bstrateg) to the box labeled Row(s): and your dependent variable (catestw1) to the box labeled Column(s):. At the bottom-left of the window, tick ☑ Display clustered bar charts. Creating bar charts is useful because it allows us to visualize the results of the chi-square test. Next, go into Statistics… and you will see the window depicted in Figure 7.5 pop up. Tick ☑ Chi-square to request the chi-square statistic and *p*-value and ☑ Phi and Cramer's V to request an effect size for your test, and then click Continue . *Effect sizes* refer to the strength of the relationship between two variables.

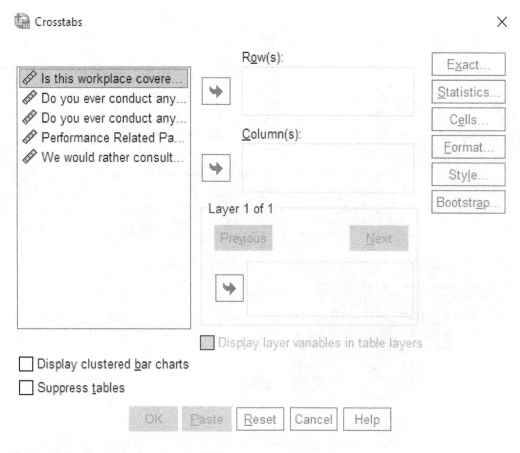

Figure 7.4 Crosstabs function in SPSS

Reprint courtesy of IBM Corporation ©

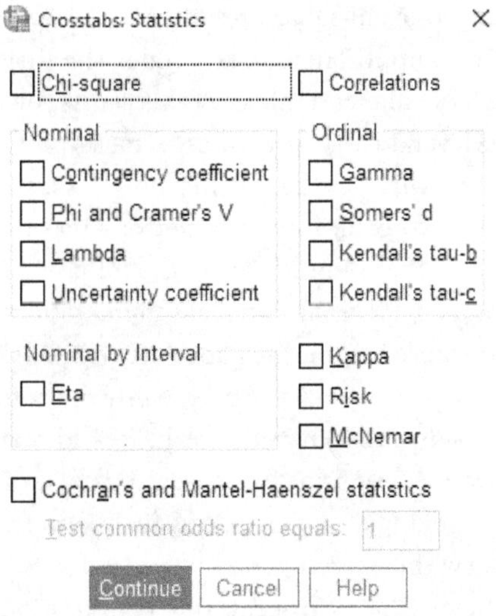

Figure 7.5 Crosstabs statistics function in SPSS

Reprint courtesy of IBM Corporation ©

Now go into [Cells]. The window in Figure 7.6 appears. You will note that ☑ Observed is ticked by default. I also want you to tick ☑ Expected and, under Percentages, tick ☑ Row and then [Continue].

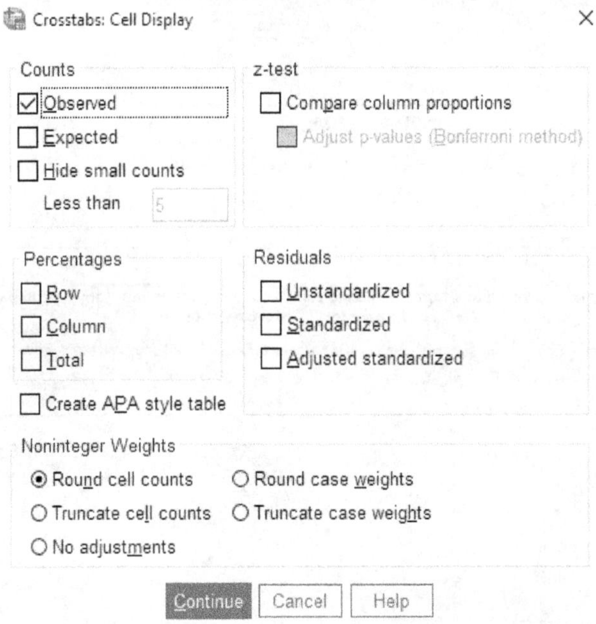

Figure 7.6 Crosstabs cell display function in SPSS

Reprint courtesy of IBM Corporation ©

Now click [OK] to request your chi-square results and you will see the output depicted in Figure 7.7. Let's go through this output, one box at a time. The first box, labeled Case Processing Summary, indicates the number of valid and missing cases across the two variables used in the test. You can see that there are 2651 valid cases in this test. The second box is the cross-tabulation of the two variables. As you can see, whether the organization has a strategic formal plan (yes/no) is listed in the rows and whether the organization uses personality or attitude tests (yes managerial/ yes nonmanagerial/no) is listed in the columns. There is a lot going on in this table. You can look at the actual and expected counts, but for purposes of interpretation, you should instead focus on the row percentages as these are more helpful than absolute numbers. The table shows that, among firms that have a formal strategic plan, 40.6% use personality or attitude tests for managerial selection, compared with only 11.8% in firms that do not have a formal strategic plan. There is very little difference between the two types of firms in respect to the use of such tests on nonmanagerial employees: 3.1% versus 3.2%. Looking at organizations that conduct no tests at all, 56.3% have a formal strategic plan, compared with 85.0% that do not have a formal strategic plan. These findings are consistent with our hypotheses. That is, it seems that organizations with a formal strategic plan in place are more likely to employ sophisticated employee selection tools such as personality and aptitude tests. But these results are confined to our sample. The key question, as always, is: Do they generalize to the wider population (e.g., all organizations in the United Kingdom)?

Crosstabs

Case Processing Summary

	Cases					
	Valid		Missing		Total	
	N	Percent	N	Percent	N	Percent
Is this workplace covered by a formal strategic plan? * Do you ever conduct any type of personality or attitude test?	2651	98.9%	29	1.1%	2680	100.0%

Is this workplace covered by a formal strategic plan? * Do you ever conduct any type of personality or attitude test? Crosstabulation

			Do you ever conduct any type of personality or attitude test?			Total
			managerial	non-managerial	no tests conducted	
Is this workplace covered by a formal strategic plan?	yes	Count	901	68	1250	2219
		Expected Count	796.9	68.6	1353.5	2219.0
		% within Is this workplace covered by a formal strategic plan?	40.6%	3.1%	56.3%	100.0%
	no	Count	51	14	367	432
		Expected Count	155.1	13.4	263.5	432.0
		% within Is this workplace covered by a formal strategic plan?	11.8%	3.2%	85.0%	100.0%
Total		Count	952	82	1617	2651
		Expected Count	952.0	82.0	1617.0	2651.0
		% within Is this workplace covered by a formal strategic plan?	35.9%	3.1%	61.0%	100.0%

Chi-Square Tests

	Value	df	Asymptotic Significance (2-sided)
Pearson Chi-Square	132.112[a]	2	.000
Likelihood Ratio	152.189	2	.000
Linear-by-Linear Association	131.523	1	.000
N of Valid Cases	2651		

a. 0 cells (0.0%) have expected count less than 5. The minimum expected count is 13.36.

Symmetric Measures

		Value	Approximate Significance
Nominal by Nominal	Phi	.223	.000
	Cramer's V	.223	.000
N of Valid Cases		2651	

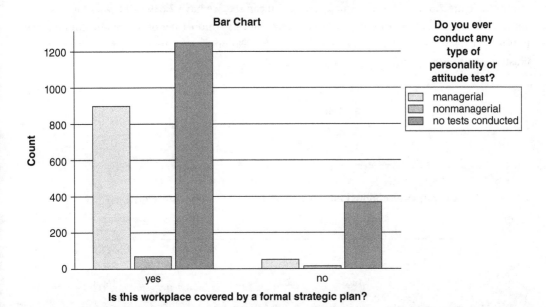

Figure 7.7 Chi-square output, ever conduct personality or attitude test by workplace covered by a formal strategic plan

The next box down, labeled Chi-Square Tests, reports the chi-square statistic and its corresponding p-value. In this case, the chi-square statistic is 132.11 and the p-value is 0.000 (which we would report as $p < 0.001$). In other words, yes, we are able to make that 'quantum leap' from sample to the population. Our two variables are indeed dependent on one another.

Moving further down Figure 7.7, under Symmetric Measures, we can find the effect sizes for this test. Both Phi and Cramer's V happen to be 0.223, indicating a moderate effect size. In other words, the effect of our independent variable on our dependent variable is not terribly strong, but it's certainly not a weak effect, either.

Finally, you can see from the bar chart at the bottom of the output that firms that are covered by a formal strategic plan use very different selection tools compared with those that are not covered by a formal strategic plan, but bear in mind that this chart reports absolute counts, rather than percentages.

And there you have it, your first chi-square test using SPSS! Shall we do another one? I'm going to assume you responded something like, 'Yes, of course! These chi-square tests are awesome!'

Let's think of another nominal outcome variable that may differ based on whether the organization has a formal strategic plan in place. The survey of organizations offers another variable, cptestw1, which asks whether the firm utilizes any performance or competency tests. As with our previous hypothesis, we can likely expect organizations with a strategic plan in place to be more likely to conduct performance or competency tests on employees.

Before you carry out the chi-square test, don't forget to have a look at the frequencies for cptestw1. Go to Analyze, Descriptive Statistics, and Frequencies…. Move the variable into the right-hand column by double clicking and make sure pie chart is ticked under Charts . Then click OK . The output in Figure 7.8 reports the frequencies. As you can see, we have 2,659 valid cases for this variable and 21 missing cases. In total, 51.2% of organizations conduct performance and competency tests for managerial staff, 15.5% for employees, and 33.3% conduct no such tests at all. The pie chart illustrates this distribution.

Statistics

Do you ever conduct any type of performance or competency test?

N	Valid	2659
	Missing	21

Do you ever conduct any type of performance or competency test?

		Frequency	Percent	Valid Percent	Cumulative Percent
Valid	managerial	1362	50.8	51.2	51.2
	non-managerial	411	15.3	15.5	66.7
	no tests conducted	886	33.1	33.3	100.0
	Total	2659	99.2	100.0	
Missing	Don't know	5	.2		
	Item not applicable	16	.6		
	Total	21	.8		
Total		2680	100.0		

Do you ever conduct any type of performance or competency test?

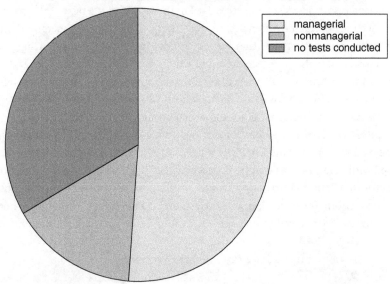

managerial
nonmanagerial
no tests conducted

Figure 7.8 Frequencies, ever conduct performance or competency test

Reprint courtesy of IBM Corporation ©

To conduct the chi-square test, go to Analyze, Descriptive Statistics, and Crosstabs.... In the window depicted in Figure 7.9, you may need to remove the previous variable, catestw1, from Column(s): and replace it with cptestw1. Make sure ☑ Display clustered bar charts is ticked. Also, go into Statistics... and make sure ☑ Chi-square and ☑ Phi and Cramer's V are ticked and then click Continue. Now into Cells... and make sure ☑ Observed, ☑ Expected, and ☑ Row percentages are all ticked. If so, click Continue and then OK.

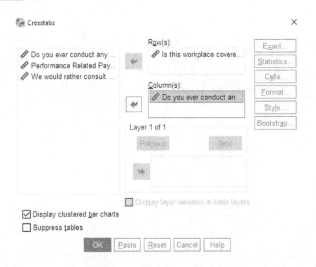

Figure 7.9 Crosstabs function in SPSS

Reprint courtesy of IBM Corporation ©

The results of your chi-square test appear in Figure 7.10. As seen in the Case Processing Summary, we have 28 missing cases and 2652 valid cases used in the test. Looking next at the cross-tabulation, you can again see the observed frequencies, expected frequencies, and the marginals, but our main concern is with the row percentages that we requested. The results once again suggest that organizations with a strategic plan in place are more likely to conduct performance and competency tests. Specifically, it was found that 58.2% of such organizations carry out such tests on managerial employees, compared with only 16.2% in organizations without a formal strategic plan. Curiously, organizations without a strategic plan are more likely to carry out such tests on nonmanagerial employees (21.8% vs. 14.2% in organizations with a formal strategic plan). But organizations without a strategic plan are also much more likely (62.0%) to conduct no performance and competency tests compared with organizations that do have a strategic plan in place (27.6%). Looking at the big picture, this cross-tabulation clearly suggests that, overall, more 'strategic' organizations are more likely to conduct performance and competency tests, but, again, does this finding generalize to the wider population? Are we allowed to make that 'quantum leap' from sample to population?

Case Processing Summary

| | Cases | | | | | |
| | Valid | | Missing | | Total | |
	N	Percent	N	Percent	N	Percent
Is this workplace covered by a formal strategic plan? * Do you ever conduct any type of performance or competency test?	2652	99.0%	28	1.0%	2680	100.0%

Is this workplace covered by a formal strategic plan? * Do you ever conduct any type of performance or competency test? Crosstabulation

| | | | Do you ever conduct any type of performance or competency test? | | | |
			managerial	non-managerial	no tests conducted	Total
Is this workplace covered by a formal strategic plan?	yes	Count	1291	316	613	2220
		Expected Count	1139.3	343.2	737.5	2220.0
		% within Is this workplace covered by a formal strategic plan?	58.2%	14.2%	27.6%	100.0%
	no	Count	70	94	268	432
		Expected Count	221.7	66.8	143.5	432.0
		% within Is this workplace covered by a formal strategic plan?	16.2%	21.8%	62.0%	100.0%
Total		Count	1361	410	881	2652
		Expected Count	1361.0	410.0	881.0	2652.0
		% within Is this workplace covered by a formal strategic plan?	51.3%	15.5%	33.2%	100.0%

Chi-Square Tests

	Value	df	Asymptotic Significance (2-sided)
Pearson Chi-Square	266.250[a]	2	.000
Likelihood Ratio	281.512	2	.000
Linear-by-Linear Association	259.472	1	.000
N of Valid Cases	2652		

a. 0 cells (0.0%) have expected count less than 5. The minimum expected count is 66.79.

Symmetric Measures

		Value	Approximate Significance
Nominal by Nominal	Phi	.317	.000
	Cramer's V	.317	.000
N of Valid Cases		2652	

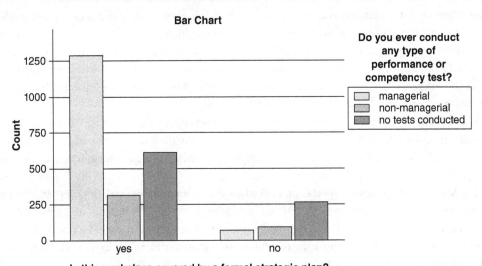

Figure 7.10 Chi-square output, ever conduct performance or competency test by workplace covered by a formal strategic plan

Reprint courtesy of IBM Corporation ©

The next box down reports a chi-square statistic of 266.25 and a corresponding p-value of 0.000, which we would report as $p < 0.001$. This chi-square statistic is even larger than the one from our previous test (132.11), suggesting that we should perhaps find a larger effect size (i.e., strength of relationship). Indeed, when looking at the Phi and Cramer's V statistics in the next box, we find evidence of an even stronger relationship. Both statistics are 0.317, which can be considered evidence of a strong effect size. This can be seen in the bar chart we requested, which appears at the bottom of Figure 7.10. It seems that the relative difference between firms that conduct managerial performance and competency tests and firms that conduct no such tests is reversed across the two categories (those with a formal strategic plan and those without). It would appear, once again, that strategic thinking is associated with more rigorous and sophisticated performance evaluation.

Alternative Nonparametric Tests

There are any number of nonparametric statistical tests. Chi-square, by far, is the most popular and widely used, but it's not the only one at your disposal. Another nonparametric test that's worth learning is the Mann–Whitney U test. This one is a bit like a cross between the independent samples t-test and the chi-square test.

There is a very fine line indeed between the t-test and Mann–Whitney. You'll recall that the independent variable in an independent samples t-test must be nominal with two categories and the dependent variable must be either ordinal or scale. You'll also recall that, as a parametric test, the t-test makes certain assumptions about the shape, or distribution, of the ordinal or scale dependent variable. More specifically, they must be (roughly) normally distributed in the form of a bell curve. But what happens if you are interested in examining differences across an ordinal variable that is not at all normally distributed? In such cases, the independent samples t-test would be inappropriate as the inferences would be potentially invalid in light of distributional nonnormality. But fear not, because the Mann–Whitney test comes to the rescue.

Mann–Whitney requires a two-category nominal independent variable (just like the t-test) and an ordinal dependent variable that can be nonnormally distributed. It essentially asks the same fundamental question as in a t-test: Is there a significant difference in outcomes across these two groups?

The Mann–Whitney test is especially useful when your sample size is small. Recall that, when the sample size is very large, a parametric test can cope with nonnormality because of the central limit theorem, which assumes that the sampling distribution of sample means will be normally distributed. Small samples are rarely normally distributed, so it makes sense to use a statistical method that does not assume normality, like Mann–Whitney.

The mathematical computation of Mann–Whitney U is not something that I consider to be essential learning. In short, instead of calculating and comparing mean scores (as with the t-test), Mann–Whitney calculates the rank-ordering and comparison of scores. The bigger the difference in rank-ordering between the two groups or samples, the more likely the difference is statistically significant. If you're interested in how to do the mathematics of this test 'by hand', you can check out Chapter 11 of Healey (1999). For now, I'll show you how we can instruct SPSS to do the test for us.

To illustrate the Mann–Whitney *U* test using SPSS, we'll be using two variables that can be found in the Chapter 7 dataset: prp (performance-related pay) and antiunion (the extent to which the employer would rather consult directly with employees than with the union). Go into the Variable View for a moment to see how these two variables were measured and coded. Performance-related pay, our independent variable, is coded 1 = *yes* (offered) and 2 = *no* (not offered). Antiunion asks respondents' agreement on whether they would rather consult directly with employees than with unions, where 1 = *strongly disagree*, 2 = *disagree*, 3 = *neither agree nor disagree*, 4 = *agree*, and 5 = *strongly agree*.

Let's stop and think for a moment. We might hypothesize that managers who would prefer to avoid unions and consult directly and individually with employees are also more likely to offer performance-related pay. We could also reason that employers who are more antiunion are also more likely to be successful in avoiding a union, thus facilitating performance-related pay. Let's see if we can corroborate this hypothesis.

First, let's request frequencies for both variables. Go to Analyze, Descriptive Statistics, and Frequencies… . Move both variables to the right. Go into Charts and tick ⊙ Histograms:. Since this is a nonparametric test, you don't need to request means and standard deviations, so click Continue and then OK to produce the output in Figure 7.11. Have a look at the output briefly to familiarize yourself with the two variables. You will note that the histogram for antiunion, our ordinal dependent variable, appears nonnormally distributed, which is not a problem for Mann–Whitney.

Statistics

		Performance Related Pay	We would rather consult employees directly than deal with unions
N	Valid	2676	2667
	Missing	4	13

Frequency Table

Performance Related Pay

		Frequency	Percent	Valid Percent	Cumulative Percent
Valid	yes	1142	42.6	42.7	42.7
	no	1534	57.2	57.3	100.0
	Total	2676	99.9	100.0	
Missing	missing	4	.1		
Total		2680	100.0		

(Continued)

Figure 7.11   (Continued)

We would rather consult employees directly than deal with unions

		Frequency	Percent	Valid Percent	Cumulative Percent
Valid	Strongly Disagree	68	2.5	2.5	2.5
	Disagree	484	18.1	18.1	20.7
	Neither agree nor disagree	436	16.3	16.3	37.0
	Agree	807	30.1	30.3	67.3
	Strongly Agree	872	32.5	32.7	100.0
	Total	2667	99.5	100.0	
Missing	missing	13	.5		
Total		2680	100.0		

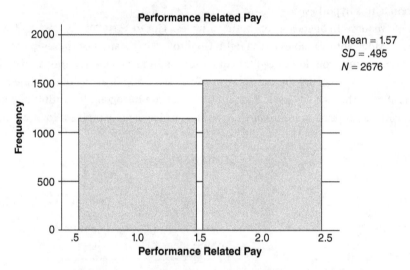

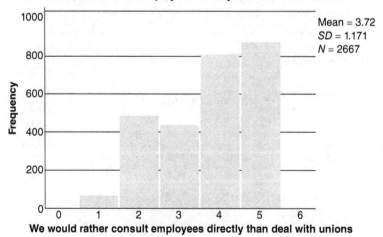

Figure 7.11   Frequencies, performance-related pay and rather consult directly

Now, to carry out the statistical test, go to A̲nalyze, N̲onparametric Tests, L̲egacy Dialogs, and 2̲ Independent Samples…. In the new window shown in Figure 7.12, you will see that Mann–Whitney *U* is already ticked by default under Test Type. Now move antiunion over into the T̲est Variable List: and prp (performance-related pay) over into G̲rouping Variable:. As with the *t*-test, you will now need to click into Define Groups… . Given that prp is coded 1 = *yes* and 2 = *no*, we will enter a 1 and 2, as illustrated in Figure 7.13. When you are ready to see the results of your Mann–Whitney, just click Continue and OK and check out the output in Figure 7.14.

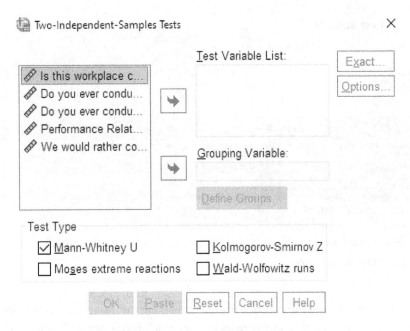

Figure 7.12 Mann–Whitney *U* function in SPSS

Reprint courtesy of IBM Corporation ©

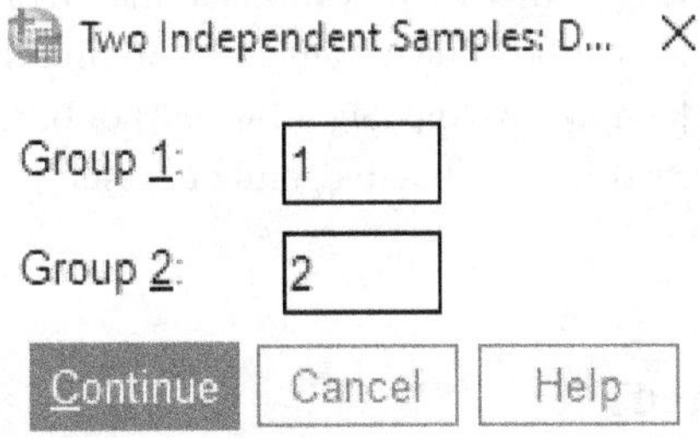

Figure 7.13 Mann–Whitney *U*, Group 1 and Group 2

Reprint courtesy of IBM Corporation ©

Mann-Whitney Test

Ranks

Performance Related Pay		N	Mean Rank	Sum of Ranks
We would rather consult employees directly than deal with unions	yes	1134	1400.52	1588194.00
	no	1529	1281.18	1958922.00
	Total	2663		

Test Statistics[a]

	We would rather consult employees directly than deal with unions
Mann-Whitney U	789237.000
Wilcoxon W	1958922.000
Z	-4.114
Asymp. Sig. (2-tailed)	.000

a. Grouping Variable: Performance Related Pay

Figure 7.14 Mann–Whitney U output, performance-related pay by rather consult directly

Reprint courtesy of IBM Corporation ©

We won't get into the mathematics or meaning underlying the 'Mean Rank'. Basically, you just need to look at the two numbers in that column to determine which is bigger. The bigger mean rank, 1400.52, corresponds to 'yes' (the organization offers performance-related pay), and the smaller mean rank, 1281.18, corresponds to 'no' (the organization does not offer performance-related pay). What this means is that performance-related pay is associated with an increased likelihood of preferring to consult directly with employees, rather than with unions. This result is as we hypothesized; however, we still need to determine whether we can make that 'quantum leap' and generalize to the wider population. Go to the next box down. Here you will find the Mann–Whitney test statistic, 789,237.00, and a p-value [denoted Asymp. Sig. (2-tailed)] of 0.000, which we would report as $p < 0.001$. Therefore, our hypothesis is corroborated, and our result generalizes.

What Have You Learned?

When running nonparametric statistical tests like the chi-square and Mann–Whitney U, forget about means, mean differences, standard deviations, and normal (bell-shaped) distributions. These are all irrelevant. Nonparametric tests are thus nicely suited to research questions that involve nominal variables, ordinal variables, or some combination of the two. They also work quite well when you're dealing with small samples (e.g., less than 200 cases).

The two nonparametric tests described in detail in this chapter, chi-square and Mann–Whitney *U*, are widely used among statisticians and data scientists. The chi-square test works well with nominal and ordinal variables, as long as there are not too many categories. Once a variable has, say, greater than four categories, the test becomes a bit unwieldy and difficult to interpret. The Mann–Whitney *U* test, much like the independent samples *t*-test, requires an independent variable that is nominal with only two categories and a dependent variable that is ordinally measured.

You have done excellent work thus far, my friend. You're shaping up to be a formidable applied statistician! We're now moving onto our last bivariate test in this textbook: simple regression and Pearson's *r*. Both tests are parametric, so we'll once again be concerned with mean scores and standard deviations and normal distributions. Before you move on to the next chapter, take a short break. You've earned it!

Further Reading

Berkson, J. (1938). Some difficulties of interpretation encountered in the application of the chi-square test. *Journal of the American Statistical Association, 33*(203), 526-536.

Franke, T. M., Ho, T., & Christie, C. A. (2012). The chi-square test: Often used and more often misinterpreted. *American Journal of Evaluation, 33*(3), 448-458.

Gibbons, J. D., & Chakraborti, S. (1991). Comparisons of the Mann-Whitney, Student's *t*, and alternate *t* tests for means of normal distributions. *The Journal of Experimental Education, 59*(3), 258-267.

Lewis, D., & Burke, C. J. (1949). The use and misuse of the chi-square test. *Psychological Bulletin, 46*(6), 433-489.

Sharpe, D. (2015). Chi-square test is statistically significant: Now what? *Practical Assessment, Research, and Evaluation, 20*(1), Article 8, 1-10.

In-Class Discussion Questions

1. What is a chi-square test? How is a chi-square statistic calculated and interpreted?
2. What types of variables can and cannot be used in the context of a chi-square test?
3. What is the difference between a parametric statistical test and a nonparametric statistical test? What kind of test is chi-square?
4. List out five research questions that a management scientist might answer using a chi-square test.
5. Further to Question 4, list out the 10 variables associated with those five research questions. Show how you would measure and code those variables in a questionnaire.
6. How would you report the results of a chi-square test? Which statistics would you include and how would you interpret the results?

8

Simple Regression and Pearson's *r*

Regression analysis is, by far, the most commonly used statistical method on planet earth. In this chapter, you will learn all about simple regression and Pearson's *r* correlation coefficient. Both methods are bivariate statistical tests. They are essentially the same method, except for two key differences: (1) simple regression specializes in prediction, whereas Pearson's *r* excels at explanation, and (2) simple regression expresses the relationship between two variables (X and Y) in unstandardized (raw) terms, whereas Pearson's *r* expresses the relationship between X and Y in standardized terms. Don't worry if you don't know what I mean by this just yet. You will understand at the end of the chapter.

Like the previous bivariate tests that we've studied thus far, simple regression and Pearson's *r* correlation coefficient only work with certain types, or combinations, of variables. More specifically, these two tests are designed to look at the relationship between an ordinal or scale-independent variable, X, and an ordinal or scale-dependent variable, Y – although some hardliners will argue that Y must only be scale level. There is one curious exception to this rule – that is, simple regression – and Pearson's *r* can also be used when X is a nominal, two-category variable (also referred to as a dummy variable). We will return to this exception in Chapter 9, where we will learn about multiple regression analysis. Although, in practice, an independent variable in regression analysis can be nominal with two categories, it can never be nominal with more than two categories, and, moreover, the dependent variable, Y, can never be nominal, no matter how many categories. In other words, the outcome variable in a regression analysis must always be ordinal or, preferably, scale. These are the unescapable parameters of the statistical tests we'll be looking at in this chapter.

When carrying out a simple regression or Pearson's *r* test, you will be answering three key questions: (1) Is there a generalizable relationship between X and Y? (2) Is the relationship between X and Y positive, neutral, or negative? (3) How strong is the relationship between X and Y? Let's look at each one of these questions in detail.

With respect to (1), you will almost always find some type of relationship between X and Y in your data, but the key question, as always, pertains to whether that relationship generalizes to the wider population. In carrying out both tests, you will find a 'coefficient' or 'weight' that serves as the result of the test. In simple regression, the coefficient is called 'b,' and in Pearson's r, the coefficient is called (surprise, surprise) 'r.' As with previous tests, attached to these statistics, you will find a p-value. If $p < 0.05$, then we can conclude that the result (b or r) generalizes. Otherwise, we assume that the relationship is simply an artifact of our sample data.

With respect to (2), relationships between X and Y in both tests can be positive, neutral, or negative. Technically, if we find a neutral relationship between X and Y, this implies that the result of the test is not significant. A perfectly neutral result in simple regression is when $b = 0$, and a perfectly neutral result in Pearson's r is when $r = 0$. In both cases, your p-values will necessarily be +0.999 and thus not generalizable. In practice, relationships are rarely found to be perfectly neutral. They are almost always positive or negative, but to varying degrees. A *positive* relationship between X and Y means that, as values of X increase, values in Y also increase. A *negative* relationship between X and Y means that, as values of X increase, values in Y decrease. In simple regression, a positive relationship between X and Y is illustrated by a b coefficient that is a positive number, and a negative relationship is illustrated by a b coefficient that is a negative number. The same is also true for Pearson's r: a positive r implies a positive relationship, and a negative r implies a negative relationship.

With respect to (3), I'm afraid that simple regression, in expressing the relationship between X and Y using coefficient b, isn't able to speak to the strength of the relationship. Because b is an unstandardized (raw) statistic, its value depends on the scales used to measure the two variables. In other words, a higher (or lower) b value in simple regression doesn't always imply a stronger relationship relative to other b values. However, Pearson's r, being what is called a standardized statistic, is a value that is always between -1 and 1. Thus, Pearson's r statistics that are close to 1 and -1 indicate stronger positive and negative relationships, respectively.

In sum, both simple regression and Pearson's r are bivariate tests designed to assess the relationship between X and Y, where both the predictor and outcome variables are ordinal or (preferably) scale in measurement. The relationship between X and Y is expressed by either b or r, two coefficients that also have p-values attached to them. If $b = 0$ and $r = 0$, then there is no relationship between X and Y and thus nothing to generalize. If b and r are positive numbers with statistically significant p-values, then the relationship between X and Y is positive and generalizable. If b and r are negative numbers with statistically significant p-values, then the relationship between X and Y is negative and generalizable.

Correlational Studies in Management Research

If two variables are correlated with one another, they can be said to *covary*. This means that changes in one are associated with concomitant changes in the other. Of course, correlation does not imply causation. In other words, even if we can establish that X is significantly correlated with Y, we still cannot claim that X causes Y. If X is positively correlated with Y, this means that, as X goes up, values in Y also go up. If X is negatively correlated with Y, this means that, as X goes up, values in Y go down.

It's pretty easy to see how we could apply the principle of correlation to various matters that are important to management researchers.

First, let's think of two variables that ought to be positively correlated. Age and income are classic examples. Imagine you've administered a survey asking two questions:

How old are you?

What is your annual income?

Your X variable (age) and your Y variable (income) are both measured at the scale level, so we know that they are appropriate for both simple regression and Pearson's r. In fact, even if you measured both variables ordinally (e.g., age measured as 18–24, 25–34, 35–44 years, and so on and income measured as less than \$5000, \$5001–\$10,000, \$10,001–\$20,000, and so on) they could still both be used in both tests, in theory.

Let's think about our expectations for this test. We might assume that, as age increases, income should also increase, generally speaking. Of course, there may be exceptions. Some people age and make poor career decisions, thus resulting in a lower salary in later life. But, overall, we expect a positive relationship between age and income. As people age, they gain more experience and, therefore, are able to earn more money. To test this relationship, we can run a simple regression and/or a Pearson's r correlation coefficient test. If our coefficients are positive numbers and the p-values associated with them are significant (i.e., $p < 0.05$), then we can assume that the positive relationship we found in our sample generalizes to the population. In fact, this is a widely established finding in the management sciences. Among working age people, as age increases, earning power simultaneously goes up.

We could do a similar kind of thought experiment for variables that we might expect to be negatively related to one another. How about job satisfaction and intention to leave? If we administered a survey to a sample of employees and included these two variables, we would likely expect to find negative coefficients in a simple regression or Pearson's r. In other words, as job satisfaction increases, an employee's intention to leave decreases. Note that this research question could equally be articulated in reverse: as job satisfaction decreases, does intention to leave increase? Real-world data would very likely find this to be true.

Here are some other research questions that could be answered using a simple regression or Pearson's r test:

- Is working hours per week positively correlated with likelihood of burnout? In this case, working hours per week is the independent variable, and likelihood of burnout the dependent variable.
- Is the smelliness of an employee negatively related with number of friends at work? In this case, employee smelliness is the independent variable, and number of friends at work is the dependent variable.
- Is income positively correlated with job satisfaction? In this case, income is the independent variable and job satisfaction, the dependent variable.
- Is income negatively correlated with number of written warnings? In this case, income is again the independent variable, and number of written warnings is the dependent variable.
- Is IQ positively correlated with performance appraisal ratings. In this case, the independent variable is IQ, and the dependent variable is performance appraisal ratings.

- Is body weight negatively correlated with perceived competence? In this case, the independent variable is body weight, and the dependent variable is perceived competence.

- Is organizational commitment positively correlated with working hours per week? In this case, organizational commitment is the independent variable, and working hours per week is the dependent variable.

- Is number of children negatively correlated with productivity? In this case, number of children is the independent variable and some measure of productivity, the dependent variable.

- Is shop floor cleanliness positively correlated with a consumer's propensity to consume? In this case, shop floor cleanliness is the independent variable and propensity to consume, the dependent variable.

- Is number of hours of health and safety training negatively correlated with number of accidents at work? In this case, the independent variable is number of hours of health and safety training, and the dependent variable is number of accidents.

- Is employee attractiveness positively correlated with income? In this case, the independent variable is attractiveness, and the dependent variable is income.

You will have likely noticed that the common thread across all the variables in these research questions is that they are all ordinal or scale in measurement. Let's take a closer look at the last question in this list to illustrate the foundations of regression analysis.

Basic Concepts in Regression Analysis

The best way to get your head around regression analysis is through visualizing the relationship between your two variables. But first, let's think about how we might measure attractiveness and income.

You might be tempted to administer a survey asking respondents to rate themselves on attractiveness using a Likert scale (say, 1 = *not at all attractive* to 7 = *extremely attractive*). Is this really attractiveness, though? One could argue that self-reports of attractiveness do not necessarily measure attractiveness. Relying on self-reports would introduce *common method bias* (CMB), also referred to as *common method variance* (CMV). CMB (or CMV) is defined as a systematic error in measurement that typically happens when only one method of data collection is used. To get around this problem, let's imagine that we took photographs of 20 respondents and then asked 100 people to rate them on perceived attractiveness using the same 1 to 7 scale as above. We then average these scores, creating 20 separate averages for each individual depicted in the photograph. Boom! We have just measured our independent variable, X. Our dependent variable, Y, is easier to measure. We ask the 20 respondents to report their yearly income. Let's say we collected the following (hypothetical) data depicted in Table 8.1.

To visualize the relationship between X and Y, we create a scatterplot. A *scatterplot* is a two-dimensional graph with the independent variable, X, plotted along the horizontal X-axis and the dependent variable, Y, plotted along the vertical Y-axis. Figure 8.1 depicts this graph. As you can see, there appears to be a generally positive relationship between attractiveness and income. In other words, as we move along the X-axis (from less attractive to more attractive), income also appears to move in an upward direction: as attractiveness increases, so does income. But 'eye-balling' a bunch of dots on a graph isn't very scientific now, is it?

Table 8.1 Attractiveness and income data

Respondent	Attractiveness score	Income (USD)
1	4.26	57,000
2	3.56	38,000
3	6.58	78,000
4	3.44	34,000
5	2.12	50,000
6	4.18	45,000
7	3.12	24,000
8	6.22	72,000
9	3.00	34,000
10	4.34	38,000
11	1.78	45,000
12	5.97	60,000
13	3.78	38,000
14	4.55	49,000
15	4.04	42,000
16	6.99	58,000
17	2.66	22,000
18	4.07	35,000
19	6.71	72,000
20	4.00	44,000

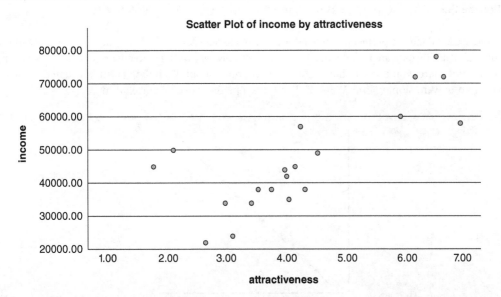

Figure 8.1 Scatterplot displaying relationship between attractiveness and income

If you really want to understand the relationship between attractiveness and income, you will need to impose a line-of-best-fit on this scatterplot. The *line-of-best-fit*, also referred to as the *least-squares regression line*, can be defined, in this context, as a straight line through the data with the minimal distance between the line and each data point, where this distance is referred to as a *residual*. In other words, the best-fit line comes as close as possible to the dots in the scatterplot. Figure 8.2 depicts the same data points as in Figure 8.1; only this time, I have included the line-of-best-fit among the data points. The fact that the line slopes upward, from left to right, confirms that the relationship between *X* and *Y* is positive. Note that we still don't know if this result generalizes or not. That is a question for *p*-values to determine, and we'll get to that soon enough. But for now, I want you to understand what a positive, neutral, and negative relationship in regression analysis look like.

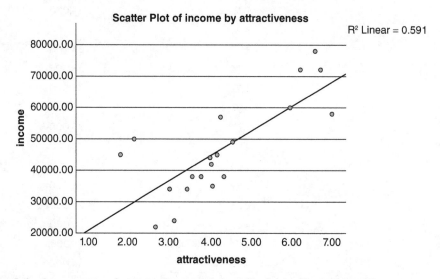

Figure 8.2 Same scatterplot as in Figure 8.1, but displaying line-of-best-fit

Figure 8.3 depicts a perfect positive relationship between *X* and *Y*. This is, of course, purely hypothetical. Real-life data are full of variation and noise and very unlikely to create such a clean-looking scatterplot. Here, you can see that there are no residuals at all. Each data point is situated perfectly along an upward sloping line. We would call this a perfect positive correlation.

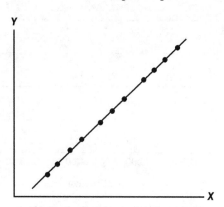

Figure 8.3 Perfect positive correlation

Figure 8.4 depicts a strong positive relationship between X and Y. As you can see, there are some residuals here, but generally speaking, the data points cluster nicely along the line-of-best-fit, and the line itself is upward sloping, again suggesting that as X increases, so does Y.

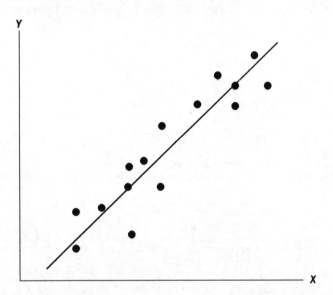

Figure 8.4 Strong positive correlation

Figure 8.5 depicts a weak positive relationship between X and Y. The residuals are quite sizeable, with significant distance between the line-of-best-fit and the data points. But you can still see a weak upward slope here.

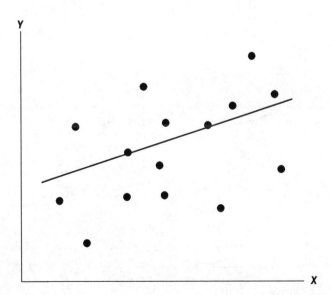

Figure 8.5 Weak positive correlation

Figure 8.6 depicts a perfectly neutral relationship between X and Y. Again, this is purely hypothetical. In the real world, we would be unlikely to encounter a correlation of zero. We know that this is a neutral relationship because the line-of-best-fit is perfectly horizontal. That is, as X increases, there is no effect (positive or negative) on Y. The two variables appear to be completely unrelated to each other.

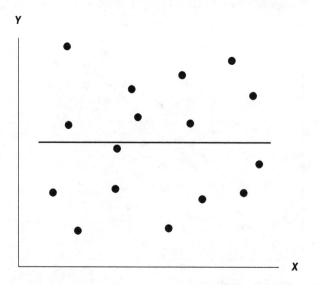

Figure 8.6 No (or neutral) correlation

Figure 8.7 depicts a weak negative relationship between X and Y. The distribution of the data points is similar to that in Figure 8.5 in terms of residuals; only, this time, you can identify a slight downward slope, indicating that as X increases, values in Y decrease.

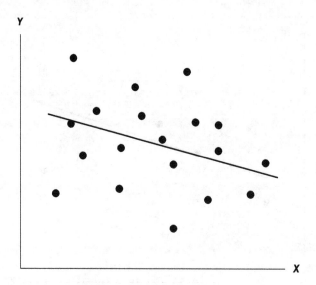

Figure 8.7 Weak negative correlation

Figure 8.8 depicts a strong negative relationship between X and Y. The residuals are relatively small, and most of the data points cluster around a downward sloping line.

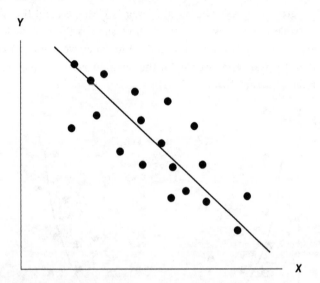

Figure 8.8 Strong negative correlation

Finally, Figure 8.9 depicts a perfect negative relationship between X and Y. All the data points sit on a downward sloping line-of-best-fit. For every one-unit increase in X, there is a corresponding decrease in Y.

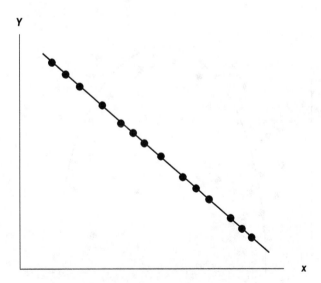

Figure 8.9 Perfect negative correlation

You will note that all the lines in Figures 8.3 through 8.9 are straight lines. This is because regression analysis is predicated on the assumption that the relationship between X and Y is linear. Of course, in reality, many bivariate relationships are curvilinear. Figures 8.10 and 8.11 illustrate what are called quadratic regression lines, where the former is U-shaped and the latter is an inverted U-shape. It is also possible to fit a cubic regression line, such as the one depicted in Figure 8.12. Curvilinear regression is a pretty advanced method, so for now, we're going to set nonlinear relationships between X and Y aside and assume, for the remainder of this chapter, that we're dealing exclusively with variables that are linearly related.

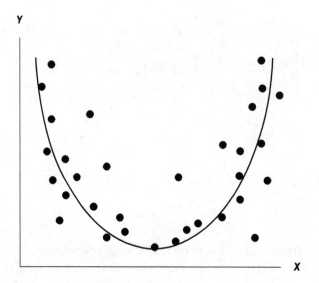

Figure 8.10 Quadratic U-shaped curvilinear relationship

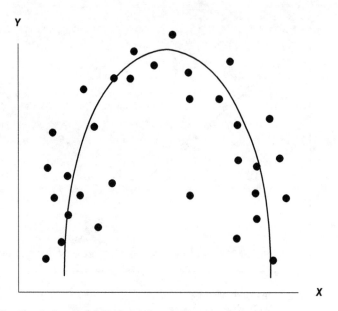

Figure 8.11 Quadratic inverted U-shaped curvilinear relationship

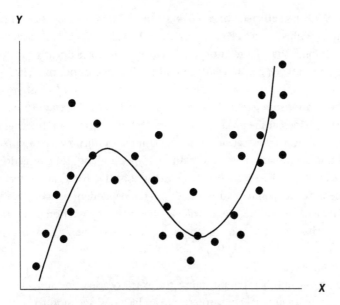

Figure 8.12 Cubic regression line

The Mathematics Underlying Simple Regression

How can we accurately estimate the line-of-best-fit in a scatterplot? Surely, there must be a way in which we can mathematically capture the linear relationship between (any) *X* and (any) *Y*, right? I'm so glad you asked! Yes, there is a mathematical formula for describing the best linear relationship between two ordinal- or preferably scale-level variables. In fact, you may very well already be familiar with Equation (8.1).

$$Y = bX + a + e \qquad\qquad\qquad (8.1)$$

In this equation,

    Y = the dependent variable

    b = the slope

    X = the independent variable

    a = the *y*-intercept

    e = an error term

You already know all about *X* and *Y*, but you may or may not be familiar with the other components of the simple regression equation. Let's look at them one at a time.

As noted above, b is a coefficient that refers to the slope of the regression line. If the slope is perfectly horizontal (as illustrated in Figure 8.6), then the value of b is necessarily zero. If b is a positive number, this implies that the relationship between X and Y is linearly positive: that is, when X increases, Y also increases. If b is a negative number, this means that the relationship between X and Y is linearly negative: that is, as X increases, Y decreases. Note that a positive or negative b does not mean that the relationship generalizes to the population in this way. To make such an inference, we would have to look at the p-value associated with the coefficient. In other words, a positive or negative b only indicates a positive or negative relationship within your sample. The best way to describe b is that it is a number that says something important about the directional nature of the relationship between X and Y. A b coefficient, whether positive or negative, speaks to the type of association between the independent variable, X, and the dependent variable, Y. It should be noted that the value of b depends on the scale of the variables used in Equation (8.1). Thus, b is going to be a larger number when using income measured as a true scale than when income is measured as an ordinal variable (e.g., 1 = *$0 to $10,000 per annum*, 2 = *$10,001 to $25,000 per annum*, 3 = *$25,001 to $40,000 per annum*, etc.).

The y-intercept, a, is a number that pinpoints the exact location on the Y-axis where the line-of-best-fit (described by b) touches it. The y-intercept can be a positive number or a negative number, as illustrated in Figures 8.13a and b, respectively. This number, a, doesn't describe the relationship between X and Y, so it's not terribly important for purposes of explanation. However, as we'll soon find out, it is essential if you want to use Equation (8.1) for purposes of predicting a value of Y based on a value of X. You cannot make any predictions without first knowing the value of the y-intercept.

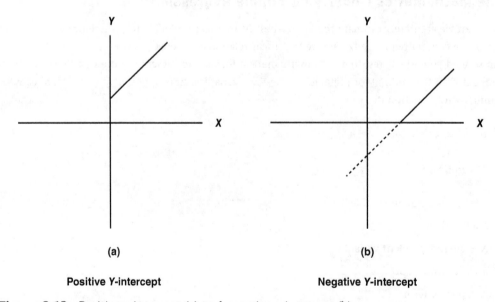

(a)   (b)

Positive Y-intercept   Negative Y-intercept

Figure 8.13 Positive y-intercept (a) and negative y-intercept (b)

Finally, e is appended to the end of Equation (8.1). In fact, it's not essential and doesn't really need to be there at all. So, let's drop it and use Equation (8.2) instead:

$$Y = bX + a \qquad\qquad (8.2)$$

The e in Equation (8.1) refers to an *error term*, which is basically all the other factors, apart from X, that also influence Y. Think about an error term in this way. We're assuming that X explains some of the variation in Y, but certainly not *all* the variation in Y. For example, attractiveness may predict income, but there are myriad other factors, or variables, that also predict income (such as education, father's income, mother's income, IQ, conscientiousness, etc.). In short, the e in Equation (8.1) refers to all those other variables. The error term simply demonstrates that you are aware that an infinite number of other factors covary with Y, not just X, and that you obviously haven't included all of them in your equation. But, again, it is not mathematically necessary to include e in your equation because it is not a number or statistic and it cannot ever be measured. So, for now, let's just leave it aside.

You might be wondering at this stage how to calculate b and a. Well, ask and you shall receive. We'll start with the computational equation for b because we first need to compute b in order to subsequently compute a.

Due to the fact that we can employ any number of algebraic transformations, there are several ways of expressing the formula for calculating the slope, b. But no matter which equation we use, all formulas essentially examine the nature of the relationship between X and Y. Equation (8.3) expresses what I consider to be the clearest mathematical expression of covariation between X and Y.

$$b = \frac{N\Sigma XY - (\Sigma X)(\Sigma Y)}{N\Sigma X^2 - (\Sigma X)^2} \qquad\qquad (8.3)$$

where

b = slope

N = total number of cases in the sample

ΣXY = addition of the cross-products of X and Y

ΣX = addition of all the scores of X

ΣY = addition of all the scores of Y

ΣX^2 = addition of the squared scores of X

Now, don't panic. It looks like there is a heck of lot going on in this equation, but it's pretty manageable if we break it down into its individual parts and use a calculation table. To illustrate how to calculate b, we first need some data. Let's use the data from Table 8.1, looking at the relationship between attractiveness (X) and income (Y).

Table 8.2 Calculation table for b

Respondent	X	Y	X²	XY
1	4.26	57,000	18.15	242,820
2	3.56	38,000	12.67	135,280
3	6.58	78,000	43.30	513,240
4	3.44	34,000	11.83	116,960
5	2.12	50,000	4.49	106,000
6	4.18	45,000	17.47	188,100
7	3.12	24,000	9.73	74,880
8	6.22	72,000	38.69	447,840
9	3.00	34,000	9.00	102,000
10	4.34	38,000	18.84	164,920
11	1.78	45,000	3.17	80,100
12	5.97	60,000	35.64	358,200
13	3.78	38,000	14.29	143,640
14	4.55	49,000	20.70	222,950
15	4.04	42,000	16.32	169,680
16	6.99	58,000	48.86	405,420
17	2.66	22,000	7.08	58,520
18	4.07	35,000	16.56	142,450
19	6.71	72,000	45.02	483,120
20	4.00	44,000	16.00	176,000
$N = 20$	$\Sigma X = 85.37$	$\Sigma Y = 935,000$	$\Sigma X^2 = 407.81$	$\Sigma XY = 4,332,120$

To simplify the calculation of b, we create Table 8.2.

You will notice that the first three columns of this table are identical to those in Table 8.1. From the first column, we already know one of the key values to use in Equation (8.3): $N = 20$, because there are 20 subjects in our sample. The second and third columns are the raw scores of X and Y, respectively, with the sum of these scores listed at the bottom of the columns. The fourth column reports the square of every value of X and the sum of the square of every value of X at the bottom. The last column lists the product of X and Y, with the sum of XY at the bottom. With all these numbers in place, we are now in a position to simply plug the relevant values into Equation (8.3). Thus,

$$b = \frac{N\Sigma XY - (\Sigma X)(\Sigma Y)}{N\Sigma X^2 - (\Sigma X)^2}$$

$$b = \frac{(20)(4,332,120) - (85.37)(935,000)}{(20)(407.81) - (85.37)^2}$$

$$b = \frac{86,642,400 - 79,820,950}{8156.20 - 7288.04}$$

$$b = \frac{86,642,400 - 79,820,950}{8156.20 - 7288.04}$$

$$b = \frac{6821,450}{868.16}$$

$$b = 7857.37$$

See? I told you it wasn't that hard! You've just calculated your first slope. Ace work!

Now, how do we interpret a b of 7857.37? Remember that the outcome variable, income, is in US dollars. Therefore, if $b = 7857.37$, this implies that, for every unit increase in X, attractiveness, participants enjoy an extra $7857.37 in income. Hence, it pays to be good looking! Because the line-of-best-fit is linear, this increase holds at every increase in X. For example, if we compare participants with an attractiveness score of 1 and 2, the person rated as a 2 on attractiveness will make, according to our model, $7857.37 more per year than a person rated as 1. Similarly, if we compare participants with an attractiveness score of 4 and 5, the person rated as a 5 on attractiveness will earn, according to our model, $7857.37 more per year than a person rated as a 4. The value of b, as noted above, says something about the nature of the relationship between X and Y. In this case, the fact that we found a positive number in our slope implies a positive relationship between X and Y; as X increases, so does Y. If, hypothetically, we had found that b was a negative number, then this would imply a negative relationship between X and Y. But, again, whether this relationship generalizes to the wider population depends on the corresponding p-value, which we'll get to shortly. For now, I just want you to understand how to solve Equation (8.3).

You'll notice that, although we've solved for b, we still don't know the value of a, our y-intercept. The equation we use to solve for a is described in Equation (8.4).

$$a = \bar{Y} - b\bar{X} \tag{8.4}$$

Solving for the y-intercept is pretty easy. We already know $b = 7857.37$, so we just need to calculate the mean of Y, also known as $\bar{Y}$ (pronounced Y-bar), and the mean of X, also known as $\bar{X}$ (pronounced X-bar).

To calculate $\bar{Y}$, just take the sum of the Y scores divided by the total number of cases in the sample. Looking at Table 8.2, you can see that the sum of $Y = 935,000$, and the total number of cases = 20. Therefore, $\bar{Y} = 935,000/20 = 46,750$.

To calculate $\bar{X}$, just take the sum of the X scores divided by the total number of cases in the sample. Looking once again at Table 8.2, the sum of $X = 85.37$, and the total number of cases = 20. Therefore, $\bar{X} = 85.37/20 = 4.27$.

Now simply plug the numbers into Equation (8.4) to find the y-intercept.

$$a = \bar{Y} - b\bar{X} \tag{8.4}$$

$$a = 46,750 - (7857.37)(4.27)$$

$$a = 46,750 - 33,550.97$$

$$a = 13,199.03$$

In other words, the line-of-best-fit, with a slope of 7857.37, touches the Y-axis at 13,199.03. Boom! You've just modeled your first simple regression equation. How does it feel to be such a superstar?

What's great about simple regression is that, once you've calculated b and a, you can then use the equation for purposes of predicting values of Y given a hypothetical value of X. Let me show you what I mean. If you look through Table 8.2, you'll see that the person with the lowest attractiveness value is participant 11, with an attractiveness value of 1.79 (again, on a seven-point scale). What if we were interested in estimating the income of some hypothetical person with an attractiveness value of 1.00 (corresponding to 'not at all attractive')? In this case, we could simply assign a value of 1.00 to X, our attractiveness variable, to predict what his or her income, Y' (pronounced Y prime), would be.

Thus,

$Y' = bX + a$

$Y' = (7857.37)(1) + 13,199.03$

$Y' = 7857.37 + 13,199.03$

$Y' = 21,056.40$

In other words, according to our line-of-best-fit, if an individual had an attractiveness (X) value of 1 ('not at all attractive'), then we can assume, based on the slope, b, and y-intercept, a, that his or her yearly income is likely to be around \$21,056.40. Of course, this is only an estimate. We cannot predict Y' with 100% accuracy. But we are likely to be much closer to the actual value than if we were just guessing without access to the data.

The fact that we can use the values of b and a for purposes of prediction is a real strength of simple regression. However, there is also a major limitation of this method of expressing the relationship between X and Y – namely, that b is not an indicator of the *strength* of the relationship between X and Y. A larger b value does not necessarily imply a stronger relationship. The reason for this is that the value of b depends on the scale used to measure the dependent variable, Y. In the case of the example we've been looking at, our b value is comparatively large because we've measured income as our outcome variable. If our outcome was, like our independent variable, another seven-point ordinal scale, then our value of b is likely to be much smaller.

Although the slope in simple regression cannot speak to the strength of the relationship between X and Y, there is another 'sister' method we can estimate that can: Pearson's r correlation coefficient.

The Mathematics Underlying Pearson's *r*

Whereas the b in simple regression is an unstandardized coefficient (meaning it has, technically, an unlimited scale and is dependent on Y values), Pearson's r is a standardized coefficient. Accordingly, r is always a value between -1 and 1, where -1 implies a perfect negative correlation (see Figure 8.9),

0 implies no correlation (see Figure 8.6), and 1 implies a perfect positive correlation (see Figure 8.3). The fact that r cannot, mathematically speaking, ever be larger than 1 or smaller than -1 means that we can evaluate the strength of the relationship (positive or negative) between X and Y by looking at how close the coefficient gets to 1 or -1. The closer r gets to 1 or -1, the stronger the positive or negative relationship, respectively.

As with simple regression, there are several formulas that can be used to calculate r, but the easiest one is that found in Equation (8.5):

$$r = \frac{N\Sigma XY - (\Sigma X)(\Sigma Y)}{\sqrt{[N\Sigma X^2 - (\Sigma X)^2][N\Sigma Y^2 - (\Sigma Y)^2]}} \tag{8.5}$$

where

r = Pearson's r correlation coefficient

N = number of cases in the sample

ΣXY = addition of the cross-products of X and Y

ΣX = addition of all the scores of X

ΣY = addition of all the scores of Y

ΣX^2 = addition of the squared scores of X

$(\Sigma X)^2$ = addition of all the scores of X, squared

ΣY^2 = addition of the squared scores of Y

$(\Sigma Y)^2$ = addition of the scores of Y, squared

This is probably the most complicated equation we've covered in this book, but even then, it's not that complicated. As with Equation (8.3), we can simplify it by using a table and breaking it down into its constituent parts. In fact, we could almost use Table 8.2, as it contains all the values we need, except for Y^2. To make the calculation of r easier, I have reproduced Table 8.2 and included an extra column for Y^2 (see Table 8.3).

From Table 8.3, we get the following:

$N = 20$

$\Sigma X = 85.37$

$\Sigma Y = 935,000$

$\Sigma X^2 = 407.81$

$\Sigma Y^2 = 48,245,000,000$

$\Sigma XY = 4,332,120$

Table 8.3 Calculation table for r

Respondent	X	Y	X²	Y²	XY
1	4.26	57,000	18.15	3,249,000,000	242,820
2	3.56	38,000	12.67	1,444,000,000	135,280
3	6.58	78,000	43.30	6,084,000,000	513,240
4	3.44	34,000	11.83	1,156,000,000	116,960
5	2.12	50,000	4.49	2,500,000,000	106,000
6	4.18	45,000	17.47	2,025,000,000	188,100
7	3.12	24,000	9.73	576,000,000	74,880
8	6.22	72,000	38.69	5,184,000,000	447,840
9	3.00	34,000	9.00	1,156,000,000	102,000
10	4.34	38,000	18.84	1,444,000,000	164,920
11	1.78	45,000	3.17	2,025,000,000	80,100
12	5.97	60,000	35.64	3,600,000,000	358,200
13	3.78	38,000	14.29	1,444,000,000	143,640
14	4.55	49,000	20.70	2,401,000,000	222,950
15	4.04	42,000	16.32	1,764,000,000	169,680
16	6.99	58,000	48.86	3,364,000,000	405,420
17	2.66	22,000	7.08	484,000,000	58,520
18	4.07	35,000	16.56	1,225,000,000	142,450
19	6.71	72,000	45.02	5,184,000,000	483,120
20	4.00	44,000	16.00	1,936,000,000	176,000

With these values, you can now simply plug the numbers into Equation (8.5) to calculate r. Before we calculate r, we already know that the value will be a positive number (because our slope, b, is a positive number) that is greater than 0 but less than 1. Let's calculate r using the values in Table 8.3.

$$r = \frac{N \sum XY - (\sum X)(\sum Y)}{\sqrt{\left[N \sum X^2 - (\sum X)^2 \right]\left[N \sum Y^2 - (\sum Y)^2 \right]}}$$

$$r = \frac{(20)(4,332,120) - (85.37)(935,000)}{\sqrt{\left[(20)(407.81) - (85.37)^2 \right]\left[(20)(48,245,000,000) - (935,000)^2 \right]}}$$

$$r = \frac{86,642,400 - 79,820,950}{\sqrt{\left[8156.20 - 7288.04 \right]\left[964,900,000,000 - 874,225,000,000 \right]}}$$

$$r = \frac{6,821,450}{\sqrt{\left[868.16 \right]\left[90,645,000,000 \right]}}$$

$$r = \frac{6{,}821{,}450}{\sqrt{78{,}694{,}363{,}200{,}000}}$$

$$r = \frac{6{,}821{,}450}{8{,}870{,}984.34}$$

$$r = 0.77$$

As you can see, our Pearson's r correlation coefficient is indeed a positive number (indicating a positive relationship between attractiveness and income), and it is less than 1. There are no hard and fast rules in terms of the strength of the relationship between X and Y, but, generally speaking, a Pearson's r value of 0.7 or –0.7 is considered strong; 0.5 or –0.5 is moderate; and 0.3 or –0.3 is considered weak. These figures are just indicative, and, ultimately, you should refer to your corresponding p-value to determine whether the result (positive or negative) generalizes (more on this in the next section).

A very useful statistic deriving from r is called the coefficient of determination. The *coefficient of determination* is defined as the amount of variation in Y explained by X. It's also very easy to calculate: you simply square your calculation of r:

Coefficient of determination = r^2

Given that the r we just calculated is 0.77, $r^2 = 0.59$. If we convert 0.59 into a percentage (100×0.59), we get 59%. The way we would interpret this coefficient of determination is that our independent variable, attractiveness, explains 59% of the total variation in our dependent variable, income. Another way of saying this is that 41% of the variation in income is explained by factors other than one's attractiveness.

Think about the coefficient of determination in this way. Every dependent variable, Y, has variation. Some participants will score higher on Y, and others will score lower. We want to understand how scores on Y covary with scores on X. Therefore, we divide the variation in Y into two components. *Systematic variation* refers to the scores on Y that are explained as a function of the scores on X. *Stochastic variation* refers to the unexplained variation in Y, which can be attributed to all the other variables that were not included in your model or, alternatively stated, to your error term, e, included in Equation (8.1). Stochastic variation in Y is random, whereas systematic variation in Y is explainable by virtue of one's scores on X. In this case, 59% of one's income is attributable to attractiveness, with the remaining 41% attributable to the many other factors that also covary with income, such as, education, IQ, conscientiousness, working hours per week, and so on.

All else being equal, the coefficient of determination is a useful indicator in terms of understanding how important X is. Obviously, if $r = 0$, then $r^2 = 0$, meaning that your independent variable explains 0% of Y. Similarly, if $r = 1$ or $r = -1$, then $r^2 = 1$, meaning that your independent variable explains 100% of the variation in Y. The higher your r^2 value, the stronger your explanatory regression model.

Okay, hot shot. I think you now have a strong understanding of simple regression and Pearson's r correlation coefficient, at least a strong enough one to know that doing the math by hand is no good. So, let's learn how to use IBM SPSS Statistics Software (SPSS) to carry out these two statistical tests.

Pearson's *r* and Simple Regression Using SPSS

Let's start by learning how to use SPSS to carry out a Pearson's *r* correlation coefficient test, and then, we'll learn how to do a simple regression. In my view, Pearson's *r* is, ironically, simpler than a 'simple' regression.

First, we need to open the dataset. We'll be using the survey of employees for both these tests covered in this chapter. Go to the online Companion Website and open file chap8data. Before we begin, you should satisfy yourself that all the variables in this file are either ordinal or scale in measurement. This can be verified by going into Variable View and checking the second column from the right, labeled Measure.

Let's start with the assumption, or hypothesis, that when managers are perceived to listen to employees and give them a voice at work, employees are likely to report higher levels of job satisfaction. In other words, we are assuming a positive relationship between the provision of voice at work and job satisfaction: as the amount of voice given increases, so does job satisfaction, or, alternatively stated, the more managers listen to employees, the higher the employees' job satisfaction. This makes sense, right?

In the Variable View, have a look at our independent variable, voice1, and our dependent variable, jobsatcomp. Recall that job satisfaction is measured using eight items:

The dependent variable in this dataset, jobsatcomp, is a composite measure of these eight items, meaning that we added them all together and divided by eight. I've already done this for you, but if you'd like to do this yourself using chap8data, follow the instructions in Box 8.1.

Box 8.1: Creating the
Job Satisfaction Composite Variable

The survey of employees contains 8 single item indicators of job satisfaction:

1. jobsat1: How satisfied are you with . . . The sense of achievement from work?
2. jobsat2: How satisfied are you with . . . The scope for using your own initiative?
3. jobsat3: How satisfied are you with . . . The amount of influence you have over the job?
4. jobsat4: How satisfied are you with . . . The training you receive?
5. jobsat5: How satisfied are you with . . . The opportunity to develop your skills in your job?
6. jobsat6: How satisfied are you with . . . The amount of pay you receive?
7. jobsat7: How satisfied are you with . . . Your job security?
8. jobsat8: How satisfied are you with . . . The work itself?

Each variable is measured on a five-point Likert scale, such that 1 = *strongly disagree*, 2 = *disagree*, 3 = *neither agree nor disagree*, 4 = *agree*, and 5 = *strongly agree*.

What we want to do is to create a single composite variable that incorporates all eight dimensions of job satisfaction. We will call this new composite job satisfaction variable *jobsatcomp*. To create a composite variable, we simply add all the scores of all eight variables together and divide by 8. Technically, we don't have to divide by 8, but we will do this to maintain the original five-point scale. If we don't divide by eight, the composite variable will have a low score of 8 (e.g., for respondents who answered 'strongly disagree' on all eight items: $1+1+1+1+1+1+1+1 = 8$) and a high score of 40 (e.g., for respondents who answered 'strongly agree' on all eight items: $5 + 5 + 5 + 5 + 5 + 5 + 5 = 40$).

To create our composite job satisfaction variable in SPSS, go to Transform and then Compute Variable. Under Target Variable:, write jobsatcomp. Now you need to tell SPSS that you want to add all the eight job satisfaction variables together and divide by 8. You can do this using the point-and-click method and the calculator in the window, but it's easier simply to write out the following equation under Numeric Expression:

(jobsat1 + jobsat2 + jobsat3 + jobsat4 + jobsat5 + jobsat6 + jobsat7 + jobsat8)/8

When you are ready to create your composite, click OK . Boom! You just created a composite variable called jobsatcomp! Don't forget to go into Variable View and include your Values and Missing values.

The independent variable, voice1, posits: 'Managers here . . . Are sincere in attempting to understand employees' views' and asks respondents to report on a five-point scale whether they *strongly agree = 5, agree = 4, neither agree nor disagree = 3, disagree = 2,* or *strongly disagree = 1.*

Before we run the Pearson's *r* test, go ahead and request frequency distributions and descriptive statistics for both variables. I'm not going to report the tables here because you should already be a pro at this, but just to jog your memory, you can request these by going to Analyze, Descriptive Statistics, and Frequencies. Move voice1 (found at the top of the list of variables) and jobsatcomp (found at the bottom of the list of variables) from the left column to the right column. Go into Statistics and tick ☑ Mean and ☑ Std. deviation, and then click Continue . Now go into Charts and tick ◉ Histograms: and ☑ Show normal curve on histogram. Click Continue and then OK .

Looking at the output, you should see that voice1 has a mean of 3.40 and a standard deviation of 1.06; jobsatcomp has a mean of 3.56 and a standard deviation of 0.72. Both distributions are reasonably normally distributed, at least at first glance.

At this point, we're now ready to carry out our Pearson's r correlation coefficient test. It is very simple. Go to Analyze, Correlate, and Bivariate. The window depicted in Figure 8.14 appears. Identify your two variables of interest, voice1 and jobsatcomp, in the left-hand column and move them to the right-hand column by either double clicking them or using ➡ . Note that there is no particular order in which you need to do this, but typically, we would place the independent variable, voice1, first and the dependent variable, jobsatcomp, second. You will notice that, by default, under Correlation Coefficients, ☑ Pearson is ticked. Under Test of Significance, ◉ Two-tailed is also the default. Two-tailed tests are generally preferable to one-tailed ones because they are more conservative and less prone to Type I error. Finally, ☑ Flag significant correlations is also ticked by default, so that our output will tell us whether or not the Pearson's r correlation coefficient is statistically significant and thus generalizable to the wider population. Now go into Options and tick ☑ Means and standard deviations . You already requested this information above, but I thought I'd show you this useful shortcut. You should also tick ◉ Exclude cases listwise, and then Continue and OK . Boom! You've just run your first Pearson's r test!

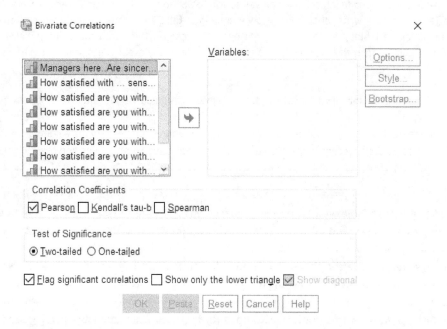

Figure 8.14 Bivariate correlations function in SPSS

Have a look at the output depicted in Figure 8.15. Below the descriptive statistics, you will find a correlations table. It is a 2 × 2 table, with both variables listed in the columns and the rows. In summary, there are four Pearson's *r* values reported here, but two are redundant. The key correlation coefficient is 0.579, which describes the nature of the relationship between voice1 and jobsatcomp. The '**' after the Pearson's *r* coefficient indicates that this result is statistically significant and thus generalizable from the sample to the population. A Pearson's *r* of 0.579 can be considered a moderate correlation between *X* and *Y*, as described in Table 8.4.

Descriptive Statistics

	Mean	Std. Deviation	N
Managers here..Are sincere in attempting to understand employees' views	3.40	1.060	20339
Job Satisfaction Composite Variable	3.5568	.72143	20339

Correlations[b]

		Managers here..Are sincere in attempting to understand employees' views	Job Satisfaction Composite Variable
Managers here..Are sincere in attempting to understand employees' views	Pearson Correlation	1	.579**
	Sig. (2-tailed)		.000
Job Satisfaction Composite Variable	Pearson Correlation	.579**	1
	Sig. (2-tailed)	.000	

**. Correlation is significant at the 0.01 level (2-tailed).

b. Listwise N=20339

Figure 8.15 Descriptive statistics and correlation between managers are sincere in attempting to understand employees' views and job satisfaction composite variable

Reprint courtesy of IBM Corporation ©

Table 8.4 Pearson's *r* effect sizes

	Pearson's r coefficient
Very weak	0.00–0.19
Weak	0.20–0.39
Moderate	0.40–0.59
Strong	0.60–0.79
Very strong	0.80–1.00

The way we interpret a correlation of 0.579 is that, as voice increases, job satisfaction also increases. Thus, our hypothesis is confirmed. Voice1 can be said to be moderately, albeit significantly, positively correlated with job satisfaction.

You will also notice in the correlations table that job satisfaction and job satisfaction are correlated at 1.00 and, in similar vein, voice1 and voice1 are correlated at 1.00. This information is useless to us, for all practical purposes, but it does shed some light on the nature of Pearson's r. It makes sense that if we are correlating the same variable with itself, it should have a perfect correlation. Bearing in mind that all Pearson's r values are necessarily between –1 and 1, we can see from the table that correlating a variable with itself must result in a perfect positive correlation, and indeed, this can be confirmed in the table. But, again, the key correlation that we use to answer our research question is the one between voice1 and job satisfaction: 0.579 (where $p = 0.000$, which we would report as $p < 0.001$).

Now let's say we want to see if some other voice variables are similarly positively correlated with job satisfaction. We might do these extra analyses to see if employee voice is 'robustly' positively correlated with job satisfaction. There are three other voice variables in this dataset whose effects we can evaluate. These are voice2, voice3, and voice4. Rather than examining these one at a time, I'm going to show you how to evaluate them simultaneously, alongside voice1.

The three variables, voice2, voice3, and voice4, are measured as follows:

In fact, these three measures are imperfect, as described in Timming (2009), but they are good enough for our purposes.

Go ahead and request the descriptive statistics and frequency distributions for these variables before carrying out the Pearson's r tests. Again, I'm not going to reproduce these data here because you should already know how to do this (Analyze, Descriptive Statistics, and Frequencies). Make sure you request the ☑ Mean and ☑ Std. deviation in Statistics , and tick ⊙ Histograms: and ☑ Show normal curve on histogram in Charts . When you are ready, click Continue and OK . Do these three variables seem reasonably normally distributed?

Now, to carry out these bivariate tests simultaneously, go to Analyze, Correlate, and Bivariate. The window depicted in Figure 8.16 appears on your screen. You may notice that your two variables from the previous Pearson's r test, voice1 and jobsatcomp, are still in the Variables: column. Click Reset to revert the window to its natural state, as depicted in Figure 8.14. Now we simply want to add our variables in the following sequence: jobsatcomp, voice1, voice2, voice3, and voice4. Highlight them on the left-hand side and move them to the right by either double clicking or using

. Everything else should be ready to go (to be absolutely sure, you can quickly go into Options... and make sure that ☑ Means and standard deviations and ⦿ Exclude cases listwise are ticked), so click OK to produce the output depicted in Figure 8.17.

Figure 8.16 Bivariate correlation function in SPSS with managers are sincere in attempting to understand employees' views and job satisfaction composite variable

Reprint courtesy of IBM Corporation ©

Descriptive Statistics

	Mean	Std. Deviation	N
Job Satisfaction Composite Variable	3.5510	.72876	18994
Managers here..Are sincere in attempting to understand employees' views	3.39	1.070	18994
Overall, how good are managers at seeking views of employees/employees reps	3.28	1.144	18994
Overall, how good are managers at responding to suggestions from employees/worker reps	3.18	1.125	18994
Overall, how good are managers at allowing employees/worker reps influence final decision	2.95	1.108	18994

(Continued)

Figure 8.17 (Continued)

Correlations[b]

		Job Satisfaction Composite Variable	Managers here..Are sincere in attempting to understand employees' views	Overall, how good are managers at seeking views of employees/e mployees reps	Overall, how good are managers at responding to suggestions from employees/w orker reps	Overall, how good are managers at allowing employees/w orker reps influence final decision
Job Satisfaction Composite Variable	Pearson Correlation	1	.585**	.571**	.586**	.577**
	Sig. (2-tailed)		.000	.000	.000	.000
Managers here..Are sincere in attempting to understand employees' views	Pearson Correlation	.585**	1	.696**	.710**	.674**
	Sig. (2-tailed)	.000		.000	.000	.000
Overall, how good are managers at seeking views of employees/employees reps	Pearson Correlation	.571**	.696**	1	.831**	.777**
	Sig. (2-tailed)	.000	.000		.000	.000
Overall, how good are managers at responding to suggestions from employees/worker reps	Pearson Correlation	.586**	.710**	.831**	1	.839**
	Sig. (2-tailed)	.000	.000	.000		.000
Overall, how good are managers at allowing employees/worker reps influence final decision	Pearson Correlation	.577**	.674**	.777**	.839**	1
	Sig. (2-tailed)	.000	.000	.000	.000	

**. Correlation is significant at the 0.01 level (2-tailed).

b. Listwise N=18994

Figure 8.17 Descriptive statistics and correlations between various employee voice variables and job satisfaction composite variable

Reprint courtesy of IBM Corporation ©

After briefly looking through the descriptive statistics, move down to the correlation table below it. There is a lot of information here to digest. First of all, it needs to be remembered that, even though there are multiple variables in this table, this is not a multivariate test. Instead, it is a series of bivariate tests (Pearson's r tests, to be more specific). Again, you'll see all five variables (jobsat-comp, voice1, voice2, voice3, and voice4) across the columns and down the rows. Starting at the top left and moving down diagonally to the bottom right, you will see once again a series of correlation coefficients (Pearson's r values) of 1. This means that each variable, when correlated with itself, is obviously perfectly correlated. You will also notice that the Pearson's r values above that diagonal line and below that diagonal line are identical. In other words, the table is like a mirror, with the top-right coefficients identical to the bottom-left coefficients.

For our specific purposes, we only need to follow the first row, labeled 'Job Satisfaction Composite Variable,' across from left to right (or you could also arrive at the same results by following the first column down from top to bottom). Moving from left to right, you will see that job satisfaction is significantly positively correlated with voice1 ($r = 0.585$, $p < 0.001$), voice2 ($r = 0.571$, $p < 0.001$), voice3 ($r = 0.586$, $p < 0.001$), and voice4 ($r = 0.577$, $p < 0.001$). Those of you with a good eye for detail will notice that the Pearson's r value between voice1 and job satisfaction changed slightly from $r = 0.579$ to $r = 0.585$. The reason for this slight change is that, by adding more variables and using listwise deletion of cases, we changed the total number of cases involved in the analyses from $n = 20,339$ to $n = 18,994$. How would we interpret these results? In short, all four voice variables (voice1, voice2, voice3, and voice4) are moderately, positively, and significantly correlated with job satisfaction. That is, the different dimensions of voice we examined all appear to be associated with an increase in overall job satisfaction.

What's interesting about the data depicted in Figure 8.17 is that we have information not only on the bivariate tests of primary interest to us (reported in the preceding paragraph), but also on how each of the four voice variables are correlated with each other. You can see, for example, that voice3 and voice4 are very strongly correlated ($r = 0.839$, $p < 0.001$). In fact, all four of the voice variables are significantly, positively, and strongly correlated with each other. This should not be surprising. If managers offer voice in one dimension, they are also likely to offer voice in other dimensions as well.

Now that you are a pro at using SPSS to carry out Pearson's r tests, let's redo these analyses, but this time using simple regression instead. Before we do this, let's think about how these analyses might be different. As you already know, Pearson's r values are always standardized between -1 and 1, whereas B coefficients in simple regression are raw, or unstandardized, meaning that they can, in theory, take any value, positive or negative. Both Pearson's r and B coefficients have p-values attached to them to indicate significance and generalizability, but only the former can indicate the strength of the relationship between X and Y.

Simple regression reports not only the unstandardized B coefficients, but also a standardized coefficient called Beta. Beta and Pearson's r are identical. Both are standardized between -1 and 1, both say something about the strength of the relationship between X and Y, and both have p-values attached that suggest significance and generalizability. A key distinction is that standardized Beta and Pearson's r values cannot be used for prediction, whereas B coefficients can. Still confused? No worries! It will become clearer as we work through the examples and look at the output.

To carry out a simple regression, go to A̲nalyze, R̲egression, and L̲inear. The window depicted in Figure 8.18 appears. The first step is to identify our dependent variable – in this case, jobsatcomp – from the left column and move it to the right under D̲ependent:. Next, we need to highlight our independent variable – let's start with voice1 – and move it to the right under I̲ndependent(s):. Now go into Statistics... (see the new window depicted in Figure 8.19). Note that ☑ Estimates and ☑ Model fit are ticked by default. In addition, tick ☑ D̲escriptives and then Continue . Before we click OK , let's think a bit about what we can expect based on the Pearson's r test we've already conducted. We know that the relationship between X (voice1) and Y (job satisfaction), expressed as an unstandardized B coefficient in a simple regression, must be a positive number and statistically significant. We also know that the standardized Beta coefficient will be equivalent to our Pearson's r value (in this case, $r = 0.579$). Let's confirm that this is indeed the case. Click OK and have a look at the output in Figure 8.20.

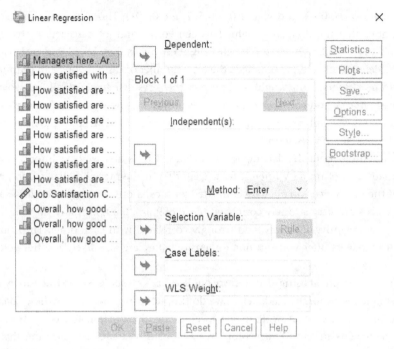

Figure 8.18 Linear regression function in SPSS

Reprint courtesy of IBM Corporation ©

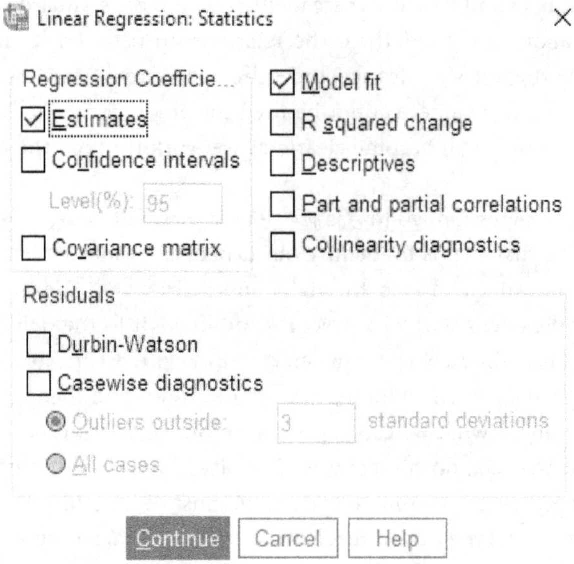

Figure 8.19 Linear regression statistics function in SPSS

Reprint courtesy of IBM Corporation ©

Descriptive Statistics

	Mean	Std. Deviation	N
Job Satisfaction Composite Variable	3.5568	.72143	20339
Managers here..Are sincere in attempting to understand employees' views	3.40	1.060	20339

Correlations

		Job Satisfaction Composite Variable	Managers here..Are sincere in attempting to understand employees' views
Pearson Correlation	Job Satisfaction Composite Variable	1.000	.579
	Managers here..Are sincere in attempting to understand employees' views	.579	1.000
Sig. (1-tailed)	Job Satisfaction Composite Variable	.	.000
	Managers here..Are sincere in attempting to understand employees' views	.000	.
N	Job Satisfaction Composite Variable	20339	20339
	Managers here..Are sincere in attempting to understand employees' views	20339	20339

Variables Entered/Removed[a]

Model	Variables Entered	Variables Removed	Method
1	Managers here..Are sincere in attempting to understand employees' views[b]	.	Enter

a. Dependent Variable: Job Satisfaction Composite Variable

b. All requested variables entered.

(Continued)

Figure 8.20   (Continued)

Model Summary

Model	R	R Square	Adjusted R Square	Std. Error of the Estimate
1	.579[a]	.335	.335	.58811

a. Predictors: (Constant), Managers here..Are sincere in attempting to understand employees' views

ANOVA[a]

Model		Sum of Squares	df	Mean Square	F	Sig.
1	Regression	3551.031	1	3551.031	10266.941	.000[b]
	Residual	7033.966	20337	.346		
	Total	10584.997	20338			

a. Dependent Variable: Job Satisfaction Composite Variable

b. Predictors: (Constant), Managers here..Are sincere in attempting to understand employees' views

Coefficients[a]

Model		Unstandardized Coefficients B	Std. Error	Standardized Coefficients Beta	t	Sig.
1	(Constant)	2.215	.014		159.675	.000
	Managers here..Are sincere in attempting to understand employees' views	.394	.004	.579	101.326	.000

a. Dependent Variable: Job Satisfaction Composite Variable

Figure 8.20   Descriptive statistics and simple regression, X = voice1 and Y = jobsatcomp

Reprint courtesy of IBM Corporation ©

Figure 8.20 consists of six separate, but interrelated, boxes. Let's look at them one at a time. The first box, Descriptive Statistics, gives the mean, standard deviation, and number of analysis cases for our two variables (both N = 20,339). The second box, labeled Correlations, includes (surprise, surprise!) the Pearson's r correlation coefficients that we requested previously. Here you can indeed verify that the Pearson's r value is still 0.579. The third box, Variables Entered/Removed, simply lists out the independent variables included in the simple regression equation, in this case only voice1. The fourth box, Model Summary, provides some interesting data. You will note that big 'R' is the same as Pearson's r – for example, 0.579. When we square R, we get what is referred to as the *coefficient of determination*, R^2, defined as the amount of variation in our dependent variable that is explained by our independent variable. In this case, the coefficient of determination is 0.335. This coefficient is interpreted as the amount of variation in Y (job satisfaction) that is explained by X (voice1). In other words, voice1 explains about 33.5% of job satisfaction, meaning that 66.5% of job satisfaction is explained by other variables. The next table, ANOVA, is fairly unnecessary for applied statisticians. In short, if the p-value is significant (in this case, $F = 10{,}266.94$, $p < 0.001$), then we can conclude that the independent variable significantly predicts the dependent variable. Finally, in the last table, Coefficients, we arrive at the results of our simple regression analysis. This is where you will report on the nature of the relationship between X and Y.

Recall that the simple regression equation is $Y = bX + a$. It is in the Coefficients box that we can find all the ingredients for this equation. The row labeled '(Constant)' provides a, the y-intercept. For whatever reason, a is labeled as 'unstandardized B,' so the constant is 2.22. This particular value has no interpretive meaning and is only needed for purposes of predicting values of Y from given values of X. The second component of the simple regression equation, b, is also labeled 'unstandardized B,' corresponding to 0.394. Thus, the fully specified simple regression equation for these two variables is $Y = (0.394) X + 2.22$, where 0.394 indicates the positive nature of the relationship between X and Y, and 2.22 indicates where on the Y-axis the line-of-best-fit crosses. Alternatively stated, for every one-unit increase in X, Y changes by 0.394 units, and this line crosses the Y-axis at 2.22.

Further over in the Coefficients box, you will see a column labeled Standardized Coefficients Beta. This is the standardized coefficient expressing the relationship between X and Y and, as noted above, the value is indeed identical to Pearson's r, 0.579 (note that the constant, a, has no standardized coefficient). The advantage of using standardized Beta over unstandardized B is that the former is always a number between −1 and 1, and so it speaks clearly to the strength of the relationship between X and Y.

In the next column over in the Coefficients box, we have the t-statistic (whereby a stronger relationship between X and Y corresponds to a larger t-statistic), and in the very last column, we finally have the p-value (denoted Sig.), which indicates whether or not our result (a positive relationship between voice1 and job satisfaction) generalizes. The fact that the constant, a, is statistically significant is not terribly relevant. However, that the independent variable ($B = 0.394$/Beta $= 0.579$) is statistically significant ($p < 0.001$) indicates that voice1, as expected, is positively and significantly related to job satisfaction. Of course, we knew this to be the case already because of the Pearson's r test we ran, but now you know how to express the relationship between X and Y using both Pearson's r and simple regression.

Let's carry out three further simple regressions using voice2, voice3, and voice4 as the independent variables and job satisfaction as the dependent variable. This time, we'll focus on just the Model Summary and Coefficients output and set aside the rest.

Go to Analyze, Regression, and Linear again to see the window depicted in Figure 8.21. We can leave the dependent variable, jobsatcomp, as is, but we will need to return voice1 to the list on the left by highlighting it and using ↵. Next, find voice2 and move it to where voice1 used to be by highlighting it and using ⇨. Recall that, when analysing Pearson's r, we were able to move voice2, voice3, and voice4 all at once to create a set of bivariate tests. We cannot do the same in simple regression because moving more than one independent variable at a time into the right-hand column will create a single multivariate regression model (which we will learn about in the next chapter). For now, let's look only at the relationship between voice2 and job satisfaction. When both variables are in place, click OK to see the output depicted in Figure 8.22.

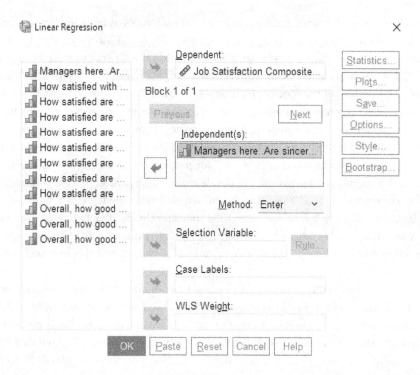

Figure 8.21 Linear regression function in SPSS with dependent and independent variable

Reprint courtesy of IBM Corporation ©

Model Summary

Model	R	R Square	Adjusted R Square	Std. Error of the Estimate
1	.566[a]	.320	.320	.59604

a. Predictors: (Constant), Overall, how good are managers at seeking views of employees/employees reps

Coefficients[a]

Model		Unstandardized Coefficients B	Std. Error	Standardized Coefficients Beta	t	Sig.
1	(Constant)	2.371	.013		185.004	.000
	Overall, how good are managers at seeking views of employees/employees reps	.360	.004	.566	97.654	.000

a. Dependent Variable: Job Satisfaction Composite Variable

Figure 8.22 Selected descriptive statistics and simple regression, X = voice2 and Y = jobsatcomp

Reprint courtesy of IBM Corporation ©

Looking first at the Model Summary box, you will find that the R^2 value of 0.320 means that 32% of the variability in job satisfaction is explained by voice2. This is not hugely different from the R^2 value in our previous simple regression model with voice1 (where 33% of the variation of Y was explainable by X).

Now looking at the Coefficients box, our unstandardized B for voice2 is 0.360, our standardized Beta is 0.566 (the same as Pearson's r), and $p < 0.001$. In other words, voice2 is significantly positively correlated with job satisfaction, but, again, we already knew this from our previous Pearson's r tests. The way we would interpret this simple regression analysis is that for every one unit increase in voice2, Y changes by 0.360. The regression line crosses the Y-axis at 2.37 (which is denoted Unstandardized B in the output, and corresponds to a, the y-intercept).

Let's do another simple regression, but this time, with voice3 as the independent variable. Go to Analyze, Regression, and Linear. Remove voice2 and replace it with voice3. Then click OK to see the (selected) output in Figure 8.23.

Model Summary

Model	R	R Square	Adjusted R Square	Std. Error of the Estimate
1	.583[a]	.340	.340	.58853

a. Predictors: (Constant), Overall, how good are managers at responding to suggestions from employees/worker reps

Coefficients[a]

Model		Unstandardized Coefficients		Standardized Coefficients		
		B	Std. Error	Beta	t	Sig.
1	(Constant)	2.354	.013		187.576	.000
	Overall, how good are managers at responding to suggestions from employees/worker reps	.377	.004	.583	101.394	.000

a. Dependent Variable: Job Satisfaction Composite Variable

Figure 8.23 Selected descriptive statistics and simple regression, X = voice3 and Y = jobsatcomp

Reprint courtesy of IBM Corporation ©

From this output, we can glean the following information. The R^2 of 0.340 suggests that 34% of the variation in job satisfaction is attributable to voice3. The unstandardized $B = 0.377$, the standardized Beta = 0.583 (the same as the Pearson's r), and $p < 0.001$. Thus, we conclude that voice3 is positively and significantly related to job satisfaction, as we expected. For every one-unit increase in X, values in Y change by 0.377. The regression line crosses the Y-axis at 2.35, which is denoted Unstandardized B and represents a, the y-intercept.

Try and see if you can figure out how to run a simple regression with voice4 as the independent variable. I'm not going to give you exact instructions, but if you do this correctly, you should find an R^2 of 0.331, an Unstandardized B of 0.378, a standardized Beta of 0.576, and a p-value of <0.001. Did you do it right? Of course you did, hot shot. Nice work! You are now an expert in using SPSS to carry out simple regression.

What Have You Learned?

This chapter described the last two bivariate tests covered in this book: Pearson's r and simple regression. These are two ways of expressing the nature of the relationship between X and Y when both variables are ordinal or preferably scale level. Both tests are predicated on the assumption that the relationship between the independent and dependent variables is linear in nature. The 'result' of both tests is a coefficient. In the case of Pearson's r, the coefficient is standardized between −1 and 1, where the closer the number is to −1 and 1, the stronger the relationship. In the case of simple regression, two coefficients are provided: an unstandardized B and a standardized Beta, the latter of which is identical to Pearson's r. In both tests, a positive coefficient implies a positive relationship between X and Y: thus, as values in X increase, so do values in Y. A negative coefficient implies a negative relationship between X and Y: thus, as values in X increase, values in Y simultaneously decrease. Note that we cannot say that X causes Y, but we can conclude that X is associated with Y (or correlated with Y) provided that the p-value attached to these coefficients is < 0.05. The lower the p-value, the more confident we are that the positive or negative relationship we found generalizes to the population. If the coefficients (either r, unstandardized B, or standardized Beta) equal or approximate zero, then the p-value will very likely be nonsignificant, suggesting that there is no relationship between X and Y. In other words, we would be unable to make that quantum leap from the sample to the population.

Bivariate tests like Pearson's r and simple regression are obviously limited in one very important way – namely, a single outcome, Y, is usually associated with more than one independent variable. Indeed, in each of the tests we examined in this chapter, we learned from the coefficient of determination (R^2) that the independent variable (whether voice1, voice2, voice3, or voice4) only explains a certain percentage of the variation in Y (job satisfaction). This, by definition, implies that multiple X variables likely work together in their association with Y. To model real-life relationships, bivariate correlations are not enough because real life is more complex. When we consider how multiple independent variables simultaneously might predict a single dependent variable, we enter into the realm of multivariate tests. The remainder of this book focuses on the main multivariate tests that are at our disposal: multiple regression, logistic regression, factor analysis, and structural equation modeling. Are you up to the challenge? I think you are. Let's do it!

Further Reading

Berk, R. A. (2004). *Regression analysis: A constructive critique* (Vol. 11). Sage.

Chatterjee, S., & Hadi, A. S. (2015). *Regression analysis by example*. John Wiley.

Darlington, R. B., & Hayes, A. F. (2017). *Regression analysis and linear models*. Guilford.

Huck, S. W., Ren, B., & Yang, H. (2007). A new way to teach (or compute) Pearson's r without reliance on cross-products. *Teaching Statistics, 29*(1), 13-16.

Kader, G., & Franklin, C. (2008). The evolution of Pearson's correlation coefficient. *The Mathematics Teacher, 102*(4), 292-299.

Rawlings, J. O., Pantula, S. G., & Dickey, D. A. (2001). *Applied regression analysis: a research tool*. Springer Science & Business Media.

In-Class Discussion Questions

1. What are simple regression and Pearson's r correlation coefficient? When can they be used and with what types of variables? How can you interpret the results?
2. What is the difference between a standardized and an unstandardized coefficient? Why and when would we use one over the other?
3. List out five research questions that a management scientist might answer using either simple regression or Pearson's r.
4. Further to 3, list out how you would measure the 10 variables associated with those research questions. How would you measure and, where relevant, code them?
5. What is a scatterplot? What are residuals? How can we calculate the line-of-best-fit?
6. How and why would you create a composite variable in SPSS?

PART IV
MULTIVARIATE MODELING

Okay, no more fun and games. Let's get serious. Bivariate models are a good introduction to statistics, but serious modeling is almost always multivariate in nature. The world is complex. Rarely, if ever, will you find a single variable that is associated with a single predictor. For this reason, bivariate statistics are severely limited. There is no simple relationship between X and Y because X and Y are simultaneously related to any number of other predictors or outcomes. If you are really interested in understanding the relationship between X and Y, you will have to consider both variables in their wider context. This necessitates multivariate modeling. A multivariate model can be any simultaneous equation containing three or more variables. You may be focusing on the relationship between X and Y while holding constant, or controlling for, other variables, or you may be interested in multiple predictors ($X_1, X_2, X_3 \ldots X_i$) or even multiple outcomes ($Y_1, Y_2, Y_3 \ldots Y_i$). In the remainder of this book, we'll be looking at four of the most commonly used multivariate methods.

In Chapter 9, you will learn about multiple regression analysis. This is just an extension of simple regression (from Chapter 8) that includes multiple independent variables predicting a single dependent variable. It would not be unfair to say that multiple regression is very likely the most common multivariate statistical test in the world. It is (relatively) simple, versatile, and good when it comes to both explanation and prediction. It is also the foundation of any number of other advanced multivariate statistical tests. If you want to consider yourself a serious statistician, you must master this method.

In Chapter 10, we'll be looking at the fundamentals of logistic regression. This multivariate method is based on the concept of maximum likelihood estimation. It is arguably even more versatile than multiple regression (in that it has less restrictive assumptions associated with its use), but it is constrained to the prediction of a single, binary (yes/no, either/or) dependent variable. Whenever you are attempting to predict the likelihood of outcome 1 versus outcome 2, logistic regression is your method.

In Chapter 11, we will have a look at latent variables, or factors. These are unobservable variables that are composed of multiple single-item indicators that 'hang together' logically and empirically. There are two methods we'll look at in this chapter. Exploratory factor analysis, also commonly referred to as principal components analysis, involves the exploratory identification of factors based on the input of any number of single-item indicators. By rotating the factor solution, we can identify a number of wider factors within our dataset. Confirmatory factor analysis, on the other hand, is a deductive approach that tests whether a set of variables 'hang together' in a wider measurement model. This latter method fits under the family of structural equation modeling, also referred to as analysis of covariance structures.

Finally, in Chapter 12, we will extend confirmatory factor analysis, which measures the existence of latent variables, into structural equation modeling, which examines the relationship among a set of latent variables. In short, structural equation modeling is a lot like multiple regression, but instead of using observable variables or composites, the variables are latent and thus unobservable (i.e., assumed to exist by virtue of their relationship with a set of single-item variables that 'hang together' logically and empirically).

Okay, buckle up, my friend. We're about to get real.

9

Multiple Regression

If you've made it this far in the book, you must be resilient. We're ready to move into Part III and are nearing the home stretch. Now that you're an expert in bivariate statistical tests, you're ready to explore the heretofore elusive multivariate tests that have been periodically mentioned in previous chapters. In this chapter, we'll be looking at the single most important multivariate test in all of the social sciences: multiple regression analysis, also referred to as *multiple ordinary least squares (OLS)* regression analysis. Simply put, multiple regression is just a multivariate extension of simple regression. By 'multivariate', I mean that we are including more than one independent variable simultaneously in our equation. How many independent variables can we include in a single model? The general consensus is that each variable requires at least 10 cases, subjects, or respondents in our sample. Therefore, if our analysis sample is $n = 100$, we shouldn't have any more than 10 variables in our equation, but if our sample is $n = 1000$, we can have up to 100 variables in a single equation, and so on.

As we learned from the previous chapter, there are some hard and fast rules to simple regression analysis, and these also hold for multiple regression as well. For example, we can only predict or explain one dependent variable, Y, at a time. Moreover, Y must be a metric variable, for example, either ordinal or preferably scale in measurement, and roughly normally distributed. Our independent variables $(X_1, X_2 \ldots X_i)$ must be linearly related to Y and also ordinal or scale with one curious exception: it is possible, as alluded to in the previous chapter, to include binary, also referred to as dichotomous or 'dummy', independent variables, with only two categories. Multicategory nominal variables (three or more categories) cannot ever be used in multiple regression analyses, but they can be converted into a series of dummy variables, as we'll learn later in this chapter. For now, just realize that multiple regression is invalid where any independent variable, X, is nominal with more than two categories. Multiple regression is a parametric test, and so is predicated on variables with meaningful mean scores and standard deviations (again, with the exception of dummy variables).

Now, I have some bad news and some good news to report. The bad news is that multiple regression is much more complex than simple regression. You're really going to have to stretch your mind to understand the ins and outs of this method of analysis. The good news, however, is that multiple regression is so complex that it would be utterly pointless to demonstrate the mathematics underlying the test. Thus, you won't be expected to do much math in this chapter, and for the remaining ones. We'll be focusing exclusively on 'applied statistics' from here on out, and letting IBM SPSS Statistics Software (SPSS) do all of the heavy lifting for us.

Before I introduce some basic concepts in multiple regression, let's first think about how this method can be used in management research. The possibilities are truly endless, as you'll see.

Multiple Regression in Management Research

As we have already learned, regression analysis can be used for both prediction and explanation. Let's say we have a series of independent variables and we want to use those to predict some dependent variable. We can do this by running a multiple regression analysis and calculating a, the y-intercept, as well as the unstandardized B coefficients associated with each X variable. Then we simply plug the relevant values of X into the equation, multiply each value by its unstandardized coefficient, and add the y-intercept to predict an estimated value of Y. Such a technique might be useful for organizations trying to predict a future outcome based on past or present data. For example, a restaurant might want to estimate how many pizzas will be ordered on a given day so that they can optimize their supply chain. You might look at variables such as temperature outside, total rainfall that day, previous pizza orders, customer satisfaction trends, and so on, and then use those factors to predict the number of pizzas likely to be ordered.

For management researchers, like us, we are usually less concerned than practitioners with predicting values of Y and more concerned with explaining how a set of independent variables relate to an outcome. Most of our research questions will center around the extent to which a group of independent variables are associated with a single dependent variable. We tend to think of these associations as positive, neutral, or negative. Thus, one independent variable, X_1, might be positively related to Y (as values in X go up, so do values in Y), another independent variable, X_2, might be negatively related to Y (as values in X go up, values in Y go down), and yet another independent variable, X_3, might be unrelated to Y (variation in the values of X_3 are not associated in any systematic way with values in Y). The following are a set of research questions that would benefit from the use of multiple regression analysis. You will notice that these questions are more general than the bivariate ones from the previous chapters. This is because research questions in multivariate research do not typically mention all of the variables included in a model.

- What are the predictors of individual job satisfaction? In this case, possible independent variables might include contract type (X_1), working hours per week (X_2), work intensity (X_3), work-life balance (X_4), stress (X_5), job monotony (X_6), availability of assistance from supervisors (X_7), job autonomy (X_8), creativity (X_9), job complexity (X_{10}), employee voice (X_{11}), job insecurity (X_{12}), pay satisfaction (X_{13}), and opportunities for learning and development (X_{14}), and the dependent variable is a measure of job satisfaction (Timming, 2010b).

- What are the predictors of individual productivity? In this case, possible independent variables might include years of education (X_1), whether or not the employee graduated from an Ivy League university (X_2), intelligence as measured by IQ (X_3), father's education (X_4), mother's education (X_5), conscientiousness (X_6), working hours per week (X_7), mental health (X_8), and the number of hours spent surfing the web during the workday (X_9), and the dependent variable is a measure of individual productivity.

- What are the organization-level predictors of total sales? In this case, possible independent variables might include organization size (X_1), total population within a 25-mile radius of the organization (X_2), percentage of the workforce with a university degree (X_4), and advertising budget (X_5), and the dependent variable is the total number of sales in dollars for each organization.

- What are the predictors of individual income? In this case, possible independent variables might include age (X_1), education (X_2), height (X_3), weight (X_4), aptitude (X_5), race (X_6, noting that this must be a dummy variable, e.g., white vs. nonwhite), marital status (X_7, again, noting that this must be a dummy variable, e.g., married vs. not married), and number of hours per week spent watching television (X_8), and the dependent variable is yearly annual income.

- What are the predictors of individual employee trust in managers? In this case, possible independent variables might include job autonomy (X_1), employee voice (X_2), employment relations climate (X_3), salary (X_4), and job satisfaction (X_5), and the dependent variable is a measure of employee trust in managers.

- What are the organization-level predictors of total profits? In this case, possible independent variables might include percentage of labor force with a university degree (X_1), a dummy variable measuring whether the firm is in the manufacturing sector or not (X_2), number of years since the founding of the organization (X_3), whether or not the organization has access to credit (X_4), and size of the organization (X_5), and the dependent variable is a measure of total profits in dollars.

Let's take a closer look at how a management scientist might answer this last question. Imagine that you have a unique dataset containing the responses to these variables of 200 organizations. That is, you have measures of total profit (Y), percentage of labor force with a university degree (X_1), whether the firm are in the manufacturing sector (X_2), number of years since the founding of the organization (X_3), whether or not the organization has access to credit (X_4), and size of the organization (X_5).

First, ask yourself, what kind of bivariate relationships might we expect? We may hypothesize:

Hypothesis 1: The higher the percentage of employees with a university degree, the more profitable the organization.

Hypothesis 2: Organizations in the manufacturing sector are less profitable than organizations in the service sector.

Hypothesis 3: The older the company, the more profitable it is.

Hypothesis 4: Organizations that have access to credit will be more profitable than organizations that do not have access to credit.

Hypothesis 5: The larger the organization, the more profitable it is.

Now, we could do four separate Pearson's *r* tests to answer these questions, but the problem with that approach is that we couldn't then see how the independent variables might affect each other. By running a multiple regression analysis, we can look at the pure effect of each independent variable on the dependent variable while holding constant, or parceling out, the influence of the other covariates. A *covariate* is also referred to as a *control variable*. Sometimes control variables are interesting in and of themselves, and sometimes they just 'hang out' in the background of a multiple regression so that their influence can be accounted for.

To answer this research question using multiple regression analysis, our unstandardized Equation (9.1) looks like this:

$$Y = B_1(X_1) + B_2(X_2) + B_3(X_3) + B_4(X_4) + B_5(X_5) + a \tag{9.1}$$

where

Y = total profit

X_1 = Percentage of the labor force with a university degree

B_1 = a coefficient describing the relationship between X_1 and Y with the influence of X_2, X_3, X_4, and X_5 held constant

X_2 = whether the firm is in the manufacturing sector (or not)

B_2 = a coefficient describing the relationship between X_2 and Y with the influence of X_1, X_3, X_4, and X_5 held constant

X_3 = age of the organization

B_3 = a coefficient describing the relationship between X_3 and Y with the influence of X_1, X_2, X_4, and X_5 held constant

X_4 = whether or not the organization has access to credit

B_4 = a coefficient describing the relationship between X_4 and Y with the influence of X_1, X_2, X_3, and X_5 held constant

X_5 = number of employees

B_5 = a coefficient describing the relationship between X_5 and Y with the influence of X_1, X_2, X_3, and X_4 held constant

a = y-intercept

Now, we would use this equation if we wanted to predict profitability based on these five inputs. After running the multiple regression, we would simply insert our values of X_{1-5}, multiply by each unstandardized coefficient, and add the y-intercept. It's that easy!

But, as noted above and in Chapter 8, we are usually more interested in explaining the relationship between our independent variables and our dependent variables. To do this, we would instead use the standardized Equation (9.2):

$$Y = \text{Beta}_1(X_1) + \text{Beta}_2(X_2) + \text{Beta}_3(X_3) + \text{Beta}_4(X_4) + \text{Beta}_5(X_5) \tag{9.2}$$

You'll notice that this equation is very similar to Equation (9.1), save that the y-intercept is missing and the coefficients are now reported as standardized Betas, rather than unstandardized B coefficients. Using Equation (9.2), we can explain the relationship between each X variable and Y by looking at the Beta coefficient, which, like Pearson's r, is always a number between -1 and 1, where -1 is a perfect negative correlation, 0 is no correlation, and 1 is a perfect positive correlation. Thus, if B_1, B_2, B_3, B_4, and B_5 are all positive numbers (i.e., greater than 0 but less than 1), and their corresponding p-values are all significant, then we would conclude that all five independent variables are significantly positively related to profitability. Boom! That wasn't so hard now, was it?

Now that you get the general idea surrounding multiple regression analysis, let's delve a little deeper into some basic concepts pertaining to this statistical technique. From here on out, we'll be referring to standardized regression equations only, meaning that we'll be focusing on Beta coefficients, rather than unstandardized B coefficients.

Let's do this!

Basic Concepts in Multiple Regression

Multiple regression analysis entails the prediction of one dependent variable, Y, by the combination of multiple (i.e., two or more) independent variables simultaneously. We have already learned that we cannot simply add an infinite number of independent variables into our model. The larger the sample size, the more independent variables we can include. Two key questions at this preliminary stage are (1) which independent variables should we add to the model and (2) how should they be selected from our list of potential independent variables?

Confirmatory Versus Exploratory Multiple Regression Models

To answer these two questions, we must consider whether we wish to build a confirmatory multiple regression model or an exploratory multiple regression model. A *confirmatory model* is one where the variables are chosen entirely on the basis of theory. Thus, if a theory suggests that a set of variables may be related to an outcome, then you simply include those variables in the model and test the relationships. Both the model as a whole and the individual predictors can be confirmed or disconfirmed. Even if you end up with a 'bad' model (e.g., one that poorly predicts or explains the dependent variable), that's perfectly fine with the confirmatory approach to model building.

The exploratory approach to model building means you allow SPSS (or whatever statistical package you're using) to help you statistically identify 'good' predictors from a larger set of potential independent variables. Let's say, for example, you have 99 potential independent variables and one dependent variable. Using an exploratory approach, you can carry out a stepwise *forward exploration* or a *backward exploration*. The forward method adds one variable to the model at a time and assesses how that addition affects overall model fit. If an included variable adds value, it remains in the model; if an included variable fails to add value, then it is removed from the model. At the end of the process, you will be left with a series of 'good' independent variables. The backward process takes the opposite approach. It starts with all 99 independent variables in the model and then removes one predictor at a time to see how that affects overall model fit. If a removed variable increases model fit, it is retained, and vice versa. Using a stepwise, exploratory approach, virtually guarantees that you will have a strong model because, whichever approach you use, independent variables that are weakly correlated with the dependent variable are removed, leaving only the 'good' predictors.

So which approach is better? The confirmatory approach or the exploratory approach? Opinions on this matter may differ, but it is the view of this author that a confirmatory, theory-driven approach should always be used as a first course of action. Exploratory stepwise approaches to model building are akin to a fishing expedition. Sure, you may end up with a better model fit than with the confirmatory approach, but just because a model is statistically strong doesn't imply that it is meaningful. A stepwise approach might identify a bunch of predictors that are strongly, but nonsensically, correlated with the outcome. My advice is that all modeling should be theory- and hypothesis-driven.

Control Variables

Another consideration in building a multiple regression model concerns which *control variables*, or *covariates*, should be included. A control variable is an independent variable whose value is held constant in the analysis. What does this mean and why would anyone want to do such a crazy thing?

Imagine that you are interested in studying the relationship between education and income. You want to know, for every one-unit increase in education (e.g., an extra year of education), how much more money an individual will earn. You could evaluate this question with a simple regression equation (where $X = education$ and $Y = income$), but doing so would only tell part of the story. After all, there are many, many factors that also are associated with earnings, like age, intelligence, and conscientiousness. Now let's say you want to evaluate the pure effect of education on income while holding age, intelligence, and conscientiousness constant. In this case, age, intelligence, and conscientiousness are considered control variables, or covariates, in a multiple regression equation. You may not be interested necessarily in the effects of age, intelligence, and conscientiousness on income, but you still want their effects to be taken into account in your analysis. Hence, you run a multiple regression with four independent variables ($X_1 = education$, $X_2 = age$, $X_3 = intelligence$, and $X_4 = conscientiousness$) and one dependent variable ($Y = income$). Such an equation will produce four coefficients (Betas), each describing the strength of the relationship between the independent variable and dependent variable. By including the three extra covariates, the Beta coefficient describing the relationship between education and income has held constant, or parceled out, the influence of age, intelligence, and conscientiousness. You could also report the relationship between age and income, intelligence and income, as well as conscientiousness and income, or you could just let them 'hang out' in the background of the equation. Either way, the benefit of using control variables is that you are reducing the possibility of *omitted variable bias* in your model. Omitted variable bias refers to a situation in which important or relevant covariates are left out of a model.

On the whole, control variables are very important. As noted above, you should use theory to inform which control variables you include in your model. Try to include as many relevant controls as possible, but don't just throw in a bunch of random controls. Make sure that your choice of covariates is driven by hypotheses.

Multivariate Outliers

You will recall that we previously discussed univariate outliers and why they are bad for parametric models such as regression analysis. To briefly recap, univariate outliers are values that are very, very high or very, very low, relative to the mean score of an ordinal or, more likely, a scale-level variable. We don't like univariate outliers because they 'drag' the mean score up (or down), resulting in a positively (or negatively) skewed distribution. This is a problem, statistically speaking, because parametric tests depend on normally distributed variables. We also discussed various ways of dealing with univariate outliers, like deleting the extreme scores, winsorizing them, or mathematically transforming them.

Now that we are moving into the realm of multivariate analyses, it makes sense at this stage to introduce the concept of a *multivariate outlier*. A multivariate outlier refers to a case (subject, respondent, participant, organization, or whatever the unit of analysis might be) that contains an unusual combination of scores. What do I mean by an unusual combination of scores? Let's consider an example.

Say you have a dataset composed of 100 randomly drawn private sector organizations in the United States. In this case, the unit of analysis is the organization. Now, within this dataset, it may be perfectly normal and reasonable to have a firm that employs 15 people. This is what could be described as an SME. There is nothing odd about that. It may also be perfectly normal and reasonable to have another firm with a yearly turnover of $500,000,000. There are some seriously profitable companies in the United States, so there is nothing unusual about this amount of money. However, if you were to identify a single case (i.e., a private sector company) that employs only 15 people and has a yearly turnover of $500,000,000, this would be unusual. Such a case should immediately raise red flags.

If such a case (called a multivariate outlier) is identified, you should immediately double check your data. Maybe, after double checking, you find that, indeed, there is a firm that employs 15 people and has yearly revenue of $500,000,000. In that case, simply retain the case and proceed with your regression analysis. However, many identifiable multivariate outliers are the result of simple data entry errors. Maybe, after double checking the dataset, you find that the firm actually employs 15,000 employees and has a yearly revenue of $500,000,000. This would make a bit more sense. In that case, you can fix the data entry error and then move on with the analysis.

The most common method of identifying multivariate outliers is through a test called Mahalanobis's distance. You will learn how to run this test in a multiple regression analysis using SPSS below.

Least Squares and the Coefficient of Determination

Up to this point, I've referred a few times to a good fitting multiple regression model. What does that mean? How can we evaluate or assess whether a multivariate model is a good fit? To answer these questions, let's review a bit of what we already learned about simple regression from the previous chapter.

Regression analysis (both simple and multivariate) is grounded in a very important concept that we refer to as *ordinary least squares*, or OLS. OLS is the mathematical logic underlying essentially all linear regression analyses. The aim, or objective, of any regression analysis is to generate B (or Beta) coefficients that minimize the amount of error in the model. You might recall that in Chapter 8 we discussed the *line of best fit*. The line of best fit, in short, is the one line that describes the nature of the relationship between X and Y in a way that best minimizes the residuals, or errors. The closer the individual dots in a scatterplot are to the line of best fit, the stronger the relationship between X and Y and the better the overall model fit. In a bivariate context, this is reflected in Pearson's r, which is always a value between –1 and 1. Recall that, when we square the value of r, we get the amount of variation in Y that is explained by X. Thus, if $r = 0.374$, then $r^2 = 0.140$, meaning that X explains 14% of the variation in Y ($0.140 \times 100 = 14.0\%$).

The same logic of OLS also applies to multivariate regression analysis, only this time, there are multiple lines of best fit (corresponding to multiple B or Beta weights) that describe the relationships between the independent variables and the dependent variable while the values of the other covariates in the equation are held constant, as discussed above.

Just as lower-case r describes the relationship between X and Y in a bivariate model, 'big' R similarly describes the relationship between a series of independent variables (e.g., X_1, X_2, X_3, X_4 . . . X_i) and Y in a multivariate model. More important, just as lower-case r^2 explains the amount of variation in Y explained by X in a bivariate model, big R^2 explains the amount of variation in Y explained, simultaneously, by all independent X variables in a multivariate regression equation. R^2, also referred to as the *coefficient of determination*, is a single positive number (always between 0 and 1) that is an indicator of overall model fit. The higher the value of R^2, the better the overall model fit, which means that the errors, or residuals, are lower. Conversely, the lower the value of R^2, the worse the model fit and the higher the residuals, or errors.

R^2 is the most important statistic of overall model fit in regression analysis, but it does have one fairly significant limitation. It can be artificially inflated, or propped up. Now, of course, you would never do such a thing on purpose! But it can still happen without your being aware. Let me explain. If you have one X and one Y, then little r^2 is straightforward and easy to interpret. But if you add an extra variable (X_1 and X_2), then your big R^2 will improve. If you add a third, fourth, and fifth independent variable (X_1, X_2, X_3, X_4, and X_5), each additional variable will increase the value of R^2. This may not seem like much of a problem to you, but it is. This problem is often referred to as *overfitting*, whereby too many irrelevant independent variables are added to a model, thus inflating the R^2. Imagine, for example, that only X_1 and Y are statistically significantly related in the multiple regression equation. Even if the remaining X variables do not significantly predict Y, they will still increase R^2. This is what I mean when I say that R^2 can be artificially propped up, simply by adding more independent variables into the model. To offset this possibility, researchers often report *adjusted R^2*, rather than just R^2. Adjusted R^2 has a built-in correction to avoid the artificial inflation of R^2 just based on the addition of more independent variables.

In short, especially when you are building large multivariate models with lots of independent variables, you should always report adjusted R^2 as your measure of overall model fit.

Coefficients and Confidence Intervals

It should come as no surprise to you that a multiple regression analysis has multiple 'results'. The overall model fit, R^2, is one useful result. It tells you how much variation in Y is explained by your independent variables and allows you to compare the overall fit between different models. But, in and of itself, it does not predict, nor does it explain.

Prediction and explanation are made possible by B and Beta coefficients, respectively. If you have 10 independent variables in your multiple regression model, then you will have 10 separate coefficients. In fact, you will have 20 coefficients: 10 B weights and 10 Beta weights. You will recall that B and Beta express the exact same relationship, but in different terms: the B weight (or coefficient) is an unstandardized slope and the Beta weight (or coefficient) is a standardized slope.

As with simple regression, each coefficient will have attached to it a t-statistic (generated from a t-test) and a corresponding p-value. If your coefficient for a given variable, say, X_n, has a significant p-value attached to it (where $p < 0.05$), then you can conclude that X_n is statistically significantly correlated with Y while holding constant the influence of the other independent variables. If your coefficient for X_n is not significant (i.e., $p > 0.05$), then you can conclude that X_n is not significantly related to Y, or that it does not significantly predict Y.

If you use a stepwise (forward or backward) approach to model building (see Box 9.1), then it is very likely that all of your independent variables will be significantly related to Y. However, if you use a strictly confirmatory approach, then it is possible that only some, or even none, of your independent variables will be significantly related to Y.

Box 9.1: Enter Versus Stepwise Methods of Model Building

Multiple regression models can be built in one of two ways. First, they can be strictly confirmatory. This means that the inclusion of independent variables is based completely on theory and hypotheses. You might assume, for example, that, based on extant research, five variables (X_1, X_2, X_3, X_4, and X_5) significantly predict Y. Thus, when building your multiple regression model, you use something called the 'Enter' method. This means that you're including all five variables in your model, regardless of whether or not all are good predictors of your dependent variable.

The second method, or rather series of methods, is more exploratory than confirmatory. Instead of using theory to construct your final multiple regression model, you can use a stepwise forward or stepwise backward method to help you identify only those independent variables that do a good job predicting your dependent variable. For example, let's say you have 25 X variables ($X_1 \ldots X_{25}$) that could predict Y. Using a stepwise forward method, SPSS will add one variable at a time, starting with X_1, and only retaining each variable if it significantly predicts Y. Thus, the good predictors will be retained in the final model and the poor predictors excluded. Similarly, using a stepwise backward method, SPSS will start by adding all 25 X variables and then gradually remove variables that poorly predict Y. Either

(Continued)

way, you will 'explore' different combinations of X variables to find the best model fit, that is, the highest R^2 value.

Personally, I strongly advise against the use of stepwise methods. Yes, all of your predictors will significantly predict your dependent variable. But many researchers view this as a sloppy 'fishing' expedition. It's best to use a strictly confirmatory approach to multiple regression model building by using the Enter method. That is to say, you should always use theory to decide which variables to include and which to exclude and report honestly if some of your predictors (independent variables) are poor predictors of Y.

As with simple regression, if B is a positive number and the corresponding p-value is significant, then you conclude that that particular independent variable is positively related to Y (while holding constant the other variables in the equation). If B is a negative number and the corresponding p-value is significant, then you conclude that that particular variable is negatively related to Y (while holding constant the other variables in the equation). If B is zero, or very close to zero, and the p-value is not statistically significant, then you conclude that there is no generalizable relationship between that independent variable and Y.

The same logic applies to Beta coefficients, except that with Betas, the value will always be between –1 and 1, where the more extreme the value (i.e., the closer to 1 or –1), the stronger the relationship between the independent variable and the dependent variable (again, while holding constant the values of the covariates).

One problem, as we've already learned, is that these coefficients are just estimates based on the sample data. The value of B represents the effect on Y of every one-unit increase in X. But remember that this value is calculated on sample data, even though what we really care about is what the value of B is in the wider population. Fortunately, in addition to getting an estimate of B, multiple regression analysis can also provide us with *confidence intervals* surrounding that estimate. A confidence interval refers to a range of values, from lower bound to upper bound, around which we express some degree of confidence that the true, population value falls. Most confidence intervals in inferential statistics are expressed at 95%. In other words, a 95% confidence interval means that we can be 95% confident that the true, population value of B is somewhere within a given range of scores. Don't worry too much if you don't quite understand this concept just yet. It will be made clearer when we start running multiple regression models using SPSS. Just bear with me a bit longer as we move through some of the more technical concepts related to this method.

Multicollinearity

Multicollinearity is a serious problem in multiple regression analysis. It sounds like a big, complicated word, but it's actually pretty easy to understand. *Multicollinearity* refers to a multivariate model in which the independent variables are excessively highly correlated with each other. What does 'excessively highly correlated' mean? In an ideal world (which, of course, doesn't exist), we want all of our X variables to be independent and completely uncorrelated with each other. That way, we could easily understand the 'pure' effect of each X variable on Y (while holding constant the other covariates in the equation). If the bivariate correlation among all your X variables is zero (a hypothetical situation that will almost never be the case), then the model is *additive*. That is, each coefficient adds up to calculate R^2. Similarly, if all of your X variables are perfectly correlated with each other, this refers to an equally hypothetical situation referred to as *singularity*. It is technically impossible to run a multiple regression analysis under the condition of singularity. The reason it is impossible is that, insofar as all of your X variables are perfectly correlated with one another, this would make it equally impossible to identify unique effects of each X variable on Y.

But let's get back to the real world. Singularity (perfect multicollinearity) and zero correlation among your independent variables (perfect independence) is extremely rare in real-life data. Much more likely, you will find correlations among your X variables that are partial, rather than absolute. But even partial correlations can be problematic for your multiple regression model. To understand why this is the case, let's consider an example.

Imagine that you are thinking of using three standardized tests as part of the selection procedure in your company: (1) an IQ test, (2) a verbal reasoning test, and (3) a numeric ability test. To see whether these tools help predict employee performance, you ask your existing workforce to take these three tests and then use them to predict actual performance as measured by their current performance appraisal scores. In this case, the three test scores are the X variables (X_1, X_2, and X_3) and employee performance is your Y variable.

The problem with such a model should be immediately apparent. While scores on the verbal test and the numeric test are likely to be somewhat correlated, you might expect scores on both tests to be very highly correlated with the IQ test. The reason you might expect this is that IQ tests often measure both verbal and numeric ability.

Okay, at this stage, you might be thinking, 'so what'? Why should this even matter? Think about it in these terms. If the IQ test is 'excessively highly correlated' with the verbal test and the numeric test, then you won't be able to easily untangle which one best predicts Y. In other words, the fact that some of your independent variables are highly correlated with each other masks, or obscures, the separate correlations with the dependent variable. Alternatively stated, when there is too much 'overlap' in correlations among the independent variables, it becomes difficult (and, in the case of singularity, impossible) to unpack what is truly associated with the outcome variable, Y. For this reason, you ideally want to select independent variables that are not 'excessively highly correlated'.

But what exactly do we mean by 'excessively highly correlated'? You could just throw all of the independent variables into a bivariate correlation table and compare the Pearson's r scores. The problem with this approach, however, is that it's not clear-cut how high of a correlation is too high. Is it 0.900? Almost certainly. 0.750? Possibly. 0.500? Maybe. 0.250? Not likely. Fortunately, we have a much better way to more objectively assess whether multicollinearity is a problem. The *variance inflation factor*, also referred to as VIF, is a common statistical method used to identify independent variables that are 'excessively highly correlated'. You will learn more about this method below when you use SPSS to carry out a multiple regression analysis.

Redundancy, Complementarity, and Suppression

Beyond multicollinearity, another feature of multivariate regression analysis pertaining to the relationship among independent variables is the extent to which the variables are redundant, complementary, or suppressed. Let's take a look at what each of these looks like.

Redundancy refers to a situation in which a set of independent variables predict the dependent variable better individually than they do together. In other words, the sum of their bivariate correlations with Y is greater than the sum of the multivariate correlations. This is similar to multicollinearity, but not the same. It is similar in that it implies that the presence of another variable adds no further value to the model. The variable is, in a word, redundant. You can assess redundancy by adding a variable and seeing what happens to the R^2 value. If R^2 remains unchanged with the addition of another variable, then that variable is redundant and no longer needed in the model. It should be noted that the redundant variable does not need to be perfectly correlated with another independent variable, but they are usually fairly highly correlated. To illustrate redundancy, consider the following example. Say you're implementing a selection procedure to hire a computer programmer. As part of the selection procedure, you administer a series of tests to candidates for the position. Imagine that, among the tests you are administering is a coding test and a mathematics test. Now, because coding requires a high level of mathematical ability, you may find the mathematics test redundant (or vice versa). You can check whether this is the case by including first the coding test scores in your model and then the coding test scores and the mathematics test scores. If the R^2 does not improve (i.e., if it does not get larger, thus explaining greater variation in the dependent variable), then you can conclude that the mathematics test is redundant in the model in that it does not appear to add any predictive value beyond the other independent variable.

Complementarity is, in many ways, the opposite of redundancy. It refers to a situation in which a set of independent variables predict the dependent variable better together than they do individually. In other words, the bivariate correlations with Y may be small or even insignificant, but when the multivariate correlations are modeled together, they predict even better. It is conceivable, for example, that two independent variables, X_1 and X_2, are each uncorrelated (or weakly correlated) with Y in a bivariate context, but when placed together in a multivariate model, they become strongly correlated with Y. This increase in predictive power is due to the influence of the other covariate. In combination, they work well to predict the outcome variable. Let's consider an example of complementarity. This time, imagine that you are trying to predict whether a university professor (like me) will be a good teacher. Say you have some teaching evaluation scores to serve as the outcome and your two independent variables are (1) knowledge of the material and (2) the extent to which one is an engaging speaker. Now, independently, these two factors might not be enough to predict good teaching. One can have a lot of knowledge of the material, but is not an engaging speaker. Equally, one can be an engaging speaker, but not have much knowledge about the material. But when the two are combined into a multivariate model, they predict the outcome more strongly than they could individually. This would be evident, for example, by comparing Pearson's r correlations (bivariate) with Beta values (multivariate). If the Beta values are greater than the sum of the two Pearson's *r* correlation coefficients, then you have complementarity in your model.

Finally, *suppression* (more commonly referred to as *suppressor effects*) refers to a situation where a bivariate correlation changes direction when it is placed in a multivariate model as a result of the influence of the other covariates. This is a rare, but not unheard of, occurrence. What's happening with suppression is that another covariate (or combination of covariates) is suppressing the effect of an independent variable on Y. Normally when this happens, you will find that, in a bivariate context, there is no significant correlation between X_1 and Y, but when placed in a multivariate context, the relationship becomes significant. Less frequently, you will find that, in a bivariate context, X_1 and Y are significantly positively correlated, but when placed in a multivariate context, they become significantly negatively correlated, or vice versa. As I said, this doesn't occur regularly in multivariate models. Most typically, there is a general agreement between bivariate and multivariate results. But, on occasion, you will find the presence of other independent variables changes the nature of the relationship between X and Y.

Homoscedasticity (and Heteroscedasticity)

One of the assumptions of regression (both simple and multiple) is that the relationship between X and Y must be homoscedastic. This concept is not an easy one to grasp and, for an applied statistics textbook, I'm not sure that a long-winded mathematical explanation is necessary. So I'll break this concept down to the bare bones, if I may. In short, homoscedasticity is good and heteroscedasticity is bad. *Homoscedasticity* means that the residuals, or error terms (also referred to as disturbances), between X and Y are randomly (or roughly evenly) distributed across all values of X. By contrast, *heteroscedasticity* means that the error terms between X and Y are nonrandomly (or systematically) distributed across all values of X. Thus, a heteroscedastic relationship between X and Y is one in which the error terms are greater (or lower) at some values of X compared with others. If this still isn't very clear, let me explain this concept visually. I'm going to carry out this explanation using a bivariate example, but the same logic holds in a multiple regression, save that you will have multiple X variables and their relationship with Y to evaluate.

Recall from Chapter 8 that a residual is the distance between the actual data points and the OLS line of best fit in a scatterplot. When X and Y are perfectly positively (or negatively) correlated, then there are no residuals at all. Most of the time, there will be some error between the actual data points and the line of best fit (resulting in a Pearson's *r* that is greater than −1 but less than 1).

Figure 9.1 illustrates a homoscedastic relationship between X and Y. Remember, this is a good thing. You can see that X does not perfectly predict Y because there are errors between the data points and the line of best fit. However, in this case, the error terms appear to be randomly distributed. That is to say, there is no 'pattern' that emerges in this scatterplot. Some lines are closer to the line of best fit, and some lines are further way. The distances between each data point and the error line average themselves out. These are the kinds of residuals we want to see in our regression analyses because they suggest homoscedasticity.

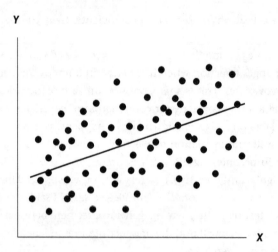

Figure 9.1 Homoscedasticity

Now, Figure 9.2 illustrates a heteroscedastic relationship between X and Y. This is a bad thing. You can see that X does not perfectly predict Y, but – more important – you can also see a pattern that emerges in the scatterplot. As X increases, the error terms in predicting Y become more variable; that is, the values in Y are located further from the line of best fit at higher X values, but closer to the line of best fit at lower X values, meaning that the error terms are not randomly distributed across all values of X. You can see a 'funnel' shape emerging here, where the error terms become larger as X increases. Anytime you see a funnel shape or a 'bow-tie' shape when plotting or comparing residuals, this is an indication of heteroscedasticity.

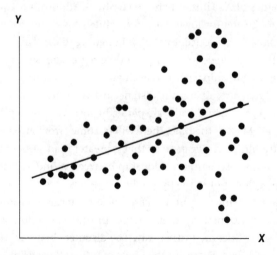

Figure 9.2 Heteroscedasticity

If this isn't entirely clear, don't worry too much. You'll understand the concept better when we look at actual data.

Linearity (and Nonlinearity)

Another key assumption of regression analysis (both simple and multivariate) is that the relationship between X and Y must be linear. I'm not going to dwell too much on this assumption because it has already been discussed in Chapter 8. In short, the line of best fit in a standard regression analysis is a straight line describing the anticipated change in Y for every one-unit increase in X.

This may seem like a curious assumption, given many relationships between variables are, in fact, naturally nonlinear. In such cases, a straight line will suggest a poor fit, when in fact there is a strong fit that is undetected by the use of linear regression. This has previously been referred to as Type II error, where you fail to find a relationship that really exists. Consider the following example of a nonlinear relationship between working hours per week and wages. In this case, the independent variable, X, is working hours and the dependent variable Y, is income. Now, you might assume that this is a linear positive relationship; that is, as working hours increase, so do wages. But if employees receive overtime (e.g., time and a half) beyond a certain number of hours, then the relationship can become nonlinear.

Nonlinear relationships can be U-shaped (see Figure 9.3), inverted U-shaped (see Figure 9.4), and even S-shaped (see Figure 9.5).

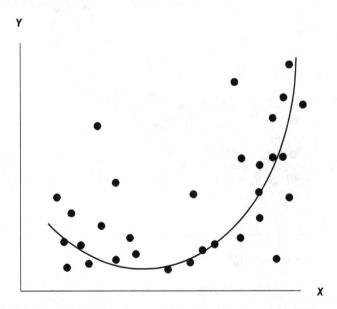

Figure 9.3 U-shaped relationship

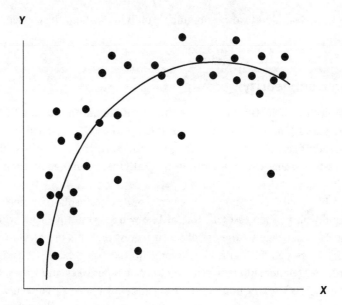

Figure 9.4 Inverted U-shaped relationship

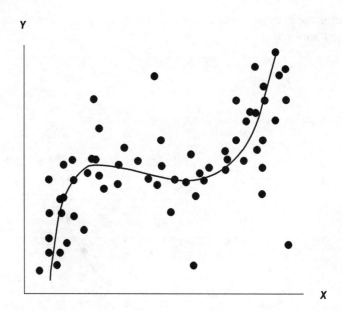

Figure 9.5 S-shaped relationship

When you are dealing with nonlinear relationships, you cannot use standard linear regression. Instead, you have to make more advanced modifications to the model to enable it to estimate nonlinear relationships. These modifications are, in fact, fairly easy to do. To assess whether a relationship between X and Y is nonlinear, you can simply square all the values of X (i.e., X^2) or, in the event of an S-shaped curve, you can cube all the values of X (i.e., X^3). If your R^2 value increases with an X^2 or an X^3, then the relationship between X and Y is likely nonlinear. We'll test this out below, so don't worry if this concept is still unclear.

Dummy Variables

As alluded to above, there is a specific type of variable that, for whatever reason, statisticians have agreed can violate the assumptions of regression and still be used. A *dummy variable* is a two-category nominal variable. By definition, including a dummy variable in your multiple regression model guarantees that you cannot satisfy the assumption of linearity, nor homoscedasticity. When there are only two categories in a variable, it can obviously never be said to be normally distributed. By all accounts, we shouldn't be able to use dummy variables, but, hey, we can anyway because, as a community of data scientists, we've agreed that it's okay to use them, despite their limitations.

There are, however, some rules with using dummy variables in regression analysis. Dummies can only be used as independent variables. If your dependent variable only has two categories, then you cannot use multiple regression analysis, but instead you can use logistic regression (to be discussed in Chapter 10). Additionally, dummies must only have two categories. Any nominal variable with three or more categories cannot be used as a single, stand-alone variable in a multiple regression analysis.

If you have a multicategory nominal variable and you want to study its effects in a multiple regression analysis, then you must first turn it into a series of dummy variables. To do this, you simply take $k - 1$, where k = the number of categories in that multicategory nominal variable. For example, imagine if you have a multicategory variable like race, measured as such:

1 = *white*

2 = *black*

3 = *East Asian*

4 = *South Asian*

5 = *Native American*

6 = *mixed race*

In this case, you have six categories, so you will need to create five dummy variables ($6 - 1 = 5$). To do this, you need to select one reference category. Let's use 'white' as the reference category. Your five dummy variables deriving from this variable are thus:

Variable 1: 1 = *white*, 0 = *black*

Variable 2: 1 = *white*, 0 = *East Asian*

Variable 3: 1 = *white*, 0 = *South Asian*

Variable 4: 1 = *white*, 0 = *Native American*

Variable 5: 1 = *white*, 0 = *mixed race*

You will note that dummy variables should always be coded 0 and 1, although, in theory, they can be coded using any two numbers. The advantage of coding 0 and 1 is that the results of the regression analysis are more easily interpretable.

The interpretation of dummy variables is not straightforward using unstandardized B coefficients. In short, because there are only two categories (0 and 1), you can no longer interpret the effect on Y of a one-unit increase in X. Instead, you would interpret B as the difference between the category coded 1 vis-à-vis the category coded 0. Using Variable 1 as an example, if B is a positive number and significant, then you would conclude that whites score significantly higher than blacks in whatever relationship you're examining. Similarly, if B is a negative number and significant, then you would conclude that whites score significantly lower than blacks in that relationship.

Don't worry too much if you still don't understand dummy variables. You will by the end of this chapter.

Moderation

We could argue that simple regression (where there is one X variable and one Y variable) is, well, rather too 'simple' to truly understand a relationship between a predictor and an outcome. Multiple regression is certainly an improvement on simple regression because the former allows for the incorporation (and holding constant) of other X variables simultaneously. But even multiple regression is still, arguably, an oversimplification of those relationships in real life. Fortunately, there are additional methods of looking at more complex relationships in the context of a multiple regression. To this end, moderated models offer a deeper, more intricate analysis of the relationship between a set of predictors and a single outcome. Let's look at what moderation in multiple regression models looks like.

A *moderation* refers to a situation in which the relationship between, say, X_1 and Y changes in some way as a result of the presence of another independent variable, say, X_2. In other words, X_2 is said to moderate the relationship between X_1 and Y. Another way of saying this is that X_1 and X_2 interact with each other, such that the latter changes the strength or the nature of the former's relationship with Y. What, exactly, does it mean?

Perhaps the best way to explain a moderated regression analysis is visually. Figures 9.6a and b demonstrate what a moderation looks like. Figure 9.6a illustrates a simple, positive relationship between total hours of training that an employee receives per year and job performance. As you can see, the more training received, the higher the job performance, generally speaking. Figure 9.6b illustrates a moderation effect between hours of training (X_1), IQ (X_2), and job performance (Y). As you can see from the two lines (line 'A' depicting the relationship between training and performance for high-IQ employees and line 'B' depicting the relationship between training and performance for low-IQ employees), both are positively related to job performance, but employees with higher IQs (line 'A') enjoy a stronger positive relationship with job performance than employees with lower IQs (line 'B'). We define high and low IQ as individuals 1 *SD* above and below the mean, respectively.

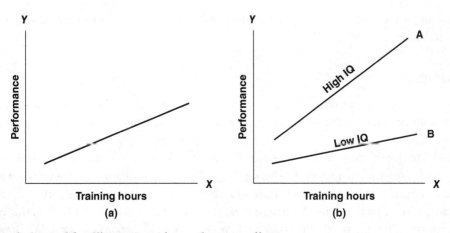

Figure 9.6a and b   Illustration of a moderation effect

As you can see in Figure 9.6b, we have a predictor (X_1 = hours of training), a moderator (X_2 = IQ, broken down into two levels: high and low IQ), and an outcome variable (Y = job performance). If X_2 (IQ) were to fail to moderate the relationship between X_1 (hours of training) and Y (job performance), this means that X_2 (IQ) does not change the nature of the relationship between X_1 (hours of training) and Y (job performance). In other words, regardless of how high or low a respondent scores on X_2 (IQ), the relationship between X_1 (hours of training) and Y (job performance) remains the same and would look like the one depicted in Figure 9.6a. However, as clearly illustrated in Figure 9.6b, X_2 (IQ) can be shown to moderate the relationship between X_1 (hours of training) and Y (job performance), meaning that the relationship between X_1 (hours of training) and Y (job performance) looks different when interacted with the moderator, X_2 (IQ). For example, you can see in Figure 9.6a that the relationship between X_1 (hours of training) and Y (job performance) is positive and significant. But when we incorporate X_2 (IQ) as a moderator in Figure 9.6b, we find that the relationship between X_1 (hours of training) and Y (job performance) is very strong when values of X_2 (IQ) are high, but when values of X_2 (IQ) are low, the positive relationship between X_1 (hours of training) and Y (job performance) is much weaker.

To calculate whether or not your model has a significant interaction effect, you simply have to take the *product* of your two X variables and insert that new variable (the interaction of X_1 and X_2) into your multiple regression model. In other words, you take X_1 and multiply it by X_2 or, alternatively stated, take the values of X_1 times the values of X_2 to create your new interaction term. If this new interaction variable is statistically significant (e.g., $p < 0.05$), then you can confidently conclude that you have a significant interaction effect in your model, and that the relationship between X_1 and Y depends on the level of X_2. To test for the presence of an interaction effect, your regression equation will look like the one in Equation (9.1):

$$Y = B_1X_1 + B_2X_2 + B_3(X_1 \times X_2) + a \qquad (9.3)$$

If you run this regression and your interaction term is statistically significant ($p < 0.05$), then this means that X_2 moderates the relationship between X_1 and Y. You can plot this moderation using what are called simple slopes, as depicted in lines 'A' and 'B' in Figure 9.6b.

Wow, this is pretty difficult material, my friend, but don't worry. It will become clearer when we run a moderation analysis in SPSS.

Mediation

Mediation refers to the statistical process by which we examine the underlying mechanism linking an independent variable (X) and a dependent variable (Y). Sometimes there is a *direct relationship* between the two variables, X and Y. We cannot (normally) go so far as to say that X causes Y, but sometimes it's pretty clear that X influences Y, especially when X is a temporal antecedent to Y. Other times, however, the relationship between X and Y is *indirect*; that is, it is mediated by a third variable, Z. In an indirect effect, Z is referred to as the mediator or the mediating variable. A mediation can be *full* or *partial*. A full mediation means that the relationship between X and Y is fully explained by Z. In other words, the relationship between X and Y is nonsignificant, but through Z it becomes significant. A partial mediation, on the other hand, means that Z significantly mediates the relationship between X and Y, but the relationship between X and Y is still statistically significant (but weaker in light of the introduction of the mediator, Z).

If you're still confused about mediation, it may help to consider the *path diagram* represented in Figure 9.7. A path diagram is a graphical representation of a set of variables, where the relationships are represented by lines and arrows. In most multiple regression path diagrams, the independent variables start on the left-hand side and the dependent variable is located on the right-hand side.

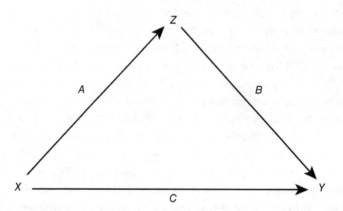

Figure 9.7 Illustration of a mediation effect

Looking at the mediation depicted in Figure 9.7, you can see the direct effect of X on Y labeled C, and the indirect effect of X on Y labeled A and B, where A describes the relationship between X and Z and B describes the relationship between Z and Y. Alternatively stated, C represents the direct relationship between X and Y, and B + C represent the indirect relationship between X and Y through Z. The indirect effect is calculated by taking the product of A and B (i.e., A × B) and comparing that value to C.

Okay, I think you now have enough background information on multiple regression analysis that we can hand over the heavy lifting to SPSS.

Multiple Regression Using SPSS

Let's have a look at the survey of organizations. Go to the Companion Website and open the dataset labeled chap9data. Here you will find nine variables that I've taken from the wider dataset. Go into the Variable View and have a look at them.

Now that we've reached multivariate analyses, for this chapter and the remainder of the book, I won't be showing you how to run descriptive statistics for each variable. If you've been a diligent reader, and I know you have been, then you should already be able to ask SPSS to pull descriptives, frequencies, and histograms for each of these variables. Before you proceed, take a few moments to request this information yourself.

We also won't be bothering with any data transformations in light of nonnormality. Again, if you'd like to request skewness and kurtosis statistics on your own and then transform nonnormal distributions, feel free to do so, but please note that this will slightly change the results reported in the rest of this chapter, which are based on raw (unmodified) data.

What we will do now, before we get to the multiple regression analyses, is to go through our variables and tentative hypotheses. Once these are clear, I'll show you how to run a series of multiple regression analyses using SPSS.

Our dependent variable, perform1, is a measure of the organizations' financial performance (for the moment, just ignore perform2). Now, I should say that some researchers will argue that multiple regression should only be used with a scale-level dependent variable, but the consensus is that ordinal variables also typically 'work' in such models. So we're going to go ahead and use this variable, where financial performance is measured on a five-point scale (where 1 = *a lot below average* and 5 = *a lot better than average*). In short, we are trying to predict which factors might be significantly associated with the financial performance of an organization.

We have seven possible independent variables: (1) prp, whether the firm offers performance-related pay, (2) antiunion, the extent to which management would rather consult with workers directly than deal with unions, (3) innovat, the extent to which the workplace is innovative in its product or service, (4) contractr, whether contractors are doing work that used to be done in-house five years ago, (5) diversity, whether the workplace has a formal diversity/equal opportunities policy, (6) appraise, the proportion of nonmanagerial employees whose work is formally appraised, and (7) infoshar, the extent to which managers share staffing information with employees.

It should be noted that variables (1), (4), and (5) are dichotomous (dummy) variables, coded 0 = *no* and 1 = *yes*. Spend some time now looking through the Variable View to see how all of the independent variables are measured.

Now, let's look at each hypothesis to set our expectations.

Hypothesis 1: We expect that firms offering performance-related pay will report higher levels of financial performance compared with firms not offering performance-related pay. More motivated employees work harder, thus contributing positively to financial performance.

Hypothesis 2: We expect that organizations that would rather consult directly with workers than with unions will report higher levels of financial performance. Their resistance to union presence suggests that they are more cost-conscious, thus contributing positively to financial performance.

Hypothesis 3: We expect that organizations that are more innovative deliver higher financial performance. Innovation drives performance improvement, thus contributing positively to financial performance.

Hypothesis 4: We expect that organizations that are increasingly using contractors will report higher levels of financial performance. The use of contractors suggests that managers are cost-conscious, thus contributing positively to financial performance.

Hypothesis 5: We expect that organizations that have a formal diversity/equal opportunities policy report higher financial performance. Diversity is a strong asset that organizations can leverage, thus contributing positively to financial performance.

Hypothesis 6: We expect that organizations that use formal performance appraisals will also deliver higher financial returns. Appraising employee performance embeds a culture of continuous improvement and promotes accountability, thus contributing positively to financial performance.

Hypothesis 7: We expect that organizations that share staffing information with employees will report higher levels of financial performance. Information sharing builds trust and organizational commitment, thus contributing positively to financial performance.

You might be tempted just to run a single multiple regression model to test these seven hypotheses, and you could do so. But to really show you how to build a model, we're going to run a series of models, each of which adds another independent variable. But before we do that, let's first ask SPSS to create a bivariate correlation table with all of these variables. This will allow us to evaluate the Pearson's *r* values for each hypothesis.

Go to Analyze, Correlate, and Bivariate. The window depicted in Figure 9.8 appears. Simply highlight the top eight variables in the left-hand column (excluding perform2, at the bottom of the list) and move them to the right using ➡. Now quickly go into Options and click ☑ Means and standard deviations. Click Continue and then OK. Have a look at the output in Figure 9.9.

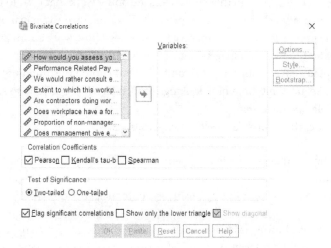

Figure 9.8 Bivariate correlations function in SPSS

Descriptive Statistics

	Mean	Std. Deviation	N
How would you assess your workplace's financial performance?	3.5733	.81753	2456
Performance Related Pay	.4268	.49470	2676
We would rather consult employees directly than deal with unions	3.7240	1.17055	2667
Extent to which this workplace leads the way in developing new products/services	3.3542	1.19928	1787
Are contractors doing work which would have been done in-house 5 yrs ago?	.2478	.43182	2248
Does workplace have a formal written policy on diversity/equal opportunities?	.9033	.29554	2659
Proportion of non-managerial employees whose performance is formally appraised	5.6668	.93660	2221
Does management give employees information about staffing plans?	.7014	.45774	2679

(Continued)

(Continued)

Correlations

		How would you assess your workplace's financial performance?	Performance Related Pay	We would rather consult employees directly than deal with unions	Extent to which this workplace leads the way in developing new products/services	Are contractors doing work which would have been done in-house 5 yrs ago?	Does workplace have a formal written policy on diversity/equal opportunities?	Proportion of non-managerial employees whose performance is formally appraised	Does management give employees information about staffing plans?
How would you assess your workplace's financial performance?	Pearson Correlation	1	.058**	.001	.193**	-.006	.054**	.045*	.018
	Sig. (2-tailed)		.004	.960	<.001	.788	.008	.044	.364
	N	2456	2453	2444	1681	2078	2439	2033	2455
Performance Related Pay	Pearson Correlation	.058**	1	.077**	.053*	.035	.025	.027	-.028
	Sig. (2-tailed)	.004		<.001	.026	.095	.199	.205	.149
	N	2453	2676	2663	1786	2244	2655	2217	2675
We would rather consult employees directly than deal with unions	Pearson Correlation	.001	.077**	1	-.038	-.113**	-.165**	.053*	-.163**
	Sig. (2-tailed)	.960	<.001		.112	<.001	<.001	.013	<.001
	N	2444	2663	2667	1776	2236	2647	2209	2666
Extent to which this workplace leads the way in developing new products/services	Pearson Correlation	.193**	.053*	-.038	1	.067**	.153**	.025	.079**
	Sig. (2-tailed)	<.001	.026	.112		.010	<.001	.357	<.001
	N	1681	1786	1776	1787	1489	1770	1382	1787
Are contractors doing work which would have been done in-house 5 yrs ago?	Pearson Correlation	-.006	.035	-.113**	.067**	1	.089**	-.020	.024
	Sig. (2-tailed)	.788	.095	<.001	.010		<.001	.397	.246
	N	2078	2244	2236	1489	2248	2232	1882	2247
Does workplace have a formal written policy on diversity/equal opportunities?	Pearson Correlation	.054**	.025	-.165**	.153**	.089**	1	.049*	.111**
	Sig. (2-tailed)	.008	.199	<.001	<.001	<.001		.020	<.001
	N	2439	2655	2647	1770	2232	2659	2212	2658
Proportion of non-managerial employees whose performance is formally appraised	Pearson Correlation	.045*	.027	.053*	.025	-.020	.049*	1	.017
	Sig. (2-tailed)	.044	.205	.013	.357	.397	.020		.434
	N	2033	2217	2209	1382	1882	2212	2221	2220
Does management give employees information about staffing plans?	Pearson Correlation	.018	-.028	-.163**	.079**	.024	.111**	.017	1
	Sig. (2-tailed)	.364	.149	<.001	<.001	.246	<.001	.434	
	N	2455	2675	2666	1787	2247	2658	2220	2679

**. Correlation is significant at the 0.01 level (2-tailed).

*. Correlation is significant at the 0.05 level (2-tailed).

Figure 9.9 SPSS output, descriptive statistics and bivariate correlations, multiple variables vis-à-vis Perform1

Reprint courtesy of IBM Corporation ©

The first thing you might notice under descriptive statistics is that N (the total number of cases) is different for each variable. This is due to the difference in missing values across the items in the survey of organizations. Have a look at the means and standard deviations for each variable.

Under Correlations, you'll see a rather large matrix with every possible combination of Pearson's r correlations. The ones that we are interested in run from left to right across the top row of this table. Here you can see how each independent variable, on its own, correlates with the dependent variable, perform1. Reading from left to right, you can see that three variables have **, implying a reasonably strong Pearson's r correlation where $p < 0.01$: it seems financial performance is positively related to performance-related pay ($r = 0.058$, $p < 0.001$), innovation ($r = 0.193$, $p < 0.01$), and the presence of a formal diversity/equal opportunity policy ($r = 0.054$, $p < 0.01$). Financial performance is also positively related, at the $p < 0.05$ level, to the proportion of employees whose work is formally appraised ($r = 0.045$, $p < 0.05$), although this relationship has * instead of **, implying weaker, but still statistically significant, generalizability of the finding. The remaining variables are not significantly related to financial performance. Now, this information is interesting, but it does not adequately address the hypotheses. To do this, we'll need to run the multiple regression models.

The first model, in fact, is a simple regression model, so you should already be familiar with this process from Chapter 8. Go to Analyze, Regression, and Linear. The window depicted in Figure 9.10 appears. Highlight perform1 (the first variable in the left column) and move it to the right under Dependent:. Then highlight performance-related pay on the left and move it to the right under Independent(s):. Now go into Statistics... and you'll see a new dialogue box, depicted in Figure 9.11. Tick ☑ Confidence intervals and click Continue. Then click OK. Boom! Have a look at the output in Figure 9.12.

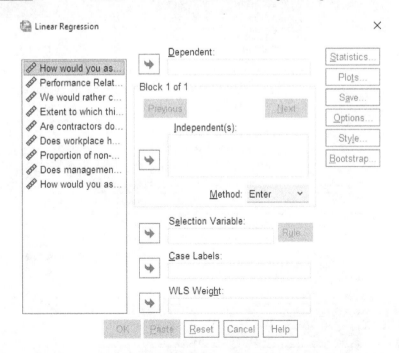

Figure 9.10 Linear regression function in SPSS

Reprint courtesy of IBM Corporation ©

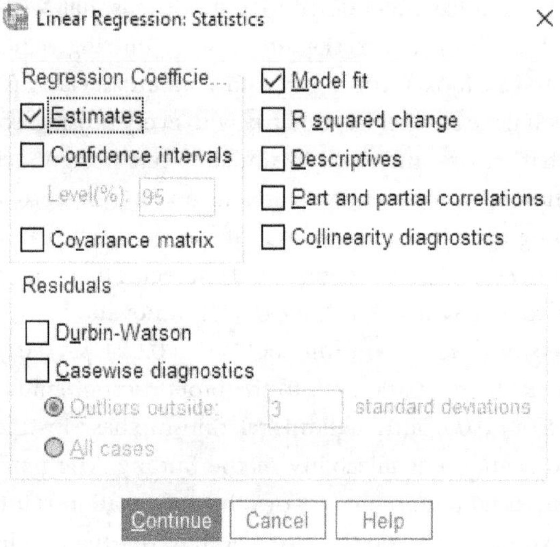

Figure 9.11 Linear regression statistics function in SPSS

Reprint courtesy of IBM Corporation ©

Variables Entered/Removed[a]

Model	Variables Entered	Variables Removed	Method
1	Performance Related Pay[b]	.	Enter

a. Dependent Variable: How would you assess your workplace's financial performance?

b. All requested variables entered.

Model Summary

Model	R	R Square	Adjusted R Square	Std. Error of the Estimate
1	.058[a]	.003	.003	.81657

a. Predictors: (Constant), Performance Related Pay

ANOVA[a]

Model		Sum of Squares	df	Mean Square	F	Sig.
1	Regression	5.518	1	5.518	8.276	.004[b]
	Residual	1634.302	2451	.667		
	Total	1639.821	2452			

a. Dependent Variable: How would you assess your workplace's financial performance?

b. Predictors: (Constant), Performance Related Pay

Coefficients[a]

Model		Unstandardized Coefficients		Standardized Coefficients			95.0% Confidence Interval for B	
		B	Std. Error	Beta	t	Sig.	Lower Bound	Upper Bound
1	(Constant)	3.533	.022		161.881	.000	3.490	3.576
	Performance Related Pay	.096	.033	.058	2.877	.004	.031	.161

a. Dependent Variable: How would you assess your workplace's financial performance?

Figure 9.12 SPSS output, simple regression, performance-related pay predicts financial performance

Reprint courtesy of IBM Corporation ©

The first box just reminds you which two variables were entered into the equation. The second box provides the overall model summary. Here you can see the R is the exact same value as Pearson's r, 0.058. Squaring this gives 0.003, which means that only 0.3% of the variation in financial performance can be explained by the presence of performance-related pay schemes. The next box down, labeled ANOVA, tells us that the model significantly predicts financial performance. All you need to pay attention to here is the p-value of 0.004. Finally, you get the 'results' of the simple regression under the box labeled Coefficients. Here you can see what you already know. The standardized coefficient, Beta, is exactly the same as your Pearson's r value, 0.058. The corresponding t-statistic is 2.88 and the p-value is 0.004. The unstandardized coefficient, B, is 0.096. This can be interpreted as follows: firms that offer performance-related pay score 0.096 higher on financial performance than those that do not.

As I said, this is nothing new to you because you already learned how to do simple regression in Chapter 8. But now we're going to run a series of multiple regressions, each of which adds a new independent variable into the equation. I'm not going to reproduce all of the output in this chapter, but I will show the output of the final multiple regression model when we get there. For now, let's start by adding one more variable, antiunion, to the simple regression model we just built.

Go to Analyze, Regression, and Linear.. Find antiunion and move it to the right under Independent(s):. We're going to keep everything the same and just click OK. Looking at the output, you will note, under Model Summary, that our R and R^2 are the exact same values, 0.058 and 0.003, respectively. In other words, we already know that adding antiunion to the model, in effect, added no value at all. In fact, our ANOVA, which tests overall model fit, suggests that the overall model got slightly worse, as evidenced by the higher p-value of 0.017. As expected, under Coefficients, our B and Beta values for antiunion are nonsignificant ($p = 0.817$), but performance-related pay is still significant and positive ($p = 0.004$).

Let's add a third independent variable into the analysis: innovat. Go to Analyze, Regression, and Linear.. Find innovat in the left-hand column and move it to the right under Independent(s):, and then click OK. You will immediately see under Model Summary that our R value has shot up from 0.058 to 0.201, suggesting that innovation likely strongly predicts financial performance. The corresponding R^2 of 0.041 means that now 4.1% of the variation in financial performance can be explained by our three independent variables, although we can bet that most of this explanatory power is driven by the inclusion of innovat. The ANOVA is significant at $p < 0.001$, which suggests a very good fit, overall, for this model. Finally, moving down to Coefficients, you will see that antiunion is still insignificant (Beta = 0.004, $p = 0.874$), performance-related pay is still significant, but at roughly the same value (Beta = 0.062, p = 0.010), and innovat is strongly significant (Beta = 0.188, $p < 0.001$).

Let's add another independent variable to the model: contractr. Go to Analyze, Regression, and Linear.. Find contractr and move it to the right under Independent(s):, and then click $\boxed{\text{OK}}$. As you will see, the values of R and R^2 have barely moved to 0.204 and 0.042, respectively. It looks like we've added another dud into our multiple regression model! The overall ANOVA value is still significant at $p < 0.001$, but we can probably assume that this is because innovat does such a good job predicting financial performance. Looking at Coefficients, performance-related pay and innovat are still statistically significant, but antiunion and contractr are insignificant (p = 0.543 and p = 0.478, respectively).

Now we're going to add another independent variable to the multiple regression model: diversity. Looking back at our bivariate correlations table, this variable was a significant predictor of financial performance (r = 0.054, $p < 0.01$). Let's see if it remains a significant predictor in the presence of the other covariates. Go to Analyze, Regression, and Linear.. Find diversity and move it to the right under Independent(s):, and then click $\boxed{\text{OK}}$. Now here is where the model gets really interesting. Our model summary suggests that there is not much improvement in R and R^2, whose values are now 0.209 and 0.044, respectively. Our overall model fit, as expressed by the ANOVA, is still significant at $p < 0.001$. Moving down to our coefficients, you can see that innovat and performance-related pay are both still significant predictors, but the other three variables, including diversity, are nonsignificant, with p-values of 0.430, 0.477, and 0.472. What this means is that we have identified a suppressor effect. Diversity and financial performance were both positively and significantly correlated in a bivariate context (r = 0.054, $p < 0.01$), but when diversity is placed alongside the other independent variables and their influence is thus controlled for, the relationship between diversity and financial performance disappears and becomes nonsignificant (Beta = 0.019, p = 0.472). In other words, the presence of the other covariates in the model is suppressing the effect of diversity on financial performance. Pretty cool, eh?

Let's add another variable to the model and see what happens: appraise. Go to Analyze, Regression, and Linear.. Find appraise from the list on the left and move it to the right under Independent(s):, and then click $\boxed{\text{OK}}$. This time, you will notice a modest reduction in the values of R and R^2, to 0.200 and 0.040, respectively. In other words, we can already assume that the addition of this new independent variable into the equation adds no value (and, in fact, takes away value!). Our ANOVA value, which is indicative of overall model fit, is still significant at $p < 0.001$, but, again, this significance is likely driven by our two significant predictors, performance-related pay and innovat. Looking now at Coefficients, you can see that appraise is not significantly related to financial performance, given that Beta = 0.002 and p = 0.960. Innovat is still strongly significant (Beta = 0.190, $p < 0.001$), but, interestingly, performance-related pay is only barely significant (Beta = 0.059, p = 0.049), recalling that 0.05 is the cutoff for statistical significance. What this means is that there is evidence of a bit of redundancy now vis-à-vis performance-related pay. In other words, the presence of the other variables slightly weakens the relationship between performance-related pay and financial performance.

At last, we arrive at our full multiple regression model! This one will be set up slightly differently from the previous ones because I'll be adding some extra bells and whistles. Thus, I will include all of the output.

As always, go to Analyze, Regression, and Linear.. Find infoshare (this should be second from the last in the list of variables) in the left-hand column and move it to the right under Independent(s):. Now go into $\boxed{\text{Statistics}}$ and tick ☑ Descriptives and ☑ Collinearity diagnostics, and then $\boxed{\text{Continue}}$. Next go into [S̲ave…] and have a look at the window depicted in Figure 9.13. There are lots of cool options here for experimentation, but for now I want you to tick ☑ Ma̲halanobis so we can check for multivariate outliers. Click [C̲ontinue] and when you are ready to run the full multiple regression model, click [OK].

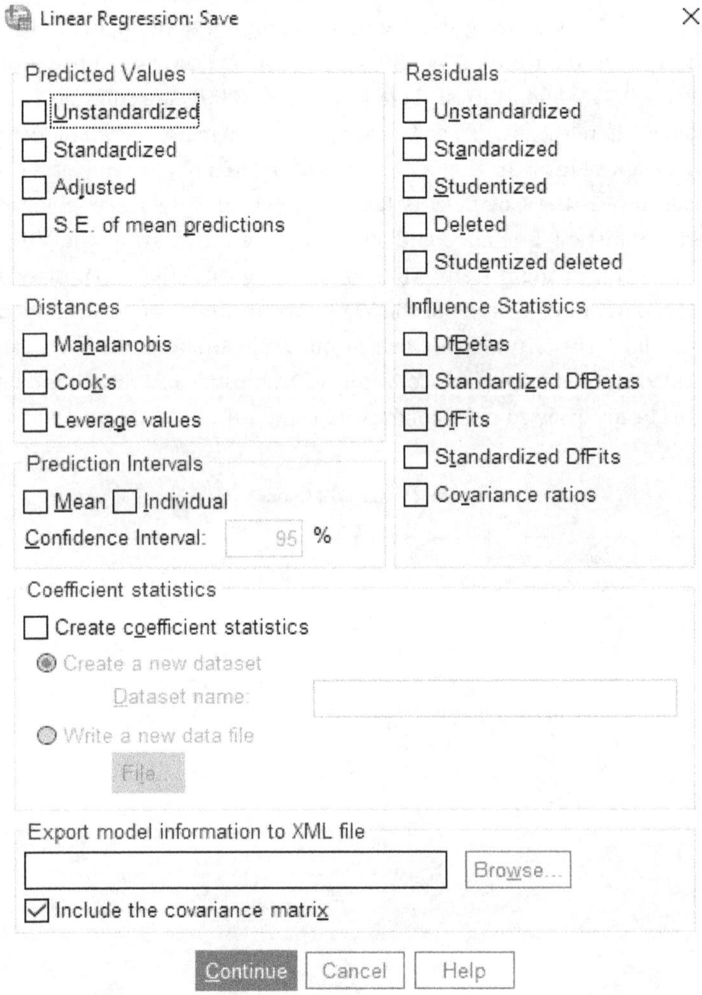

Linear Regression: Save   ✕

Predicted Values
- ☐ U̲nstandardized
- ☐ Standar̲dized
- ☐ Adj̲usted
- ☐ S.E. of mean p̲redictions

Residuals
- ☐ U̲nstandardized
- ☐ St̲andardized
- ☐ S̲tudentized
- ☐ De̲leted
- ☐ Stud̲entized deleted

Distances
- ☐ Ma̲halanobis
- ☐ Coo̲k's
- ☐ Leverag̲e values

Influence Statistics
- ☐ DfB̲etas
- ☐ Standardiz̲ed DfBetas
- ☐ Df̲Fits
- ☐ S̲tandardized DfFits
- ☐ Co̲variance ratios

Prediction Intervals
- ☐ M̲ean ☐ I̲ndividual
- C̲onfidence Interval: [95] %

Coefficient statistics
- ☐ Create c̲oefficient statistics
  - ◉ Create a new dataset
    - D̲ataset name: [   ]
  - ○ Write a new data file
    - [Fi̲le…]

Export model information to XML file
[   ] [Bro̲wse…]
☑ Include the covariance matri̲x

[C̲ontinue] [Cancel] [Help]

Figure 9.13 Linear regression save function in SPSS

Reprint courtesy of IBM Corporation ©

The output is reported in Figure 9.14. The first box provides some descriptive statistics. Here you will see that, using listwise deletion of cases, the total number of organizations included in these analyses is $n = 1086$, suggesting that there is quite a bit of missing data in this regression analysis. You can skip the correlations table and Variables Entered/Removed and go straight down to the Model Summary. Here you will see that adding infoshare has had a negligible effect on the model.

The new R is 0.201 and R^2 is 0.040, implying that our full multiple regression model explains roughly 4% of the total variation in financial performance. Alternatively stated, those independent variables not measured and therefore not included in our model explain 96% of the variation in financial performance. The ANOVA, which assesses the overall model fit, is still statistically significant, but, again, this is likely driven by our two significant predictors, performance-related pay and innovat. If you scroll down to Coefficients, you will confirm that the addition of infoshare did not add value to the model. Thus, sharing staffing information does not appear to be associated with changes in financial performance (Beta = –0.022, p = 0.467). However, both performance-related pay (Beta = 0.059, p = 0.048) and innovat (Beta = 0.192, p < 0.001) are still significant predictors of the outcome variable. Therefore, we can conclude that the two most important factors in determining financial performance are (1) having a performance-related pay scheme and (2) innovation of product or service. Also in the Coefficients table, you will find two new columns on the right labeled Collinearity Statistics: Tolerance and VIF. Pay close attention to the VIF scores to assess multicollinearity. As a rule of thumb, any VIF score that is greater than 10 indicates that multicollinearity is a problem. In our case, none of the VIF scores are anywhere near that cutoff, so we can assume that multicollinearity is not a problem in our multivariate model. You can skip the final two boxes in Figure 9.14, the first labeled Collinearity Diagnostics and the second labeled Residuals Statistics. We have already assessed multicollinearity using VIF.

Descriptive Statistics

	Mean	Std. Deviation	N
How would you assess your workplace's financial performance?	3.6050	.82670	1086
Performance Related Pay	.5479	.49793	1086
We would rather consult employees directly than deal with unions	4.0700	1.03696	1086
Extent to which this workplace leads the way in developing new products/services	3.4926	1.13000	1086
Are contractors doing work which would have been done in-house 5 yrs ago?	.2293	.42056	1086
Does workplace have a formal written policy on diversity/equal opportunities?	.9319	.25210	1086
Proportion of non-managerial employees whose performance is formally appraised	5.6713	.97131	1086
Does management give employees information about staffing plans?	.6713	.46997	1086

Correlations

		How would you assess your workplace's financial performance?	Performance Related Pay	We would rather consult employees directly than deal with unions	Extent to which this workplace leads the way in developing new products/services	Are contractors doing work which would have been done in-house 5 yrs ago?	Does workplace have a formal written policy on diversity/equal opportunities?	Proportion of non-managerial employees whose performance is formally appraised	Does management give employees information about staffing plans?
Pearson Correlation	How would you assess your workplace's financial performance?	1.000	.056	.009	.189	-.012	.021	.010	-.005
	Performance Related Pay	.056	1.000	.024	-.012	.025	-.033	.096	.010
	We would rather consult employees directly than deal with unions	.009	.024	1.000	-.011	-.100	-.056	.145	-.047
	Extent to which this workplace leads the way in developing new products/services	.189	-.012	-.011	1.000	.067	.060	.004	.088
	Are contractors doing work which would have been done in-house 5 yrs ago?	-.012	.025	-.100	.067	1.000	.061	-.032	.009
	Does workplace have a formal written policy on diversity/equal opportunities?	.021	-.033	-.056	.060	.061	1.000	.029	-.003
	Proportion of non-managerial employees whose performance is formally appraised	.010	.096	.145	.004	-.032	.029	1.000	-.013
	Does management give employees information about staffing plans?	-.005	.010	-.047	.088	.009	-.003	-.013	1.000
Sig. (1-tailed)	How would you assess your workplace's financial performance?		.032	.388	<.001	.343	.244	.367	.437
	Performance Related Pay	.032		.216	.351	.210	.141	.001	.368
	We would rather consult employees directly than deal with unions	.388	.216		.354	.000	.033	.000	.060
	Extent to which this workplace leads the way in developing new products/services	.000	.351	.354		.014	.025	.446	.002

(Continued)

(Continued)

Are contractors doing work which would have been done in-house 5 yrs ago?	.388	.147	.023	.	.014	.000	.343
Does workplace have a formal written policy on diversity/equal opportunities?	.467	.171	.	.023	.025	.033	.244
Proportion of non-managerial employees whose performance is formally appraised	.336	.	.171	.147	.446	.000	.367
Does management give employees information about staffing plans?	.	.336	.467	.388	.002	.060	.437
N							
How would you assess your workplace's financial performance?	1086	1086	1086	1086	1086	1086	1086
Performance Related Pay	1086	1086	1086	1086	1086	1086	1086
We would rather consult employees directly than deal with unions	1086	1086	1086	1086	1086	1086	1086
Extent to which this workplace leads the way in developing new products/services	1086	1086	1086	1086	1086	1086	1086
Are contractors doing work which would have been done in-house 5 yrs ago?	1086	1086	1086	1086	1086	1086	1086
Does workplace have a formal written policy on diversity/equal opportunities?	1086	1086	1086	1086	1086	1086	1086
Proportion of non-managerial employees whose performance is formally appraised	1086	1086	1086	1086	1086	1086	1086
Does management give employees information about staffing plans?	1086	1086	1086	1086	1086	1086	1086

Variables Entered/Removed[a]

Model	Variables Entered	Variables Removed	Method
1	Does management give employees information about staffing plans?, Does workplace have a formal written policy on diversity/equal opportunities?, Proportion of non-managerial employees whose performance is formally appraised, Are contractors doing work which would have been done in-house 5 yrs ago?, Performance Related Pay, Extent to which this workplace leads the way in developing new products/services, We would rather consult employees directly than deal with unions[b]	.	Enter

a. Dependent Variable: How would you assess your workplace's financial performance?

b. All requested variables entered.

(Continued)

(Continued)

Model Summary[b]

Model	R	R Square	Adjusted R Square	Std. Error of the Estimate
1	.201[a]	.040	.034	.81244

a. Predictors: (Constant), Does management give employees information about staffing plans?, Does workplace have a formal written policy on diversity/equal opportunities?, Proportion of non-managerial employees whose performance is formally appraised, Are contractors doing work which would have been done in-house 5 yrs ago?, Performance Related Pay, Extent to which this workplace leads the way in developing new products/services, We would rather consult employees directly than deal with unions

b. Dependent Variable: How would you assess your workplace's financial performance?

ANOVA[a]

Model		Sum of Squares	df	Mean Square	F	Sig.
1	Regression	29.983	7	4.283	6.489	<.001[b]
	Residual	711.550	1078	.660		
	Total	741.533	1085			

a. Dependent Variable: How would you assess your workplace's financial performance?

b. Predictors: (Constant), Does management give employees information about staffing plans?, Does workplace have a formal written policy on diversity/equal opportunities?, Proportion of non-managerial employees whose performance is formally appraised, Are contractors doing work which would have been done in-house 5 yrs ago?, Performance Related Pay, Extent to which this workplace leads the way in developing new products/services, We would rather consult employees directly than deal with unions

Coefficients[a]

Model		Unstandardized Coefficients		Standardized Coefficients	t	Sig.	95.0% Confidence Interval for B		Collinearity Statistics	
		B	Std. Error	Beta			Lower Bound	Upper Bound	Tolerance	VIF
1	(Constant)	3.029	.206		14.699	<.001	2.625	3.434		
	Performance Related Pay	.099	.050	.059	1.977	.048	.001	.196	.988	1.012
	We would rather consult employees directly than deal with unions	.005	.024	.006	.206	.837	-.043	.053	.965	1.037
	Extent to which this workplace leads the way in developing new products/services	.141	.022	.192	6.400	<.001	.098	.184	.985	1.016
	Are contractors doing work which would have been done in-house 5 yrs ago?	-.052	.059	-.027	-.881	.379	-.168	.064	.982	1.019
	Does workplace have a formal written policy on diversity/equal opportunities?	.044	.098	.013	.446	.655	-.149	.237	.988	1.012
	Proportion of non-managerial employees whose performance is formally appraised	.001	.026	.001	.045	.964	-.049	.052	.968	1.033
	Does management give employees information about staffing plans?	-.038	.053	-.022	-.728	.467	-.142	.065	.990	1.010

a. Dependent Variable: How would you assess your workplace's financial performance?

(Continued)

(Continued)

Collinearity Diagnostics[a]

Model	Dimension	Eigenvalue	Condition Index	Variance Proportions							
				(Constant)	Performance Related Pay	We would rather consult employees directly than deal with unions	Extent to which this workplace leads the way in developing new products/services	Are contractors doing work which would have been done in-house 5 yrs ago?	Does workplace have a formal written policy on diversity/equal opportunities?	Proportion of non-managerial employees whose performance is formally appraised	Does management give employees information about staffing plans?
1	1	6.354	1.000	.00	.01	.00	.00	.01	.00	.00	.01
	2	.743	2.924	.00	.01	.00	.00	.97	.00	.00	.00
	3	.421	3.885	.00	.91	.00	.00	.00	.00	.00	.07
	4	.286	4.717	.00	.06	.01	.01	.00	.01	.00	.89
	5	.084	8.717	.00	.00	.09	.87	.01	.03	.01	.01
	6	.068	9.693	.00	.00	.31	.01	.01	.63	.00	.00
	7	.034	13.603	.02	.01	.48	.03	.00	.19	.44	.01
	8	.011	24.197	.97	.00	.11	.07	.00	.13	.54	.02

a. Dependent Variable: How would you assess your workplace's financial performance?

Residuals Statistics[a]

	Minimum	Maximum	Mean	Std. Deviation	N
Predicted Value	3.1500	3.9075	3.6050	.16623	1086
Std. Predicted Value	-2.737	1.820	.000	1.000	1086
Standard Error of Predicted Value	.043	.161	.067	.020	1086
Adjusted Predicted Value	3.1416	3.9179	3.6049	.16672	1086
Residual	-2.72829	1.81219	.00000	.80982	1086
Std. Residual	-3.358	2.231	.000	.997	1086
Stud. Residual	-3.364	2.256	.000	1.001	1086
Deleted Residual	-2.73760	1.85335	.00005	.81597	1086
Stud. Deleted Residual	-3.380	2.260	.000	1.001	1086
Mahal. Distance	1.990	41.546	6.994	5.577	1086
Cook's Distance	.000	.018	.001	.002	1086
Centered Leverage Value	.002	.038	.006	.005	1086

a. Dependent Variable: How would you assess your workplace's financial performance?

Figure 9.14 SPSS output, full multiple regression model predicting Perform1

Reprint courtesy of IBM Corporation ©

Recall that we also asked SPSS to search for multivariate outliers using Mahalanobis's Distance. You won't find this information in the output in Figure 9.14. Instead, go back to Data View in your spreadsheet. You will notice that a new column labeled MAH_1 has been created. At the moment, this new column is just a bunch of random numbers, with several missing values. The missing values in the MAH_1 column are from variables with missing cases. What we are going to do is to sort that column in descending order by right clicking on MAH_1 and clicking on Sort Descending. Now you will see the Mahalanobis's Distance values numbered from a high of 41.55 to a low of 1.99. As a general rule, the higher and more 'unusual' looking the value, the more likely it is a multivariate outlier. You could just delete the first few high values, but another way to more objectively decide whether to delete a case is to use a chi-square test to create a p-value that can be used to determine whether a case is a multivariate outlier. To do this, you will need to know the degrees of freedom, which in this case is simply the number of independent variables in your multiple regression equation; that is, $df = 7$. Now, to calculate the p-values for Mahalanobis's Distance, go to Transform and Compute Variable. The window depicted in Figure 9.15 appears. Under Target Variable:, type 'MAH_2' to create a new variable with your chi-square p-values. Now, click once in the box under Numeric Expression: and type: 1 –. Then under Function Group: click All, and then under Functions and Special Variables:, scroll down and double click on Cdf.Chisq. Your numeric expression will now look like this: 1 - CDF.CHISQ(?,?). Now, for the first ?, we want to delete it and replace it with

MAH_1. For the second ?, we want to delete it and replace it with our degrees of freedom, which is 7. So your final equation under Numeric Expression: is 1 – CDF.CHISQ(MAH_1,7). When you are ready to create your new MAH_2 variable (which contains only p-values), click OK . Now, go back to Data View and you will see that you have created a new variable, MAH_2, with p-values for each value of MAH_1. We will use a p-value cutoff of $p < 0.01$, so any value in MAH_2 that is <0.01 can be deleted as a multivariate outlier. As it happens, the first 47 cases in our dataset have $p < 0.01$ (i.e., $p = 0.00$), so you could delete them, but for now, let's just keep the multivariate outliers in the equation to simplify the next SPSS function.

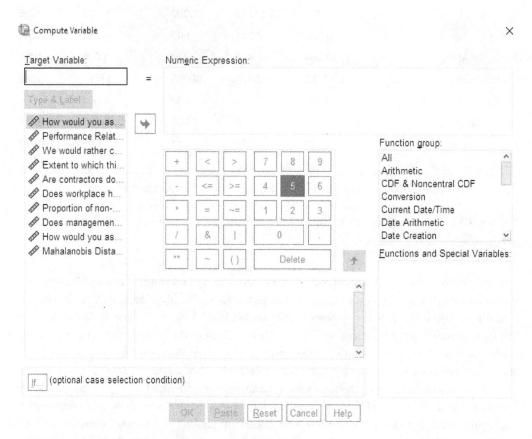

Figure 9.15 Compute variable function in SPSS to assess Mahalanobis's Distance

Reprint courtesy of IBM Corporation ©

So far, we have used the 'Enter' method to construct our multiple regression equation, meaning that we have entered all seven independent variables. But, as mentioned above, we could also use an exploratory 'stepwise' method in which we allow SPSS to include variables that are significantly related to the outcome and exclude variables that are not significantly related to the outcome. To do this, go to Analyze, Regression, and Linear. You should have your dependent variable, perform1, under Dependent: and your seven independent variables under Independent(s). Immediately, below the Independent(s) box, you will see Method: Enter. Click on this and select Forward and then OK . Looking at the output, you'll see that, using the Forward technique, only innovat survives as an independent variable. Do the same thing now, but this time under Method:, click Backward. In the output, you'll see that the sixth model, consisting of performance-related pay and innovat is the best one.

You will notice that the dataset we've been using has another variable labeled perform2. This is an alternate measure of performance that asks the respondents (i.e., the HR managers): How would you assess your workplace's labor productivity, where 1 = *a lot below average* to 5 = *a lot better than average*. Try to run the multiple regression model again, but this time using the 'Enter' method and perform2 as the dependent variable. How is this model different from the one we estimated using perform1 as the dependent variable?

Okay, the last thing I want to teach you before drawing this chapter to a close is how to do mediation and moderation/interaction analyses in SPSS. The easiest way to do this is to install Andrew Hayes's (2017) PROCESS Macro for SPSS. This extension is free, but it requires administrator rights to install onto your computer. You may have to request authorization from your IT support team to enable the use of this function. If you do have administrator rights, you can install the Hayes PROCESS Macro for SPSS on your PC by following this short instructional video:

www.youtube.com/watch?v=11tNWOJPCzo

If you have installed PROCESS correctly, you should see PROCESS v3.5 by Andrew F. Hayes when you go to Analyze and Regression. Using SPSS to do mediation and moderation analyses is pretty advanced. If you do wish to learn how to use these functions, you can read all about it in Box 9.2.

Box 9.2: Using Hayes's PROCESS Macro in SPSS to Do Mediation and Moderation Analyses

The PROCESS Macro in SPSS is a groovy tool. It enables researchers to conduct advanced regression analyses, including mediations, moderations, and even moderated mediations. The user interface is simple and easy-to-use, in spite of the fact that the analyses are highly advanced. PROCESS comes with 91 model templates, most of which are complex moderated mediations. Given that this is an applied statistics textbook, I'm only going to show you how to do a simple mediation (Model 4) and a simple moderation (Model 1). For anyone interested in learning more complex methods, I urge you to read Hayes (2017).

We won't be using the WERS datasets for these analyses. Instead, you can find another dataset in the Companion Website called chap9PROCESS.sav. This dataset contains responses from local government professionals in Western Australia (*n* = 289), most of whom are chief executive officers. Spend a little time in Variable View going through the list of variables included in this dataset and verify how they

(Continued)

were measured. You will see that there are four variables in this dataset: AUTOND (a composite measure of job autonomy, where 1 = *less autonomy* and 5 = *more autonomy*), MHI (a composite measure of mental health, where 1 = *poorer mental health* and 5 = *better mental health*), INCIV (a composite measure of workplace incivility, where 1 = *less incivility* and 5 = *more incivility*), and PHYSYMPT (a composite measure of physical symptoms, where 1 = *fewer physical symptoms* and 5 = *more physical symptoms*). Before proceeding, think for a moment how these four variables might be related to one another.

I'm first going to show you how to conduct a simple moderation (Model 1) followed by a simple mediation (Model 4) using PROCESS. Let's do this!

Using SPSS PROCESS to Estimate a Simple Moderation (Model 1)

Recall that a moderating variable, *M*, changes the nature of the relationship between your independent variable, *X*, and your dependent variable, *Y*. Alternatively stated, the relationship between *X* and *Y* changes at different levels of *M*. For example, when *M* is high, *X* might be positively related to *Y*, but when *M* is low, *X* might be unrelated to *Y* or even negatively related to *Y*. In short, a moderation means that the relationship between *X* and *Y* depends on *M*. This is also commonly referred to as an interaction effect, where *X* and *M* are said to interact in their relationship with *Y*. To assess statistically whether there is a significant interaction effect, you simply include the product of *X* and *M* in your regression equation:

$$Y = B_1 X_1 + B_2 M_2 + B_3 (X_1 \times M_2) + a + e$$

where *Y* is the dependent variable, $B_1 X_1$, the relationship between *X* and *Y*, $B_2 M_2$, the relationship between *M* and *Y*, $B_3 (X_1 \times M_2)$, the interaction term between *X* and *M*, *a*, the y-intercept, and *e*, the error term.

Visually, a simple moderation looks like this:

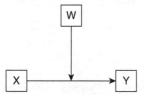

Okay, now let's test a simple moderation using the chap9PROCESS.sav dataset, which you can download from the Companion Website. Our *X* variable is going to be job autonomy, our *Y* variable is going to be mental health, and our moderator, *W*, is going to be workplace incivility. Visually, our hypotheses will look like this:

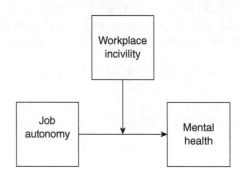

In short, we will hypothesize that job autonomy is positively associated with mental health (i.e., the more autonomy an individual has, the higher his or her level of mental health). We will also hypothesize that workplace incivility interacts with job autonomy to reduce mental health (i.e., when workplace incivility is high, the positive relationship between job autonomy and mental health is weakened).

To assess this moderation, go to Analyze, Regression, and PROCESS v3.5 by Andrew F. Hayes. You will see the following window:

Now, move AUTOND (job autonomy) under X variable:, move MHI (mental health) under Y variable:, and move INCIV (workplace incivility) under Moderator variable W:. Now, if you click under Model number:, you'll see that there are 92 different models that PROCESS can estimate. We are going to stay at Model 1 because that aligns with the simple moderation we're conducting. We're also going to leave Confidence intervals at 95, so we can estimate 95% confidence intervals. Finally, we're going to leave Number of bootstrap samples at 5000. This means that our confidence intervals will be estimated by SPSS running the analysis 5000 times. Now, go into ⌷ Options ⌷ and tick ☑ Generate code for visualizing interactions and ⊙ All variables that define products. ⊙ -1SD, Mean, +1SD. In short, ☑ Generate code for visualizing interactions will allow us to produce a graph illustrating our interaction effect; ⊙ All variables that define products will mean center our variables to mitigate against multicollinearity; and ⊙ -1SD, Mean, +1SD will report the relationship between X and Y when W is at +1 SD, the mean, and at –1 SD. When you are ready to estimate your moderation, click Continue and OK.

(Continued)

Please note that it takes a few seconds for SPSS to produce PROCESS output. Let's look at this output, one section at a time.

In the following section, you will see a summary of your model and sample size:

```
Model : 1
    Y : MHI
    X : AUTOND
    W : INCIV


Sample
Size: 250
```

Next, you will see the results of the moderation:

```
OUTCOME VARIABLE:
 MHI

Model Summary
       R        R-sq       MSE         F        df1        df2          p
    .5443      .2962      .2570     34.5152    3.0000    246.0000      .0000

Model
             coeff        se          t          p        LLCI        ULCI
constant    3.7311      .0324    115.1136      .0000      3.6673      3.7949
AUTOND       .2184      .0425      5.1393      .0000       .1347       .3022
INCIV       -.3806      .0540     -7.0540      .0000      -.4869      -.2743
Int_1       -.3126      .0840     -3.7200      .0002      -.4781      -.1471

Product terms key:
 Int_1   :       AUTOND    x        INCIV

Test(s) of highest order unconditional interaction(s):
        R2-chng         F         df1        df2          p
X*W      .0396     13.8383     1.0000    246.0000      .0002
----------
    Focal predict: AUTOND   (X)
        Mod var: INCIV   (W)

Conditional effects of the focal predictor at values of the moderator(s):

      INCIV     Effect        se          t          p        LLCI        ULCI
     -.4808      .3687      .0592      6.2322      .0000       .2522       .4853
      .0000      .2184      .0425      5.1393      .0000       .1347       .3022
      .6012      .0305      .0654       .4664      .6413      -.0984       .1594
```

Under Model Summary, you will see an R^2 value of 0.2962, meaning that our two independent variables, job autonomy and workplace incivility, explain 29.62% of the variation in mental health. Under

Model, you can see the coefficient, standard error, t-statistics, p-value, lower confidence interval (95%), and upper confidence interval (95%). Job autonomy positively predicts mental health ($B = 0.2184$, $p < 0.0001$), meaning that higher levels of job autonomy are associated with improved mental health, as we expected. Incivility negatively predicts mental health ($B = -0.3806$, $p < 0.0001$), meaning that higher levels of workplace incivility are associated with lower levels of mental health. The interaction between job autonomy and incivility (denoted Int_1) is also statistically significant at $p = 0.0002$, meaning that the relationship between X (job autonomy) and Y (mental health) depends on values of workplace incivility (W), but at this stage, we still don't know exactly how W moderates the relationship between X and Y.

A little bit further down the output, under Conditional effects of the focal predictor at values of the moderator(s):, you will see exactly how workplace incivility moderates the relationship between job autonomy and mental health. The three rows here report the relationship between X and Y at (1) low workplace incivility ($-1\ SD$), (2) average workplace incivility (the mean), and (3) high workplace incivility ($+1\ SD$).

Looking at the first row (the relationship between X and Y when workplace incivility is low), you can see that job autonomy positively and significantly predicts mental health ($B = 0.3687$, $p < 0.0001$). In other words, in workplaces with a low level of incivility, job autonomy improves mental health.

Looking at the second row (the relationship between X and Y when workplace incivility is average), you can see that job autonomy still positively and significantly predicts mental health ($B = 0.2184$, $p < 0.0001$). In other words, even at average levels of workplace incivility, job autonomy still improves mental health.

Looking at the third row (the relationship between X and Y when workplace incivility is high), you can see that the relationship between job autonomy and mental health is not statistically significant ($p = 0.6413$). In other words, the protective effect of job autonomy on mental health is significantly weakened in workplaces with high levels of incivility.

For some people, this information is enough to understand the nature of the moderation. But for others, it helps visualize this interaction effect. If you want to produce a graph that illustrates this interaction effect, you can copy and paste the following text into an SPSS syntax window.

```
DATA LIST FREE/
    AUTOND      INCIV       MHI           .
BEGIN DATA.
        -.7618      -.4808      3.6332
         .0000      -.4808      3.9141
         .7618      -.4808      4.1950
        -.7618       .0000      3.5647
         .0000       .0000      3.7311
         .7618       .0000      3.8975
        -.7618       .6012      3.4790
         .0000       .6012      3.5022
         .7618       .6012      3.5255
END DATA.
GRAPH/SCATTERPLOT=
    AUTOND   WITH     MHI      BY       INCIV   .
```

(Continued)

Simply double click on the output, highlight everything from DATA LIST FREE/ to INCIV . and copy by right clicking on your mouse. Don't forget to include the full stop/period after INCIV! Once you have copied the above text, go to File, New, and Syntax. When the syntax window opens, simply paste the text into it, highlight the text, and then click ▶. Note that if you fail to highlight the text before clicking ▶, your graph will not look right. If you've properly highlighted the syntax and clicked ▶, you should see a new graph appear in your output:

Graph

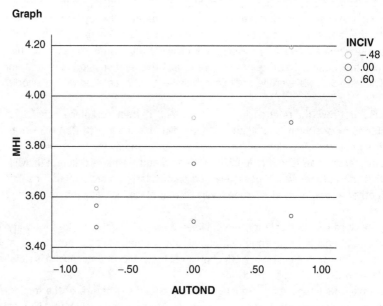

Reprint courtesy of IBM Corporation ©

Here you can vaguely see three lines, one for each level of workplace incivility. If you double click on the graph, then go to Elements, click Interpolation Line, and then close the window, you should see lines on your graph now:

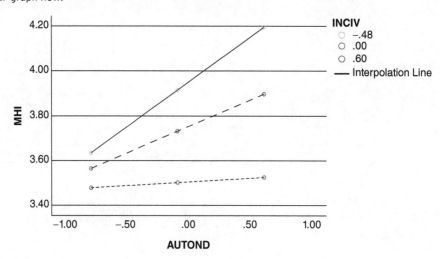

Reprint courtesy of IBM Corporation ©

The top line shows the positive and significant relationship between job autonomy and mental health when workplace incivility is low (–1 SD). The middle line shows the positive and significant relationship between job autonomy and mental health when workplace incivility is average (mean). The bottom line shows the nonsignificant relationship between job autonomy and mental health when workplace incivility is high (+1 SD).

There you have it! You just did a simple moderation using the Hayes SPSS PROCESS Macro. Nice work! Now let's see how we can estimate a simple mediation.

Using SPSS PROCESS to Estimate a Simple Mediation (Model 4)

You will recall that mediation refers to a situation in which the relationship between X and Y can be explained either entirely or partially by a third variable, M. In the case of a full mediation, the relationship between X and Y flows entirely through M. In other words, in a full mediation, the direct relationship between X and Y is nonsignificant, but the indirect relationship, through M, is significant. In the case of a partial mediation, the relationship between X and Y is significant, but so is the indirect relationship through M. Mediation models excel at uncovering the mechanism through which X relates to Y. A simple mediation model looks like this:

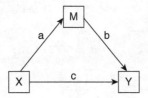

Here, you can see three direct relationships, where $X \rightarrow M$ is explained by a, $M \rightarrow Y$ is explained by b, and $X \rightarrow Y$ is explained by c. You can also see an indirect relationship between X and Y through M, which is explained by the product of a and b, that is, $a \times b$.

Using Model 4 in PROCESS, we can test a simple mediation model. Looking again at our dataset, chap9PROCESS, let's build a simple mediation model in which X = *job autonomy*, Y = *physical pain*, and M = *mental health*. Visually, this model looks like this:

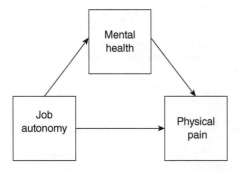

We might hypothesize that there is a weak relationship, if any relationship at all, between job autonomy and physical pain. We might also hypothesize (as we discovered in our moderation analysis,

(Continued)

above) that there is a positive relationship between job autonomy and mental health (i.e., high levels of job autonomy are associated with higher levels of mental health) and a negative relationship between mental health and physical pain (i.e., higher levels of mental health are associated with lower levels of physical pain). Thus, we are hypothesizing an indirect effect of job autonomy on physical pain through mental health.

To carry out this simple mediation using Model 4 in PROCESS, go to Analyze, Regression, and PROCESS v3.5 by Andrew F. Hayes. If you've recently done the moderation analysis using Model 1, you might need to click on Reset to start afresh with the simple mediation analysis. First, under Model number:, change it from 1 to 4. Second, move AUTOND (job autonomy) to the right under X variable:. Third, move PHYSYMPT to the right under Y variable:. Fourth, move MHI (mental health) to the right under Mediator(s) M:. Now, go into Options and tick ☑ Show total effect model and then Continue. When you're ready to run your simple mediation, click OK.

Once again, it may take several seconds for SPSS to produce the output.

Let's examine this output one section at a time. The first section reminds you which model you're using (Model 4), which variables you're using, and what your sample size is:

```
Model   : 4
    Y   : PHYSYMPT
    X   : AUTOND
    M   : MHI


Sample
Size:  237
```

The next section only reports the direct relationship between X (job autonomy) and M (mental health). Here you can see that job autonomy is significantly and positively related to mental health ($B = 0.2471$, $p < 0.0001$). In other words, higher levels of job autonomy are associated with improved mental health, as we hypothesized:

```
OUTCOME VARIABLE:
 MHI

Model Summary
          R        R-sq        MSE          F        df1         df2          p
      .3090       .0955       .3313    24.8144     1.0000    235.0000       .0000

Model
                coeff         se          t          p        LLCI        ULCI
constant       2.8085       .1940    14.4742       .0000      2.4262      3.1908
AUTOND          .2471       .0496     4.9814       .0000       .1494       .3448
```

The next section reports the direct relationships between X (job autonomy) and Y (physical pain), and M (mental health) and Y (physical pain). As you can see, job autonomy is not related to physical pain ($p = 0.9731$), meaning that there is no association between these two variables. However, mental health is significantly and negatively related to physical pain ($B = -0.4084$, $p < 0.0001$). In other words, higher levels of mental health are significantly associated with lower levels of physical pain, as we hypothesized:

```
OUTCOME VARIABLE:
PHYSYMPT

Model Summary
          R        R-sq       MSE         F        df1         df2          p
      .2790      .0778      .7304     9.8757     2.0000    234.0000       .0001

Model
              coeff        se          t          p        LLCI        ULCI
constant     3.6139     .3962     9.1205      .0000      2.8332      4.3945
AUTOND       -.0026     .0774     -.0337      .9731      -.1552       .1499
MHI          -.4084     .0969    -4.2162      .0000      -.5992      -.2175
```

Reprint courtesy of IBM Corporation ©

The next section reports the total effects model. This model combines the direct effects and the indirect effects to give an overall assessment of the total effects. The relevant part of this model is that the total effects have a nonsignificant p-value of 0.1758. This nonsignificant overall p-value is likely a function of the fact that there is no significant direct effect between job autonomy and physical pain:

```
************************** TOTAL EFFECT MODEL ****************************
OUTCOME VARIABLE:
PHYSYMPT

Model Summary
          R        R-sq       MSE         F        df1         df2          p
      .0882      .0078      .7826     1.8438     1.0000    235.0000       .1758

Model
              coeff        se          t          p        LLCI        ULCI
constant     2.4670     .2982     8.2725      .0000      1.8795      3.0545
AUTOND       -.1035     .0762    -1.3579      .1758      -.2537       .0467
```

Reprint courtesy of IBM Corporation ©

Finally, we arrive at the output where we can conclude whether there is a significant indirect effect of job autonomy on physical pain through mental health. Here, you will see some of what you already know. The total effect of X on Y (including direct and indirect effects) is nonsignificant ($p = 0.1758$). The direct effect of X on Y is also nonsignificant ($p = 0.9731$). The new, and most important, information is at the bottom of this section. Here you will find the indirect effect of X (job autonomy) on Y (physical pain) through M (mental health). You'll notice that there is no p-value associated with indirect effects. If you want to determine whether an indirect effect is statistically significant, you have to look at the

(Continued)

bootstrapped lower-level confidence interval (BootLLCI = −0.1795) and the bootstrapped upper-level confidence interval (BootULCI = −0.0407). If this range contains the number zero, then the indirect effects are nonsignificant. In our case, the range between the lower and upper confidence intervals do not contain zero (−0.1795 to −0.0407). Therefore, we can conclude that the indirect relationship between X (job autonomy) and Y (physical pain) through M (mental health) is indeed statistically significant. Given that the direct relationship between X (job autonomy) and Y (physical pain) is nonsignificant (p = 0.9731), we can conclude that our model is a full mediation:

```
*************** TOTAL, DIRECT, AND INDIRECT EFFECTS OF X ON Y ***************

Total effect of X on Y
      Effect          se            t            p          LLCI         ULCI
      -.1035        .0762      -1.3579        .1758        -.2537        .0467

Direct effect of X on Y
      Effect          se            t            p          LLCI         ULCI
      -.0026        .0774       -.0337        .9731        -.1552        .1499

Indirect effect(s) of X on Y:
            Effect      BootSE     BootLLCI     BootULCI
  MHI       -.1009       .0358       -.1795       -.0407
```

Reprint courtesy of IBM Corporation ©

Nice work! You just carried out your first simple moderation (Model 1) and simple mediation (Model 4) using SPSS PROCESS. Bear in mind that we've only gone through two of almost 92 different model templates in PROCESS. This macro has so much more to offer. If you're interested in learning more about moderation, mediation, and moderated mediations, have a read through Hayes (2017).

What Have You Learned?

That was some amazing work you just did there, partner. You now know how to run a multiple regression analysis. Of course, this chapter covered multiple regression for beginners. There are more advanced methods and techniques that could have been used (Tabachnick and Fidell, 2019). But you now have a good introduction to multivariate statistics. If you have a single, ordinal, or preferably scale-level dependent variable and you want to predict or explain it from a set of ordinal, scale, or dummy (e.g., two category) independent variables, then you'll know exactly what to do and how to interpret the results.

Now, you might be thinking, what do I do if my dependent variable is not continuous? What if I want to predict or explain a binary outcome? Many outcomes in management research are binary, either/or, yes/no. Did the organization go out of business or did it survive the recession? Did the employee leave for a new job, or stay? In these circumstances, it is not possible to use OLS regression because a binary, two-category dependent variable violates the fundamental assumptions of multiple linear regression. Fortunately, we have another tool in our multivariate toolbox that we can use to answer such research questions. In Chapter 10, we'll take a look at logistic regression, which is designed to model the determinants of a single, binary outcome. It's essentially like taking a dummy variable, as we learned about in this chapter, and turning it into a dependent variable.

Further Reading

Allison, P. D. (1999). *Multiple regression: A primer*. Pine Forge Press.

Berry, W. D., Feldman, S., & Stanley Feldman, D. (1985). *Multiple regression in practice* (No. 50). Sage.

Hayes, A. F. (2017). *Introduction to mediation, moderation, and conditional process analysis: A regression-based approach*. Guilford Press.

Roberts, A., & Roberts, J. M., Jr. (2020). *Multiple regression: A practical introduction*. Sage.

Timming, A. R. (2010a). Cross-national variations in the determinants of job satisfaction: How far do our results 'travel'? *International Journal of Organization Theory and Behavior, 13*(4), 525-545.

Timming, A. R., French, M. T., & Mortensen, K. (2021). Health anxiety versus economic anxiety surrounding COVID-19: An analysis of psychological distress in the early stages of the pandemic. *Journal of Affective Disorders Reports,* 5, Article 100152.

In-Class Discussion Questions

1. Why is it preferable to run a single multiple regression analysis, rather than run a set of bivariate correlations looking at the relationship of each independent variable with the dependent variable?
2. How can you use and interpret a dummy variable in the context of multiple linear regression analysis?
3. Write out a full regression equation (e.g., $Y = ...$) with six independent variables and one dependent variable. Label and describe each component of the equation. Select seven variables that could be used in your equation. What kinds of results would you expect to find from estimation of that equation? What is a moderation? How can you detect and interpret a moderating effect?
4. What is mediation? How can you detect and interpret a mediation effect?
5. What is multicollinearity? Why is it a problem? How can it be detected? What can be done about it?

10

Logistic Regression

Multiple regression analysis is pretty cool, right? As mentioned in Chapter 9, it is the most widely used statistical technique. It is accurate, informative, and easy to interpret. It is versatile as well inasmuch as it can cope with scale, ordinal, and two-category nominal (aka, dummy) independent variables. But it also has some limitations. With the exception of the inclusion of dummy variables, the rest of the independent variables must be linearly related to the dependent variable. The ordinal- or scale-level variables in a multiple regression analysis must be roughly normally distributed. Perhaps the biggest limitation of multiple regression analysis, however, is that it can only predict and/or explain a quantitative, continuous dependent variable. But what if your dependent variable only has two possible outcomes: yes or no? Pass or fail? Should I invest or not invest? Should I hire or not hire? Will the patient live or die? What is the likelihood that an employee is a high performer or a low performer? In other words, what if you want to predict or explain a dummy variable?

Now, you might be wondering, what would happen if I just ran a multiple regression analysis with a binary dependent variable? What's the worst that could happen? After all, nearly all multiple regression analyses violate one or two assumptions, right? Beyond violating the assumption of normality, it also just wouldn't make mathematical sense to run a multiple regression analysis with a binary outcome variable, as you'll soon learn.

So what is one to do if you want to model the effects of a set of independent variables on a binary outcome? Fortunately, you can use logistic regression in such occasions. Logistic regression analysis is, in many ways, similar to multiple regression. It, too, can cope with scale, ordinal, or two-category (aka, dummy) independent variables. It, too, can be used to either predict or explain a single dependent variable. It, too, provides a *B* coefficient that says something about the nature of the relationship between each independent variable and the dependent variable. This *B* coefficient, like in multiple regression, has a *p*-value associated with it that will tell us whether the result we found in our sample generalizes to the wider population.

But there are some crucial differences as well. For example, whereas multiple regression is based on the logic of *OLS* (whereby the line of best fit minimizes the residuals, or error terms), logistic regression is based on the logic of *maximum likelihood estimation*, also referred to as MLE. MLE refers to an estimation technique where the coefficients or weights are calculated based on a probability distribution, not a normal distribution. Whereas OLS regression calculates statistical significance on the basis of a t-statistic, logistic regression calculates statistical significance on the basis of what is called a Wald statistic. Moreover, whereas goodness-of-fit in multiple regression is estimated by R^2 (which corresponds to the amount of variation in Y that is explained by the independent variables), logistic regression can only yield a pseudo-R^2 value, which is kind of like an R^2 imposter. The pseudo-R^2 is an imperfect statistic and only loosely comparable to R^2 as a measure of goodness-of-fit. Perhaps one of the biggest differences between OLS regression and logistic regression is that the former assumes a linear relationship between each X variable and Y, whereas the latter assumes an S-shaped probability distribution and is based on probabilities and odds of an outcome occurring (or not occurring). Don't worry if this isn't absolutely clear to you just yet. It will be by the end of this chapter.

In short, if you want to predict an either/or, yes/no outcome, and you have a set of predictor variables that are scale, ordinal, or dummy in measurement, then logistic regression is the way to go. This method is designed to handle a two-category nominal dependent variable and can be used for prediction (how likely is outcome A or outcome B?), explanation (how does a one-unit change in X affect the odds of Y happening?), or classification (given this set of predictors ($X_1, X_2, X_3, X_i \ldots$), does this person (or organization) most likely belong to group A or group B? Before we delve further into the inner logic of logistic regression, let's have a brief look at, practically speaking, how this method might be operationalized in management research.

Logistic Regression in Management Research

Management researchers are often concerned with probability and likelihood. Many, if not most, management decisions are based on the odds of a particular outcome occurring, or not. Sometimes managers will informally estimate these odds; for example, if I make decision X, is it not at all likely/somewhat likely/likely/very likely/inevitable that Y will happen? But making management decisions based on a 'gut feeling' of the likelihood of an outcoming happening is pretty shortsighted. Other managers or management researchers use data analytics to calculate the odds of something happening. In fact, logistic regression is a commonly used method in data analytics. The better you understand the predictors (independent variables) of an outcome (dependent variable), the better your decision-making.

Here is a set of research questions that a management researcher like you might want to answer using multiple logistic regression analysis.

- What are the predictors of the likelihood of a workplace accident? In this case, possible independent variables might include organization size (X_1), presence or absence of heavy machinery (X_2), presence or absence of a formal workplace health and safety policy (X_3), presence or absence of a trade union (X_4), total number of health and safety training hours per year (X_5), and total number of accidents over the previous 12 months (X_6), and the dependent variable is the number of workplace accidents across the sample organizations.

- What are the predictors of the likelihood that an organization will turn a profit, or not? In this case, possible independent variables might include organization size (X_1), total marketing budget (X_2), total access to finance capital (X_3), whether it turned a profit last year (X_4), whether it reaches a domestic or international market (X_5), and proportion of employees with an MBA (X_6), and the dependent variable is whether the sample organizations turned a profit.
- What are the predictors of the likelihood that a Hollywood movie will turn a profit, or not? In this case, possible independent variables might include total production budget (X_1), whether or not the movie features an academy award winning actor (X_2), total length of the movie (X_3), and audience reaction to the trailer on a scale of 1 to 7, where 1 = *this movie looks boring* to 7 = *this movie looks awesome*, and the dependent variable is whether the sample movies made a net profit or a net loss.
- What are the predictors of the likelihood that a job applicant will be successful in a job interview? In this case, possible independent variables might include percentage of time making eye contact (X_1), job applicant attractiveness on a scale of 1 to 7, where 1 = *not at all attractive* and 7 = *extremely attractive* (X_2), height (X_3), whether the applicant has a four-year university degree (X_4), whether the applicant has relevant training (X_5), and whether the applicant already has social connections within the company (X_6), and the dependent variable is whether an applicant was successful in the sample interviews.
- What are the predictors of the likelihood of high or low employee performance? In this case, possible independent variables might include IQ (X_1), working hours per week (X_2), years of education (X_3), whether the individual has an Ivy League degree (X_4), conscientiousness (X_5), and average number of hours of sleep per night (X_6), and the dependent variable is a binary performance measure that categorizes the sample employees into the top 50% and the bottom 50%.
- What are the predictors of the likelihood that a patient will live or die? In this case, possible independent variables might include age (X_1), gender (X_2), mental health (X_3), whether the patient is diabetic (X_4), weight (X_5), whether the patient is taking a particular medication (X_6), number of days of hospitalization (X_7), and whether the patient has health insurance (X_8), and the dependent variable is whether the sample patients lived or died.

Let's dissect the last example to see how a logistic regression model might be built and tested. Imagine that you are a hospital administrator. There are two reasons why you might be interested in predicting the likelihood that a patient will live or die. First, obviously, you have a moral obligation to safeguard the health and well-being of patients. Second, surviving patients are good for hospital business. So you've decided to look at potential predictors. To compile your sample, you look up historical data at the hospital over the last three years, identifying patients who died (coded 0) and those who lived (coded 1). Along with the life/death data, you also have information on age, gender, mental health (as measured by a 10-item psychosocial distress scale), diabetic status, weight, whether the patient is taking a particular medication, total days spent in hospital, and whether the patient has health insurance. You will note that this list of independent variables contains a mix of scale-level variables (e.g., age), ordinal variables (e.g., mental health), and a couple of two-category nominal variables (e.g., whether the patient has health insurance and is diabetic).

With this configuration of independent variables and this particular dependent variable, you are all set to run a multiple logistic regression.

My guess (I could very well be wrong because I'm a fake doctor, not a real one!) is that the hospital administrator would find the following results:

- Patient age is associated with an increased likelihood of death.
- Being male is associated with an increased likelihood of death.
- Poor mental health is associated with an increased likelihood of death.
- Being diabetic is associated with an increased likelihood of death.
- Weight is associated with an increased likelihood of death.
- Taking a particular medication is associated with a reduced likelihood of death.
- Number of days of hospitalization is associated with an increased likelihood of death.
- Having health insurance is associated with a reduced likelihood of death.

Armed with this information, the hospital administrator can then use the results of the logistic regression analysis to implement policies and practices that can reduce the mortality rate. Examples might include designing a special care plan for patients with diabetes or improving the mental health of all patients through some sort of hospital-wide mindfulness intervention.

Okay, now that you have an idea of how management researchers might use multiple logistic regression in practice, let's have a look at the basic concepts underlying the method. We won't get too mathematical, trust me.

Basic Concepts in Logistic Regression

Why Can't We Just Use OLS Regression to Model a Binary Outcome?

You might be tempted to skip the rest of this pesky chapter and just use your newfound skills in OLS regression to model a dichotomous dependent variable. What's the worst that could happen, right? There are good reasons why this is just 'not done' in statistics, even though, technically, it could be done.

Consider the hypothetical scatterplot depicted in Figure 10.1. Here you can visually see the relationship between X (years of education) and Y (whether or not the respondent is in paid employment). As you can see, there are only two values of Y (let's call them $0 = no, not in paid employment$ and $1 = yes, in paid employment$). Using OLS regression, you can see that a line of best fit can technically be modeled. You can clearly see a clustering of cases that are 'not in paid employment' on the lower end of the education scale and a second clustering of individuals 'in paid employment' on the higher end of the education scale. But there is a logical problem with using a straight line of best fit: technically, depending on your coefficient or weight, B, values of Y can, in theory, be calculated that are greater than 1 and less than 0. This makes no sense (Pampel, 2000). Either you're employed (1), or you're not (0). You can't be more than employed (e.g., 2.80) or less than unemployed (e.g., −1.45). But depending on your unstandardized B coefficient in an OLS regression equation, it is possible to calculate an outcome of either of these numbers. The reason is that a straight line of best fit, technically, extends up infinitely and down infinitely. Hopefully this explains why OLS regression, which produces a straight line, is incapable of modeling a binary outcome.

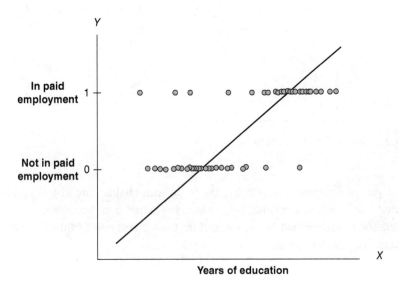

Figure 10.1 Ordinary least squares with a binary dependent variable

Instead of using a straight line, logistic regression uses an S-shaped line (also referred to as a *sigmoid* line, or function), depicted in Figure 10.2. This S-shaped line makes much more sense because it is level at the bottom (0, or not in paid employment) and again level at the top (1, in paid employment). With this curved line of best fit, it is impossible to calculate a score of greater than 1 and equally impossible to calculate a score of less than 0. You can still model the effect of X on Y, but a one-unit increase in X (in this case, an additional year of education) has differential effects on Y, the probability of being in paid employment. Near the bottom of the S-shaped curve, a one-unit increase in X doesn't have much of an effect on Y because of the flatness of the curve. The same is true at the top. A one-unit increase in education at the higher end doesn't have much of an impact on employment chances. But in the middle of the S-shaped distribution, you can see a comparatively large effect on Y of a one-unit increase in X. In this sense, logistic regression is, in fact, a type of nonlinear regression model. It assumes that changes in X will have different effects on Y (larger or smaller) depending on where one is on the X scale.

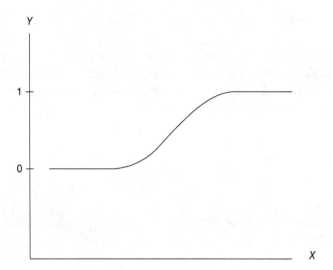

Figure 10.2 S-shaped sigmoid function

In sum, if you were thinking of skipping the rest of this chapter and just using linear OLS to model a dichotomous outcome variable, think again. For better or for worse, you will need to learn how to do logistic regression. But before we get into the ins and outs of this method, let's review some key concepts: probabilities and odds.

Probabilities Versus Odds

The S-shaped curve that I referred to above is a nonlinear function commonly called the *logit transformation*. To understand the logit transformation, you must first understand what we mean by probabilities and odds. These are not the same thing.

Probability refers to the likelihood that something will occur, or not. It is always a number between 0 and 1, which explains why we always code our dependent variable in logistic regression as 0 and 1. If a probability = 0, then there is 0% chance that something will occur. For example, if 100 readers of this book are asked if I have a good sense of humor and zero answer 'yes', then 0/100 = 0, which means the probability of a reader thinking I have a good sense of humor is 0%. Alternatively, if 100 readers of this book are asked if the author is a nerd and 100 answer 'yes', then 100/100 = 1, which means the probability of a reader thinking that I am a nerd is 100%. Now, if 100 readers of this book are asked if they've learned a lot about statistics from reading this book and 50 answer 'yes', then 50/100 = 0.5, which means that there is a 50% chance the readers learned a lot about statistics (I hope the real statistic is much higher, obviously). In short, when you divide the number of events by the number of possible outcomes, you get the probability, which is always a number between 0 (no chance) and 1 (100% chance). To convert a probability into a percentage, simply multiply it by 100. Thus, a probability of 0.47 corresponds to a 47% chance.

Another way of thinking about probabilities is through *odds*. The odds, like the probability, refer to the chances that something happens, or not, but it is expressed as a ratio to 1. To calculate the odds, you simply take the probability that something will happen divided by the probability that something will not happen. Alternatively stated, you calculate odds using Equation (10.1):

Odds = Probability $(P)/(1 - P)$ (10.1)

Probability and odds are similar in that a calculation of zero for both means that there is a 0% chance of something happening. Thus, using the preceding formula, if $P = 0$, then $0/(1 - 0) = 0$. But whereas the probability cannot ever be a number greater than 1, the odds can be significantly larger because they have no ceiling.

Let's calculate a few odds so you can better understand this concept. Imagine you're looking at an outcome with a 50% chance of occurring (like flipping a coin, heads or tails). The probability of this occurrence is 0.5. To calculate the odds, just plug $p = 0.5$ into Equation (10.1):

Odds = $0.5/(1 - 0.5) = 0.5/0.5 = 1$

So for a probability of 0.5, the odds are 1, also expressed as a ratio of 1:1. This means that an event will occur just as often as an event will not occur, just like when you flip a coin.

Now, let's calculate the odds when the probability is 0.8, or an 80% chance of something happening.

Odds = $0.8/(1 - 0.8) = 0.8/0.2 = 4$

So for a probability of .8, the odds are 4, also expressed as a ratio of 4:1. This means that an event will occur four times for every one time that it will not occur.

Finally, let's calculate the odds when the probability is 0.1, or only a 10% chance of something happening.

Odds = $0.1/(1 - 0.1) = 0.1/0.9 = 0.111$

So for a probability of 0.1, the odds are 0.111, also expressed as a ratio of 0.111:1. This means that an event will occur 0.111 times for every one time that it does not occur.

The more odds you calculate, you will begin to see a pattern. For any event that has less than a 50% chance of happening, the odds will always be between 0 and less just than 1. However, for events that have a greater than 50% chance of happening, the odds can increase indefinitely, from just over 1 to infinity.

Logged Odds

Odds are great because they are easy to interpret. That's why they are used by bookies when placing bets. But they cannot be used to model a logistic regression equation because they do not produce the right probability distribution. That is to say, they do not create that S-shaped sigmoid distribution referred to above and depicted in Figure 10.2. To produce that S-shaped distribution, we need to use something called *logged odds*, or *logits* (pronounced low-jits). Logged odds, or logits, are calculated by taking the natural log of the calculated odds. Why would anyone do such a crazy thing?

The answer to this question is that logged odds are perfectly suited to predicting the likelihood of a binary outcome because they follow an S-shaped distribution. Logged odds differ in some important ways from probabilities and odds. Let's have a look at the key differences.

Probabilities, you might recall, are always a number between 0 and 1, where zero means there is no chance of something happening, 1 means that there is a 100% chance of something happening, and 0.5 means that there is a 50% chance of something happening. Odds, you might recall, are always a number greater than 0, but they have no ceiling. That is to say, they can go up infinitely. Alternatively stated, odds, like probabilities, cannot ever be a negative number. But by taking the natural log of the odds, you can produce a probability distribution that has both negative numbers (to infinity) and positive numbers (to infinity). Furthermore, by converting probabilities into odds, and odds into logged odds, you will find larger effects in the middle of the probability distribution and smaller effects at the upper and lower ends of the distributions, as illustrated in the S-shaped distribution.

If this explanation isn't clear, perhaps it will help to calculate a few logged odds. Let's start with an event with a probability of 0.5, which means there is a 50/50 chance of it happening. A probability of 0.5 corresponds to odds to 1 (which means a 1:1 ratio). When you take the natural log of 1, you get a logged odd (or logit) of 0.

Now let's calculate the logged odds of an event with a probability of 0.3, or a 30% chance of happening. The odds of an event with a 30% chance of happening are 0.429 (which means a 0.429:1 ratio). When you take the natural log of 0.429, you get a logged odds (or logit) of –0.847.

Now let's calculate the logged odds of an event with a probability of 0.7, or a 70% chance of happening. The odds of an event with a 70% chance of happening are 2.33 (which means a 2.33:1 ratio). When you take the natural log of 2.33, you get a logged odds (or logit) of 0.827.

Do you see what's happening here? We're starting with a probability (*P*) of something happening. We then convert that *P* into odds. We then convert those odds into logged odds. By following this procedure, we can convert every probability into a number between negative infinity and positive infinity, where 0 means that there is a 50/50 chance of something happening. By removing the lower limit of 0 for probabilities and odds, and by removing the upper limit of 1 for probabilities (but not for odds), we are able to approximate an S-shaped probability distribution with tails that extend into infinity on each end. This logit transformation is what makes logistic regression possible! We've taken a fundamentally nonlinear S-shaped distribution, and we make it appear linear by taking the natural log of the odds.

The key problem with calculating logged odds is that they don't have much intuitive meaning, in and of themselves. So when we calculate logged odds in logistic regression, we know that a positive number means that there is a greater than 50% chance that something will happen and a negative number means that there is a less than 50% chance that something will happen, but we cannot say that a logged odds of 2 means that it is two times more likely to happen. To draw intuitive conclusions from the logged odds, we need to convert them back into odds. We can do this through a process called *exponentiation*, which you'll learn about in the next section.

Interpreting Logistic Regression Models and Coefficients

Now that you have some background on how logistic regression works, let's take a look at the practicalities surrounding the generation and interpretation of the results.

Basically, what we're trying to do in a logistic regression analysis is to estimate the change in probability of Y occurring for every one-unit increase in X. Alternatively stated, we want to know, if X goes up by one unit, how does that affect the probability of Y happening? If X is a binary variable, then we want to know the difference in probability that Y happens across the two levels of X. You may notice that if we build a simple logistic regression equation, with one binary X variable and one binary Y variable, we end up with an equation that mimics, in many respects, a chi-square test. But whereas a chi-square test cannot cope with an ordinal- or scale-level predictor, logistic regression can.

As with multiple regression, where we want to understand the effect on Y of a one-unit increase in X, we will need a coefficient, or weight, that describes the nature of the effect. In multiple regression, we used two key coefficients: unstandardized B and standardized Beta. Both coefficients say something to us about the nature of the relationship between X and Y.

In logistic regression, there are also two coefficients that can similarly describe the relationship between X and Y: odds and logged odds. You might be wondering why we can't also describe the relationship between X and Y using simple probabilities. Good question! Using probabilities as a coefficient is not possible. If you want to know why, check out Box 10.1.

Box 10.1: Why We Don't Use Probabilities as Coefficients in Logistic Regression

Probabilities are perhaps more intuitive than odds and are certainly more intuitive than logged odds. Most people generally understand probabilities because we can easily convert a probability into a percentage by multiplying a probability by 100. Thus, for example, a probability of 0.38 corresponds to a 38% chance of something happening. It would be great if we could use probabilities as the coefficients in a logistic regression analysis, for example, by saying that a one-unit increase in X is associated with a 2% increase in Y happening. Unfortunately, we can't get away with this because of the S-shaped sigmoid distribution we use to model maximum likelihood. The reason for this is that probabilities unfold linearly, whereas an S-shaped logit transformation is (obviously) curvilinear. That's why we use logged odds, instead of just odds or probabilities, to describe the relationship between X and Y in logistic regression analysis. Logged odds 'map' nicely onto the sigmoid function, where changes in X at the lower and higher ends result in much smaller increases in odds compared with changes in X in the middle of the distribution. You can see this clearly just by looking at the sigmoid distribution in Figure 10.2. If X increases at the bottom end, where the tail is flat, Y only barely changes. The same is true of a change in X at the top end: Y only barely changes. But a comparable change in X in the middle of the distribution results in a noticeable change in Y because the line is slanting upward. We couldn't reproduce the same nonlinear relationship between X and Y using probabilities. Like it or not, we're stuck with using logged odds for our logistic regression analyses.

When you run a logistic regression model, you will generate two key 'results', the logged odds and the odds. The logged odds are a bit like unstandardized B in a multiple regression equation. The effect of a one-unit increase in X on Y can be expressed as logged odds, where a positive number means that the probability is greater than 50% and a negative number means that the probability is less than 50%. But the logged odds, on their own, aren't very helpful because they don't say anything substantive or meaningful about the importance of different X variables. For example, you might find that the logged odds of men being promoted next year are, say, 1.98 compared with women, but this does not mean that men are nearly twice as likely to be promoted as women. Logged odds, therefore, do not offer clear and meaningful interpretation to the statistician.

Odds, on the other hand, do offer a clear and meaningful interpretation. In this sense, odds are a lot like Beta in multiple regression. They tell us more about the nature and strength of the relationship between X and Y than logged odds or unstandardized B. To transform the logged odds into odds, a process called *exponentiation* (briefly mentioned above) is needed. You don't need to know about the mathematics underlying this transformation. All you need to know is that IBM SPSS Statistics Software (SPSS) will do this transformation for you by converting the less interpretable logged odds into more interpretable odds. *Exponentiating* the logged odds simply means that you take the exponent, or antilog, of the logged odds coefficient. If you would like to do these calculations by hand, you can, of course. On most calculators, you can put in the logged odds coefficient that SPSS gives you and press the exponentiation (e^x) function button. Fortunately for us, SPSS will do this calculation and provide it in the output. Thanks, SPSS!

To interpret exponentiated odds, you apply the same logic as normal odds. In other words, an exponentiated odds of 1 (which corresponds to an odds ratio of 1:1) means you're looking at a 50/50 chance, or no effect of X on Y. An exponentiated odds of greater than 1 means that the odds are going up. For example, if the exponentiated odds is 2.00, this means that, for every one-unit increase in X, the odds of Y happening goes up by a factor of 2, or twice as much. If an exponentiated odds is less than 1, this means that the odds of Y go down for every one-unit increase in X.

Once you have calculated the logged odds and exponentiated odds (or, rather, once SPSS has calculated these for you!), you now need to consider whether these coefficients represent effects that are large enough to generalize from the sample to the population. In other words, does this change in (logged) odds of Y happening from a one-unit increase in X generalize to the wider population from which the sample was drawn? Recall that, in multiple regression, a t-statistic tells us whether unstandardized B and standardized Beta coefficients generalize. The t-statistic comes with a corresponding p-value, which, if $p < 0.05$, tells us whether we are able to make a 'quantum leap' from sample to population. In logistic regression, instead of using a t-statistic, we use something called a Wald statistic. The Wald statistic is based on a chi-square distribution. The larger the Wald statistic associated with a logged odds and/or exponentiated odds, the more likely the p-value is < 0.05, the more generalizable the result. It's that simple!

Recall that multiple regression is based on the principle of OLS. In contrast, logistic regression is based on the principle of *maximum likelihood estimation* (also commonly referred to as MLE). The mathematics underlying this concept are pretty complex and do not need to be explained in depth here. Suffice it to say that MLE is a procedure that produces coefficients (logged odds and odds) that are best able to predict Y with the observed (sample) data. The better the independent variables can predict values of Y (0 or 1), the higher the MLE. Note that, whereas OLS is based on a normal (bell shaped) distribution and t-statistics, MLE is based on a chi-square distribution and Wald statistics. Also note that, whereas OLS is based on the assumption of a linear relationship between X and Y, MLE is based on the assumption of a nonlinear (or curvilinear) relationship between X and Y, as explained above.

A final feature of logistic regression models that I'd like to discuss is overall model fit, also referred to as goodness-of-fit. Recall that, in multiple regression, we compare the total sum of squares with the error sum of squares to see if adding our independent variables improves our prediction of the dependent variable, Y. In logistic regression, we similarly compare a baseline log likelihood with a model log likelihood to see if our independent variables improve our prediction of the Y outcomes. You will also recall that, in multiple regression, we calculate multiple R and R^2 to get a 'big picture' overview of how well our model works, that is to say, how much variation in Y is explainable by our predictors. We can't exactly calculate an R^2 value for a logistic regression because, technically, our dependent variable, being binary (e.g., 0 or 1), doesn't have enough variation or variance. However, there are several alternative goodness-of-fit measures in logistic regression that act a bit like R^2. These goodness-of-fit measures are referred to as *pseudo R^2* statistics. A pseudo R^2 statistic is a number between 0 and 1, where numbers closer to 0 indicate poorer fit (our independent variables don't do such a good job predicting Y) and numbers closer to 1 indicate a better fit (our independent variables do a good job of predicting Y). Other measures of good fit we'll look at in the next section include the Cox and Snell, Nagelkerke, and Hosmer–Lemeshow statistics.

Okay, that was a lot of information, wasn't it? You can wipe the sweat off your brow because we're done with the hard part of logistic regression. From here on out, let's let SPSS do the heavy lifting. Before we move on to learn about how to use SPSS to do logistic regression, I want to summarize the key aspects of logistic regression and compare them with multiple regression, as illustrated in Table 10.1.

Table 10.1 Differences between multiple regression and logistic regression

	Multiple regression	Logistic regression
Overall model fit/ goodness-of-fit	Multiple R and R^2, which equals the amount of variation in Y explained by the independent variables	Pseudo R^2, Cox and Snell, Nagelkerke, Hosmer–Lemeshow, which mimic R^2 but cannot be interpreted as the amount of variation in Y explained by X
Model estimation	Ordinary least squares, which refers to the line of best fit that minimizes the error terms in the model	Maximum likelihood estimation, which refers to the estimation of parameters using a probability distribution that maximizes likelihood
Dependent variable	Must be ordinal or preferably scale in measurement and normally distributed	Must be dichotomous with only two options, typically reported as 0 and 1
Independent variables	Must be scale, ordinal, or dummy (dichotomous)	Must be scale, ordinal, or dummy (dichotomous)
Coefficients, or weights	Unstandardized B and standardized Beta	Logged odds and exponentiated odds
Statistical inference	The t-statistic corresponds to a p-value	The Wald statistic corresponds to a p-value
Linearity	The relationship between X and Y is based on a straight line	The relationship between X and Y is based on an S-shaped line
Interpretation	What is the effect on Y for every one-unit increase in X?	What is the effect of the likelihood of Y for every one-unit increase in X?

Logistic Regression Using SPSS

Imagine that you are a management researcher interested in equality, diversity, and inclusion in organizations. You would like to know if it's possible to predict whether an organization has a formal diversity/equal opportunities policy, or not, based on a set of organizational characteristics. In this case, your dependent variable is a simple yes/no answer to the following question: 'Does this workplace have a formal written policy on diversity/equal opportunities?' Fortunately for you, the survey of organizations asked this very question!

Go into the Companion Website and, in the Chapter 10 folder, open the dataset titled, chap-10data. This is a selection of variables taken from the wider survey of organizations. At the top of the list in Variable View, you can see our dependent variable, labeled 'diversity'. If you go into Values, you can see that answers to this question are coded 1 = *yes* and 0 = *no*. Let's quickly have a look at the frequencies for this variable. Go to Analyze, Descriptive Statistics, and Frequencies. Find diversity in the left-hand column and move it over to the right. Because this is a binary variable, we don't need to request any statistics, so just click OK . The output in Figure 10.3 shows that there are 2659 valid cases for this question (with 21 missing cases). The frequency table shows that about 90% of firms report having a formal written policy on diversity/equal opportunity and about 10% report that they do not have such a policy. The fact that these numbers are lopsided is not a problem, as it might be for OLS. Remember that MLE, which underlies logistic regression, makes no assumptions about the 'shape' or 'distribution' of the variables.

Statistics

Does workplace have a formal written policy on diversity/equal opportunities?

N	Valid	2659
	Missing	21

Does workplace have a formal written policy on diversity/equal opportunities?

		Frequency	Percent	Valid Percent	Cumulative Percent
Valid	no	257	9.6	9.7	9.7
	yes	2402	89.6	90.3	100.0
	Total	2659	99.2	100.0	
Missing	Refusal	21	.8		
Total		2680	100.0		

Figure 10.3 Frequencies for diversity

Reprint courtesy of IBM Corporation ©

What we want to do with our logistic regression is to look at factors that might be associated with an increase or decrease in the probability that an organization has a formal written policy on diversity/equal opportunities.

One such factor that comes to mind is firm size. Are larger firms more likely to have formal diversity policies than smaller firms? We can answer this question by running a simple logistic regression analysis, using firm size as the independent variable and diversity (yes/ no) as the dependent variable. If you go into Variable View, you will see a variable called *firmsize*. If you look into the Values tab, you will see only the missing data codes. This means that the variable is a true scale-level variable. In other words, if you see a 12 in the Data View column, this means that the organization employs 12 people, and so on.

Before we run the simple logistic regression, let's have a quick look at the frequencies for firmsize. Go to Analyze, Descriptive Statistics, and Frequencies. If diversity is still there, simply click Reset. Now find firmsize in the left-hand side and move it to the right-hand column. Go into Statistics and tick ☑ Mean, ☑ Median, and ☑ Std. deviation, and then click Continue. Let's ask for a histogram, too. Go into Charts and tick ⊙ Histograms. Now click Continue and then OK. Figure 10.4 depicts the frequency output for firmsize. You can see from the output that we have full information on this variable; that is, 2680 firms responded to this question, with no missing data. The average firm size is 449.30, the median is 67.00, and the standard deviation is 1213.54. We can already tell from these stats that this variable is skewed to the right (i.e., very large firms are dragging the mean score to the right). Fortunately, because we're not using OLS regression, the nonnormal distribution of this variable doesn't matter. As noted above, MLE, the procedure used for logistic regression, doesn't make assumptions about the normality of the variables.

Statistics

EPQ Q1 Currently how many employees do you have on the payroll at this workplace

N	Valid	2680
	Missing	0
Mean		449.30
Median		67.00
Std. Deviation		1213.544

(Continued)

Figure 10.4 (Continued)

EPQ Q1 Currently how many employees do you have on the payroll at this workplace

		Frequency	Percent	Valid Percent	Cumulative Percent
Valid	5	55	2.1	2.1	2.1
	6	57	2.1	2.1	4.2
	7	73	2.7	2.7	6.9
	8	53	2.0	2.0	8.9
	9	60	2.2	2.2	11.1
	10	46	1.7	1.7	12.8
	11	59	2.2	2.2	15.0
	12	34	1.3	1.3	16.3
	13	45	1.7	1.7	18.0
	14	42	1.6	1.6	19.6
	15	35	1.3	1.3	20.9
	16	35	1.3	1.3	22.2
	17	30	1.1	1.1	23.3
	18	29	1.1	1.1	24.4
	19	23	.9	.9	25.2
	20	28	1.0	1.0	26.3
	21	24	.9	.9	27.2
	22	30	1.1	1.1	28.3
	23	15	.6	.6	28.8
	24	13	.5	.5	29.3
	25	21	.8	.8	30.1
	26	20	.7	.7	30.9
	27	13	.5	.5	31.3
	28	25	.9	.9	32.3
	29	19	.7	.7	33.0
	30	26	1.0	1.0	34.0
	31	20	.7	.7	34.7
	32	26	1.0	1.0	35.7
	33	15	.6	.6	36.2
	34	12	.4	.4	36.7
	35	12	.4	.4	37.1
	36	14	.5	.5	37.6
	37	10	.4	.4	38.0

38	16	.6	.6	38.6
39	16	.6	.6	39.2
40	21	.8	.8	40.0
41	11	.4	.4	40.4
42	10	.4	.4	40.8
43	7	.3	.3	41.0
44	11	.4	.4	41.5
45	8	.3	.3	41.8
46	10	.4	.4	42.1
47	7	.3	.3	42.4
48	15	.6	.6	42.9
49	11	.4	.4	43.4
50	14	.5	.5	43.9
51	9	.3	.3	44.2
52	13	.5	.5	44.7
53	9	.3	.3	45.0
54	8	.3	.3	45.3
55	12	.4	.4	45.8
56	11	.4	.4	46.2
57	7	.3	.3	46.5
58	11	.4	.4	46.9
59	7	.3	.3	47.1
60	13	.5	.5	47.6
61	6	.2	.2	47.8
62	9	.3	.3	48.2
63	12	.4	.4	48.6
64	12	.4	.4	49.1
65	10	.4	.4	49.4
66	3	.1	.1	49.6
67	17	.6	.6	50.2
68	9	.3	.3	50.5
69	8	.3	.3	50.8
70	16	.6	.6	51.4
71	12	.4	.4	51.9
72	7	.3	.3	52.1
73	7	.3	.3	52.4
74	7	.3	.3	52.6
75	5	.2	.2	52.8

(Continued)

Figure 10.4 (Continued)

76	6	.2	.2	53.1
77	7	.3	.3	53.3
78	4	.1	.1	53.5
79	8	.3	.3	53.8
80	8	.3	.3	54.1
81	3	.1	.1	54.2
82	5	.2	.2	54.4
83	3	.1	.1	54.5
84	5	.2	.2	54.7
85	5	.2	.2	54.9
86	4	.1	.1	55.0
87	6	.2	.2	55.2
88	7	.3	.3	55.5
89	6	.2	.2	55.7
90	8	.3	.3	56.0
91	8	.3	.3	56.3
92	5	.2	.2	56.5
93	6	.2	.2	56.7
94	3	.1	.1	56.8
95	4	.1	.1	57.0
96	6	.2	.2	57.2
97	5	.2	.2	57.4
98	5	.2	.2	57.6
99	6	.2	.2	57.8
100	8	.3	.3	58.1
101	5	.2	.2	58.3
102	4	.1	.1	58.4
103	5	.2	.2	58.6
104	3	.1	.1	58.7
105	5	.2	.2	58.9
106	5	.2	.2	59.1
107	5	.2	.2	59.3
109	3	.1	.1	59.4
110	5	.2	.2	59.6
111	2	.1	.1	59.7
112	7	.3	.3	59.9
113	2	.1	.1	60.0
114	6	.2	.2	60.2

115	5	.2	.2	60.4
116	4	.1	.1	60.6
117	3	.1	.1	60.7
118	4	.1	.1	60.8
119	4	.1	.1	61.0
120	5	.2	.2	61.2
121	3	.1	.1	61.3
122	4	.1	.1	61.4
123	2	.1	.1	61.5
124	3	.1	.1	61.6
125	4	.1	.1	61.8
126	6	.2	.2	62.0
127	2	.1	.1	62.1
128	3	.1	.1	62.2
129	3	.1	.1	62.3
130	4	.1	.1	62.4
131	2	.1	.1	62.5
132	4	.1	.1	62.6
133	6	.2	.2	62.9
135	7	.3	.3	63.1
136	5	.2	.2	63.3
137	2	.1	.1	63.4
138	4	.1	.1	63.5
139	2	.1	.1	63.6
140	5	.2	.2	63.8
141	4	.1	.1	64.0
142	4	.1	.1	64.1
143	4	.1	.1	64.3
144	1	.0	.0	64.3
146	4	.1	.1	64.4
147	3	.1	.1	64.6
148	3	.1	.1	64.7
149	3	.1	.1	64.8
150	4	.1	.1	64.9
151	1	.0	.0	65.0
152	3	.1	.1	65.1
154	1	.0	.0	65.1
155	7	.3	.3	65.4

(Continued)

Figure 10.4 (Continued)

156	5	.2	.2	65.6
158	6	.2	.2	65.8
160	6	.2	.2	66.0
161	4	.1	.1	66.2
162	3	.1	.1	66.3
163	1	.0	.0	66.3
164	4	.1	.1	66.5
165	1	.0	.0	66.5
166	2	.1	.1	66.6
167	3	.1	.1	66.7
168	6	.2	.2	66.9
169	7	.3	.3	67.2
170	5	.2	.2	67.4
171	1	.0	.0	67.4
172	3	.1	.1	67.5
173	2	.1	.1	67.6
174	4	.1	.1	67.7
175	1	.0	.0	67.8
176	2	.1	.1	67.8
177	4	.1	.1	68.0
178	3	.1	.1	68.1
179	2	.1	.1	68.2
180	1	.0	.0	68.2
181	2	.1	.1	68.3
182	2	.1	.1	68.4
183	3	.1	.1	68.5
184	4	.1	.1	68.6
186	3	.1	.1	68.7
187	2	.1	.1	68.8
188	1	.0	.0	68.8
189	1	.0	.0	68.9
190	3	.1	.1	69.0
191	3	.1	.1	69.1
192	4	.1	.1	69.3
193	3	.1	.1	69.4
194	1	.0	.0	69.4
195	1	.0	.0	69.4
196	1	.0	.0	69.5

197	2	.1	.1	69.6
198	5	.2	.2	69.7
199	3	.1	.1	69.9
200	4	.1	.1	70.0
202	1	.0	.0	70.0
203	5	.2	.2	70.2
204	2	.1	.1	70.3
205	1	.0	.0	70.3
206	3	.1	.1	70.4
207	4	.1	.1	70.6
208	1	.0	.0	70.6
209	2	.1	.1	70.7
210	5	.2	.2	70.9
211	2	.1	.1	71.0
213	3	.1	.1	71.1
214	1	.0	.0	71.1
215	1	.0	.0	71.2
216	1	.0	.0	71.2
217	1	.0	.0	71.2
218	2	.1	.1	71.3
219	2	.1	.1	71.4
221	3	.1	.1	71.5
223	2	.1	.1	71.6
224	1	.0	.0	71.6
226	3	.1	.1	71.7
227	3	.1	.1	71.8
228	2	.1	.1	71.9
229	3	.1	.1	72.0
230	2	.1	.1	72.1
232	1	.0	.0	72.1
233	1	.0	.0	72.2
235	1	.0	.0	72.2
236	3	.1	.1	72.3
237	2	.1	.1	72.4
238	2	.1	.1	72.5
240	2	.1	.1	72.5
241	1	.0	.0	72.6
242	5	.2	.2	72.8

(Continued)

Figure 10.4 (Continued)

243	2	.1	.1	72.8
244	2	.1	.1	72.9
245	3	.1	.1	73.0
246	1	.0	.0	73.1
247	3	.1	.1	73.2
248	1	.0	.0	73.2
250	2	.1	.1	73.3
251	5	.2	.2	73.5
252	1	.0	.0	73.5
253	1	.0	.0	73.5
255	2	.1	.1	73.6
256	2	.1	.1	73.7
259	1	.0	.0	73.7
260	2	.1	.1	73.8
261	2	.1	.1	73.9
263	3	.1	.1	74.0
265	3	.1	.1	74.1
266	1	.0	.0	74.1
267	3	.1	.1	74.3
268	2	.1	.1	74.3
270	2	.1	.1	74.4
273	3	.1	.1	74.5
275	3	.1	.1	74.6
276	1	.0	.0	74.7
277	3	.1	.1	74.8
278	3	.1	.1	74.9
279	1	.0	.0	74.9
280	3	.1	.1	75.0
281	2	.1	.1	75.1
282	1	.0	.0	75.1
284	3	.1	.1	75.3
285	2	.1	.1	75.3
289	2	.1	.1	75.4
290	3	.1	.1	75.5
291	3	.1	.1	75.6
292	1	.0	.0	75.7
293	2	.1	.1	75.7
294	1	.0	.0	75.8

295	1	.0	.0	75.8
297	3	.1	.1	75.9
298	1	.0	.0	76.0
299	2	.1	.1	76.0
300	2	.1	.1	76.1
301	1	.0	.0	76.2
302	2	.1	.1	76.2
303	1	.0	.0	76.3
304	1	.0	.0	76.3
305	1	.0	.0	76.3
306	1	.0	.0	76.4
307	1	.0	.0	76.4
308	1	.0	.0	76.5
309	2	.1	.1	76.5
311	1	.0	.0	76.6
313	1	.0	.0	76.6
314	5	.2	.2	76.8
315	2	.1	.1	76.9
316	3	.1	.1	77.0
317	2	.1	.1	77.1
318	3	.1	.1	77.2
319	1	.0	.0	77.2
320	3	.1	.1	77.3
321	1	.0	.0	77.4
323	2	.1	.1	77.4
324	2	.1	.1	77.5
325	2	.1	.1	77.6
326	1	.0	.0	77.6
327	1	.0	.0	77.6
330	3	.1	.1	77.8
331	1	.0	.0	77.8
334	1	.0	.0	77.8
335	1	.0	.0	77.9
336	1	.0	.0	77.9
337	1	.0	.0	77.9
338	1	.0	.0	78.0
340	1	.0	.0	78.0
341	1	.0	.0	78.1

(Continued)

Figure 10.4 (Continued)

342	1	.0	.0	78.1
343	1	.0	.0	78.1
345	2	.1	.1	78.2
348	1	.0	.0	78.2
349	3	.1	.1	78.4
350	3	.1	.1	78.5
352	1	.0	.0	78.5
353	1	.0	.0	78.5
354	1	.0	.0	78.6
356	2	.1	.1	78.7
358	2	.1	.1	78.7
359	1	.0	.0	78.8
360	2	.1	.1	78.8
361	1	.0	.0	78.9
369	2	.1	.1	79.0
370	2	.1	.1	79.0
371	3	.1	.1	79.1
373	3	.1	.1	79.3
374	1	.0	.0	79.3
375	1	.0	.0	79.3
380	3	.1	.1	79.4
383	1	.0	.0	79.5
386	1	.0	.0	79.5
388	2	.1	.1	79.6
389	1	.0	.0	79.6
391	3	.1	.1	79.7
392	1	.0	.0	79.8
393	1	.0	.0	79.8
394	2	.1	.1	79.9
395	1	.0	.0	79.9
396	1	.0	.0	80.0
400	1	.0	.0	80.0
403	1	.0	.0	80.0
406	1	.0	.0	80.1
408	1	.0	.0	80.1
409	3	.1	.1	80.2
410	2	.1	.1	80.3
413	1	.0	.0	80.3

415	1	.0	.0	80.4
416	2	.1	.1	80.4
418	1	.0	.0	80.5
419	3	.1	.1	80.6
423	3	.1	.1	80.7
425	1	.0	.0	80.7
426	1	.0	.0	80.8
428	1	.0	.0	80.8
429	2	.1	.1	80.9
431	1	.0	.0	80.9
432	1	.0	.0	81.0
433	1	.0	.0	81.0
434	1	.0	.0	81.0
435	1	.0	.0	81.1
437	3	.1	.1	81.2
438	1	.0	.0	81.2
439	2	.1	.1	81.3
440	3	.1	.1	81.4
442	2	.1	.1	81.5
443	1	.0	.0	81.5
445	2	.1	.1	81.6
446	1	.0	.0	81.6
447	2	.1	.1	81.7
449	1	.0	.0	81.8
450	2	.1	.1	81.8
451	1	.0	.0	81.9
452	1	.0	.0	81.9
454	1	.0	.0	81.9
458	1	.0	.0	82.0
464	1	.0	.0	82.0
469	1	.0	.0	82.1
474	1	.0	.0	82.1
476	1	.0	.0	82.1
477	3	.1	.1	82.2
478	1	.0	.0	82.3
480	1	.0	.0	82.3
482	1	.0	.0	82.4
485	2	.1	.1	82.4

(Continued)

Figure 10.4 (Continued)

486	1	.0	.0	82.5
488	2	.1	.1	82.5
489	2	.1	.1	82.6
491	2	.1	.1	82.7
496	1	.0	.0	82.7
497	1	.0	.0	82.8
499	1	.0	.0	82.8
500	1	.0	.0	82.8
502	1	.0	.0	82.9
504	1	.0	.0	82.9
505	2	.1	.1	83.0
506	2	.1	.1	83.1
508	1	.0	.0	83.1
509	2	.1	.1	83.2
510	2	.1	.1	83.2
514	3	.1	.1	83.4
517	2	.1	.1	83.4
518	1	.0	.0	83.5
520	2	.1	.1	83.5
526	1	.0	.0	83.6
529	1	.0	.0	83.6
530	1	.0	.0	83.7
535	1	.0	.0	83.7
540	2	.1	.1	83.8
542	2	.1	.1	83.8
543	2	.1	.1	83.9
545	1	.0	.0	84.0
547	1	.0	.0	84.0
550	1	.0	.0	84.0
551	2	.1	.1	84.1
553	2	.1	.1	84.2
554	2	.1	.1	84.3
560	1	.0	.0	84.3
564	1	.0	.0	84.3
568	1	.0	.0	84.4
570	1	.0	.0	84.4
571	1	.0	.0	84.4
572	1	.0	.0	84.5

577	1	.0	.0	84.5
582	1	.0	.0	84.6
583	2	.1	.1	84.6
585	1	.0	.0	84.7
586	1	.0	.0	84.7
590	1	.0	.0	84.7
591	1	.0	.0	84.8
592	1	.0	.0	84.8
599	1	.0	.0	84.9
600	2	.1	.1	84.9
607	1	.0	.0	85.0
608	1	.0	.0	85.0
613	2	.1	.1	85.1
614	1	.0	.0	85.1
616	3	.1	.1	85.2
618	1	.0	.0	85.3
622	1	.0	.0	85.3
624	1	.0	.0	85.3
626	1	.0	.0	85.4
627	1	.0	.0	85.4
629	2	.1	.1	85.5
630	1	.0	.0	85.5
631	1	.0	.0	85.6
633	1	.0	.0	85.6
637	2	.1	.1	85.7
639	1	.0	.0	85.7
646	1	.0	.0	85.7
649	2	.1	.1	85.8
650	4	.1	.1	86.0
651	1	.0	.0	86.0
657	1	.0	.0	86.0
662	2	.1	.1	86.1
665	1	.0	.0	86.2
666	2	.1	.1	86.2
671	1	.0	.0	86.3
677	1	.0	.0	86.3
682	1	.0	.0	86.3
685	1	.0	.0	86.4

(Continued)

Figure 10.4   (Continued)

694	2	.1	.1	86.5
698	1	.0	.0	86.5
700	1	.0	.0	86.5
704	1	.0	.0	86.6
706	1	.0	.0	86.6
707	1	.0	.0	86.6
709	1	.0	.0	86.7
720	1	.0	.0	86.7
723	1	.0	.0	86.8
725	1	.0	.0	86.8
727	1	.0	.0	86.8
730	1	.0	.0	86.9
733	1	.0	.0	86.9
737	1	.0	.0	86.9
749	1	.0	.0	87.0
753	1	.0	.0	87.0
757	1	.0	.0	87.1
761	1	.0	.0	87.1
768	1	.0	.0	87.1
770	1	.0	.0	87.2
775	2	.1	.1	87.2
792	1	.0	.0	87.3
797	1	.0	.0	87.3
798	2	.1	.1	87.4
800	1	.0	.0	87.4
809	1	.0	.0	87.5
815	1	.0	.0	87.5
830	1	.0	.0	87.5
832	1	.0	.0	87.6
835	1	.0	.0	87.6
836	1	.0	.0	87.6
844	1	.0	.0	87.7
847	1	.0	.0	87.7
850	1	.0	.0	87.8
854	1	.0	.0	87.8
855	1	.0	.0	87.8
856	1	.0	.0	87.9
857	1	.0	.0	87.9

861	2	.1	.1	88.0
864	1	.0	.0	88.0
866	1	.0	.0	88.1
871	1	.0	.0	88.1
884	1	.0	.0	88.1
885	1	.0	.0	88.2
006	1	.0	.0	88.2
908	1	.0	.0	88.2
909	1	.0	.0	88.3
913	2	.1	.1	88.4
915	1	.0	.0	88.4
920	1	.0	.0	88.4
921	1	.0	.0	88.5
925	1	.0	.0	88.5
929	1	.0	.0	88.5
935	1	.0	.0	88.6
936	1	.0	.0	88.6
938	1	.0	.0	88.7
940	1	.0	.0	88.7
943	1	.0	.0	88.7
944	1	.0	.0	88.8
947	1	.0	.0	88.8
948	1	.0	.0	88.8
952	1	.0	.0	88.9
958	1	.0	.0	88.9
962	1	.0	.0	89.0
965	1	.0	.0	89.0
970	1	.0	.0	89.0
974	1	.0	.0	89.1
977	1	.0	.0	89.1
986	1	.0	.0	89.1
993	1	.0	.0	89.2
997	1	.0	.0	89.2
999	1	.0	.0	89.3
1000	2	.1	.1	89.3
1010	1	.0	.0	89.4
1013	1	.0	.0	89.4
1016	1	.0	.0	89.4

(Continued)

Figure 10.4 (Continued)

1019	1	.0	.0	89.5
1022	1	.0	.0	89.5
1023	1	.0	.0	89.6
1028	1	.0	.0	89.6
1044	1	.0	.0	89.6
1046	1	.0	.0	89.7
1047	1	.0	.0	89.7
1048	1	.0	.0	89.7
1053	1	.0	.0	89.8
1058	1	.0	.0	89.8
1060	1	.0	.0	89.9
1061	1	.0	.0	89.9
1071	1	.0	.0	89.9
1072	1	.0	.0	90.0
1082	1	.0	.0	90.0
1085	1	.0	.0	90.0
1099	1	.0	.0	90.1
1100	1	.0	.0	90.1
1103	1	.0	.0	90.1
1105	2	.1	.1	90.2
1110	2	.1	.1	90.3
1115	1	.0	.0	90.3
1116	1	.0	.0	90.4
1120	2	.1	.1	90.4
1126	2	.1	.1	90.5
1147	1	.0	.0	90.6
1148	1	.0	.0	90.6
1154	1	.0	.0	90.6
1156	1	.0	.0	90.7
1172	1	.0	.0	90.7
1176	1	.0	.0	90.7
1178	2	.1	.1	90.8
1187	1	.0	.0	90.9
1193	1	.0	.0	90.9
1200	2	.1	.1	91.0
1202	1	.0	.0	91.0
1216	1	.0	.0	91.0
1219	1	.0	.0	91.1

1224	1	.0	.0	91.1
1243	1	.0	.0	91.2
1247	2	.1	.1	91.2
1259	1	.0	.0	91.3
1264	1	.0	.0	91.3
1270	2	.1	.1	91.4
1273	1	.0	.0	01.4
1275	1	.0	.0	91.5
1283	1	.0	.0	91.5
1286	1	.0	.0	91.5
1290	1	.0	.0	91.6
1300	4	.1	.1	91.7
1306	1	.0	.0	91.8
1310	1	.0	.0	91.8
1312	1	.0	.0	91.8
1330	1	.0	.0	91.9
1338	1	.0	.0	91.9
1349	1	.0	.0	91.9
1377	1	.0	.0	92.0
1380	1	.0	.0	92.0
1387	1	.0	.0	92.1
1406	1	.0	.0	92.1
1417	1	.0	.0	92.1
1441	1	.0	.0	92.2
1476	1	.0	.0	92.2
1489	1	.0	.0	92.2
1500	1	.0	.0	92.3
1507	1	.0	.0	92.3
1509	1	.0	.0	92.4
1546	1	.0	.0	92.4
1574	1	.0	.0	92.4
1605	2	.1	.1	92.5
1620	1	.0	.0	92.5
1628	1	.0	.0	92.6
1645	2	.1	.1	92.6
1655	1	.0	.0	92.7
1656	1	.0	.0	92.7
1661	1	.0	.0	92.8

(Continued)

Figure 10.4 (Continued)

1669	1	.0	.0	92.8
1692	1	.0	.0	92.8
1693	1	.0	.0	92.9
1695	1	.0	.0	92.9
1697	1	.0	.0	92.9
1702	1	.0	.0	93.0
1719	1	.0	.0	93.0
1733	1	.0	.0	93.1
1745	1	.0	.0	93.1
1750	1	.0	.0	93.1
1753	1	.0	.0	93.2
1767	2	.1	.1	93.2
1768	1	.0	.0	93.3
1778	1	.0	.0	93.3
1820	1	.0	.0	93.4
1854	1	.0	.0	93.4
1855	1	.0	.0	93.4
1859	2	.1	.1	93.5
1891	1	.0	.0	93.5
1892	2	.1	.1	93.6
1896	1	.0	.0	93.7
1905	1	.0	.0	93.7
1910	2	.1	.1	93.8
1921	1	.0	.0	93.8
1938	1	.0	.0	93.8
1951	1	.0	.0	93.9
1975	1	.0	.0	93.9
1981	1	.0	.0	94.0
1992	1	.0	.0	94.0
2000	2	.1	.1	94.1
2010	1	.0	.0	94.1
2015	1	.0	.0	94.1
2041	1	.0	.0	94.2
2055	1	.0	.0	94.2
2059	1	.0	.0	94.3
2066	1	.0	.0	94.3
2072	1	.0	.0	94.3
2106	1	.0	.0	94.4

2123	1	.0	.0	94.4
2140	1	.0	.0	94.4
2178	1	.0	.0	94.5
2212	1	.0	.0	94.5
2228	1	.0	.0	94.6
2232	1	.0	.0	94.6
2274	1	.0	.0	94.6
2277	1	.0	.0	94.7
2292	1	.0	.0	94.7
2353	1	.0	.0	94.7
2363	1	.0	.0	94.8
2378	1	.0	.0	94.8
2382	1	.0	.0	94.9
2393	1	.0	.0	94.9
2419	1	.0	.0	94.9
2421	1	.0	.0	95.0
2426	1	.0	.0	95.0
2440	1	.0	.0	95.0
2500	1	.0	.0	95.1
2504	1	.0	.0	95.1
2522	1	.0	.0	95.1
2523	1	.0	.0	95.2
2542	1	.0	.0	95.2
2552	1	.0	.0	95.3
2558	1	.0	.0	95.3
2565	1	.0	.0	95.3
2568	1	.0	.0	95.4
2570	1	.0	.0	95.4
2585	1	.0	.0	95.4
2589	1	.0	.0	95.5
2614	1	.0	.0	95.5
2625	1	.0	.0	95.6
2714	1	.0	.0	95.6
2734	1	.0	.0	95.6
2748	1	.0	.0	95.7
2784	1	.0	.0	95.7
2792	1	.0	.0	95.7
2798	1	.0	.0	95.8

(Continued)

Figure 10.4 (Continued)

2818	1	.0	.0	95.8
2820	1	.0	.0	95.9
2886	1	.0	.0	95.9
2914	1	.0	.0	95.9
2985	1	.0	.0	96.0
3000	1	.0	.0	96.0
3008	1	.0	.0	96.0
3012	1	.0	.0	96.1
3115	1	.0	.0	96.1
3131	1	.0	.0	96.2
3141	1	.0	.0	96.2
3173	1	.0	.0	96.2
3190	1	.0	.0	96.3
3200	1	.0	.0	96.3
3207	1	.0	.0	96.3
3214	1	.0	.0	96.4
3253	1	.0	.0	96.4
3320	2	.1	.1	96.5
3326	1	.0	.0	96.5
3343	1	.0	.0	96.6
3394	1	.0	.0	96.6
3408	1	.0	.0	96.6
3450	1	.0	.0	96.7
3453	1	.0	.0	96.7
3460	1	.0	.0	96.8
3504	1	.0	.0	96.8
3520	1	.0	.0	96.8
3527	1	.0	.0	96.9
3529	1	.0	.0	96.9
3542	1	.0	.0	96.9
3554	1	.0	.0	97.0
3617	1	.0	.0	97.0
3628	1	.0	.0	97.1
3642	2	.1	.1	97.1
3650	1	.0	.0	97.2
3651	1	.0	.0	97.2
3660	1	.0	.0	97.2
3661	1	.0	.0	97.3

3672	1	.0	.0	97.3
3744	1	.0	.0	97.4
3804	1	.0	.0	97.4
3825	1	.0	.0	97.4
3830	1	.0	.0	97.5
3892	1	.0	.0	97.5
3917	2	.1	.1	97.6
3944	1	.0	.0	97.6
3945	1	.0	.0	97.6
4009	1	.0	.0	97.7
4022	1	.0	.0	97.7
4028	1	.0	.0	97.8
4048	1	.0	.0	97.8
4066	1	.0	.0	97.8
4072	1	.0	.0	97.9
4114	1	.0	.0	97.9
4131	1	.0	.0	97.9
4156	1	.0	.0	98.0
4216	1	.0	.0	98.0
4348	1	.0	.0	98.1
4368	1	.0	.0	98.1
4396	1	.0	.0	98.1
4500	1	.0	.0	98.2
4511	1	.0	.0	98.2
4523	1	.0	.0	98.2
4552	1	.0	.0	98.3
4600	1	.0	.0	98.3
4602	1	.0	.0	98.4
4700	1	.0	.0	98.4
4818	1	.0	.0	98.4
4845	1	.0	.0	98.5
4861	1	.0	.0	98.5
4876	1	.0	.0	98.5
4919	1	.0	.0	98.6
4920	1	.0	.0	98.6
4940	1	.0	.0	98.7
4996	1	.0	.0	98.7
5066	1	.0	.0	98.7

(Continued)

Figure 10.4   (Continued)

5562	1	.0	.0	98.8
5568	1	.0	.0	98.8
5659	1	.0	.0	98.8
5666	1	.0	.0	98.9
5672	1	.0	.0	98.9
5779	1	.0	.0	99.0
5963	1	.0	.0	99.0
6045	1	.0	.0	99.0
6183	1	.0	.0	99.1
6200	1	.0	.0	99.1
6417	1	.0	.0	99.1
6648	1	.0	.0	99.2
6884	1	.0	.0	99.2
6918	1	.0	.0	99.3
7028	1	.0	.0	99.3
7050	1	.0	.0	99.3
7124	1	.0	.0	99.4
7451	1	.0	.0	99.4
7775	1	.0	.0	99.4
7907	1	.0	.0	99.5
8355	1	.0	.0	99.5
8500	1	.0	.0	99.6
8520	1	.0	.0	99.6
8814	1	.0	.0	99.6
9117	1	.0	.0	99.7
9784	1	.0	.0	99.7
10319	1	.0	.0	99.7
10427	1	.0	.0	99.8
11302	1	.0	.0	99.8
11562	1	.0	.0	99.9
11566	1	.0	.0	99.9
11605	1	.0	.0	99.9
11776	1	.0	.0	100.0
20746	1	.0	.0	100.0
Total	2680	100.0	100.0	

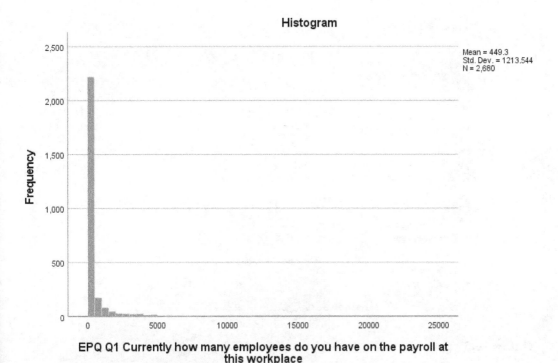

Figure 10.4 Frequencies for firmsize

Reprint courtesy of IBM Corporation ©

Okay, let's run this simple logistic regression now. Go to Analyze, Regression, and Binary Logistic. You'll see the window depicted in Figure 10.5. First, move diversity to the right under Dependent:. Second, move firmsize to the right under Covariates:. We don't have any nominal independent variables in this model, so we can skip Categorical . Now go into Options and tick ☑ Hosmer-Lemeshow goodness-of-fit and ☑ CI for exp(B): 95 % , which asks for 95% confidence intervals around our exponentiated *B* coefficient. Click Continue . Now, before we click OK , let's briefly review what we're trying to answer with this simple logistic regression test. Essentially, what we're asking is: for every one-unit increase in firm size (e.g., for every additional employee), how does that affect the odds of a company having a formal diversity/equal opportunity policy? We hypothesized that larger firms are more likely to have such a formal policy. Now, when you're ready, click OK and have a look at the output depicted in Figure 10.6.

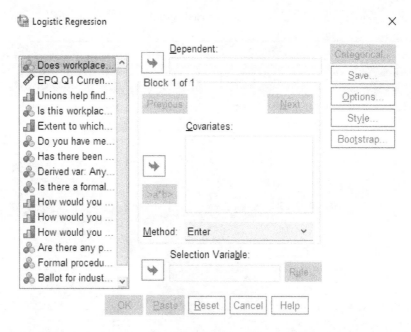

Figure 10.5 Binary logistic regression function in SPSS

Reprint courtesy of IBM Corporation ©

Case Processing Summary

Unweighted Cases[a]		N	Percent
Selected Cases	Included in Analysis	2659	99.2
	Missing Cases	21	.8
	Total	2680	100.0
Unselected Cases		0	.0
Total		2680	100.0

a. If weight is in effect, see classification table for the total number of cases.

Dependent Variable Encoding

Original Value	Internal Value
no	0
yes	1

Block 0: Beginning Block

Classification Table[a,b]

	Observed			Predicted		
				Does workplace have a formal written policy on diversity/equal opportunities?		Percentage Correct
				no	yes	
Step 0	Does workplace have a formal written policy on diversity/equal opportunities?	no		0	257	.0
		yes		0	2402	100.0
	Overall Percentage					90.3

a. Constant is included in the model.

b. The cut value is .500

Variables in the Equation

		B	S.E.	Wald	df	Sig.	Exp(B)
Step 0	Constant	2.235	.066	1159.673	1	.000	9.346

Variables not in the Equation

			Score	df	Sig.
Step 0	Variables	EPQ Q1 Currently how many employees do you have on the payroll at this workplace	27.592	1	.000
	Overall Statistics		27.592	1	.000

Block 1: Method = Enter

Omnibus Tests of Model Coefficients

		Chi-square	df	Sig.
Step 1	Step	104.842	1	.000
	Block	104.842	1	.000
	Model	104.842	1	.000

(Continued)

Figure 10.6 (Continued)

Model Summary

Step	-2 Log likelihood	Cox & Snell R Square	Nagelkerke R Square
1	1584.505[a]	.039	.082

a. Estimation terminated at iteration number 8 because parameter estimates changed by less than .001.

Hosmer and Lemeshow Test

Step	Chi-square	df	Sig.
1	207.076	8	.000

Contingency Table for Hosmer and Lemeshow Test

		Does workplace have a formal written policy on diversity/equal opportunities? = no		Does workplace have a formal written policy on diversity/equal opportunities? = yes		Total
		Observed	Expected	Observed	Expected	
Step 1	1	96	41.757	197	251.243	293
	2	67	35.938	189	220.062	256
	3	38	36.352	227	228.648	265
	4	24	34.717	239	228.283	263
	5	6	32.803	259	232.197	265
	6	8	29.851	259	237.149	267
	7	4	24.126	261	240.874	265
	8	8	15.898	257	249.102	265
	9	4	5.413	262	260.587	266
	10	2	.145	252	253.855	254

Classification Table[a]

			Predicted		
			Does workplace have a formal written policy on diversity/equal opportunities?		Percentage Correct
	Observed		no	yes	
Step 1	Does workplace have a formal written policy on diversity/equal opportunities?	no	0	257	.0
		yes	0	2402	100.0
	Overall Percentage				90.3

a. The cut value is .500

Variables in the Equation

		B	S.E.	Wald	df	Sig.	Exp(B)	95% C.I.for EXP(B) Lower	Upper
Step 1[a]	EPQ Q1 Currently how many employees do you have on the payroll at this workplace	.003	.001	34.166	1	.000	1.003	1.002	1.004
	Constant	1.771	.080	494.623	1	.000	5.878		

a. Variable(s) entered on step 1: EPQ Q1 Currently how many employees do you have on the payroll at this workplace.

Figure 10.6 Logistic regression output, predicting diversity

Reprint courtesy of IBM Corporation ©

The first box you see, Case Processing Summary, tell us that 2659 valid cases were included in this simple logistic regression (e.g., there were 21 missing cases, all of which came from diversity).

The second box you see, Dependent Variable Encoding, simply reminds us of how we coded our dependent variable, where 0 = *no* and 1 = *yes*.

Most of the information under Block 0: Beginning Block you can skip. These tables simply remind us of how many organizations have (2402) and do not have (257) formal diversity/equal opportunity policies and tell us how good the model is without firmsize included.

The real bread and butter of the logistic regression output starts under Block 1: Method = Enter. First, the Omnibus Test of Model Coefficients compared our baseline model (i.e., the model without the independent variable) with our test model (i.e., the model with the independent variable). If the chi-square associated with 'Model' is significant (and in this case, it is $\chi^2 = 104.84$, $p < 0.001$), then this tells us that the addition of our independent variable, firmsize, helps us better predict diversity compared with the baseline model without firmsize. So, in short, firmsize seems to be a reasonably good predictor of whether or not a firm has a formal diversity/equal opportunity policy in place.

Next, under Model Summary, you can find the –2 log likelihood, Cox and Snell R^2, and Nagelkerke R^2. The –2 log likelihood value of 1584.51 isn't terribly informative because it is scale dependent. It is an overall measure of goodness-of-fit and was used to compute the Omnibus Test of Model Coefficients from the preceding paragraph. The two pseudo-R^2 values, however, are useful. These statistics, like an R^2 in multiple linear regression, are always values between 0 and 1, where the higher the value, the better your model fit. In this case, the Cox and Snell R^2 is 0.039 and the Nagelkerke R^2 is 0.082. As noted above, these cannot be converted into percentage of variance explained in the dependent variable (as would be the case in multiple linear regression) because there are only two categories in our dependent variable. But they very roughly suggest that, if our dependent variable were scale, our model would explain between 3.9% (i.e., 0.039 × 100) and 8.2% (i.e., 0.082 × 100) of the variation in the outcome.

The next box reports the Hosmer–Lemeshow test. Here, you only need to focus on the *p*-value, labeled 'Sig.' in the table. Ideally, we would like to see a nonsignificant *p*-value; that is, a *p*-value that is > 0.05. Unfortunately, our *p*-value here is statistically significant ($p < 0.001$), so this suggests a problem in our model in terms of goodness-of-fit. This isn't a huge problem, though, and is likely due to the fact that the vast majority of organizations have a diversity policy compared with those that don't.

You can skip the Contingency Table for Hosmer–Lemeshow test and the Classification Table and go straight to Variables in the Equation box at the bottom of the output. Here is where we finally get the results of our simple logistic regression test. Looking closely at this table, the first feature you should note is that the relationship between firm size and diversity is statistically significant, as signaled by the p-value of 0.000 (to be reported as $p < 0.001$). The Wald statistic is 34.17, which is what SPSS used to calculate this p-value. So already we know that firm size is statistically significantly associated with whether or not an organization has a formal diversity/equal opportunity policy. The next statistic you should focus on is B, which corresponds to the logged odds change. Remember that logged odds can be positive or negative. A positive number here suggests an increase in logged odds for every one-unit increase in X and a negative number here suggests a decrease in logged odds for every one-unit increase in X. Because this value of B is positive ($B = 0.003$), we can conclude, as we expected, that larger firms are more likely to have a formal diversity/equal opportunity policy than smaller firms. Alternatively stated, for every one-unit increase in X (firm size), the logged odds of there being a formal policy increase by 0.003. Now, you will recall from our discussion above that logged odds aren't very intuitive or interpretable. For a more intuitive coefficient, check out Exp(B), the exponentiated B that converts logged odds back into normal odds. The value of Exp(B) is 1.003. This can be interpreted as an odds ratio of 1:1.003, which suggests, on the face of it, a very small, almost miniscule increase in odds, but you need to remember that this increase in odds is for every one-unit increase in X. In other words, the odds of a firm with 256 employees having a formal diversity policy is 1.003 higher than the odds of a firm with 255 employees. Every miniscule increase in odds can add up over larger numbers. Therefore, what appears like a tiny increase in odds is actually quite large. We also requested the 95% confidence intervals for Exp(B), and these are between 1.002 and 1.004. Therefore, we can conclude that as firm size increases (by one employee), so, too, does the likelihood that the firm has a formal diversity/equal opportunity policy in place. Boom! You just did your first simple logistic regression analysis. Nice work, partner!

That was so much fun. Let's do another logistic regression, but this time we'll do a multiple logistic regression with two independent variables, one of which will continue to be firmsize. This time around, let's also ask whether the presence (or absence) of a trade union has any impact on the likelihood of an organization having a formal diversity/equal opportunity policy in place. We might hypothesize that trade unions will likely push for the formalization of such policies, so we can expect organizations with a trade union to be more likely to have a formal policy than organizations without a trade union. Note that this new variable, trade union, is a dummy independent variable. So this multiple logistic regression will have one scale-level independent variable (firmsize) and one two-category nominal variable (*tradeunion*, where 0 = *no trade union* and 1 = *yes, trade union*).

Go to Analyze, Regression, and Binary Logistic again. You should still have the previous model set up. Find tradeunion in the list of variables (it should be the seventh variable from the top in the list) and move it to the right under Block 1 of 1. Now that we have added a nominal independent variable to our logistic regression model, we will need to click on Categorical . Doing so opens a new dialog box depicted in Figure 10.7. Move tradeunion from the left to the right using ➔ . You can see at the bottom of this box that the reference category is listed as 'Last'. We want to change this to ⦿ First and then click Change . This means the reference category in this analysis will be 0 = *no trade union*, rather than 1 = *yes, trade union*. In other words, the results of the logistic regression will indicate changes relative to firms that do not have a trade union. Click Continue and then OK . The output is shown in Figure 10.8.

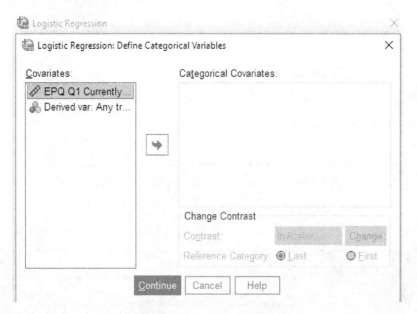

Figure 10.7 Logistic regression: define categorical variables function in SPSS

Reprint courtesy of IBM Corporation ©

Case Processing Summary

Unweighted Cases[a]		N	Percent
Selected Cases	Included in Analysis	2659	99.2
	Missing Cases	21	.8
	Total	2680	100.0
Unselected Cases		0	.0
Total		2680	100.0

a. If weight is in effect, see classification table for the total number of cases.

Dependent Variable Encoding

Original Value	Internal Value
no	0
yes	1

(Continued)

Figure 10.8   (Continued)

Categorical Variables Codings

		Frequency	Parameter coding (1)
Derived var: Any trade union/independent staff association members at workplace	no	1169	1.000
	yes	1490	.000

Block 0: Beginning Block

Classification Table[a,b]

			Predicted		
			Does workplace have a formal written policy on diversity/equal opportunities?		Percentage Correct
Observed			no	yes	
Step 0	Does workplace have a formal written policy on diversity/equal opportunities?	no	0	257	.0
		yes	0	2402	100.0
	Overall Percentage				90.3

a. Constant is included in the model.

b. The cut value is .500

Variables in the Equation

		B	S.E.	Wald	df	Sig.	Exp(B)
Step 0	Constant	2.235	.066	1159.673	1	.000	9.346

Variables not in the Equation

			Score	df	Sig.
Step 0	Variables	EPQ Q1 Currently how many employees do you have on the payroll at this workplace	27.592	1	.000
		Derived var: Any trade union/independent staff association members at workplace(1)	227.277	1	.000
	Overall Statistics		230.487	2	.000

Block 1: Method = Enter

Omnibus Tests of Model Coefficients

		Chi-square	df	Sig.
Step 1	Step	264.268	2	.000
	Block	264.268	2	.000
	Model	264.268	2	.000

Model Summary

Step	-2 Log likelihood	Cox & Snell R Square	Nagelkerke R Square
1	1425.079[a]	.095	.201

a. Estimation terminated at iteration number 8 because parameter estimates changed by less than .001.

Hosmer and Lemeshow Test

Step	Chi-square	df	Sig.
1	113.544	8	.000

Contingency Table for Hosmer and Lemeshow Test

		Does workplace have a formal written policy on diversity/equal opportunities? = no		Does workplace have a formal written policy on diversity/equal opportunities? = yes		
		Observed	Expected	Observed	Expected	Total
Step 1	1	93	51.820	156	197.180	249
	2	81	55.852	189	214.148	270
	3	41	54.410	226	212.590	267
	4	8	50.892	258	215.108	266
	5	9	18.686	258	248.314	267
	6	8	7.383	256	256.617	264
	7	5	6.973	261	259.027	266
	8	4	6.018	262	259.982	266
	9	6	4.096	260	261.904	266
	10	2	.870	276	277.130	278

(Continued)

Figure 10.8 (Continued)

Classification Table[a]

			Predicted		
			Does workplace have a formal written policy on diversity/equal opportunities?		Percentage Correct
Observed			no	yes	
Step 1	Does workplace have a formal written policy on diversity/equal opportunities?	no	0	257	.0
		yes	0	2402	100.0
	Overall Percentage				90.3

a. The cut value is .500

Variables in the Equation

		B	S.E.	Wald	df	Sig.	Exp(B)	95% C.I.for EXP(B)	
								Lower	Upper
Step 1[a]	EPQ Q1 Currently how many employees do you have on the payroll at this workplace	.001	.000	8.164	1	.004	1.001	1.000	1.002
	Derived var. Any trade union/independent staff association members at workplace(1)	2.169	.207	109.744	1	.000	8.747	5.829	13.124
	Constant	1.328	.078	287.225	1	.000	3.773		

a. Variable(s) entered on step 1: EPQ Q1 Currently how many employees do you have on the payroll at this workplace, Derived var. Any trade union/independent staff association members at workplace.

Figure 10.8 Logistic regression output (independent variables are firmsize and tradeunion, and dependent variable is diversity)

Reprint courtesy of IBM Corporation ©

We're going to skip through most of this output to focus on the key boxes. First check out Model Summary, found under Block 1: Model=Enter. By adding tradeunion to our model, the –2 log likelihood value is now 1425.08. Both the Cox and Snell pseudo-R^2 and the Nagelkerke pseudo-R^2 have also improved to 0.095 and 0.201, respectively. In other words, these statistics all tell us that adding tradeunion to our logistic regression model has improved the overall goodness-of-fit and predictive power. The Hosmer–Lemeshow test is still significant ($p = 0.000$, which should be reported as $p < 0.001$), but we're not going to worry too much about this.

Now let's cut straight to the chase by looking at the Variables in the Equation box at the bottom of the output. First, you will notice that adding tradeunion to this multivariate logistic regression equation has somewhat weakened the effect of firmsize. The Wald statistic, previously 34.17, is now 8.16, but the corresponding p-value is still significant at $p = 0.004$. This means that firm size is still positively related to the likelihood of an organization having a formal diversity/equal opportunity policy in place, even when taking into account the influence of trade union presence or absence. Now look at the effect of tradeunion on the likelihood of an organization having such a policy in place. The first thing you should notice is that the result is statistically significant ($p = 0.000$, to be reported as $p < 0.001$). The Wald statistic for tradeunion is very large, 109.74, so whatever effect we're seeing here, it's big! The B value, corresponding to the logged odds, is 2.17. What this means is that firms that have a trade union have an increased likelihood of having a formal diversity/equal opportunity policy, to the measure of 2.17 logged odds. But, again, logged odds aren't intuitive and easy to interpret, so instead let's look at the Exp(B), the exponentiated logged odds, which converts logged odds into more interpretable odds. This value is 8.75. The way we would interpret this value is as follows: organizations with a trade union are 8.75 times more likely to have a formal diversity/equal opportunity policy in place than firms without a trade union. In other words, as we expected, the presence of a trade union has a very large effect on the likelihood of having a formal policy in place.

What's that you say? You want to add one more independent variable to our multiple logistic regression model? Well, only if you insist!

Let's add another binary independent variable into the equation. This time, we'll be adding whether (or not) there is a formal procedure for dealing with discipline and dismissal. This question is similarly coded 0 = *no* and 1 = *yes*. We're going to hypothesize that having a formal discipline and dismissal policy will increase the likelihood of having a formal diversity/equal opportunity policy. This makes sense. If an organization has one policy, it probably also has the other, right?

Go again to Analyze, Regression, and Binary Logistic. Move dispolicy (which should be the eighth variable from the top of the list) to the right under Block 1 of 1. Go into Categorical... and highlight dispolicy and move it to the right using ➡. Next to Reference Category, click ⊙ First and then Change, so that our reference category will be organizations without a disciplinary and dismissal policy, coded as 0. Click Continue. and then OK. The output is depicted in Figure 10.9.

Case Processing Summary

Unweighted Cases[a]		N	Percent
Selected Cases	Included in Analysis	2657	99.1
	Missing Cases	23	.9
	Total	2680	100.0
Unselected Cases		0	.0
Total		2680	100.0

a. If weight is in effect, see classification table for the total number of cases.

Dependent Variable Encoding

Original Value	Internal Value
no	0
yes	1

(Continued)

Figure 10.9 (Continued)

Categorical Variables Codings

		Frequency	Parameter coding (1)
Is there a formal procedure for dealing with discipline and dismissals?	no	95	.000
	yes	2562	1.000
Derived var: Any trade union/independent staff association members at workplace	no	1167	.000
	yes	1490	1.000

Block 0: Beginning Block

Classification Table[a,b]

			Predicted		
			Does workplace have a formal written policy on diversity/equal opportunities?		Percentage Correct
	Observed		no	yes	
Step 0	Does workplace have a formal written policy on diversity/equal opportunities?	no	0	257	.0
		yes	0	2400	100.0
	Overall Percentage				90.3

a. Constant is included in the model.

b. The cut value is .500

Variables in the Equation

		B	S.E.	Wald	df	Sig.	Exp(B)
Step 0	Constant	2.234	.066	1158.715	1	.000	9.339

Variables not in the Equation

			Score	df	Sig.
Step 0	Variables	EPQ Q1 Currently how many employees do you have on the payroll at this workplace	27.620	1	.000
		Derived var: Any trade union/independent staff association members at workplace(1)	227.775	1	.000
		Is there a formal procedure for dealing with discipline and dismissals?(1)	492.947	1	.000
	Overall Statistics		619.571	3	.000

Block 1: Method = Enter

Omnibus Tests of Model Coefficients

		Chi-square	df	Sig.
Step 1	Step	431.406	3	.000
	Block	431.406	3	.000
	Model	431.406	3	.000

Model Summary

Step	-2 Log likelihood	Cox & Snell R Square	Nagelkerke R Square
1	1257.533[a]	.150	.319

a. Estimation terminated at iteration number 8 because parameter estimates changed by less than .001.

Hosmer and Lemeshow Test

Step	Chi-square	df	Sig.
1	64.961	8	.000

Contingency Table for Hosmer and Lemeshow Test

		Does workplace have a formal written policy on diversity/equal opportunities? = no		Does workplace have a formal written policy on diversity/equal opportunities? = yes		
		Observed	Expected	Observed	Expected	Total
Step 1	1	111	96.532	143	157.468	254
	2	71	41.655	200	229.345	271
	3	36	40.319	229	224.681	265
	4	7	38.806	259	227.194	266
	5	8	16.038	257	248.962	265
	6	7	6.366	260	260.634	267
	7	5	6.084	261	259.916	266
	8	4	5.537	262	260.463	266
	9	6	4.301	260	261.699	266
	10	2	1.361	269	269.639	271

(Continued)

Figure 10.9 (Continued)

Classification Table[a]

			Predicted		
			Does workplace have a formal written policy on diversity/equal opportunities?		Percentage Correct
Observed			no	yes	
Step 1	Does workplace have a formal written policy on diversity/equal opportunities?	no	70	187	27.2
		yes	17	2383	99.3
	Overall Percentage				92.3

a. The cut value is .500

Variables in the Equation

		B	S.E.	Wald	df	Sig.	Exp(B)	95% C.I.for EXP(B) Lower	Upper
Step 1[a]	EPQ Q1 Currently how many employees do you have on the payroll at this workplace	.001	.000	5.073	1	.024	1.001	1.000	1.001
	Derived var: Any trade union/independent staff association members at workplace(1)	1.984	.213	86.881	1	.000	7.268	4.790	11.030
	Is there a formal procedure for dealing with discipline and dismissals?(1)	3.076	.265	134.968	1	.000	21.669	12.896	36.408
	Constant	-1.380	.253	29.828	1	.000	.252		

a. Variable(s) entered on step 1: EPQ Q1 Currently how many employees do you have on the payroll at this workplace, Derived var: Any trade union/independent staff association members at workplace, Is there a formal procedure for dealing with discipline and dismissals?.

Figure 10.9 Logistic regression output (independent variables are firmsize, tradeunion, and dispolicy, and dependent variable is diversity)

Reprint courtesy of IBM Corporation ©

Scroll down to the Model Summary, under Block 1: Method=Enter. Here you can see even greater improvements in model fit, as evidenced by an even lower –2 log likelihood statistic of 1257.53 and higher pseudo-R^2 values of 0.150 and 0.319, respectively, for Cox and Snell and Nagelkerke. Overall, by adding these three independent variables into the equation, we are adding more value to the predictive power of the model. Unfortunately, though, our Hosmer–Lemeshow test statistic is still significant, a limitation that would have to be noted in our analyses.

Moving now to the Variables in the Equation box at the bottom of our output, we can see the three separate effects in our multiple logistic regression model. First, you can see that firmsize is still significant, but the *p*-value is now 0.024 and the Wald statistic is 5.07, suggesting that the effect is somewhat weakening with the inclusion of the other two independent variables. Nevertheless, it is still statistically significant. The effect of tradeunion (whether or not the organization has a trade union) is slightly weaker, but still strong by most standards (Wald statistic = 86.88, $p = 0.000$, Exp(B) = 7.27). Whereas in the previous model, organizations with a trade union were 8.75 times more likely to have a formal diversity/equal opportunity policy, in this model they are 7.27 times more likely to have such a policy in place. Finally, looking at our newest variable, dispolicy, we can see an enormous effect! The p-value of 0.000 (to be reported as $p < 0.001$) and the Wald statistic of 134.97 suggest a very strong effect of whether an organization has a disciplinary and dismissal policy or whether a firm has a diversity/equal opportunity policy. The logged odds associated with this effect suggest an increase of 3.08, but, again, these are not intuitive to interpret. The more intuitive statistic is the Exp(B), or exponentiated B, which converts the logged odds into odds. This value of 21.67 suggests that firms with a formal disciplinary and dismissal policy are nearly 22 times more likely to have a formal diversity/equal opportunity policy compared with firms that do not have a formal disciplinary and dismissal policy in place. In other words, our hypothesis was correct. Organizations that have one policy are much more likely to have both policies.

I think at this stage you have a pretty strong understanding of logistic regression and how to interpret the results in a multivariate context. There are a few more variables in the dataset and I would encourage you to experiment with them. For example, what would happen to your model if you decided to add whether (or not) an organization has a formal procedure for dealing with individual grievances? My guess is that you would find a similar result, where such firms are also much more likely to have a formal diversity/equal opportunity policy in place, but I'll leave this to you to explore this dataset a bit on your own.

Go ahead and play around with these data before you move on to the next chapter.

What Have You Learned?

Well, you made it through another intense chapter, and this was the most difficult one yet! I'm proud of you. Nice work! You are now an expert in multivariate logistic regression. The next time I need someone to predict a binary (yes/no, either/or) outcome, I know just who to approach for help . . . you!

Logistic regression is a versatile statistical technique that is used only when you have a dichotomous outcome variable. Like OLS regression, logistic regression is capable of handling multiple independent variables simultaneously. These independent variables can be scale-level, ordinal, or nominal, provided that the latter variables have only two categories. Whereas OLS regression is based on the concept of minimizing error terms, or residuals, logistic regression is based on a maximum likelihood technique that maximizes the predictive power of the model. The interpretation of a logistic regression model is rather similar to an OLS regression model: What is the effect on Y for every one-unit increase in X? But instead of explaining variation in Y (as in OLS regression), logistic regression predicts the likelihood that Y will happen, or not. The entire method is based on the logic of probability and odds. The method uses logged odds to calculate effects, but because these are not very intuitive, we exponentiate those logged odds to convert them into normal odds. Finally, whereas OLS regression provides R^2 values, which are indicative of the percentage of variation in Y explained by the independent variables, logistic regression can only offer pseudo-R^2 values, which act *as if* there were variation in the dependent variables and can be interpreted in a manner similar to OLS R^2 values.

If you thought logistic regression was cool, just hold on. In Chapter 11, we're going to change gears and learn about the measurement of latent variables. You might need to strap yourself in with a seatbelt because things are about to get crazy.

Further Reading

Hilbe, J. M. (2009). *Logistic regression models*. Chapman & Hall/CRC.

Hosmer, D. W., Jr., Lemeshow, S., & Sturdivant, R. X. (2013). *Applied logistic regression* (Vol. 398). John Wiley.

Kleinbaum, D. G., Dietz, K., Gail, M., Klein, M., & Klein, M. (2002). *Logistic regression*. Springer-Verlag.

Menard, S. (2002). *Applied logistic regression analysis* (Vol. 106). Sage.

Mood, C. (2010). Logistic regression: Why we cannot do what we think we can do, and what we can do about it. *European Sociological Review, 26*(1), 67–82.

Pampel, F. C. (2020). *Logistic regression: A primer* (Vol. 132). Sage.

In-Class Discussion Questions

1. What is logistic regression analysis and how is it similar to, and different from, multiple linear regression analysis?
2. What is a sigmoid function and why is it useful in MLE?
3. List out 10 binary outcomes that management scientists may want to predict.
4. Further to Question 3, brainstorm a few predictors for each outcome variable.
5. What is a pseudo-R^2 and how can it be interpreted in the context of multiple logistic regression analysis?
6. How would you interpret and report the results of a multiple logistic regression analysis? What statistics are important and why?

11

Exploratory and Confirmatory Factor Analyses

Multiple regression and logistic regression are multivariate statistical techniques that allow you to predict a single dependent variable from a set of independent variables. They ask how variation or change in the independent (X) variables impact variation or change in the dependent (Y) variable. In each method, the variables (both independent and dependent) are observable and directly measurable.

Factor analysis is also a multivariate method (in that it involves analysis of multiple variables simultaneously), but it levels no distinction between independent (predictor) variables and dependent (outcome) variables. In a factor analysis, we're not asking how X is related to Y or how X predicts Y. These kinds of research questions are not relevant to factor analysis because we're not trying to model statistical effects. Instead, we're trying to discover whether or not a set of variables share the same underlying structure. If they do share the same underlying structure, then the variables should 'hang together', while those that don't share the underlying structure won't fit in. For example, if we're trying to measure a construct such as job satisfaction, some items will tap that construct (e.g., 'I am satisfied with my pay' and 'I am satisfied with the amount of decision-making I have'), but other items will be measuring something else ('I am committed to my job' or 'I have a good relationship with my manager'). The latter two items (organization commitment and relationship with manager) might well be related in some way to job satisfaction, but they do not directly measure job satisfaction in the same way as the former two items do. Basically, a factor analysis asks the following question: given a set of variables, which ones 'hang together' well and which ones don't? Insofar as a set of variables 'hang together' well, we could argue that they are all measuring a different dimension of the same underlying construct (e.g., pay satisfaction and decision-making satisfaction are important dimensions of job satisfaction). Insofar as a set of variables don't 'hang together' well, then we can assume that they are measuring different underlying constructs.

If we have, say, 20 items, we can run a factor analysis to identify how many factors within those 20 items are identifiable. Maybe all 20 items measure the same factor, in which case the factor analysis will tell us that there is only one factor identifiable. Maybe half of the items measure one construct and the other half measure another construct. In this case, we end up with a two-factor solution. Or maybe five items measure factor A, five items measure factor B, five items measure factor C, and the remaining five items measure factor D. In this case, we end up with a four-factor solution to those 20 items, because four factors were identifiable. The five items of factor A 'hang together' well, meaning that they share an underlying structure, but those same five items in factor A do not 'hang together' well in factors B, C, and D. Similarly, the five items in factor B 'hang together' well but not so well with factors, A, C, and D, and so on. It is even possible that a factor analysis of the 20 items uncovers no common factors at all, meaning that all 20 items measure completely different constructs.

These 20 items are what we call observable variables. Each single indicator is an individual, observable measurement. To the extent that we are able to identify a set of common factors among those 20 items, those factors are referred to as *unobservable*, or *latent*, variables. A latent variable is a variable that is assumed to exist by virtue of its relationship to a set of observable variables, but a latent variable cannot be measured directly. It exists by virtue of its indirect relationship with a set of directly measurable indicators or items. For example, if we found two underlying factors among the 20 items (say, 12 items measuring factor A and 8 items measuring factor B), then we can conclude that we have identified two latent variables. Latent variables are distinct from composite variables, as described in Box 11.1.

Box 11.1: Latent Variables Versus Composite Variables

Some constructs are simply too complex to capture in a single item. Because the construct is multidimensional, it is composed of various elements, each of which contributes something important to the underlying structure. There are two ways of dealing with, or operationalizing, multidimensional constructs in statistical analysis. We learned about one method in previous chapters: building a composite variable. A composite variable is one that is composed by simply adding together the scores of a set of related variables. You can do this easily in the Compute function of SPSS. Let's say you have four variables that measure resilience, and each is measured on a four-point scale (where 1 = *not at all resilient* and 4 = *extremely resilient*). You could add these four variables together, giving you a composite variable with a low score of 4 (1 + 1 + 1 + 1 = 4) and a high score of 16 (4 + 4 + 4 + 4 = 16). If you wanted to, you could rescale the composite variable to the original scale by dividing the composite variable by 4. In creating a composite variable, you are basically adding up your single-item observable variables to create a new observable composite variable. Latent variables are different from composite variables. Whereas composite variables are still observable, a latent variable is unobservable, meaning that it exists only by virtue of the fact that it is composed of observable variables. A latent variable is constructed not on the basis of simply adding up the values of the single-item observable variables, but rather using more complex matrix algebra to assume its existence.

There are two types of factor analysis that we'll learn about in this chapter: exploratory factor analysis and confirmatory factor analysis. In an exploratory factor analysis, we have no idea what the underlying factor structures might look like. We're just exploring possibilities. Say we have 40 items, and we don't know how they might be related to one another. We can run an exploratory factor analysis that will tell us how many factors are identifiable within those 40 items. In the case of exploratory factor analysis, we don't have any *a priori* assumptions, one way or the other. We don't have any theory guiding our analysis. We're just exploring the underlying structures.

Confirmatory factor analysis, on the other hand, is 100% theory driven. It is a confirmatory approach, in that it is seeking to test whether our constructs are measured in the way we think that they are measured. In a confirmatory factor analysis, we might assume that, among those 40 items, we have four separate factors, or latent variables. We can then test whether the four factors really exist. One interesting feature of confirmatory factor analysis is that it can always be followed up with further exploratory factor analyses. For example, say we assume that four factors exist, but our confirmatory factor analysis suggests a poor fit for that four-factor model. We can then use what are referred to as *modification indices* to identify a better-fitting model consisting of a different set of factors (e.g., maybe there are three underlying factors among the 40 items, or maybe there are five). Modification indices are *post hoc* exploratory analyses aimed at improving model fit following a confirmatory factor analysis.

We will first use SPSS to run exploratory factor analyses, and then we will use an add-on program, AMOS, to run confirmatory factor analyses.

Let me make a quick note before we proceed. When I refer to an exploratory factor analysis in this chapter, what I'm really referring to is a *principal components analysis*. A principal components analysis (which we'll learn about here) is, in fact, a type of factor analysis, but, confusingly, there is another type of factor analysis (called a common factor analysis), which we will not learn here. So, whenever I refer to an exploratory factor analysis, what I really mean is a principal components analysis.

Factor Analysis in Management Research

When working with most economic data, factor analysis is generally an irrelevant technique. The reason it would be mostly irrelevant is that the leading economic indicators are fairly easy to measure with just one item. Accordingly, many econometricians aren't even trained in factor analysis. However, when working with psychological data, factor analysis is a core statistical technique. For this reason, it would be safe to conclude that factor analysis is mostly, in the context of management research, a statistical technique reserved for organizational psychologists interested in measuring psychological constructs in the workplace.

Let me give you an example of what I mean. We can produce an easy, one-item measure of total sales per employee. As long as we have access to the financial data within a firm, this variable is pretty easy to capture with just one measure. However, what if we would like to measure the personality of each employee to see whether such personal attributes are related to sales? How can we measure something such as personality? There is no single item, question, or statement that can validly and reliably measure something such as personality, because it is such a broad and wide-ranging construct. Fortunately, psychologists have been attempting to measure personality for as long as they have existed.

One of the most commonly used measures of personality in psychological research is the 'Big Five' factors (Gosling et al., 2003). The Big Five personalities include the following: conscientiousness, openness, agreeableness, extraversion, and neuroticism. Of course, these aren't the only five dimensions of one's personality, but they are five of the most important ones. Conscientiousness refers to one's ability to organize and systematize tasks efficiently. Openness refers to one's creativity, curiosity, and openness to new experiences. Agreeableness refers to one's ability to get along well with others. Extraversion refers to one's outgoingness and preference for social situations. Neuroticism refers to one's nervousness or anxiety.

Now, you might be thinking, why can't we just measure each one of these constructs with just one item? Well, you could, but your measurement wouldn't be very useful. For example, you could measure conscientiousness by asking,

Are you conscientious? Yes/No.

This is pretty basic and not terribly useful in tapping the underlying construct.

You also could ask something such as,

To what extent are you conscientious on a scale of 1 to 7, where 1 = *not at all conscientious* and 7 = *extremely conscientious*?

This is perhaps an improvement on the binary measurement above, but it still doesn't 'capture' the breadth and depth of conscientiousness. For example, Jackson et al. (2010) find that conscientiousness is made up of several lower-order traits such as orderliness, impulse control, industriousness, reliability, and conventionality. Each of these five subfeatures could be measured with any number of single indicators. In short, to get a good measure of conscientiousness, you might need to combine many single-item indicators, each of which 'taps' one dimension of the underlying construct. If you accidentally include an item or indicator that does not 'tap' that dimension, a factor analysis will tell you that it does not fit in with the construct.

Management researchers might use factor analysis to answer the following types of research questions:

- What is the underlying structure of *g*, also known as general mental ability (Schmidt and Hunter, 2004)? This is an important research question for managers and management scientists because *g* is an important predictor of job performance. The higher one scores on *g*, the better one's performance. There is no one item or question that measures *g*, but you could look at scores on various IQ tests, problem-solving activities, and/or verbal or quantitative reasoning tests. By combining those measures, you may identify one overarching structure of *g*, or you may identify separate factors that may relate to a 'super construct'. Either way, you will have a good latent measure of general mental ability.
- What is the underlying structure of individual job performance? Once again, a single measure of job performance may not be enough. The reason is that job performance is a multifaceted construct. Therefore, you could use factor analysis to analyse the underlying structure of individual job

performance. You might combine, for example, manager evaluations of performance with coworkers', subordinates', and customers' evaluations of performance. You might include 'hard' performance data such as sales with 'soft' performance data such as interpersonal achievements. Once you compile all your indicators of performance, a factor analysis will tell you whether you're dealing with one overall measure of performance or multiple factors, each of which contributes to, or is associated with, a wider job performance construct.

- What is the underlying structure of depression? This might be useful information for both organizational and clinical psychologists. You could just ask someone if they are depressed (yes/no) or the extent to which they feel depressed (on a Likert scale), but these single items would only provide you with limited information and wouldn't 'tap' the underlying construct. Depression involves feelings of hopelessness, despair, and sadness. It also involves physiological indicators like weight gain (or sometimes loss), sleeplessness, and changes to cardiovascular health. By combining all these indicators together, a factor analysis will tell you whether you're measuring one construct or multiple related constructs.

- What is the underlying structure of job satisfaction? Again, you could just ask an employee if they are satisfied at work or how satisfied they are on a Likert scale, but these items likely wouldn't provide you with a good measure of this complex construct. What if someone is satisfied with some dimensions of their job, but not with other dimensions? For example, you might have multiple indicators of job satisfaction, including satisfaction with pay, satisfaction with the work itself, satisfaction with supervisory support, satisfaction with training opportunities, satisfaction with autonomy, and so on. By combining all these indicators together, a factor analysis will tell you if you are dealing with one or multiple latent measures of this construct.

- What is the underlying structure of employee voice? You could ask an employee if they feel that they have a voice at work, or how much voice they have on a Likert scale, but, once again, these measures would provide you with very limited information on this construct. Employee voice can involve feelings of engagement, empowerment and autonomy, and perceptions of the ability to participate in decision-making. An employee might feel that she or he has a lot of voice on some issues and very little voice on other issues. Employee voice can be direct (e.g., do managers listen to employees) or indirect (e.g., do managers listen to trade unions that represent employees). By combining these multiple indicators, a factor analysis will tell you whether there is one overarching employee voice factor or multiple latent factors.

You can see, based on these research questions, that we're not trying to investigate or understand the nature of the relationship between X and Y, as in previous chapters. Instead, we're looking at how we can most accurately (that is to say, most validly) measure X or Y as latent variables. Accurate measurement of these constructs might be a prelude to later correlational research, of course. For example, if we are trying to understand the relationship between general mental ability (X) and individual job performance (Y), we would first need good measures of these constructs. For this reason, factor analysis is often one of the first techniques that researchers carry out before undertaking multivariate modeling. After all, it doesn't make sense to try to understand the relationship between X and Y unless you first understand what X and Y are and how they can be defined.

Let's take a brief, nonmathematical look at the logic underlying factor analysis, so you can better understand this method.

Basic Concepts in Factor Analysis

Exploratory Factor Analysis

Looking at the 'big picture', exploratory factor analysis aims to simplify data. It is also commonly referred to as a data reduction method. What exactly do I mean by simplification and data reduction? What exactly is being reduced? In essence, factor analysis reduces the dimensionality of the data. Let's say you have 50 observable indicators. It is possible that all 50 indicators, in fact, measure 50 different constructs. In such a dataset, there is no way to reduce or simplify the data. Each indicator stands alone. They might well be correlated with each other, but they do not overlap in terms of measurement. However, it is possible that some of those 50 indicators 'hang together' well and others don't. We could just look at bivariate correlations to see how much the indicators covary, but this is a pretty subjective way of doing things. Instead, we have two options, as alluded to above. First, we could run an exploratory factor analysis on those 50 indicators to see how many factors, or dimensions, emerge. That number will be anywhere between 1 (meaning that all 50 indicators measure the same construct) and 50 (meaning that all 50 indicators measure unique constructs). The fact that it is exploratory means that we have no *a priori* expectations. The second option is to run a confirmatory factor analysis. In this case, we have an *a priori* (e.g., theoretical) reason to believe that some of those 50 indicators will 'hang together' and others won't. For example, we might expect to find five factors among those 50 items, with maybe 10 items per factor. Either way (exploratory or confirmatory), we're seeing if there is a way to reduce and simplify those data. Maybe there is, or maybe there isn't. But at least we'll know if we can treat some of the variables as latent or unobserved.

Technically, exploratory factor analysis isn't an inferential technique, although it can be treated as one. In other words, we don't necessarily need to employ *p*-values in exploratory factor analysis, because it is primarily a descriptive mathematical function.

The mathematics underlying exploratory factor analysis are mind-bogglingly complex. If this were an advanced statistics textbook that you're reading, we'd all have to learn about these mathematical procedures. But, thankfully, this is an applied statistics textbook. Therefore, we can briefly summarize the math. A simple overview will suffice, which I hope to provide here.

An exploratory factor analysis starts with a data matrix. This can be a matrix of correlations (e.g., a bivariate correlation table consisting of a set of Pearson's *r* correlation coefficients) or a matrix of covariances. A *covariance* is like a correlation, but not scaled between –1 and 1. Most often, exploratory factor analysis involves a correlation matrix. Let's say you have a set of 10 items measuring overall health. To start an exploratory factor analysis, you will first look at the bivariate correlations among the 10 items. You note that five of the items measure mental health and the other five measure physical health. The question is should you treat the 10 items as an overall measure of health (e.g., one factor consisting of all 10 items), or is it better to treat these items as a two-factor solution (where physical health and mental health are measured as separate constructs)? You can look at the bivariate correlation matrix and see if the Pearson's *r* values are higher within each group than they are across each group. For example, are the five Pearson's *r* coefficients among the mental health variables higher than the correlations between the mental and physical health variables, and vice versa? If so, this might give you some indication that you're dealing with two separate factors, rather than one. But just looking at the bivariate correlations is too subjective to make any useful conclusions about data dimensionality. Instead, we can run an exploratory factor analysis using this data matrix consisting of bivariate correlations, where the key relationships are no longer the correlations among the 10 variables, but rather the factor loadings between each indicator and the wider factors, or latent variables. In short, a *factor loading* is the individual contribution of each single-item indicator (or each variable) to the wider latent factor.

Because of the mathematical nature of factor analysis, you should use ordinal- or scale-level indicators. It is technically possible to use binary (dummy) variables, but this should be avoided, if possible, because it can introduce a lot of 'noise' into the analysis. Looking at the correlation matrix, we obviously want to see that at least some of the variables are reasonably correlated with each other before we run an exploratory factor analysis. Again, it wouldn't be very sensible to just subjectively look at the bivariate correlations, but one useful option at your disposal is *Bartlett's test of sphericity*, which is a statistical test (meaning it produces a *p*-value) that tells you whether or not there are any statistically significant correlations within the bivariate correlation matrix that could lend themselves to a factor analysis.

Now we come to the mathematics underlying an exploratory factor analysis. The method of extracting factors from a set of observable items (variables) is based on the logic of distinguishing between *total variance* (i.e., all the variance among all the variables), *common variance* (i.e., variance shared with other variables in the matrix), *unique variance* (i.e., variance for a specific variable), and *error variance* (i.e., leftover variance that is, in effect, a residual error term). The procedure needs to employ a criterion for deciding how many factors are optimal for a given set of observable indicators. The criterion that is typically used in exploratory factor analysis is referred to as the *latent root criterion*, which is equivalent to an eigenvalue of greater than 1. Eigenvalue is a fancy word, but you only need to know that it entails a cutoff of 1, where an eigenvalue of greater than 1 suggests the existence of a latent factor. Thus, looking back at our example of the 10 overall health indicators, if only one factor emerges with an eigenvalue greater than 1, then we conclude that there is a one-factor solution and that overall health is best considered as a single construct or dimension. However, if two factors among these 10 indicators have eigenvalues greater than 1, then we can conclude that there is a two-factor solution and that mental and physical health should be considered as separate constructs or dimensions. The eigenvalue is, therefore, a statistical cutoff that we use in exploratory factor analysis to determine the optimum number of factors for a set of single-item indicators. We can produce a *scree plot*, which is a visual representation of the number of factors whose eigenvalues are greater than 1. Figure 11.1 demonstrates a scree plot for the two-factor health solution. In it, you'll see that two factors (physical health and mental health) are above the cutoff of an eigenvalue of 1 on the *Y*-axis. The remaining factors (3 through 10) all fall below an eigenvalue of 1, meaning that they do not constitute factors.

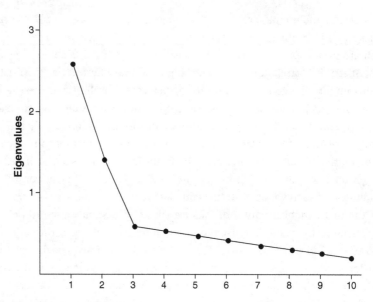

Figure 11.1 Two-factor scree plot

These eigenvalues are calculated by a process called factor *rotation*. Again, the mathematics under-lying factor rotation are too complex for this applied textbook, but rotation essentially means that you are rotating the initial (unrotated) factor solution to see if the factors extracted are theoretically mean-ingful. Don't worry about how this is accomplished. You just need to understand that an exploratory factor analysis starts with a bivariate correlation matrix, then extracts unrotated factors (which are essentially the best linear combinations of variables that can be statistically 'clumped' together), and finally these unrotated factors are mathematically 'rotated' to confirm that the number of extracted factors still make sense. In this process, the first factor extracted (factor 1) explains the most amount of shared variance. The leftover (residual) variance is then used to create the second-best factor (factor 2). The leftover (residual) variance from the first and second factors is then used to create the third-best factor (factor 3), and so on and so forth. Through this process, the aim is to optimize the factor load-ings, such that each latent factor is associated with the variables in the matrix with the highest factor loadings against it. For this reason, the first factor that is extracted in an exploratory factor analysis is usually the strongest, and the last factor extracted is usually the weakest. But all the extracted factors that are meaningful will have an eigenvalue of greater than 1. Any apparent factors with an eigen-value of less than 1 aren't really factors at all. They are not meaningful 'clumps' of variables, whereas the extracted factors are meaningful 'clumps'. That's why they are said to 'hang together'.

In exploratory factor analysis, there are different methods of rotation. The two key types of rotation are orthogonal and oblique. *Orthogonal* rotation is the simplest and most common type, where the results of the unrotated factor analysis are rotated 90 degrees on a 360 degree axis, as illus-trated in Figure 11.2. Here, you can see how the unrotated factors relate to the rotated factors. An *oblique rotation* is more flexible in that it is not constrained to a 90 degree rotation. When doing an exploratory factor analysis, it doesn't really matter whether you use an orthogonal (90 degree) rotation or an oblique (flexible) rotation. You just need to use some kind of rotation method to extract meaningful factors from the data. For this reason, the most commonly used types of rotation are orthogonal, including varimax rotation, quartimax rotation, and equimax rotation, with the first being the default method. All methods should produce fairly similar results, and all methods are available in SPSS for exploratory factor analysis.

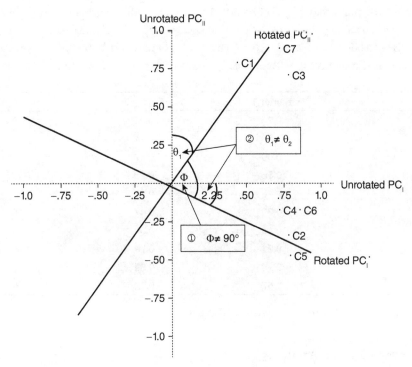

Figure 11.2 Orthogonal rotation in exploratory factor analysis

Source: Pett et al. (2003).

The last step in an exploratory factor analysis, after rotating the solution, is to identify which items 'load' onto which factor(s), bearing in mind that some items won't load onto any factors and some items might load onto both factors. Recall that a factor loading is like a correlation between the individual items and the overarching factor(s). Typically, we use a cutoff of 0.40 to determine whether or not an item loads onto a factor. If all items in a one-factor solution have a loading of greater than 0.40, then we conclude that all items load onto that factor. If we have a two-factor solution, we look for items that have a loading of 0.40 or greater and conclude that they are part of that particular factor. If an item has a factor loading of greater than 0.40 on both factors, then we need to consider whether we keep that item because it doesn't offer good *discriminant validity*. Discriminant validity means that one factor can be conceptually and statistically distinguished from another item. Some items may not load onto either factor as evidenced by a loading of less than 0.40, in which case we can drop them entirely from our measurement model.

Figure 11.3 provides a hypothetical set of already rotated factor loadings for a two-factor solution of our health variable (with mental health as factor 1 and physical health as factor 2). As you can see, items 1, 2, 3, and 4 load onto factor 1 with values of greater than 0.40, and they also all load onto factor 2 with items less than 0.40. So far, so good. We can therefore conclude that factors 1, 2, 3, and 4 'tap' mental health. Similarly, items 6, 7, 8, and 9 load onto factor 2 with values of greater than 0.40, and they also load onto factor 1 with items less than 0.40. Therefore, we can conclude that items 6, 7, 8, and 9 'tap' physical health. You will also note that item 5 does not load onto either factor with a value of greater than 0.40, so we can drop it from our measurement. Similarly, item 10 loads onto both factor 1 and factor 2 with a value of greater than 0.40, so we've dropped this one as well because it reduces the discriminant validity of our two-factor solution.

	Factor 1	Factor 2	
Item 1	0.73	0.25	✓
Item 2	0.58	0.14	✓
Item 3	0.66	0.37	✓
Item 4	0.56	0.28	✓
Item 5	0.26	0.15	✗
Item 6	0.30	0.47	✓
Item 7	0.16	0.50	✓
Item 8	0.21	0.79	✓
Item 9	0.28	0.55	✓
Item 10	0.57	0.62	✗

Figure 11.3 Two-factor solution with loadings

Confirmatory Factor Analysis

Whereas exploratory factor analysis involves no *a priori* expectations, confirmatory factor analysis is always driven by theory and, therefore, by hypotheses. In other words, by taking a confirmatory approach to measuring a latent construct or variable, we have expectations, grounded in the extant literature, that the measurement model in the population will look the way we expect it to look in the sample. We can then test whether or not we were correct in our model specification using statistical inference. However, instead of using p-values to gauge whether or not we can generalize the measurement model from the sample data to the population, we instead use something called *critical ratios*. Critical ratios are the same thing as p-values, but they are expressed in standardized z-scores. A critical ratio of beyond ±1.96 is equivalent to a p-value of < 0.05. If you don't understand this just yet, you will once we learn how to do a confirmatory factor analysis in AMOS.

Figure 11.4 illustrates what a confirmatory factor analysis might look like. In this figure, we are measuring the latent construct (job satisfaction) as a function of eight single-item indicators (qa8a, qa8b, qa8c, qa8d, qa8e, qa8f, qa8g, qa8h), each of which, we hypothesize, 'taps' an underlying dimension of the wider construct. In fact, this model maps directly onto eight variables in the WERS of employees. We'll be working on this model later in the chapter.

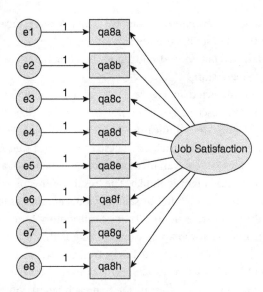

Figure 11.4 Confirmatory factor analysis, job satisfaction

In Figure 11.4, you will see that job satisfaction, our latent variable, is measured via an oval. This is typical in confirmatory factor analysis. The oval in a path diagram always represents a latent, or unobserved, variable. The eight single-item job satisfaction indicators (qa8a, qa8b, qa8c, qa8d, qa8e, qa8f, qa8g, qa8h) are measured using rectangles. Again, this is convention in path diagrams such as the one in Figure 11.4. You will also notice that each rectangle (i.e, each single item indicator [e1, e2, e3, e4, e5, e6, e7, e7, e8]) has a circle associated with it. These circles are the residual, or error, terms that are not explained by the latent variable.

In this particular measurement model, we are assuming, *a priori*, that job satisfaction is a single-factor solution consisting of these eight items, each of which 'taps' an underlying dimension of job satisfaction. As with exploratory factor analysis, we're not looking at causal relationships in the context of a confirmatory factor analysis. That is to say, we're not concerned about understanding the relationship our latent variable has with any other variables. Instead, we're just trying to get a good, accurate measurement of the variable. Once we have a good measurement of job satisfaction (or whatever latent variable we're trying to measure), we could then use it as either an independent variable or a dependent variable in a wider structural equation model, as we'll discuss in the next chapter. For now, let's just focus on the measurement of latent variables using confirmatory factor analysis and forget about the fact that the latent variables themselves can be related to each other in the same way that single-item indicators can be related to each other.

As with exploratory factor analysis, the mathematics underlying confirmatory factor analysis are way too complex for this textbook. If you really want a good, in-depth mathematical explanation of confirmatory factor analysis, you can check out Bollen (1989). For now, I'm going to give a brief summary of the mathematics underlying confirmatory factor analysis.

This statistical approach is based on matrix algebra. Lucky for us, we don't have to do any of the math! SPSS has an add-on program, called AMOS, which fortunately does the math for us. Whereas exploratory factor analysis started with bivariate correlations among the items, confirmatory factor analysis starts with an analysis of *covariances* among the items. A covariance is a bit like a Pearson's *r* correlation coefficient in that it describes the linear relationship between two variables, but, unlike Pearson's *r*, it is not standardized between –1 and 1 and therefore has no range, like an unstandardized *B* coefficient in simple regression.

Our measurement model depicted in Figure 11.4 assumes, or hypothesizes, that the latent construct job satisfaction is composed of a combination of the eight single-item indicators. The relationships between the eight single-item indicators and the latent variable are described by a set of variances and covariances/regression coefficients. These estimates of sample variances and covariances are mathematically expressed in covariance algebra to come up with a set of estimates of what the population covariance matrix might look like. The 'result' of this procedure is that we can tell whether or not the parameters identified in our sample model are similar to, or different from, the estimated parameters in the population matrix. That's confirmatory factor analysis in a nutshell.

One feature of confirmatory factor analysis worth noting is that a latent variable must have a minimum of three single-item indicators attached to it. Technically, it is possible in a more complex structural equation model to have a latent variable with only two items attached to it, but for confirmatory factor analysis, you'll just have to trust me that each latent construct must be composed of at least three observable variables. In the case of Figure 11.4, we're fine because there are eight variables measuring job satisfaction. If we only had two variables in the WERS dataset measuring job satisfaction, then it would be technically impossible to run a confirmatory factor analysis.

The reason that there always must be at least three items per latent variable in a confirmatory factor analysis is a bit complicated, but essentially, it boils down to the idea of *model identification*. Model identification refers to whether a confirmatory factor analysis (or wider structural equation model, as we'll learn in the next chapter) is overidentified, just identified, or underidentified. You don't need to understand the mathematics underlying model identification, but you do need to understand that a confirmatory factor analysis can only be run if a model is just identified or, preferably, overidentified. If a model is underidentified, this means that you technically cannot run the model. The reason why overidentified models are good is that they have enough data points and parameters (i.e., weights) to be freely estimated. A just-identified model is okay because it has the same number of data points vis-à-vis structural parameters. But an underidentified model has a mismatch between the number of data points and the structural parameters to be estimated. In other words, underidentified models don't provide enough data to answer the questions we want to ask. It's a bit like asking someone to solve the following equation: $x + y = 300$. We don't have enough information to do so. This is why three variables, at a minimum, need to be attached to each latent variable. And even if we have three variables per latent variable, we still need to fix one of the three parameters at 1.00 to enable estimation of the full model. This means that we do not freely estimate the factor loadings between all three indicators and the latent construct; only two of those are allowed to be freely estimated, while the third one is fixed at 1.00. It is not relevant which of the three indicators should be fixed. That is usually a random choice. But what is important is that, for any given latent variable with three or more items attached to it, at least one of those paths between the item and the latent variable will need to be fixed at 1.00 to ensure that the model is identifiable. In addition, you will note in Figure 11.4 that all the paths between the error terms (e1, e2, e3, e4, e5, e6, e7, and e8) and the items are fixed at 1.00 as well, meaning that they are also not allowed to be freely estimated. It sounds weird, I know. You'll just have to trust me on this one.

When you have set up your confirmatory factor analysis and selected which paths are to be fixed at 1.00, then you are finally able to run your model and generate your fit statistics and parameter estimates. As with logistic regression, we typically use MLE to run confirmatory factor analyses.

Okay, now that you know about the basic concepts underlying both exploratory and confirmatory factor analyses, let's use some real data to illustrate both methods. First I'll show you how to run an exploratory factor analysis using SPSS, and then I'll show you how to run a confirmatory factor analysis using AMOS.

Exploratory Factor Analysis Using SPSS

Open up the file labeled Chap11data.sav from the Companion Website. This data file is from the survey of employees. Spend a few minutes in Variable View looking through the variables and seeing how they are coded. You should also run some descriptive statistics, so that you can familiarize yourself with the variables in the dataset.

When you feel you are sufficiently familiar with the data, let's consider how we can use exploratory factor analysis to explore the variables.

You will notice that the dataset contains eight single items measuring job satisfaction: qa8a, qa8b, qa8c, qa8d, qa8e, qa8f, qa8g, and qa8h. These are depicted in Figure 11.5, which is taken directly from the survey of employees. Each item measures a unique dimension of job satisfaction, from satisfaction with the job itself to satisfaction with pay. If we were to run a factor analysis on these eight items, we might expect to find a one-factor solution, meaning that all eight items 'tap' the same construct: a general latent measure of job satisfaction. We don't know this for sure, though. Maybe there are two or more 'clumps' of job satisfaction that we don't see just by looking at the eight indicators. The only way to find out if we have a one-factor solution is to run the factor analysis. So, without further ado, let's do it!

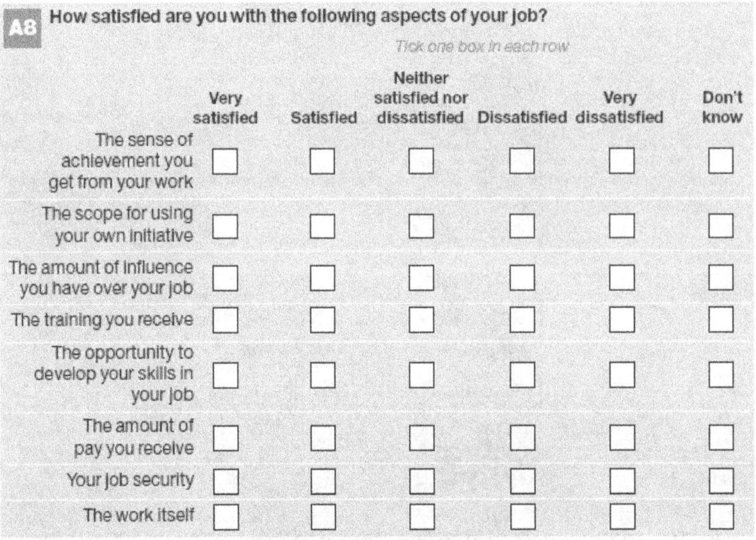
A8 How satisfied are you with the following aspects of your job?

Tick one box in each row

	Very satisfied	Satisfied	Neither satisfied nor dissatisfied	Dissatisfied	Very dissatisfied	Don't know
The sense of achievement you get from your work	☐	☐	☐	☐	☐	☐
The scope for using your own initiative	☐	☐	☐	☐	☐	☐
The amount of influence you have over your job	☐	☐	☐	☐	☐	☐
The training you receive	☐	☐	☐	☐	☐	☐
The opportunity to develop your skills in your job	☐	☐	☐	☐	☐	☐
The amount of pay you receive	☐	☐	☐	☐	☐	☐
Your job security	☐	☐	☐	☐	☐	☐
The work itself	☐	☐	☐	☐	☐	☐

Figure 11.5 Job satisfaction questions from the survey of employees

Go to Analyze, Dimension Reduction, and Factor. You will see the window depicted in Figure 11.6. Highlight the eight job satisfaction variables in the left-hand column and move them over to the right-hand column labeled Variables:. You can ignore Selection Variable:.

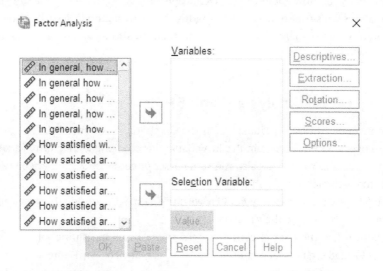

Figure 11.6 Factor analysis function in SPSS

Reprint courtesy of IBM Corporation ©

Now go into Descriptives..., as shown in Figure 11.7. Make sure that ☑Initial solution is ticked (it should be, by default) and also tick ☑Univariate descriptives, and, under Correlation Matrix, tick ☑Coefficients, ☑Significance levels, and ☑KMO and Bartlett's test of sphericity. Click Continue.

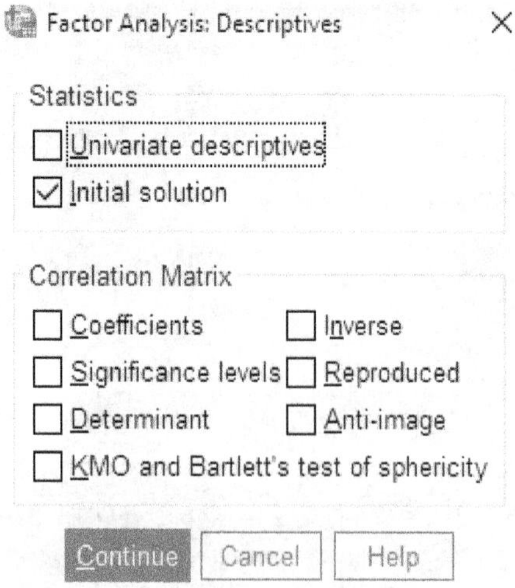

Figure 11.7 Factor analysis descriptive function in SPSS

Reprint courtesy of IBM Corporation ©

Now click [Extraction...] to see the dialog box in Figure 11.8. Here, make sure that ☑ Unrotated factor solution is ticked (it should be by default) and also tick ☑ Scree plot . Under Extract, you want to make sure that Eigenvalues greater than: [1] . Remember that this is the cutoff we use to identify factors. Click Continue .

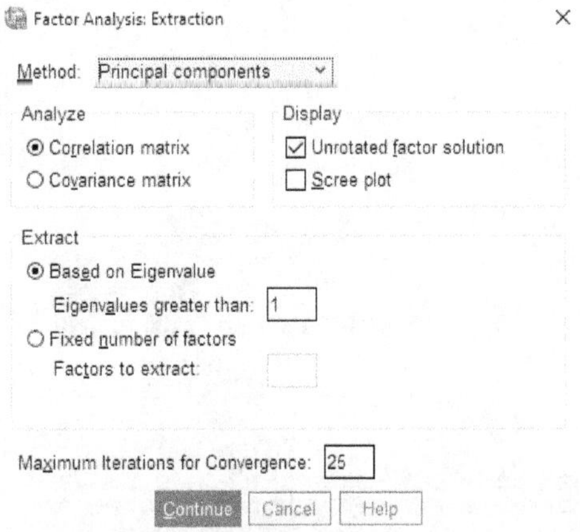

Figure 11.8 Factor analysis extraction function in SPSS

Reprint courtesy of IBM Corporation ©

Now go into [Rotation...] and tick ⦿ Varimax. You could experiment with different types of rotation, but Varimax is usually a default for many researchers. Click Continue .

When you are ready to run your first factor analysis, click [OK]. Boom! The exploratory factor analysis results are reported in the output depicted in Figure 11.9. Let's have a closer look at the output.

Descriptive Statistics

	Mean	Std. Deviation	Analysis N
How satisfied with sense of achievement from work	2.14	.919	20666
How satisfied are you with...The scope for using your own initiative	2.11	.919	20666
How satisfied are you with...The amount of influence you have over job	2.40	.961	20666
How satisfied are you with...The training you receive?	2.59	1.074	20666
How satisfied are you with…â€¦ The opportunity to develop your skills in your job	2.62	1.075	20666
How satisfied are you with...The amount of pay you receive?	2.98	1.124	20666
How satisfied are you with...Your job security?	2.59	1.072	20666
How satisfied are you with...The work itself?	2.14	.885	20666

(Continued)

Figure 11.9 (Continued)

Correlation Matrix

		How satisfied with sense of achievement from work	How satisfied are you with...The scope for using your own initiative	How satisfied are you with...The amount of influence you have over job	How satisfied are you with...The training you receive?	How satisfied are you with…The opportunity to develop your skills in your job	How satisfied are you with...The amount of pay you receive?	How satisfied are you with...Your job security?	How satisfied are you with...The work itself?
Correlation	How satisfied with sense of achievement from work	1.000	.643	.595	.403	.520	.302	.331	.693
	How satisfied are you with...The scope for using your own initiative	.643	1.000	.730	.393	.526	.291	.334	.556
	How satisfied are you with...The amount of influence you have over job	.595	.730	1.000	.444	.560	.342	.388	.539
	How satisfied are you with...The training you receive?	.403	.393	.444	1.000	.713	.329	.369	.387
	How satisfied are you with…The opportunity to develop your skills in your job	.520	.526	.560	.713	1.000	.399	.413	.490
	How satisfied are you with...The amount of pay you receive?	.302	.291	.342	.329	.399	1.000	.351	.309
	How satisfied are you with...Your job security?	.331	.334	.388	.369	.413	.351	1.000	.362
	How satisfied are you with...The work itself?	.693	.556	.539	.387	.490	.309	.362	1.000
Sig. (1-tailed)	How satisfied with sense of achievement from work		.000	.000	.000	.000	.000	.000	.000
	How satisfied are you with...The scope for using your own initiative	.000		.000	.000	.000	.000	.000	.000
	How satisfied are you with...The amount of influence you have over job	.000	.000		.000	.000	.000	.000	.000
	How satisfied are you with...The training you receive?	.000	.000	.000		.000	.000	.000	.000
	How satisfied are you with…The opportunity to develop your skills in your job	.000	.000	.000	.000		.000	.000	.000
	How satisfied are you with...The amount of pay you receive?	.000	.000	.000	.000	.000		.000	.000
	How satisfied are you with...Your job security?	.000	.000	.000	.000	.000	.000		.000
	How satisfied are you with...The work itself?	.000	.000	.000	.000	.000	.000	.000	

KMO and Bartlett's Test

Kaiser-Meyer-Olkin Measure of Sampling Adequacy.		.858
Bartlett's Test of Sphericity	Approx. Chi-Square	78054.973
	df	28
	Sig.	.000

Communalities

	Initial	Extraction
How satisfied with sense of achievement from work	1.000	.628
How satisfied are you with...The scope for using your own initiative	1.000	.628
How satisfied are you with...The amount of influence you have over job	1.000	.656
How satisfied are you with...The training you receive?	1.000	.481
How satisfied are you withâ€¦ The opportunity to develop your skills in your job	1.000	.645
How satisfied are you with...The amount of pay you receive?	1.000	.286
How satisfied are you with...Your job security?	1.000	.340
How satisfied are you with...The work itself?	1.000	.578

Extraction Method: Principal Component Analysis.

Total Variance Explained

Component	Initial Eigenvalues			Extraction Sums of Squared Loadings		
	Total	% of Variance	Cumulative %	Total	% of Variance	Cumulative %
1	4.242	53.027	53.027	4.242	53.027	53.027
2	.981	12.264	65.291			
3	.755	9.443	74.735			
4	.647	8.083	82.818			
5	.554	6.926	89.744			
6	.300	3.756	93.500			
7	.266	3.323	96.823			
8	.254	3.177	100.000			

Extraction Method: Principal Component Analysis.

(Continued)

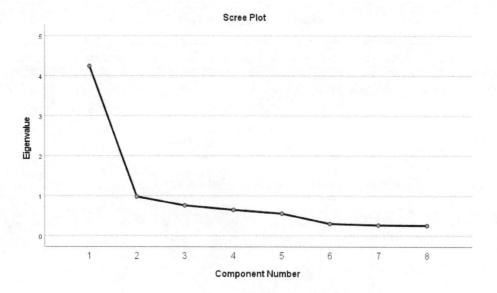

Component Matrix[a]

	Component
	1
How satisfied with sense of achievement from work	.793
How satisfied are you with...The scope for using your own initiative	.792
How satisfied are you with...The amount of influence you have over job	.810
How satisfied are you with...The training you receive?	.693
How satisfied are you withâ€¦ The opportunity to develop your skills in your job	.803
How satisfied are you with...The amount of pay you receive?	.535
How satisfied are you with...Your job security?	.583
How satisfied are you with...The work itself?	.760

Extraction Method: Principal Component Analysis.

a. 1 components extracted.

Figure 11.9   SPSS output, job satisfaction factor analysis

Reprint courtesy of IBM Corporation ©

At the top of the output, you'll notice the descriptive statistics, followed by a bivariate correlation matrix with Pearson's r values and p-values listed below. If you look closely at this table (or rather these two tables), you'll see that, as expected, all the variables are fairly highly correlated and all are statistically significant ($p < 0.001$).

Next, you'll see Kaiser–Meyer–Olkin (KMO) and Bartlett's test. Ideally, you're looking for a KMO statistic of greater than, say, 0.5 and a statistically significant p-value for Bartlett's test. In our case, the KMO value is 0.858, and the Bartlett's p-value is 0.000 (reported as $p < 0.001$). Both values indicate that a factor analysis is appropriate with these data.

You can skip the Communalities table and move on to the table labeled Total Variance Explained. Here you can see that, indeed, our exploratory factor analysis resulted in a one-factor solution. The eigenvalue for component 1 (also referred to as factor 1) is 4.24, whereas the eigenvalues for the remaining factors are all less than 1. The one component (or factor) that emerged explains 57.03% of the variance among the eight items.

The scree plot that follows visually confirms the one-factor solution. Here you can see that the first factor (Component 1) has an eigenvalue of just over 4 (it is 4.24, to be exact), well above the cutoff of 1. The remaining seven factors all have eigenvalues of less than 1, although the second factor is fairly close (its value is 0.981, still below the cutoff).

Next, you can see the component matrix. Here you can find the unrotated factor loadings, all of which are above the conventional cutoff of 0.40. This table tells us that all eight items load highly onto the underlying one-factor job satisfaction construct, as we expected.

You will finally notice that a rotated solution to the factor analysis could not be extracted because only one component (or factor) emerged from the analysis.

You've now done your first factor analysis of the eight job satisfaction items in the survey of employees, and, as we expected, all eight items load significantly onto a single latent variable, which we can call 'overall job satisfaction'. Nice work, partner!

That was so much fun. Let's do another, shall we? This time, let's see if we can find a one-factor solution for the five 'job influence' items in the survey of employees. These are displayed in Figure 11.10, which was taken directly from the WERS questionnaire.

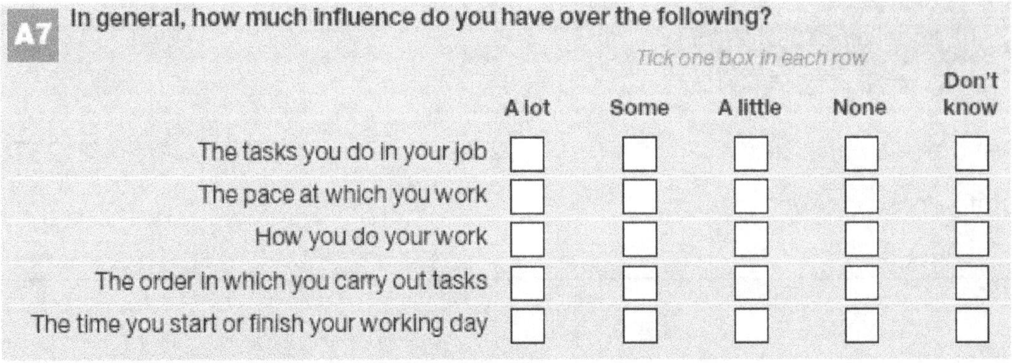

Figure 11.10 Job influence questions in the survey of employees

Each item supposedly taps a unique dimension of job influence. To find out how well these items 'hang together', let's run another exploratory factor analysis to see if we can generate another one-factor solution.

Go to Analyze, Dimension Reduction, and Factor. Remove the eight job satisfaction variables from the right-hand column and place them back in the left-hand column (do not click Reset , because that would remove the options we've already selected above). Then, select the five job influence variables (qa7a, qa7b, qa7c, qa7d, and qa7e) from the left-hand column and move them to the right-hand column. We're going to keep all the other settings the same as above, so just click OK and check out the output depicted in Figure 11.11.

Descriptive Statistics

	Mean	Std. Deviation	Analysis N
In general, how much influence do you have over the tasks you do	1.90	.931	21287
In general how much influence do you have over the pace at which you work	1.95	.971	21287
In general, how much influence do you have in how you do your work	1.68	.831	21287
In general, how much influence on order carry out tasks	1.70	.861	21287
In general, how much influence on time start/finish working day	2.42	1.193	21287

Correlation Matrix

		In general, how much influence do you have over the tasks you do	In general how much influence do you have over the pace at which you work	In general, how much influence do you have in how you do your work	In general, how much influence on order carry out tasks	In general, how much influence on time start/finish working day
Correlation	In general, how much influence do you have over the tasks you do	1.000	.591	.633	.581	.364
	In general how much influence do you have over the pace at which you work	.591	1.000	.626	.561	.358
	In general, how much influence do you have in how you do your work	.633	.626	1.000	.686	.366
	In general, how much influence on order carry out tasks	.581	.561	.686	1.000	.386
	In general, how much influence on time start/finish working day	.364	.358	.366	.386	1.000
Sig. (1-tailed)	In general, how much influence do you have over the tasks you do		.000	.000	.000	.000
	In general how much influence do you have over the pace at which you work	.000		.000	.000	.000
	In general, how much influence do you have in how you do your work	.000	.000		.000	.000
	In general, how much influence on order carry out tasks	.000	.000	.000		.000
	In general, how much influence on time start/finish working day	.000	.000	.000	.000	

KMO and Bartlett's Test

Kaiser-Meyer-Olkin Measure of Sampling Adequacy.		.849
Bartlett's Test of Sphericity	Approx. Chi-Square	43997.538
	df	10
	Sig.	.000

(Continued)

Figure 11.11   (Continued)

Communalities

	Initial	Extraction
In general, how much influence do you have over the tasks you do	1.000	.671
In general how much influence do you have over the pace at which you work	1.000	.654
In general, how much influence do you have in how you do your work	1.000	.743
In general, how much influence on order carry out tasks	1.000	.691
In general, how much influence on time start/finish working day	1.000	.340

Extraction Method: Principal Component Analysis.

Total Variance Explained

Component	Initial Eigenvalues			Extraction Sums of Squared Loadings		
	Total	% of Variance	Cumulative %	Total	% of Variance	Cumulative %
1	3.099	61.985	61.985	3.099	61.985	61.985
2	.743	14.852	76.837			
3	.453	9.062	85.899			
4	.407	8.133	94.032			
5	.298	5.968	100.000			

Extraction Method: Principal Component Analysis.

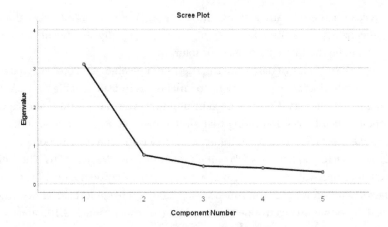

Component Matrix[a]

	Component
	1
In general, how much influence do you have over the tasks you do	.819
In general how much influence do you have over the pace at which you work	.809
In general, how much influence do you have in how you do your work	.862
In general, how much influence on order carry out tasks	.832
In general, how much influence on time start/finish working day	.583

Extraction Method: Principal Component
Analysis.

a. 1 components extracted.

Figure 11.11 SPSS output, job influence factor analysis

Let's only focus on the relevant tables in this output. You'll first notice that the correlations among the five variables are again reasonably high and statistically significant (all $p < 0.001$). We would expect this to be the case for a one-factor solution.

You'll next see a KMO value of 0.849 and a Bartlett's test p-value of 0.000 (reported as $p < 0.001$). Both statistics indicate that an exploratory factor analysis is indeed suitable for these variables.

Now moving on to the Total Variance Explained output, you can see that, once again, we have generated a one-factor solution, indicating that all five items appear to 'tap' an underlying latent variable, which we can label 'overall job influence'. The eigenvalue for component 1 (factor 1) is 3.10, and this latent factor explains 61.99% of the variation across the five items. The remaining four components all have eigenvalues of less than 1, suggesting that they do not qualify as unique factors.

The one-factor solution is again confirmed visually in the scree plot that follows, where you can see that the first factor has an eigenvalue of just over 3 (the exact value is 3.10), and the remaining factors all have eigenvalues of less than one.

Under Components Matrix, you can find the unrotated factor loadings, all of which are well above the conventional 0.40 cutoff. In other words, all five items load nicely onto the wider latent construct. Once again, a rotated solution is not available, because only one factor emerged from this factor analysis.

Wow, you are on fire! Okay, let's do one more factor analysis, but this time, let's see if we can generate a two-factor solution by putting all five job influence variables and all eight job satisfaction variables together in the same analysis. Since we have already demonstrated that both job satisfaction and job influence independently produce one-factor solutions, we can likely expect that, by adding all the items together into one exploratory factor analysis, we should be able to produce a unique two-factor solution.

Go to Analyze, Dimension Reduction, and Factor. The five job influence variables should still be under the Variables: column on the right-hand side. Select the eight job satisfaction variables from the left-hand column and move them to the right as well. Before you proceed, just count the number of variables in your Variables: list. You should have the five job influence items and the eight job satisfaction items, for a total of 13 items in the factor analysis. We're going to keep all the settings the same as above, so just click OK and check out the output depicted in Figure 11.12.

Descriptive Statistics

	Mean	Std. Deviation	Analysis N
In general, how much influence do you have over the tasks you do	1.89	.925	20261
In general how much influence do you have over the pace at which you work	1.94	.968	20261
In general, how much influence do you have in how you do your work	1.67	.826	20261
In general, how much influence on order carry out tasks	1.70	.854	20261
In general, how much influence on time start/finish working day	2.41	1.190	20261
How satisfied with sense of achievement from work	2.14	.918	20261
How satisfied are you with...The scope for using your own initiative	2.11	.919	20261
How satisfied are you with...The amount of influence you have over job	2.40	.962	20261
How satisfied are you with...The training you receive?	2.59	1.074	20261
How satisfied are you withâ€¦ The opportunity to develop your skills in your job	2.62	1.077	20261
How satisfied are you with...The amount of pay you receive?	2.98	1.124	20261
How satisfied are you with...Your job security?	2.59	1.073	20261
How satisfied are you with...The work itself?	2.14	.884	20261

(Continued)

Figure 11.12 (Continued)

Correlation Matrix

		In general, how much influence do you have over the tasks you do	In general how much influence do you have over the pace at which you work	In general, how much influence do you have in how you do your work	In general, how much influence on order carry out tasks	In general, how much influence on time start/finish working day	How satisfied with sense of achievement from work	How satisfied are you with...The scope for using your own initiative	How satisfied are you with...The amount of influence you have over job	How satisfied are you with...The training you receive?	How satisfied are you with&; The opportunity to develop your skills in your job	How satisfied are you with...The amount of pay you receive?	How satisfied are you with...Your job security?	How satisfied are you with...The work itself?
Correlation	In general, how much influence do you have over the tasks you do	1.000	.589	.633	.560	.362	.349	.466	.525	.210	.295	.189	.214	.313
	In general how much influence do you have over the pace at which you work	.589	1.000	.623	.556	.357	.287	.376	.434	.208	.256	.167	.214	.271
	In general, how much influence do you have in how you do your work	.633	.623	1.000	.694	.364	.336	.466	.490	.207	.287	.184	.214	.313
	In general, how much influence on order carry out tasks	.560	.556	.694	1.000	.384	.292	.421	.442	.179	.249	.169	.177	.264
	In general, how much influence on time start/finish working day	.362	.357	.364	.384	1.000	.164	.243	.299	.118	.184	.166	.093	.130
	How satisfied with sense of achievement from work	.349	.287	.336	.292	.164	1.000	.643	.594	.403	.520	.303	.330	.692
	How satisfied are you with...The scope for using your own initiative	.466	.376	.466	.421	.243	.643	1.000	.730	.393	.527	.289	.332	.556
	How satisfied are you with...The amount of influence you have over job	.525	.434	.490	.442	.299	.594	.730	1.000	.444	.559	.342	.387	.538
	How satisfied are you with...The training you receive?	.210	.208	.207	.179	.118	.403	.393	.444	1.000	.713	.330	.369	.386
	How satisfied are you with&; The opportunity to develop your skills in your job	.295	.256	.287	.249	.184	.520	.527	.559	.713	1.000	.400	.411	.490
	How satisfied are you with...The amount of pay you receive?	.189	.187	.184	.169	.166	.303	.289	.342	.330	.400	1.000	.350	.310
	How satisfied are you with...Your job security?	.214	.214	.214	.177	.093	.330	.332	.387	.369	.411	.350	1.000	.362
	How satisfied are you with...The work itself?	.313	.271	.313	.264	.130	.692	.556	.538	.386	.490	.310	.362	1.000
Sig (1-tailed)	In general, how much influence do you have over the tasks you do		.000	.000	.000	.000	.000	.000	.000	.000	.000	<.001	<.001	.000

Question											
In general, how much influence do you have over the pace at which you work.	000	000	000	000	000	000	000	000	000	000	000
In general, how much influence do you have in how you do your work.	000	000	000	000	000	000	000	000	000	000	000
In general, how much influence on order carry out tasks	000	000	000	000	000	000	000	000	000	000	000
In general, how much influence on time start/finish working day.	000	000	000	000	000	000	000	000	000	000	000
How satisfied with sense of achievement from work.	000	000	000	000	000	000	000	000	000	000	000
How satisfied are you with... The scope for using your own initiative	000	000	000	000	000	000	000	000	000	000	000
How satisfied are you with... The amount of influence you have over job	000	000	000	000		000	000	000	000	000	000
How satisfied are you with... The training you receive?	000	000	000	000	000	000	000	000	000	000	000
How satisfied are you with... The opportunity to develop your skills in your job	000	000	000		000	000	000	000	000	000	000
How satisfied are you with... The amount of pay you receive?	000	000	000	000	000	000	000	000	000	000	000
How satisfied are you with... Your job security?	000	000	000	000	000	000	000	000	000	000	000
How satisfied are you with... The work itself?	000	000	000	000	000	000	000	000	000	000	000

(Continued)

Figure 11.12 (Continued)

KMO and Bartlett's Test

Kaiser-Meyer-Olkin Measure of Sampling Adequacy.		.897
Bartlett's Test of Sphericity	Approx. Chi-Square	127522.054
	df	78
	Sig.	.000

Communalities

	Initial	Extraction
In general, how much influence do you have over the tasks you do	1.000	.669
In general how much influence do you have over the pace at which you work	1.000	.628
In general, how much influence do you have in how you do your work	1.000	.731
In general, how much influence on order carry out tasks	1.000	.683
In general, how much influence on time start/finish working day	1.000	.341
How satisfied with sense of achievement from work	1.000	.610
How satisfied are you with...The scope for using your own initiative	1.000	.636
How satisfied are you with...The amount of influence you have over job	1.000	.689
How satisfied are you with...The training you receive?	1.000	.549
How satisfied are you with…The opportunity to develop your skills in your job	1.000	.682
How satisfied are you with...The amount of pay you receive?	1.000	.309
How satisfied are you with...Your job security?	1.000	.367
How satisfied are you with...The work itself?	1.000	.569

Extraction Method: Principal Component Analysis.

Total Variance Explained

Component	Initial Eigenvalues			Extraction Sums of Squared Loadings			Rotation Sums of Squared Loadings		
	Total	% of Variance	Cumulative %	Total	% of Variance	Cumulative %	Total	% of Variance	Cumulative %
1	5.563	42.789	42.789	5.563	42.789	42.789	3.997	30.744	30.744
2	1.901	14.621	57.410	1.901	14.621	57.410	3.467	26.666	57.410
3	.959	7.379	64.789						
4	.758	5.831	70.620						
5	.741	5.702	76.322						
6	.620	4.773	81.095						
7	.505	3.886	84.980						
8	.456	3.506	88.487						
9	.387	2.976	91.463						
10	.301	2.313	93.776						
11	.296	2.278	96.054						
12	.264	2.029	98.083						
13	.249	1.917	100.000						

Extraction Method: Principal Component Analysis.

(Continued)

Figure 11.12 (Continued)

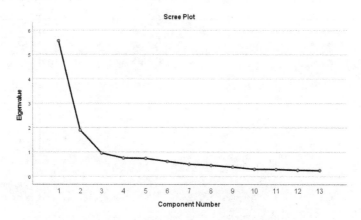

Scree Plot

Component Matrix[a]

	Component	
	1	2
In general, how much influence do you have over the tasks you do	.687	.443
In general how much influence do you have over the pace at which you work	.634	.475
In general, how much influence do you have in how you do your work	.695	.498
In general, how much influence on order carry out tasks	.642	.520
In general, how much influence on time start/finish working day	.426	.399
How satisfied with sense of achievement from work	.722	-.296
How satisfied are you with...The scope for using your own initiative	.791	-.104
How satisfied are you with...The amount of influence you have over job	.827	-.075
How satisfied are you with...The training you receive?	.583	-.458
How satisfied are you with…The opportunity to develop your skills in your job	.703	-.433
How satisfied are you with...The amount of pay you receive?	.471	-.296
How satisfied are you with...Your job security?	.509	-.329
How satisfied are you with...The work itself?	.682	-.322

Extraction Method: Principal Component Analysis.

a. 2 components extracted.

Rotated Component Matrix[a]

	Component	
	1	2
In general, how much influence do you have over the tasks you do	.230	.785
In general how much influence do you have over the pace at which you work	.169	.774
In general, how much influence do you have in how you do your work	.200	.831
In general, how much influence on order carry out tasks	.146	.813
In general, how much influence on time start/finish working day	.062	.581
How satisfied with sense of achievement from work	.740	.248
How satisfied are you with...The scope for using your own initiative	.667	.438
How satisfied are you with...The amount of influence you have over job	.674	.484
How satisfied are you with...The training you receive?	.740	.035
How satisfied are you with…The opportunity to develop your skills in your job	.815	.132
How satisfied are you with...The amount of pay you receive?	.550	.084
How satisfied are you with...Your job security?	.600	.084
How satisfied are you with...The work itself?	.727	.202

Extraction Method: Principal Component Analysis.
Rotation Method: Varimax with Kaiser Normalization.[a]
a. Rotation converged in 3 iterations.

Component Transformation Matrix

Component	1	2
1	.757	.654
2	-.654	.757

Extraction Method: Principal Component Analysis.
Rotation Method: Varimax with Kaiser Normalization.

Figure 11.12 SPSS output, job influence and job satisfaction factor analysis

You'll see a rather sizable correlation matrix with Pearson's *r* values for all 13 items. A quick scan of this matrix shows that, in general, the job satisfaction items appear to be more highly correlated with each other than they are with the job influence items, and vice versa. But, still, the job satisfaction items are all significantly correlated with the job influence items. This is likely because employees who feel that they have a lot of influence over their work are also likely to feel more satisfied.

Moving your way down the output, you'll see that the KMO (0.897) and Bartlett's test ($p = 0.000$, reported as $p < 0.001$) both look good. These statistics suggest that an exploratory factor analysis on these variables is suitable.

Under Total Variance Explained, you can see that a two-factor solution emerged in this analysis, as we expected. The first two components (factors 1 and 2) have eigenvalues of greater than 1 (5.56 and 1.90, respectively). You'll also notice that, because we have a two-factor solution, we also have new columns in this output, found under 'Rotation Sum of Squares Loadings'. The rotated eigenvalues for component (factor) 1 and component (factor) 2 are 4.00 (rounded up) and 3.47, respectively, and together they cumulatively explain 57.41% of the total variance among the 13 items in the factor analysis.

A bit further down, the scree plot visually confirms the two-factor solution. Factors 1 and 2 have eigenvalues greater than 1, while factors 3 through 13 have eigenvalues less than 1.

This time, we're going to skip the (unrotated) component matrix (since it is not very interpretable) and go straight to the rotated component matrix to see how each variable, or item, loads onto the two factors. Looking first at the five job influence items, you can see that all five load well onto component (factor) 2, with all the loadings being above the cutoff of 0.40, and, similarly, all five load poorly onto component (factor) 1, with all loadings being below the cutoff of 0.40. Now looking at the last eight job satisfaction items, you can see that all eight load well onto component (factor) 1, with all eight loadings being above the 0.40 cutoff. Looking at the loading onto component (factor) 2, the majority of them load poorly onto it, although the first two are just slightly above 0.40 (these being 0.44 and 0.48). This slight overlap is reflected in the fact that job influence likely predicts job satisfaction, leading to some degree of overlap. These results generally confirm what we expected: that the underlying latent structure of overall job satisfaction differs from the underlying latent structure of overall job influence and that both constructs have reasonably good discriminant validity. Accordingly, you could use composites of both constructs in a wider correlational model.

You can skip the final table, labeled Component Transformation Matrix, because it only tells us how the factor matrix was rotated.

Nice work! You did a great job learning exploratory factor analysis. I'm sure you'll do an equally amazing job learning how to do a confirmatory factor analysis with AMOS. Are you ready?

Confirmatory Factor Analysis Using AMOS Graphics

Let's keep working with the same data file from the survey of employees to illustrate how to run a confirmatory factor analysis in AMOS Graphics.

In file chap11data from the Companion Website, you'll see that, in addition to the five job influence items and the seven job satisfaction items (analysed above), there are also four items that measure how well management shares information with employees (qb6a, qb6b, qb6c, and qb6d) and another three items that measure how trustworthy management are perceived to be (qc2a, qc2b, and qc2c). Let's run separate confirmatory factor analyses on both these latent variables using AMOS.

The first latent variable, which we'll call info, is measured by the following four single items:

- How good are managers at telling staff about changes in how the organization is run?
- How good are managers at informing employees about changes in staffing?
- How good are managers at informing staff about changes in the way you do your job?
- How good are managers at informing staff about financial matters?

These four items were measured on a five-point Likert scale, where 1 = *very poor* and 5 = *very good* (you can confirm this by looking in Values in Data View). Before we open AMOS to run this confirmatory factor analysis, take a few moments in SPSS to run descriptive statistics, frequencies, and bivariate correlations among these four variables. I won't show you how to do this here, because you should already know how. When you have had a look at the data, open 'IBM SPSS Amos Graphics' on your computer. We will be using AMOS Graphics because this purely graphical interface is easiest to use. It works by creating figures that represent a confirmatory factor analysis (or wider structural equation model, as you'll learn in the next chapter).

When you open AMOS Graphics, you'll see the interface depicted in Figure 11.13. For a comprehensive understanding of the AMOS environment and its functionality, I recommend that you read Byrne (2010). For now, I'm just going to show you how to run a confirmatory factor analysis on info using the four items in the survey of employees.

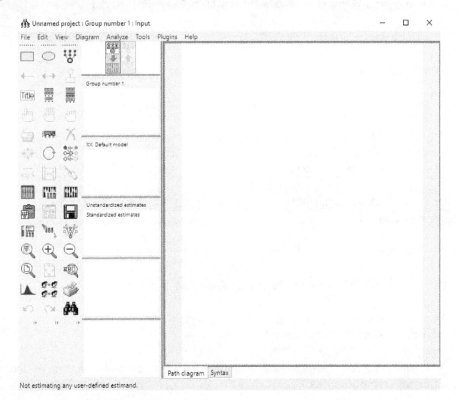

Figure 11.13   AMOS Graphics interface

Before you move on, take a few moments to review the icon descriptions in AMOS Graphics in Box 11.2.

Box 11.2: Icons in AMOS Graphics

Here is a list of the key icons in AMOS Graphics and a short description of what they do. Note that I have not listed all the icons, but rather just the ones that are typically used for factor analysis.

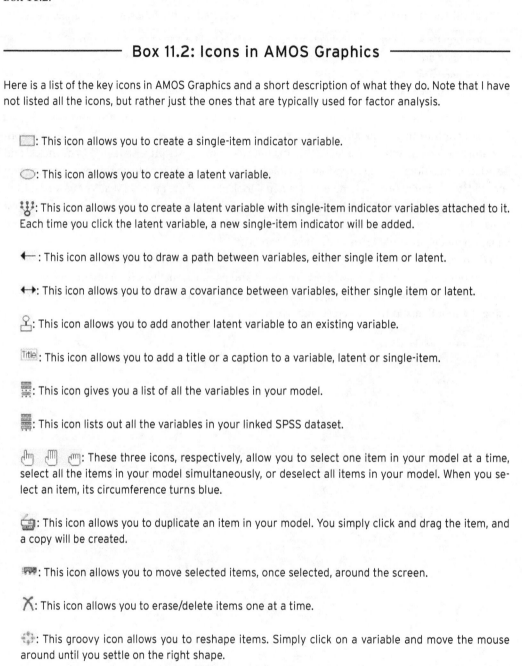

□: This icon allows you to create a single-item indicator variable.

◯: This icon allows you to create a latent variable.

: This icon allows you to create a latent variable with single-item indicator variables attached to it. Each time you click the latent variable, a new single-item indicator will be added.

←: This icon allows you to draw a path between variables, either single item or latent.

↔: This icon allows you to draw a covariance between variables, either single item or latent.

: This icon allows you to add another latent variable to an existing variable.

Title: This icon allows you to add a title or a caption to a variable, latent or single-item.

: This icon gives you a list of all the variables in your model.

: This icon lists out all the variables in your linked SPSS dataset.

: These three icons, respectively, allow you to select one item in your model at a time, select all the items in your model simultaneously, or deselect all items in your model. When you select an item, its circumference turns blue.

: This icon allows you to duplicate an item in your model. You simply click and drag the item, and a copy will be created.

: This icon allows you to move selected items, once selected, around the screen.

✗: This icon allows you to erase/delete items one at a time.

: This groovy icon allows you to reshape items. Simply click on a variable and move the mouse around until you settle on the right shape.

◯: This icon allows you to rotate the single-item indicators around a latent variable. The indicators move clockwise every time you click.

: This icon allows you to reflect the indicators of a latent variable. It's not terribly helpful, to be honest.

: This groovy icon is magical. With a single click, it touches up your variables and makes the model look pretty and symmetrical.

: This icon allows you to select a data file. You will need to start here before doing any work in AMOS Graphics, so that you can link your SPSS file to AMOS.

: This important icon is where you tell AMOS Graphics what kinds of analyses you want it to carry out. It allows you to give the program its instructions.

: When you have linked your dataset, built your model, and specified the types of analyses you want to carry out, this important icon tells AMOS to carry out the analysis. It's the equivalent of clicking OK in SPSS.

: This icon allows you to copy what you've created in AMOS Graphics to clipboard.

: This icon (obviously) allows you to save your files.

: This icon allows you to edit object properties. It's not terribly useful because if you double click any variable, the object properties box will automatically open.

: This icon allows you to preserve symmetries in your path diagram.

: These icons allow you to zoom in and out.

: This icon allows you to show the entire page on the screen.

: This groovy icon resizes the path diagram to fit on the screen.

: This icon gives you a magnifying glass. It is useful for very large path diagrams, so you can zoom in a bit on the elements.

: This icon gives you access to Bayesian statistics. This method is pretty advanced and beyond the scope of this textbook.

: This icon gives you access to multigroup analysis of covariance methods. Again, this is pretty advanced and beyond the scope of this textbook.

: This icon (obviously) allows you to print.

: This icon allows you to undo a mistake.

: This icon allows you to search specifications.

AMOS Graphics is so easy to use, it's almost silly. The first thing we need to do is to link AMOS with our SPSS file. To do this, click on the 🔳 icon. The window in Figure 11.14 appears. Go into File Name , find the Chap11data.sav file, double click, and then click OK . Too easy.

Data Files

Group Name	File	Variable	Value	N
Group number 1	\<working>			

File Name	Working File	Help
View Data	Grouping Variable	Group Value
OK		Cancel

☐ Allow non-numeric data   ☐ Assign cases to groups

Figure 11.14 Linking your SPSS file to AMOS Graphics

Next, we need to graphically create our latent variable and the four single-item indicators that it's composed of. Again, this is too easy! Click on the 🔧 icon, move your cursor to the middle of the white space of the graphical interface, click once and hold down, then move your mouse a little bit down and to the right. This action creates a circle or oval shape, which will serve as the latent variable, info. Next go into that circle and click four times. Each time you click, a new indicator variable is added. You should have created a figure similar to the one depicted in Figure 11.15.

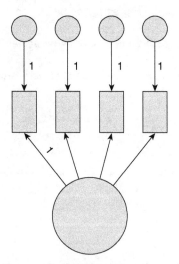

Figure 11.15 A latent variable with four single-item indicators attached

Now click on the ⟳ icon, and then move your mouse over the latent variable circle. Click three times to rotate the four single item indicators around, so that the figure in Figure 11.16 is visible.

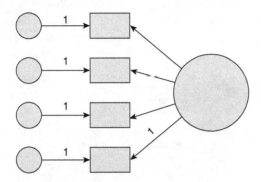

Figure 11.16   A rotation of Figure 11.15

Let's move our confirmatory factor analysis structure to the middle of the page. First, click 🖐 and then click 🚛 . Use your mouse to click the figure and move it to the middle of the page. Now unclick 🚛 and then click 🖐 to deselect the objects.

The next thing we have to do is to define our variables and indicators. Let's start by labeling our latent variable, info. Double click on the circle/oval to open the Object Properties box depicted in Figure 11.17. Under Variable Name, just write info. Feel free to adjust the font size if you'd like (I set mine at size 24), and then just close the box. In all confirmatory factor analyses, the latent variables are always circle or oval shaped.

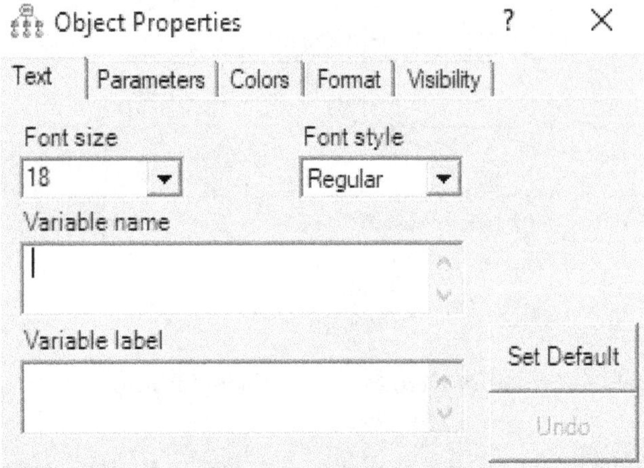

Figure 11.17   Object properties in AMOS Graphics

Now click, one at a time, on each of the four rectangles. A rectangle always represents a single-item indicator in confirmatory factor analysis. Recall from our SPSS file that we have four single items that measure info: qb6a, qb6b, qb6c, and qb6d. Double click on the first rectangle, and under Variable name, write in qb6a, then close the box. Double click on the next rectangle down, and this time, write in qb6b, then close the box. Do the same for the next two rectangles down, labeling them qb6c and qb6d. At this point, the confirmatory factor analysis model should look like the one in Figure 11.18.

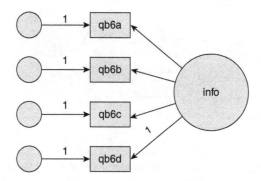

Figure 11.18 Info as a latent variable with indicators labeled

You'll notice that, to the left of each rectangle, there are four corresponding little circles. These are the *error terms* – basically, whatever variation in each rectangle that is not explained by the latent construct, info. Name each one of these, from top to bottom, e1, e2, e3, and e4, by double clicking in each circle and entering these labels into Variable name, and then closing each Object Properties box. The final confirmatory factor analysis model is depicted in Figure 11.19.

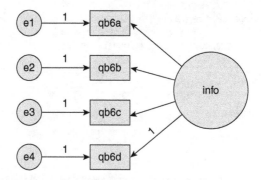

Figure 11.19 Final confirmatory factor analysis model for info

Let's examine this model. There are eight arrows in Figure 11.19. Four arrows go from the latent variable, info, to the four single-item indicators, and another four go from the error terms to the same indicators. You'll also notice that some of those paths (five of them, to be precise) are fixed at 1. This means that they will not be freely estimated. The reason we have to fix these five paths with a coefficient of 1 is that this configuration makes the model *overidentified*. Alternatively stated, if we were to remove those five fixed coefficients, then we wouldn't have enough information in the model to estimate any of the paths, and it would thus be *underidentified*. It's a strange thing, I know, and it seems a little wrong, doesn't it? But it's not wrong. You'll just have to trust me. So we're going to leave those five paths fixed at 1 and let the other three paths (between the latent variable, info, and qb6a, qb6b, and qb6c) be freely estimated by the data.

To run the confirmatory factor analysis, first click on the ▦ icon. The window in Figure 11.20 appears. Under the Estimation tab, tick ☑ Estimate means and intercepts, which is necessary when we have missing data. Now tick on the Output tab. Tick ☑ Standardized estimates, and then just close the box.

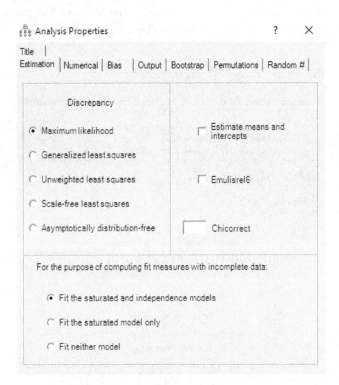

Figure 11.20 Analysis properties in AMOS Graphics

At this point, you're ready to run the results of your first ever confirmatory factor analysis using AMOS Graphics. To do so, simply click the ▦ icon. Note that it is possible that you may be asked to save your model at this point. If you aren't prompted, and you get a warning message, just save your model and then try clicking ▦ again. Boom! You'll notice that the paths have numbers (coefficients or weights) associated with them. The numbers next to the circles and boxes are variances, which aren't so important for purposes of interpretation. You can express the results in both unstandardized terms and in standardized terms by simply toggling between [Unstandardized estimates] [Standardized estimates]

on the AMOS Graphics interface. For purposes of interpretation, it is better to look at standardized coefficients, so click on Standardized estimates .

You can see that that latent variable, info, appears to load well onto our four single-item indicators, with standardized coefficients of 0.91, 0.89, 0.85, and 0.77 for items qb6a, qb6b, qb6c, and qb6d, respectively. To get even more information about your model, click on the ▦ icon. The initial output is illustrated in Figure 11.21. The first statistic of overall model fit is contained in 'Notes for Model', which you'll find depicted in Figure 11.22. Here you can see that our chi-square statistic is 108.31, with a p-value of 0.000 (reported as $p < 0.001$). Ideally, the best-fitting models will have a nonsignificant chi-square, but with very large samples (e.g., the survey of employees), they are almost always statistically significant, such as this one, so not to worry. The rest of the information on this page tells you that the model is overidentified, which is a good thing.

Notes for Model (Default model)

Computation of degrees of freedom (Default model)

Number of distinct sample moments: 14
Number of distinct parameters to be estimated: 12
Degrees of freedom (14 - 12): 2

Result (Default model)

Minimum was achieved
Chi-square = 108.309
Degrees of freedom = 2
Probability level = .000

Figure 11.21 Initial confirmatory factor analysis output

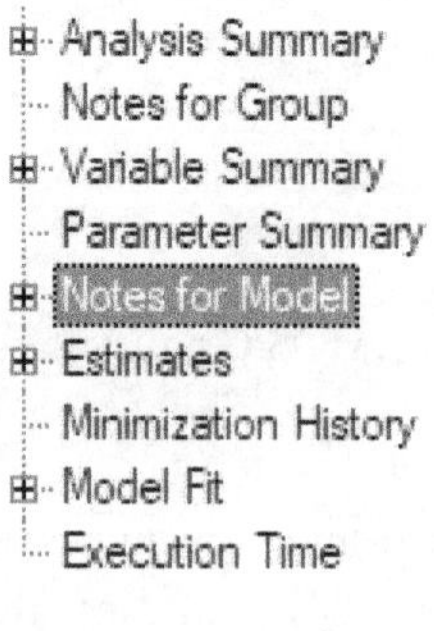

⊞ Analysis Summary
⋯ Notes for Group
⊞ Variable Summary
⋯ Parameter Summary
⊞ Notes for Model
⊞ Estimates
⋯ Minimization History
⊞ Model Fit
⋯ Execution Time

Figure 11.22 Output options on AMOS Graphics

The options above 'Notes for Model' in Figure 11.22 are optional. You can go ahead and check them out if you like. When you are ready, click on 'Estimates', where you can find the relevant coefficients depicted in the paths you specified in your confirmatory factor analysis. The most important statistics on this page are the 'Regression Weights' and the 'Standardized Weights' (see Figure 11.23). These coefficients are the same as you saw on the model in the graphical interface, but here they contain the standard errors (denoted S.E.) and critical ratios (denoted C.R.). Recall that a critical ratio is a *p*-value expressed as a *z*-score, and the equivalent of a $p < 0.05$ is a critical ratio of greater than 1.96 or less than –1.96. In this output, you can see that our freely estimated critical ratios are 132.55 (for qb6c), 140.78 (for qb6b), and 143.34 (for qb6a). All these critical ratios are well beyond the 1.96 cutoff, suggesting that these three single-item indicators significantly load onto our latent variable, info. Note that there is no critical ratio for qb6a because we fixed that coefficient at 1 to enable model overidentification.

Regression Weights: (Group number 1 - Default model)

			Estimate	S.E.	C.R.	P Label
qb6d	<---	info	1.000			
qb6c	<---	info	.993	.007	132.546	***
qb6b	<---	info	1.133	.008	140.781	***
qb6a	<---	info	1.152	.008	143.335	***

Standardized Regression Weights: (Group number 1 - Default model)

			Estimate
qb6d	<---	info	.774
qb6c	<---	info	.848
qb6b	<---	info	.892
qb6a	<---	info	.907

Figure 11.23 Regression weights and standardized regression weights in AMOS Graphics

Finally, click on 'Model Fit' from Figure 11.22 to get some additional overall model fit statistics to complement the chi-square statistic we saw in the 'Notes for Model'. Now, there are lots of overall model fit statistics on this page, but not all of them are necessary to report. Moreover, there are no hard-and-fast cutoffs for what constitutes 'good' and 'bad' model fit, but rather just a guided consensus that has emerged among statisticians. Box 11.3 reports some of the key overall goodness-of-fit statistics and how to interpret them.

Box 11.3: Confirmatory Factor Analysis ————— and Structural Equation Modeling ————— Goodness-of-Fit Statistics

Although there are no hard-and-fast cutoffs for model fit when doing confirmatory factor analysis and structural equation modeling, there are some guidelines that are generally agreed upon. These are summarized here:

(Continued)

- The chi-square (CMIN) p-value should be greater than 0.05. Alternatively stated, the critical ratio value should be either greater than 1.96 or less than –1.96.
- The SRMR should be less than 0.05 for good fit and less than 0.08 for mediocre fit.
- The GFI should be close to 1.00, typically greater than 0.90.
- The AGFI should be close to 1.00, typically greater than 0.90.
- The PGFI should be greater than 0.50.
- The NFI should be greater than 0.95, with values as low as 0.90 acceptable.
- The CFI should be greater than 0.95, with values as low as 0.90 acceptable.
- The IFI should be greater than 0.95, with values as low as 0.90 acceptable.
- The RFI should be greater than 0.95.
- The TLI should be greater than 0.95, with values as low as 0.90 acceptable.
- The PRATIO should be greater than 0.50.
- The PNFI should be greater than 0.50.
- The PCFI should be greater than 0.50.
- The RMSEA should be less than 0.05 for good fit, with anything above 0.05 and below 0.10 indicating mediocre fit.
- The PCLOSE should be greater than 0.50.
- The AIC, BCC, BIC, and CAIC default model statistics should be smaller than the values for both the saturated and independence models.
- Hoelter's 0.05 should be greater than 200.
- Hoelter's 0.01 should be greater than 200.

These are just a few of the commonly used fit statistics in confirmatory factor analysis/structural equation modeling. Not all of them are reported by AMOS, but I thought I'd reproduce them here anyway. At a bare minimum, you should report RMSEA, which is probably the most common fit statistic associated with this method.

The key goodness-of-fit statistics from the Model Fit output correspond to the row of data called **Default model**, which is our model. Have a look through the statistics and cross-check them with the cutoffs articulated in Box 11.3. The NFI Delta 1 is 0.998 (where a 'good' fit is defined as any number above 0.95). The TLI is 0.991 (where a 'good' fit is again defined as any number above 0.95). The CFI is 0.998 (where a 'good' fit is defined as any number above 0.90). The RMSEA is 0.049 (where a 'good' fit is defined as any number below 0.08). The PCLOSE is 0.549 (where a 'good' fit is defined as any number above 0.50). The Hoelter's 0.05 is 1216, and the Hoelter's 0.01 is 1870 (where a 'good' fit is defined as any number above 200). Strangely, the PRATIO value of 0.200 indicates poor fit (where good fit is any value over 0.50). It is not usual to see the occasional indicator of poor fit.

Looking at all these goodness-of-fit statistics, we can conclude that info is a 'good' latent variable (or, in exploratory factor analysis terms, a 'good' one-factor solution). The goodness-of-fit statistics, with the exception of the chi-square test and PRATIO, all indicate good model fit. Therefore, we can conclude that these four items nicely load ('hang together') onto info and that our latent variable is valid. Nice work! You just ran your first confirmatory factor analysis!

Let's do one more confirmatory factor analysis before we draw this chapter to a close. We'll take a few shortcuts in AMOS this time around.

Start a new project in AMOS Graphics by going to File, New. (You may be asked to save the confirmatory factor analysis we just ran.) This time, we're going to run another confirmatory factor analysis, but using the job influence items we already examined in the context of our exploratory factor analysis. Recall that, in the survey of employees, the following five items measure different dimensions of job influence:

- In general, how much influence do you have over the tasks you do?
- In general, how much influence do you have over the pace at which you work?
- In general, how much influence do you have in how you do your work?
- In general, how much influence do you have on order carry out tasks?
- In general, how much influence do you have on time start/finish working day?

These five items are measured on a four-point Likert scale, where 1 = *none*, 2 = *a little*, 3 = *some*, and 4 = *a lot*.

We need to build the measurement model, but first we need to link the Chap11.sav file to AMOS Graphics again. Click on the ▦ and then on File Name. Find Chap11data.sav and double click, and then OK.

To draw the measurement model, click on the 👥 icon and drag and click an oval in the white space. Then, go inside the oval and click five times to create five indicator variables (with error terms). Then, click on the ◯ icon, and, hovering over the newly created latent variable, click on the oval three times, so that the error terms and five single-item indicators rotate to the left side of the measurement model and the latent variable is on the right, as depicted in Figure 11.24. Make sure you click ◯ again to turn off the rotate function.

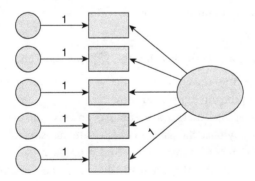

Figure 11.24 A latent variable with five indicators and error terms attached

We now need to name our latent variable, influence. To do this, click on the oval, and when the Object Properties window comes up (Figure 11.17), under Variable Name, just write the word Influence, and then, close Object Properties by clicking the ×.

Now for a groovy shortcut. Click on the ▥ icon, which lists out all variables in the linked SPSS dataset. (Note that you may need to resize this box by expanding it). Scroll through the list of variables, and when you find the five job influence variables (qa7a, qa7b, qa72c, qa7d, and qa7e), simply drag and drop them, one-by-one, into the five rectangles in your model. You can get rid of the annoying long labels by double clicking on each rectangle, opening Object Properties, and deleting the text beneath Variable label . When you close each Object Properties window, you should be left with the short variable names inside the rectangles. You can also now close the ﹐Variables in Dataset window.

Next, we need to name our error terms (the little circles attached to the rectangles), and there's yet another groovy shortcut we can take to do this. Simply go to Plugins (to the right of File, Edit, etc.) and click Name Unobserved Variables . This should create e1, e2, e3, e4, and e5 in the corresponding circles (never mind if they start at e5 from the top). The measurement model is now ready to be run. We're going to leave the six fixed paths (five between the error terms and the rectangles and one between the latent variable and one rectangle) at 1 to ensure that our model is overidentified. Your model should look like the one depicted in Figure 11.25.

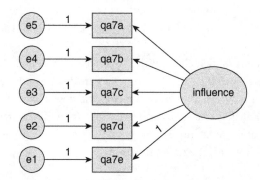

Figure 11.25 Full measurement model for job influence

Now go into Analysis Properties by clicking the ▦ icon, and under the Estimation tab, tick ☑ Estimate means and intercepts . Now go into the Output tab, tick ☑ Standardized estimates, and then, simply close the box by clicking the × in the top right-hand corner.

Before running the model, click on the save icon, 💾, and save the file somewhere on your computer. Now, when you're ready, click the ▦ icon to calculate the estimates and generate the output.

The Unstandardized estimates view is a bit busy, so click on standardized estimates . As you can see, the items appear to load reasonably well onto the latent variable, with the exception of qa7e, which has a standardized loading of 0.46.

To explore the output a bit further, click on the ▦ icon. The Notes for Model report a chi-square of 416.14 ($p = 0.000$, which would be reported as $p < 0.001$). Remember, we want to find a non-significant chi-square to conclude a good model, but when the sample size is very large (as it is in the survey of employees), we are almost always going to find a significant chi-square value. Click on Estimates, and you will see that all four freely estimated items load significantly onto the latent variable, with critical ratios between 64.43 and 67.43, clearly above the 1.96 threshold. Now click on Model Fit, and you will see the numerous goodness-of-fit statistics. These statistics are not quite as good as the ones for info, but they're not bad either. The NFI is 0.991 (where a 'good' fit is defined as any number above 0.95). The TLI is 0.972 (where a 'good' fit is again defined as any number above 0.95). The CFI is 0.991 (where a 'good' fit is defined as any number above 0.90). The RMSEA is 0.061 (where a 'good' fit is defined as any number below 0.08). The Hoelter's 0.05 is 585, and the Hoelter's 0.01 is 797 (where a 'good' fit is defined as any number above 200). But the PRATIO and PCLOSE are not great at 0.333 and 0.000, respectively.

In short, what we have produced here is a fairly good measurement model of job influence. This result should not be surprising to us, given that we have already confirmed through exploratory factor analysis that these items 'hang together' well as a reasonably good one-factor solution.

You now know how to run and interpret both exploratory and confirmatory factor analyses using SPSS and AMOS, respectively. That's no easy task, partner. Very well done! Take a bow!

What Have You Learned?

You made it to the end of Chapter 11. I know this chapter wasn't terribly easy to get through, but you did it. You now know all about latent variables, which are unobserved constructs that cannot be measured directly, but we assume that they exist by virtue of their relationship to observable variables that are measured as single-item indicators. It is important that you know how to measure latent variables because some constructs are simply too complex and too multidimensional to measure with just one item. Granted, you don't need any more than one item to measure something as simple as age. One item ('How old are you?') should give you a good (valid and reliable) measure of age. But many attitudinal and personality constructs cannot be adequately measured with just one item or question. Instead, you need to combine multiple items or questions into one latent variable. One way of doing this is to simply create a single composite variable by adding together a set of single-item variables, but another way is to create latent variables, as we've demonstrated here.

We considered two ways of assessing latent variables. In exploratory factor analysis, we have no preconceived notions of what the underlying factor structure might look like. Hence, we are exploring how the single items might 'hang together'. We might find a one-factor solution (all the items 'hang together' well), or we might find a solution with two or more factors (some of the items 'clump together' to the exclusion of other items). In confirmatory factor analysis, in contrast, we have *a priori* ideas about how the items should, in theory, load onto a latent construct. Confirmatory factor analysis is a simple (believe it or not) type of structural equation modeling (also referred to as *analysis of covariance structures*), but it only involves measurement models. A *measurement model* is an assessment of how a set of single-item indicators load onto a latent construct, whereas a *structural model* is an assessment of how a set of latent constructs are related to each other or to other observed variables. This is what we'll be looking at in Chapter 12. Are you ready?

Further Reading

Brown, T. A. (2015). *Confirmatory factor analysis for applied research*. Guilford Press.

Costello, A. B., & Osborne, J. (2005). Best practices in exploratory factor analysis: Four recommendations for getting the most from your analysis. *Practical Assessment, Research, and Evaluation, 10*(1) Article 7, 1-9.

Fabrigar, L. R., & Wegener, D. T. (2011). *Exploratory factor analysis*. Oxford University Press.

Harrington, D. (2009). *Confirmatory factor analysis*. Oxford University Press.

Hurley, A. E., Scandura, T. A., Schriesheim, C. A., Brannick, M. T., Seers, A., Vandenberg, R. J., & Williams, L. J. (1997). Exploratory and confirmatory factor analysis: Guidelines, issues, and alternatives. *Journal of Organizational Behavior, 18*(6), 667-683.

Jolliffe, I. T., & Cadima, J. (2016). Principal component analysis: A review and recent developments. *Philosophical Transactions of the Royal Society A: Mathematical, Physical and Engineering Sciences, 374*(2065), 20150202.

In-Class Discussion Questions

1. Why would one use exploratory factor analysis over confirmatory factor analysis, and vice versa?
2. What is a latent variable? How is it different from an observable variable?
3. What is the role of the eigenvalue in exploratory factor analysis?
4. How do you report and interpret the results of an exploratory factor analysis?
5. Why do we have to 'fix' some paths in a confirmatory factor analysis at 1.00? What purpose does this serve?
6. How do you report and interpret the results of a confirmatory factor analysis?

12

Structural Equation Modeling

You made it to Chapter 12, the final chapter of this book. You went from knowing next to nothing about statistics to being an applied statistics guru. I'm proud of you. There is a light at the end of the tunnel, but we still have this one last chapter. In what follows, we'll be taking a close look at structural equation modeling, also commonly referred to as analysis of covariance structures. You are already familiar with this term because confirmatory factor analysis, which we learned about in the previous chapter, is a form of structural equation model (hereafter SEM). Whereas confirmatory factor analysis focuses only on the measurement model (i.e., do we have a good measure of a latent variable or set of latent variables?), SEM focuses on the structural model (i.e., how do these latent variables relate to each other and to other observable, single-item variables?). In essence, SEM is like multiple regression analysis, except instead of using all single-item variables, it uses either all latent variables or some combination of latent and single-item variables in the context of a path diagram. In both SEM and multiple regression, the idea is to use a set of variables to predict or explain an outcome. In multiple regression, we used the terminology of independent (predictor) variables and dependent (outcome) variables. In SEM, the independent (predictor) variables are called *exogenous variables* and the dependent (outcome) variables are called *endogenous variables*.

One key difference between multiple regression and SEM is that the latter is typically expressed in a *path diagram* (Kline, 2015). A path diagram is a visual representation of the expected relationships among the latent and (where relevant) observable variables. In a path diagram, the exogenous (independent) variables are usually on the left-hand side and the endogenous (dependent variable) is usually on the right-hand side. The latent variables are represented by oval or circle shapes, as we saw in confirmatory factor analysis, and the observable (single-item indicator) variables are represented by rectangles. The relationships among the latent and observable variables are described by arrows, which start from the exogenous variables and make their way through (sometimes multiple) paths to the endogenous variable, hence the term *path analysis*. The arrows are characterized by a coefficient (which can be standardized or unstandardized) that tells us something about the nature of the relationship among the variables (i.e., positive, neutral, or negative). As with confirmatory factor analysis, p-values are generally expressed as critical ratios (CRs), where a $p < 0.05$ is equivalent to a CR of ±1.96. In other words, if the coefficient associated with a path has a CR that is greater than 1.96 or less than –1.96, then this suggests that the relationship between the variables is statistically significant and therefore generalizable.

Whereas overall model fit in multiple regression is assessed using R^2 (which corresponds to the amount of variation in Y that is explained by the X variables), SEM uses a diverse set of goodness-of-fit statistics, with which you are already familiar because they are the same ones we looked at in relation to confirmatory factor analysis.

Unlike multiple regression, SEM does not use OLS to estimate the model parameters. Instead, it typically uses MLE, which is another term with which you should already be familiar. It is the same estimation technique that we learned about in our study of logistic regression analysis.

Let's have a look at how management researchers like you might use SEM to better understand organizations and organizational behavior.

Structural Equation Modeling in Management Research

In many ways, the sorts of research questions one might ask using SEM are similar to the sorts of research questions one might ask using multiple regression. In both methods, a single outcome is predicted (or explained) by a set of independent, or exogenous, variables. The key difference, as noted above, is that SEM enables latent (directly unobservable) variables to be modeled.

Some textbooks will argue that SEM is more suitable than multiple regression for unpacking causal relations among variables. I'm not sure that I agree with that argument. It is true that SEM typically employs path analysis that appears to show cause-and-effect relationships, but you should still be careful, in my view, never to draw causal conclusions in management research, especially if the sample is cross-sectional. Indeed, even with longitudinal data, it is still not technically possible to infer airtight causal influence because of the threat of *omitted variable bias* (e.g., your 'causal' relationship could, in fact, be explained by some other variable or set of variables that you've not yet measured). In short, don't assume that, just because you're using SEM, you can conclude that your X variables cause Y.

The research process for SEM invariably always starts with theory. Remember, SEM is a confirmatory (deductive) approach – meaning that you start with a set of hypotheses and then assess whether or not you can make that 'quantum leap' from sample to population. Once you have designed your questionnaire (which can consist of both latent variables like job satisfaction and simple, observed variables like age) and administer it, the next step is to run a set of confirmatory factor analyses (see Chapter 11) on your latent variables. It wouldn't make sense to immediately start building a structural model (in which you're comparing relationships among latent variables) unless you can first confirm that your latent variables are good measures of the constructs you're trying to measure. If you cannot produce good measurement models at this preliminary stage of analysis, then you shouldn't bother running your structural model because it wouldn't yield useful information.

Let's assume that you've articulated your theory and specific hypotheses, designed your survey, collected the data, and verified, through confirmatory factor analysis, that you have measured a set of good latent variables. Now you are in a position to build your multivariate SEM. The following is a sample of research questions that a management researcher might answer using SEM. You will note that they are fairly similar to the multiple regression research questions from Chapter 9.

- What are the predictors of employee trust in management? In this case, potential exogenous (independent) variables might include the extent to which management shares information with employees (latent variable), the extent to which employees feel involved in decision-making (latent variable), the amount of influence employees have over their jobs (latent variable), their level of satisfaction with their jobs (latent variable), and their degree of organizational commitment (latent variable), and the endogenous (dependent) variable is some latent measure of employee trust in management (Timming, 2012).

- What are the predictors of pro-democracy affect (e.g., how good someone feels about democracy)? In this case, potential exogenous (independent) variables might include the extent to which employees can participate in decision-making (latent variable), trade union membership (observable, single-item indicator), the extent to which employees feel that they can take their own initiative at work (observable, single-item indicator), and wider interest in politics (latent variable), and the endogenous (dependent) variable is some latent measure of support for democracy (Timming and Summers, 2020).

- What are the predictors of pro-product affect (e.g., how good someone feels about buying a particular product or good)? In this case, potential exogenous variables might include product cost (observable, single-item indicator), perceived product usefulness (latent variable), perceived product aesthetic beauty (latent variable), and the atmospherics of the store (latent variable), and the endogenous (dependent) variable is some latent measure of how much the consumer likes the product.

- What are the predictors of statistical knowledge? In this case, potential exogenous (independent) variables might include intelligence (latent variable), whether or not one has read this book (observable, single-item indicator), conscientiousness (latent variable), creativity (latent variable), and openness to new knowledge (latent variable), and the endogenous (dependent) variable is some latent measure of statistical knowledge.

- What are the predictors of employee depression? In this case, potential exogenous (independent) variables might include age (observable, single-item indicator), income (observable, single-item indicator), gender (observable, single item indicator), whether or not the employee is taking antidepressant medication (observable, single-item indicator), and whether or not the employee is married (observable, single-item indicator), and the endogenous (dependent) variable is some latent measure of employee depression.

You might have noticed, in respect to the last research question, that the only latent variable in that model is the endogenous factor, employee depression. The rest of the variables are standard, single-item indicators, some of which are simple dummy variables. This is still considered a structural model, even though there are no latent exogenous (independent) variables. Alternatively, you could predict a single-item endogenous variable and a set of latent exogenous variables and that, too, would still be considered an SEM. A structural model must have at least one latent variable, but it could also have all latent variables in it. Oftentimes it involves a combination of both latent and observable, single-item indicators.

The primary advantage of management researchers in using SEM is that it allows us to model latent, unobservable variables alongside observable ones to get a bigger picture than can be offered by standard multiple regression, where latent constructs are often analysed by creating a single, composite variable.

Let's take a look at some basic concepts underlying SEM. Again, you should already be vaguely familiar with these after reading Chapter 11.

Basic Concepts in Structural Equation Modeling

The same basic principles that apply to confirmatory factor analysis also apply to SEM. This is because they are both part of a wider family of methods known as *analysis of covariance structures*. If, for whatever reason, you've not read Chapter 11 yet, then I strongly encourage you to stop reading this chapter and go back to that one.

I'm not going to repeat at length the basic principles discussed in Chapter 11, but I'll summarize them briefly here before diving into the unique attributes of SEM. In short, both confirmatory factor analysis and SEM are confirmatory methods, at least initially (more on this later). This means that they are always theory- and hypothesis-driven. Both SEM and confirmatory factor analysis involve latent (unobserved) variables that are composed of a series of single-item indicators. Both confirmatory factor analysis and SEM are operationalized, mathematically, using matrix algebra. The key relationships are covariances, not correlations (as is the case in multiple regression). Both confirmatory factor analysis and SEM can only be run if the models are just-identified or overidentified. That is, underidentified models are impossible to calculate, as we discussed briefly in Chapter 11. For this reason, some of the factor loadings between the single-item (observable) variables and the latent (unobserved) variables must be fixed at 1. An *underidentified model* is one in which there are simply not enough pieces of information (degrees of freedom) to enable the calculation of a result. A *just-identified model* means that there is just enough information to enable the calculation of a result. An *overidentified model* means that there are more than enough pieces of information (degrees of freedom) to enable the calculation of the result. Ideally, a good confirmatory factor analysis/ SEM should be overidentified. For practical purposes, it's not necessary that an applied statistician like you must understand everything about model identification, but you should be aware of the concept. The reason you don't need to sweat too much if you still don't grasp model identification is that AMOS Graphics will not run an underidentified model. If your model is flagged as underidentified, it's likely because you don't have enough indicators per latent variable. This is why I recommended in Chapter 11 that each latent variable should be composed of a minimum of three single-item indicators. The last similarity between confirmatory factor analysis and SEM is that they both use the same exact goodness-of-fit statistics that we reviewed in Chapter 11. If you don't recall what these statistics are, check out Box 11.3.

Okay, now that we've covered the basic principles that are shared between confirmatory factor analysis and SEM, we can now turn to the unique attributes of analysis of covariance structures that are associated with structural models. As I noted above, the key difference between confirmatory factor analysis and SEM is that the latter investigates not just measurement models (e.g., how well do a set of indicators 'hang together' to form a latent variable) but also structural models (e.g., how do a set of latent variables relate to each other or to other observable variables).

The first unique attribute of SEM is that it is based on the logic of *path analysis*. Path analysis refers to a type of visual statistical modeling in which a diagram illustrates how the variables might theoretically be related to one another. This visual diagram is also referred to as a *path diagram*. You should already be familiar with the concept of path analysis because we discussed it briefly in Chapter 9 in the context of multiple regression. In fact, there is no need in path analysis that only latent variables are used. It works perfectly well with only observable variables or some combination of the two types.

I noted at the start of this chapter that SEM is sometimes referred to as causal modeling, but I cautioned you against using this terminology because, technically, there is no way to 'prove' any causality between two variables, especially in cross-sectional studies. This is what makes path analysis so deceptive. A path diagram looks as if it is graphically articulating a set of causal relationships among variables. Consider the path diagram exemplified in Figure 12.1.

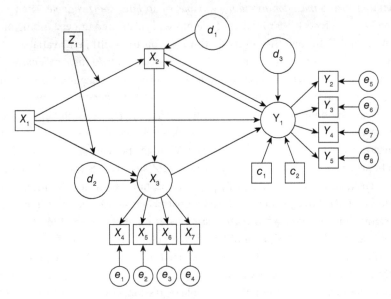

Figure 12.1 A hypothetical example of a path diagram

There is a lot going on in Figure 12.1, so let's take it one piece at a time. Based on the diagram, it appears that our X variables (X_1, X_2, and X_3, the latter of which is latent) are sequentially influencing each other, ultimately causing the outcome, Y (also a latent variable). Now, there are, of course, no guarantees that the relationships hypothesized here are causal. When reporting the results of a path analysis, it's best to use tempered language, such as 'X_1 is positively associated with X_2,' rather than bolder, and potentially misleading, language, such as 'X_1 causes changes in X_2'. It is possible, in the context of a path analysis, that the variables along the chain are indeed influencing, or causing, the modeled outcomes, but there is no way definitively to verify causality with 100% certainty, so, again, I advise against it.

Looking at Figure 12.1, you will notice two mechanisms (with which you should already be familiar from Chapter 9, when we learned about the PROCESS Macro) stand out. The first mechanism is a mediation and the second is a moderation. Let's review each of these mechanisms again, briefly, in the context of Figure 12.1.

A *mediation* refers to a situation in which the indirect effect of X_1 on Y through X_2 is stronger than the direct effect of X_1 on Y. You can see in Figure 12.1 that four separate paths can potentially explain the relationship between X_1 and Y_1: (1) X_1 can have a direct relationship with Y_1; (2) X_1 can have an indirect relationship on Y_1 through X_2; (3) X_1 can have an indirect relationship on Y_1 through X_3; and (4) X_1 can have an indirect relationship on Y_1 through X_2 and then X_3.

Sometimes there is no statistically significant direct relationship between X_1 and Y, but there is a significant indirect relationship between X_1 and X_2 and, in turn, between X_2 and Y. This is referred to as a *full mediation*, meaning that the relationship between X_1 and Y is explained fully by X_2. Other times, there may be a significant direct relationship between X_1 and Y, but the indirect relationship through X_2 is stronger than the direct relationship. This is referred to as a *partial mediation*. In either case, X_2 is referred to as a *mediator, mediating variable*, or an *intervening variable*. The whole point of testing for mediation effects is that it allows for a more sophisticated understanding of the mechanism between X_1 and Y through the effect of a third (or fourth or fifth, etc.) variable.

The second mechanism evident in Figure 12.1 is a *moderator, moderation,* or a *moderating effect*. A potential moderation is evident in light of variable Z_1 in the path diagram. Consider the relationships among X_1, Z_1, and X_2, and among X_1, Z_1, and X_3. In this diagram, Z_1 serves as a moderator. Where a significant moderation is found, this means that the relationship between X_1 and X_2/X_1 and X_3 changes depending on the value of Z_1. For example, when values of Z_1 are low (say, 1 SD below the mean), the relationship between X_1 and X_2 might be neutral, that is to say, there is no relationship between the two variables. When values of Z_1 are average (say, at the mean), the relationship between X_1 and X_2 might be slightly positive, but not statistically significant. When values of Z_1 are high (say, 1 SD above the mean), the relationship between X_1 and X_2 might be positive and statistically significant. In other words, where a moderating effect can be found, the relationship between X_1 and X_2/X_1 and X_3 changes at different levels of a third variable, Z_1.

Another unique feature of the path analysis depicted in Figure 12.1 is the presence of what are called *disturbance* terms. These are denoted by d_1, d_2, and d_3 in the figure. A disturbance term is analogous to the residuals, or error terms, in multiple regression. However, unlike in multiple regression, disturbance terms are always explicitly modeled in path diagrams, rather than just assumed. The rule surrounding disturbance terms is that you must always include one for each endogenous (dependent) variable in your model. Alternatively stated, you do not need to include a disturbance term for your exogenous (independent) variable(s). In Figure 12.1, X_2, X_3, and Y_1 are endogenous variables, with the former two (X_2 and X_3) serving simultaneously as exogenous and endogenous variables. A variable in a path diagram can be both endogenous (predicted by another variable) and exogenous (it predicts another variable). As long as a variable is predicted or explained by another variable, even if it subsequently predicts or explains an outcome, the former needs to have a disturbance term associated with it. The coefficient between the disturbance term and the endogenous (dependent) variable is always fixed at 1 to facilitate model identification.

The disturbance terms basically remind you that there are many, many other causes of an outcome beside the one predicting it. A disturbance is the sum of all other variables, not included in your model, that are associated with an endogenous variable. Obviously, we cannot account for every factor that predicts a variable (latent or observable). The world is just too complex, and we don't have a survey instrument large enough to measure all possible exogenous (independent) variables. This is why we incorporate disturbance terms in SEM. The disturbance term represents the sum of every other exogenous (independent) variable, not measured in your model, that explains the variance in your endogenous (dependent) variable(s).

In addition to explicitly modeling disturbance terms in path analysis, you must also explicitly model all your control variables, or covariates. This is a big departure from multiple regression, where control variables can just 'hang out' in the background of the analysis. For example, you might run a multiple regression with 25 independent variables in it ($X_1, X_2 \ldots X_{25}$), but your only interest is in the relationship between X_1 and Y. The other covariates ($X_2 \ldots X_{25}$) are just controls that 'hang out' in the background. You include your 24 control variables in multiple regression so that you can look at the pure effect of X_1 and Y, taking into account the presence of the other covariates, which are present, but situated in the background of the model. With path analysis, however, those control variables need to be factored explicitly into the model, as illustrated in C_1 and C_2 (two hypothetical control variables, or covariates) in Figure 12.1. Control variables in SEM look a bit like disturbance terms. In fact, incorporating explicit control variables should, in theory, weaken your disturbance terms because those control variables, were they not incorporated, would have been lumped into the disturbance terms. You can place your control variables anywhere in the model you think it makes the most conceptual sense to place them.

Another feature that is unique to SEM models is that they are able to estimate both recursive and nonrecursive relationships. A *recursive* structural model is one in which the directionality of relationships goes only one way. Typically, a recursive model is one that starts with the variable(s) on the left-side and gradually works its way forward through a series of mediations to the right-hand side, where you will find the endogenous (dependent) variable. Most SEM models are recursive because they are the easiest to build and estimate. A *nonrecursive* structural model (e.g., the one depicted in Figure 12.1), in contrast, is one that includes two-way feedback loops between some of the variables (see the bidirectional relationship between X_2 and Y_1). This type of model is useful when directionality is theoretically unclear (e.g., Does X precede Y, or vice versa?).

I've already warned you not to draw causal inferences when using SEM, and I stand by that warning (especially when using cross-sectional data). However, nonrecursive SEM models will give you the strongest possible claims to causality because they assess potentially bidirectional relationships and reverse causality. Nonrecursive models still don't give you the quantitative ammunition you need to infer causation, but they get you as close as possible to such an inference. In Figure 12.1, you will notice the two arrows, running in opposite directions, between X_2 and Y_1. Given the complexities surrounding nonrecursive SEM models compared with the relatively simpler recursive SEM models, we won't be looking at how to create the former in this textbook. A good resource for learning more about nonrecursive SEM models is Holmes Finch and French (2015). In fact, there are other advanced SEM methods, such as mean structures analysis and other multigroup methods (Yung and Bentler, 1996), that are not covered in this textbook.

The last feature that distinguishes SEM from multiple regression analysis is that the former uses modification indices. *Modification indices* refer to a statistical technique that enables us to improve model fit by respecifying (e.g., adding, deleting, or covarying) some of the relationships, items, or variables in the structural and/or measurement model. Recall that I previously told you that SEM is a confirmatory technique, not an exploratory one. As a confirmatory technique, the researcher uses theory to build and test a model, which can be rejected or accepted. Well, this is generally true. SEM, in and of itself, is deductive and thus theory-driven. But what happens if your theory is wrong and you end up with a poor-fitting model? You could just accept that your model is wrong and report that, or you could use modification indices to explore, *post hoc*, what exactly is wrong with your model and how the fit could be improved by respecifying some of the relationships. Thus, SEM can also be, to some extent, exploratory, but that doesn't mean that it should be, or must be, exploratory. My personal view is that SEM models are best evaluated through a strictly confirmatory lens. If your model is poor, then it's poor. That's science, and there is no harm in that. But if you would like to better understand why it's poor, you can ask AMOS Graphics to generate a set of modification indices, which are statistics that can help you identify 'problematic' relationships, for example, among error terms or among indicators or latent variables. You can then use those modification indices to 'tinker' with the SEM model until it produces an acceptable fit. Again, I urge caution in using modification indices because the practice, in my eyes, is not very scientific. This kind of *post hoc* 'tinkering' may be acceptable provided that you explain exactly what you changed in your SEM to create the better fit, and why. But it is not acceptable to haphazardly use modification indices to find a better-fitting model and then report that one as if it were the first model you had built. The potential to mislead others by concealing the use of modification indices is high, which is, again, why I urge caution in using this statistical technique. Another important qualification to using modification indices is that your dataset must be complete. Alternatively stated, if you have missing values in your dataset, you cannot generate modification indices. This leaves you with the option of imputing values that are missing to artificially make your dataset complete, which, in my view, is another technique that you should use with caution.

Okay, I think you now have a reasonably good grasp of the basic principles underlying SEM using path analysis. At this stage, I think we should move on to using AMOS Graphics to illustrate how to build a structural model. You should already be familiar with these techniques because they are basically the same ones we used to build a confirmatory factor analysis. We're not going to build a complex (e.g., nonrecursive) structural model because these are beyond the scope of this applied textbook. But we will look at a mediation model using WERS data. Let's do it!

Structural Equation Modeling Using AMOS Graphics

From the Companion Website, open the file chap12data.sav. You will notice that this file is very similar to the chap11data.sav file from Chapter 11. The same variables are contained in both files, with one key difference. In the chap12data.sav file, all the missing cases have been dealt with using imputation. If you'd like to see how I used IBM SPSS Statistics Software (SPSS) to impute the missing values from chap11data.sav, check out Box 12.1, where I walk you through the process.

Box 12.1: Imputation of Missing Data in SPSS

As noted above, one of the requirements of using modification indices in SEM is that the dataset is complete with no missing values. Alternatively stated, if you have even one missing value, then you are not able to access modification indices to help you improve model fit. With this limitation in mind, if you would like to learn how to use modification indices (please say yes, please say yes!), then we will have to figure out how to deal with the missing values in the survey of employees. The best way to deal with them is to use a method of *imputation*, a technique whereby missing values are replaced with values that are 'likely' or 'typical' in the dataset.

There are many different methods of imputation. Mean imputation implies that you simply replace all missing values with the mean of that particular variable. This is quick and easy, but not ideal because it promotes regression to the mean and reduces variability, especially when there is a large number of missing cases to deal with. A better method is to use *multiple imputation*, which is based on Monte Carlo simulations that start with the mean of each variable and then throw random error into those values. The problem with multiple imputation is that it doesn't work well with large datasets, such as the survey of employees. A third method is to use *regression imputation*, a statistical technique that estimates what missing values should look like using information from the other variables in the dataset for purposes of prediction. This is the imputation method that I've opted to use to convert chap11data.sav with all its missing values into chap12data.sav with no missing values at all. In chap12data.sav, you will find that the missing values have all been replaced by estimated values that were informed by regressing the variable with missing values onto the other variables in the dataset. Let me show you how I did this.

Open chap11data.sav from Chapter 11 on the Companion Website. The first thing we're going to need to do is to find out which variables in the dataset have missing values. To check this, go to Analyze, Descriptive Statistics, and Frequencies. Highlight all the variables in the left-hand column and move them to the right. Then just click OK. You'll see in the output that all variables have some missing values, with a low of 222 missing cases for 'How satisfied with sense of achievement from work' and a high of 1405 for 'How good are managers at informing staff about financial matters'. We need to replace all those missing values to be able to run modification indices in SEM.

Luckily, the process by which to use regression imputation in SPSS is easy as pie. First, go to Transform and Replace Missing Values. Highlight the variables in the list on the left-hand side and move them into the right-hand column labeled New Variable(s):. The default imputation method in SPSS is Series Mean, which simply replaces all missing values with the mean for that variable. We want to use regression imputation instead. To do this, you're going to have to click on each variable, one-by-one, and then next to Method:, change Series mean to Linear interpolation. Note that you will have to scroll all the way to the top of the New Variable(s): column.

You will have to click Change for each variable, or else the regression imputation will not work. When you have changed all the variables from Series mean to Linear interpolation, just click OK and you'll have a new dataset that contains the old data and the new (imputed) data. The new data have no missing

(Continued)

values anywhere, which means that the dataset is ideally suited for SEM. If you want to double check that the imputation worked, just compare the old variables with missing values to the new variables without missing values by scrolling across in Data View. Case 88 in the dataset is a good example. You'll see the old −9 values are now valid scores that have been estimated through regression imputation. Pretty cool, huh?

If you really want to see for yourself that all missing values have been replaced in the newly created variables, then go to Analyze, Descriptive Statistics, and Frequencies. Move your newly created (imputed) variables into the right-hand column and click OK. If you follow the table at the top of the output across to the end, you will see all the new variables have no missing values. At this stage, you are ready to learn how to build structural models.

To build a structural model using chap12data, we will need to open AMOS Graphics, like we did in Chapter 11. You will see a blank AMOS workspace. What we need to do is get from the blank workspace to the fully specified structural model depicted in Figure 12.2. As you can see, there are a lot of bits and bobs in our fully specified model, and so it may take you a while to re-create it. If you really would like to skip straight to the fully specified SEM, I've saved the model in the Companion Website as Chap12sem1.amw. However, I strongly advise that you re-create the model yourself so that you can improve your skills in working within the AMOS Graphics interface. I'll explain how to re-create the model in Figure 12.2 now. Please note that you may need to use the ⊕ ⊖ icons to scroll back and forth because it is a 'busy' model that is hard to see from a distance.

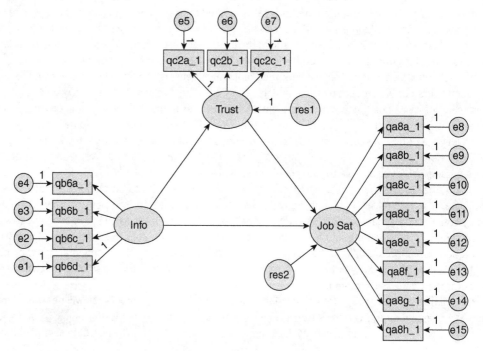

Figure 12.2 Full structural mediation model

We are going to build a structural model that contains three latent variables: (1) information (which consists of four single-item indicators that measure the extent to which employees think managers share information with them), (2) trust in management (which consists of three single-item indicators that measure how much trust employees have in managers), and (3) job satisfaction (which consists of eight single-item indicators that measure different dimensions of satisfaction with work). In the fully specified model, we're trying to understand whether sharing information with employees is associated with increased job satisfaction. You can see a test for a direct relationship between information and job satisfaction, as well as an indirect relationship through trust in managers. The logic here is that, to the extent that information sharing on the part of managers is associated with higher job satisfaction on the part of employees, this may be a result of the fact that receiving information from management increases trust in management, which in turn promotes job satisfaction. This is a potential mediation. In this case, trust in management is a mediating variable, where it is assumed that the relationship between information and job satisfaction may potentially flow through trust in management.

You will notice in Figure 12.2 that the three latent variables (Info, Trust, and JobSat) are specified with ovals and the single-item indicators are specified with rectangles. You will also notice that each rectangle has a circular error term (labeled e1 . . . e15), which, in aggregate, represent all the other variables (not measured in our model) that explain some variation in our single-item indicators. One final feature worth noting is that you will see two additional circles, labeled res1 and res2. These are also error terms (also referred to as disturbances), but they are predicting two of our latent variables, trust in management and job satisfaction. These error terms are also called residuals (which is why I've labeled them res), but you could also call them e16 and e17 if you prefer, or even d1 and d2 (for disturbance 1 and disturbance 2). You need to create these residual measures for every endogenous (dependent) variable in your model, but not for the exogenous (independent) variables. In the case of Figure 12.2, information is an exogenous (independent) variable, meaning that no other variable is predicting it. Therefore, it does not require a residual term to be added. However, trust in management is endogenous because it is predicted by information, and job satisfaction is endogenous because it is predicted by information and trust in management. As a result, you need to create these two residuals for those two latent variables, but not for information. To enable model identification (discussed in Chapter 11), we have to fix some of the paths at 1, but luckily AMOS Graphics does this automatically for us when we build the model. Specifically, the two paths from the residuals to the latent variables are fixed at 1, all the paths from the error terms to the single-item indicators are fixed at 1, and one of the paths from the latent variables to their single-item indicators is fixed at 1. By constraining these parameters to 1.00, you have an overidentified structural model for which a statistical solution can be freely estimated. Hypothetically, if you take away those fixed paths and let them be estimated freely, the model simply will not run because it will be underidentified, and therefore does not contain enough information points (or degrees of freedom) to be solved. AMOS would just give you an error message in that case.

I'm not going to walk you through, step-by-step, exactly how to create this path analysis because there is an almost infinite number of ways it could be created. But I will tell you the basic steps that you should take.

Creating a Structural Mediation Model in AMOS Graphics

First, create your three latent variables, using Figure 12.2 as a guide. Use the ◯ icon to create a single oval. Then use the 🖫 icon to create two more of these (for a total of three latent variables) by clicking and dragging each oval. You want all three ovals to form a triangle on the AMOS Graphics workspace. Make sure you click 🖫 again to turn off the copy variable function. If needed, you can use the 🚚 icon to move around your ovals.

Second, double click each oval, one-by-one, to open 'Object Properties' and label the variables 'Info', 'Trust', and 'JobSat'. Info should be in the bottom-left oval, trust should be in the top oval, and JobSat should be in the bottom-right oval. When you are done with the 'Object Properties' window, just click the X to close it. Note that you cannot have a space between Job and Sat (i.e., 'Job Sat'), or else AMOS will not run your model. So far, your path diagram should look like the one depicted in Figure 12.3.

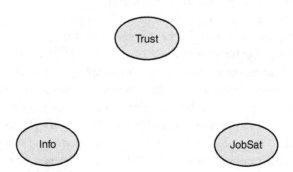

Figure 12.3   Three labeled latent variables without indicators

Third, use the ← icon to draw three arrows by clicking and dragging from one oval to another. The first arrow should connect Info and JobSat, the second should connect Info and Trust, and the third should connect Trust and JobSat. Be sure to click on the ← icon to turn it off when you are done. The model should now look like the one depicted in Figure 12.4.

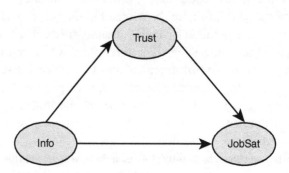

Figure 12.4   Three latent variables without indicators, but with paths specified

Fourth, you now need to create your indicator variables and associated error terms. Recall that Info is composed of four indicators, Trust is composed of three indicators, and JobSat is composed of eight indicators (for a total of 15 rectangles). Click on the 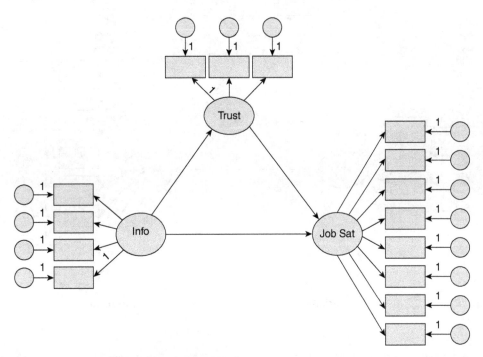 icon, hover over Info, and click four times to create four indicators. Now click on the ⟲ icon and click three times on Info so the indicators are repositioned to the left of the oval. Next, click again on the icon, hover over Trust, and click three times to create three single-item indicators. These you will want to leave as they are above that oval. Finally, click eight times on the JobSat variable. Click the ⟲ icon once to move them to the right of that latent variable. If your path diagram is too big, click ▣ to fit it to the page. It should now look like the one depicted in Figure 12.5.

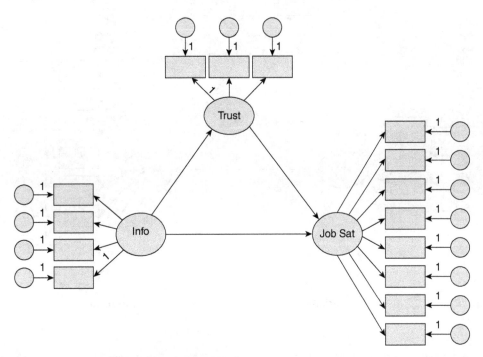

Figure 12.5 Three latent variables with indicators and error terms

Fifth, you will need to label your error terms (the little circles that individually link up to each rectangle). These error terms represent all the other variables that predict your single-item indicators aside from the latent variables that they are also linked to. There is an easy shortcut to create these error terms. Go to Plugins and click Name Unobserved Variables. You should see e1 . . . e15.

Sixth, you will need to manually create two residual terms (also referred to as disturbances) that load onto your two endogenous variables: Trust and JobSat. Click on the ⚲ icon, hover over Trust, and click three times. The first time should create your new residual variable and the other two clicks should move the variable just to the right of Trust. Click ⚲ again to turn off this function. Now double click inside the new circle to open 'Object Properties' and label it Res1. This residual term represents all the other latent variables that predict Trust. Do the same for JobSat. Click on the 👤 icon, hover over JobSat, and click six times. The first click creates the new residual and the next five move it below JobSat. Again, click 👤 to turn off this function. Double click inside that new circle to open 'Object Properties' and label it Res2. Click the X to close the 'Object Properties' box. At this point, your structural model should look like the one depicted in Figure 12.6.

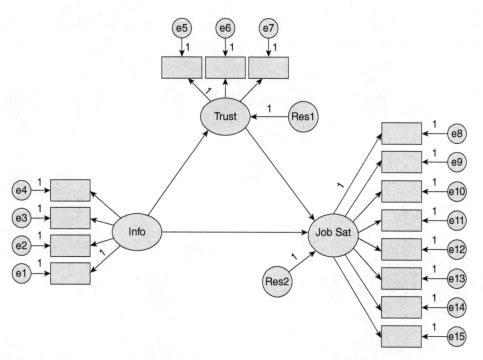

Figure 12.6 Three latent variables with indicators, error terms, and residuals

Seventh, click on the ▦ icon to link your AMOS path diagram to the SPSS data file, chap12data. sav. Click on | File Name | to select the data file and link it up by double clicking the data file and then clicking | OK |.

Eighth, you will need to name each single-item indicator. To do this, simply type the names of each variable into each rectangle, again using 'Object Properties' to label them. For example, write qb6a_1, qb6b_1, qb6c_1, and qb6d_1 into the four Info rectangles, and so on. Note that, if your rectangles are too small for the text, you can go to Plugins and click Resize Observed Variables.

Boom! You just created your first structural model on AMOS Graphics. You may need to do some tinkering here and there, for example, going into Object Properties and changing the size of the font so everything fits in the circles and squares in your path diagram. But the final path diagram, depicted in Figure 12.2, is good to go. Now, you're ready to run the SEM. But before you can do it, save your model by clicking on the 💾 icon. Name it whatever you want.

Using Modification Indices to Improve Model Fit

The first thing we're going to do now is to learn how to use modification indices to improve model fit. However, as I've noted previously, I urge caution in using this tool. You don't want to mindlessly tinker with your model to improve it. Also remember that you will need to have a dataset with no missing values to access this feature of AMOS Graphics.

To request modification indices, click on the 🔢 icon and then click on the Output tab, as illustrated in Figure 12.7. Make sure that ☑ Standardized estimates and ☑ Modification indices are ticked. Now click on the Estimation tab and make sure you tick ☑ Estimate means and intercepts . Then simply close the analysis properties box. Save your model once more. When you are done, click on the 🔢 icon to run your model. Note that this may take some time, maybe even up to a minute or more, because the survey of employees is very large. When you click on 🔢, your path diagram will look really busy, with lots of numbers, including variances and covariances being calculated. The default is to first produce Unstandardized estimates , but by clicking on Standardized estimates , you can create the equivalent of beta coefficients with a floor of –1 and a ceiling of 1 to get an indication of the strength of the relationships in your structural model. At this stage, rather than looking at the relationships among the three latent variables, we're going to instead focus on the relationships between the single-item indicators and each latent variable.

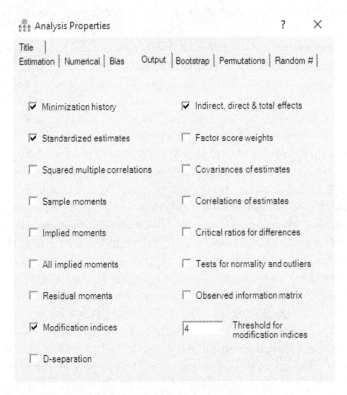

Figure 12.7 Output tab in AMOS Graphics' analysis properties

You will notice that most of the standardized estimates appear to be fairly strong, with the majority well above 0.7 or so, with a few exceptions. This is good news. Variable qa8f_1, one of the indicators of job satisfaction, is a bit of an outlier, with a standardized estimate of only 0.46. Similarly, qa8g_1 has a standardized estimate of only 0.50. But overall, your measurement models are fairly tight, with little apparent error at first glance.

Now click on the 📊 icon to view the AMOS output for this analysis. Before checking the modification indices, let's look at Model Fit by clicking on it. In fact, these model fit statistics already look reasonably good, don't they? If you compare the model fit statistics with the SEM cutoff values listed in Box 11.3, you can see we're already doing pretty good, but, of course, we can always do better. Rather than looking at how our modifications to the model affect each goodness-of-fit statistic individually, let's focus specifically on how it affects the chi-square statistic for the model. Remember, a better-fitting model means a lower chi-square value. So whatever changes we make to the model through the modification indices, we want to see a reduction in the chi-square value, which currently stands at 15,792.73.

Now click on Modification Indices in your text output. There's a lot going on here, so let me walk you through these statistics. Basically, you have two different tables: modification indices for covariances and, further down the output, modification indices for regression weights. I do not recommend using the regression weights information to modify your model because this gets way too close to *post hoc* model tinkering, which can result in an *overfitted* model (a model that artificially fits too well as a result of tinkering). Instead, focus on the first table, which lists out modification indices for covariances. The first column shows you which relationship is under examination and the second column lists the modification indices. To improve model fit, what you want to do is to look through the first column of numbers (starting 72.303) and look for 'big' numbers as you move down that column. What does 'big' mean? Well, there is no strict cutoff (especially because modification indices vary depending on sample size). Just look for values that clearly stand out. You'll know them when you see them. Each value in that column of numbers is AMOS' estimate of how much the chi-square statistic (mentioned in the previous paragraph) will go down (i.e., improve model fit) if the variables identified are allowed to covary. Remember from our preceding paragraph that the current chi-square is 15,792.73. Thus, if, in theory, we found a modification index number that is, hypothetically, 792.73, then allowing those two variables to covary should reduce the chi-square value by 792.73, to 15,000. But there are some rules to using modification indices. I'm quite conservative when it comes to using this tool, so I recommend only allowing error terms to covary with each other and only when the error terms are associated with each other within the same factor.

Let's see what this looks like in action. If you follow the modification index column down to the error terms, you'll see a few abnormally large values. For example, e11 ↔ e12 have a huge modification index of 5533.04, which means that, if we allowed them to covary, our overall chi-square statistic should fall by 5533.04 (approximately). You can see from Figure 12.2 that e11 and e12 are both associated with the same latent variable, JobSat, so we can covary them. You will also see that e9 ↔ e10 have a fairly big statistic of 2751.50, and e8 ↔ e15 have a statistic of 2867.10. Both of these error terms could be covaried because they are both linked to JobSat. Now, let's go ahead and covary all three of these error terms. All three statistics add up to 11,161.64

(i.e., 5533.04 + 2751.50 + 2867.10 = 11,161.64). If our modification estimates are correct, by cova-rying these error terms, we should see a reduction in the overall chi-square value to around 4631.09 (i.e., 15,792.73 – 11,161.64 = 4631.09).

To covary e11 and e12, go back to your path diagram. Click the ⬇ icon to transition away from your output (results) model and back to your input (specified) model. Now click on the ↔ icon to covary these two error terms. Now simply connect e11 and e12 with the double-headed arrow. Do the same now by connecting e9 and e10, and then connect e8 and e15. The respecified model should look like the one depicted in Figure 12.8. I have also saved it as chap12sem2 on the Companion Website. Now, simply click the ▦ icon to recalculate your estimates (this may take some time while AMOS is thinking). Boom! You will notice that your chi-square statistic has dropped from previously 15,792.73 to 4831.52! This is an even better fit (i.e., lower chi-square value) than AMOS originally anticipated and a fine improvement of model fit. You can verify this new chi-square statistic of 4831.52 simply by clicking on the ▦ icon and looking at the Notes for Model. In theory, you could now go on to respecify the modification indices again and keep looking for offending error terms that are highly correlated, or another option is that we could remove qa8g_1 (one of the JobSat indicators that doesn't load as highly as the others onto the latent variable), but I'm not a supporter of this kind of mindless empiricism. Therefore, I'm going to propose that we now proceed to look at the results of our mediation analysis.

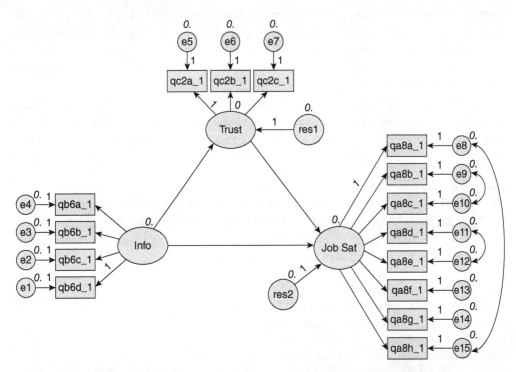

Figure 12.8 Fully specified structural model with covaried error terms

Mediation Analysis Using Structural Equation Modeling

Finally, we arrive at the point at which we can evaluate the mediation results of our structural model. Although we've already run the model with modification indices, we're going to run it again to make sure that the settings are correct. Click on the 🎹 icon. Under the Output tab, make sure you tick ☑ Indirect, direct & total effects . Now under the Bootstrap tab, make sure that you tick ☑ Perform bootstrap and ☑ Bias-corrected confidence intervals . On this same tab, you also want to make sure that Number of bootstrap samples is set at 2000 and BC confidence level is set at 95 (the default is 90). Let me explain briefly why we're doing this. A confidence interval of 90 is equivalent to a *p*-value of 0.10, whereas a 95% confidence interval is equivalent to a *p*-value of 0.05. Therefore, a 95% confidence interval is more in line with what researchers typically describe as statistically significant. The bootstrap that we're instructing AMOS to do as part of this analysis is what enables us to generate these confidence intervals in the first instance. Without the bootstrap, we have no useful confidence interval that can be used to assess whether our mediation is significant. *Bootstrapping* is a statistical process based on Monte Carlo simulations, whereby your sample is treated like a population, and a number of subsamples are repeatedly drawn from it (in our case, 2000 subsamples) to produce something like a sampling distribution and standard errors around the estimates. The number of subsamples that you could draw as part of a bootstrap could be anything, but we've instructed AMOS to take 2000 subsamples from the original sample of almost 22,000 for the survey of employees. In other words, by bootstrapping, you're asking AMOS to carry out 2000 iterative analyses and then you're using the results of these analyses to estimate standard errors that can be used to determine whether or not your mediation model is significant.

Okay, now that your analysis properties are correctly set up for mediation analysis, close the box by ticking the X and simply rerun the model by clicking on the 🎹 icon.

Before we look at the model notes in the output, let's just look briefly at the path diagram, which should now display numbers attached to each path. These are the coefficients that describe the relationships among the variables (both latent and observed). You can toggle back and forth between Unstandardized estimates / Standardized estimates. After looking at the standardized estimates, now have a look at the unstandardized estimates.

To evaluate a proposed mediation, we're now going to look at relationships among the latent variables in our model. The three paths (from Info to JobSat, from Info to Trust, and from Trust to JobSat) are where we can evaluate the mediation. Looking at the unstandardized coefficients displayed in Figure 12.9, I want you to focus on three effects.

1. The direct effect from Info to JobSat is 0.22
2. The direct effect from Info to Trust is 0.81
3. The direct effect from Trust to JobSat is 0.33

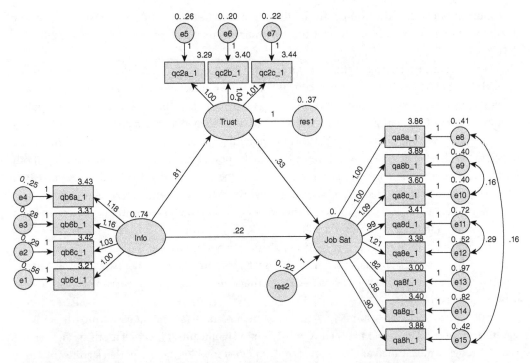

Figure 12.9 Fully specified structural model with unstandardized estimates

Okay, so we have three direct effects among our latent variables. To find out whether they are statistically significant, click on the 🖿 icon and then click on Estimates. Under Regression Weights, you can see all three of these direct effects alongside an *SE* (standard error) and CR. Remember that the CR is the same thing as a *p*-value, but it's expressed as a *z*-score. So a CR of >1.96 or <−1.96 is equivalent to a *p*-value of <0.05. In this case, all three *p*-values are way higher than 1.96 (Info → JobSat = 27.45, Info → Trust = 102.46, and Trust → JobSat = 43.86). Therefore, we can conclude that all three direct effects are positive and statistically significant. That is, information sharing is associated with higher levels of trust and job satisfaction and trust is associated with higher levels of job satisfaction.

So far, so good, but we have more than just three direct effects in our model. We also have a possible indirect effect between Info and JobSat that flows through Trust. In other words, we're assuming that information sharing is associated with higher job satisfaction at least in part because the former promotes trust in management, which, in turn, is also associated with increased job satisfaction.

Recall from above that the direct effect of Info on JobSat is 0.22. To calculate the indirect effect of Info on JobSat through Trust, we simply multiply the two regression weights that describe that indirect effect. In other words, we multiply the direct effect of Info on Trust (0.81) by the direct effect of Trust on JobSat (0.33). Thus, the indirect effect of Info on JobSat through Trust is $0.81 \times 0.33 = 0.27$.

So we have a direct effect of Info on JobSat of 0.22 and an indirect effect of Info on JobSat through Trust of 0.27. We can therefore conclude that the indirect effect through Trust is comparatively stronger than the direct effect, because 0.27 is slightly higher than 0.22. This evidence points to some degree of mediation, whereby the effect of our exogenous variable (Info) on our endogenous variable (JobSat) flows through a third intervening variable (Trust). You can confirm these direct and indirect effects by scrolling down the Estimates output until you get to Direct Effects (both unstandardized and standardized) and Indirect Effects (both unstandardized and standardized) at the bottom of the output. Here you can confirm that the three direct effects listed above are correct and the indirect effect is 0.269 (found in the second to last table in the output, labeled 'Indirect Effects: Group number 1 – Default model').

Therefore, we can see some evidence of a mediation in our model, but we still don't know if that mediation is statistically significant . . . yet. This is why we carried out the bootstrap, so that we can generate standard errors and p-values to tell us whether Trust significantly mediates the relationship between Info and JobSat.

Recall that there are two forms of significant mediation. A *full mediation* is when there is no significant direct relationship between X and Y, but a significant indirect relationship between X and Y through a mediating variable, Z. A *partial mediation* is when there is both a significant direct relationship between X and Y and a significant indirect relationship between X and Y through a mediating variable, Z. Now, we already know that there is a significant direct relationship between X (Info) and Y (JobSat) because we already reported that CR as above 1.96. If you scroll up the output, you'll see that the CR between Info and JobSat is 27.45, which is equivalent to a p-value of <0.05. So, at best, we can only hope to find a partial mediation in our model. A full mediation would require no statistical significance between Info and JobSat (e.g., a CR of <1.96 or >−1.96).

To find out if the indirect relationship between Info and JobSat through Trust is statistically significant, go back to the results output. You'll see that some of the findings are grayed out:

- Estimates/Bootstrap
  - Estimates
  - Bootstrap standard errors
  - Bootstrap Confidence

This is where you can find out whether your indirect relationship is statistically significant. To access that grayed-out section, you first need to double click on Estimates, then double click on Matrices, and then finally click on Indirect Effects (please don't ask me why this is so complicated!). When you do that, the grayed out Estimates/Bootstrap section becomes black and you can expand those findings. Click on Bootstrap Confidence and then Bias-corrected percentile method, and you'll see three options, as depicted in Figure 12.10: (1) Lower Bounds BC, (2) Upper Bounds BC, and (3) Two Tailed Significance BC. As long as the range of your lower-bound estimate and upper-bound estimate does not contain 0, you can conclude that you have a statistically significant indirect effect. Your lower-bound estimate of the indirect relationship between Info and JobSat through Trust is 0.253 and your upper-bound estimate of the indirect relationship between Info and JobSat through Trust is 0.283, as evidenced in the tables. These estimates were generated by the 2000 bootstraps that we instructed AMOS to carry out, and we would interpret them as follows: we are 95% confident that the true (population) estimate of the indirect relationship between Info and JobSat through Trust falls somewhere between 0.253 and 0.283. Because this range doesn't include 0, we can now conclude a statistically significant indirect relationship between Info and JobSat through Trust. Therefore, there is evidence of a partial mediation in our model: that Trust partially mediates the relationship between Info and JobSat. Pretty cool, huh?

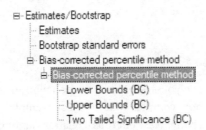

Figure 12.10 Bias-corrected percentile method for assessing indirect effects

Now, I'm going to give you a little shortcut to reaching that conclusion. Instead of looking at the Lower- and Upper-Bound estimates as in (1) and (2) above, you can just click on Two Tailed Significance (BC) in the AMOS output, with the output table depicted in Figure 12.11. Here you can see the *p*-value, which is 0.001. In other words, the indirect relationship between Info and JobSat through Trust is statistically significant at $p < 0.001$.

Indirect Effects - Two Tailed Significance (BC) (Group number 1 - Default model)

	Info	Trust	JobSat
Trust	...	...	...
JobSat	.001	...	...
qa8h_1	.001	.001	...
qa8g_1	.001	.001	...
qa8f_1	.001	.001	...
qa8e_1	.001	.001	...
qa8d_1	.001	.001	...
qa8c_1	.001	.001	...
qa8b_1	.001	.001	...
qa8a_1	.001	.001	...
qc2c_1	.001	...	...
qc2b_1	.001	...	...
qc2a_1	.001	...	...
qb6a_1	...	...	...
qb6b_1	...	...	...
qb6c_1	...	...	...
qb6d_1	...	...	...

Figure 12.11 Two tailed significance BC for assessing indirect effects

Well, there you have it, my friend. You've just carried out a simple mediation model using structural equation modeling. This may be the last statistical test you'll carry out as part of this textbook, but let's not get sentimental and cry just yet. You can always carry out further mediation tests on your own. For example, why not replace Trust as a mediator with job influence? You can find these data in chap12data.sav. What happens when you run that mediation? Or, if you were really feeling daring, you could add two mediations in the same model: What is the relationship between Info and JobSat through both Trust and Influence? If you can carry out that kind of analysis, your skills are approaching those of an accomplished applied statistician! Do you think you can do it? I do. Go for it!

What Have You Learned?

This chapter was designed to give you a very basic introduction to structural equation modeling. Obviously, SEM can be much more complex than this. For example, as noted above, nonrecursive models with feedback loops can better tease out causal relations among variables, but they are much more complicated to build than the simple mediation model in this chapter (which, frankly, wasn't so simple!). It is also possible to incorporate moderating variables into structural models, but, again, I thought that this might be outside the scope of an applied statistics textbook and, besides, you already learned moderation in Chapter 9 where we discussed the PROCESS Macro. There is a whole family of SEM-related methods that we have not covered here, including mean structures analysis, a multigroup method that is essentially like a *t*-test or an ANOVA, but with a latent outcome variable. Even though we didn't cover these methods here, I encourage you to keep reading and keep learning. Statistics *are* the future because they enable us to understand and *predict* the future.

Well, we've now reached the end of the book. I promised myself I wouldn't cry, but we've been through so much together. From Chapter 1, where you knew little or nothing about statistics, to Chapter 12, where you are now building advanced multivariate models, I think it's fair to say that you've come a long way. I'm not one for long good-byes, so let me be frank in saying that I'm proud of you for making it this far and I sincerely hope you have a new appreciation for statistics and data science. Thank you for the time and effort you've put into this epic journey.

Further Reading

Bollen, K. (1989). *Structural equations with latent variables*. John Wiley.

Byrne, B. M. (2010). *Structural equation modeling with AMOS: Basic concepts, applications, and programming (multivariate applications series)*. Taylor & Francis.

Hu, L. T., & Bentler, P. M. (1999). Cutoff criteria for fit indexes in covariance structure analysis: Conventional criteria versus new alternatives. *Structural Equation Modeling: A Multidisciplinary Journal*, 6(1), 1-55.

Kline, R. B. (2012). *Principles and practice of structural equation modeling*. Guilford.

Sivo, S. A., Fan, X., Witta, E. L., & Willse, J. T. (2006). The search for 'optimal' cutoff properties: Fit index criteria in structural equation modeling. *Journal of Experimental Education, 74*(3), 267-288.

Timming, A., & Summers, J. (2020). Is workplace democracy associated with wider pro-democracy affect? A structural equation model. *Economic and Industrial Democracy, 41*(3), 709-726.

In-Class Discussion Questions

1.   What is structural equation modeling (also commonly referred to as analysis of covariance structures)? Why and when is it preferable to the use of linear regression analysis?
2.   To which types of variables in an SEM do you need to add a residual term? What does the residual term signify? How is it typically displayed in an SEM?
3.   What are modification indices? Why should they be used cautiously in structural equation modeling? Do they pose a threat to the 'confirmatory' nature of structural equation modeling?
4.   How do you test for mediation in the context of an SEM?
5.   Articulate some research questions that management scientists might answer using structural equation modeling? Why types of variables, observed and unobservable, might be included on those models?
6.   How do you report and interpret the results of an SEM?

Appendix A

The
Workplace
Employment
Relations
Study

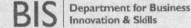

BIS | Department for Business Innovation & Skills

Workplace Employment Relations Study 2011

Carried out for the Department for Business, Innovation and Skills*

SURVEY OF EMPLOYEES

Completing this questionnaire

This is a national survey of people at work. We are interested in your views about your job and your workplace.

 You can also complete the questionnaire online. Please see the accompanying letter for information on how to do this.

Everything that you say in this questionnaire will remain confidential.

The questionnaire should take no more than 15 minutes to fill in.

Please use a blue or black pen to complete the questionnaire, and try to answer every question.

Please try to return the completed questionnaire within the next two weeks.

Thank you for your help.

*In collaboration with Acas, UK Commission for Employment and Skills, the Economic and Social Research Council, and the National Institute of Economic and Social Research.

A. ABOUT YOUR JOB

A1 How many years in total have you been working at this workplace? By workplace we mean the site or location at, or from, which you work.

Less than 1 year	1 to less than 2 years	2 to less than 5 years	5 to less than 10 years	10 years or more
☐	☐	☐	☐	☐

A2 Which of the phrases below best describes your job here?

Tick one box only

Permanent ☐
Temporary – with no agreed end date ☐
Fixed period – with an agreed end date ☐

A3 What are your basic or contractual hours each week in your job at this workplace, excluding any paid or unpaid overtime?

Contracted hours (to nearest hour) ☐☐

A4 How many hours do you usually work in your job each week, including overtime or extra hours? *Exclude meal breaks and time taken to travel to work.*

Usual hours per week (to nearest hour) ☐☐

A5 Do you agree or disagree with the following statements about your job?

Tick one box in each row

	Strongly agree	Agree	Neither agree nor disagree	Disagree	Strongly disagree	Don't know
My job requires that I work very hard	☐	☐	☐	☐	☐	☐
I never seem to have enough time to get my work done	☐	☐	☐	☐	☐	☐
I feel my job is secure in this workplace	☐	☐	☐	☐	☐	☐

A6 Think about how people in your kind of job progress – for example get a promotion. Do you agree or disagree that people in this workplace who want to progress usually have to put in long hours?

Tick one box only

Strongly agree	Agree	Neither agree nor disagree	Disagree	Strongly disagree
☐	☐	☐	☐	☐

A7 In general, how much influence do you have over the following?

Tick one box in each row

	A lot	Some	A little	None	Don't know
The tasks you do in your job	☐	☐	☐	☐	☐
The pace at which you work	☐	☐	☐	☐	☐
How you do your work	☐	☐	☐	☐	☐
The order in which you carry out tasks	☐	☐	☐	☐	☐
The time you start or finish your working day	☐	☐	☐	☐	☐

A8 How satisfied are you with the following aspects of your job?

Tick one box in each row

	Very satisfied	Satisfied	Neither satisfied nor dissatisfied	Dissatisfied	Very dissatisfied	Don't know
The sense of achievement you get from your work	☐	☐	☐	☐	☐	☐
The scope for using your own initiative	☐	☐	☐	☐	☐	☐
The amount of influence you have over your job	☐	☐	☐	☐	☐	☐
The training you receive	☐	☐	☐	☐	☐	☐
The opportunity to develop your skills in your job	☐	☐	☐	☐	☐	☐
The amount of pay you receive	☐	☐	☐	☐	☐	☐
Your job security	☐	☐	☐	☐	☐	☐
The work itself	☐	☐	☐	☐	☐	☐

A9 Thinking of the past few weeks, how much of the time has your job made you feel each of the following?

Tick one box in each row

	All of the time	Most of the time	Some of the time	Occasionally	Never
Tense	☐	☐	☐	☐	☐
Depressed	☐	☐	☐	☐	☐
Worried	☐	☐	☐	☐	☐
Gloomy	☐	☐	☐	☐	☐
Uneasy	☐	☐	☐	☐	☐
Miserable	☐	☐	☐	☐	☐

B. ABOUT YOUR WORKPLACE

B1 In the last 12 months, have you made use of any of the following arrangements, and if not, are they available to you if you needed them?

Tick one box in each row

	I have used this arrangement	Available to me but I do not use	Not available to me	Don't know
Flexi-time	☐	☐	☐	☐
Job sharing (sharing a full-time job with someone)	☐	☐	☐	☐
The chance to reduce your working hours (e.g. full-time to part-time)	☐	☐	☐	☐
Working the same number of hours per week across fewer days (e.g. 37 hours in four days instead of five)	☐	☐	☐	☐
Working at or from home in normal working hours	☐	☐	☐	☐
Working only during school term times	☐	☐	☐	☐
Paid leave to care for dependents in an emergency	☐	☐	☐	☐

B2 Now thinking about both your commitments at this workplace and outside of work, do you agree or disagree with the following?

Tick one box in each row

	Strongly agree	Agree	Neither agree nor disagree	Disagree	Strongly disagree
I often find it difficult to fulfil my commitments outside of work because of the amount of time I spend on my job	☐	☐	☐	☐	☐
I often find it difficult to do my job properly because of my commitments outside of work	☐	☐	☐	☐	☐

B3 Apart from health and safety training, how much training have you had during the last 12 months, either paid for or organised by your employer? *Please only include training where you have been given time off from your normal daily work duties to undertake the training.*

Tick one box only

None	Less than 1 day	1 to less than 2 days	2 to less than 5 days	5 to less than 10 days	10 days or more
☐	☐	☐	☐	☐	☐

B4 How well do the work skills you personally have match the skills you need to do your present job?

Tick one box only

	Much higher	A bit higher	About the same	A bit lower	Much lower
My own skills are	☐	☐	☐	☐	☐

B5 Did any of the following happen to you as a result of the most recent recession, whilst working at this workplace?

Tick all that apply

I was not working at this workplace during the recession ☐ → Go to **B6**

My workload increased ☐

My work was reorganised ☐

I was moved to another job ☐

My wages were frozen or cut ☐

My non-wage benefits (e.g. vehicles or meals) were reduced ☐

My contracted working hours were reduced ☐

Access to paid overtime was restricted ☐

I was required to take unpaid leave ☐

Access to training was restricted ☐

None of the above ☐

B6 In general, how good would you say managers at this workplace are at keeping employees informed about the following?

Tick one box in each row

	Very good	Good	Neither good nor poor	Poor	Very poor	Don't know
Changes to the way the organisation is being run	☐	☐	☐	☐	☐	☐
Changes in staffing	☐	☐	☐	☐	☐	☐
Changes in the way you do your job	☐	☐	☐	☐	☐	☐
Financial matters, including budgets or profits	☐	☐	☐	☐	☐	☐

B7 Overall, how good would you say managers at this workplace are at...

Tick one box in each row

	Very good	Good	Neither good nor poor	Poor	Very poor	Don't know
Seeking the views of employees or employee representatives	☐	☐	☐	☐	☐	☐
Responding to suggestions from employees or employee representatives	☐	☐	☐	☐	☐	☐
Allowing employees or employee representatives to influence final decisions	☐	☐	☐	☐	☐	☐

B8 Overall, how satisfied are you with the amount of involvement you have in decision-making at this workplace? *Tick one box only*

Very satisfied	Satisfied	Neither satisfied nor dissatisfied	Dissatisfied	Very dissatisfied
☐	☐	☐	☐	☐

C. YOUR VIEWS ABOUT WORKING HERE

C1 To what extent do you agree or disagree with the following statements about working here?

Tick one box in each row

	Strongly agree	Agree	Neither agree nor disagree	Disagree	Strongly disagree	Don't know
Using my own initiative I carry out tasks that are not required as part of my job	☐	☐	☐	☐	☐	☐
I share many of the values of my organisation	☐	☐	☐	☐	☐	☐
I feel loyal to my organisation	☐	☐	☐	☐	☐	☐
I am proud to tell people who I work for	☐	☐	☐	☐	☐	☐

C2 Now thinking about the managers at this workplace, to what extent do you agree or disagree with the following?

Tick one box in each row

Managers here...	Strongly agree	Agree	Neither agree nor disagree	Disagree	Strongly disagree	Don't know
Can be relied upon to keep to their promises	☐	☐	☐	☐	☐	☐
Are sincere in attempting to understand employees' views	☐	☐	☐	☐	☐	☐
Deal with employees honestly	☐	☐	☐	☐	☐	☐
Understand about employees having to meet responsibilities outside work	☐	☐	☐	☐	☐	☐
Encourage people to develop their skills	☐	☐	☐	☐	☐	☐
Treat employees fairly	☐	☐	☐	☐	☐	☐

C3 In general, how would you describe relations between managers and employees here?

Tick one box only

Very good	Good	Neither good nor poor	Poor	Very poor
☐	☐	☐	☐	☐

D. REPRESENTATION AT WORK

D1 Are you a member of a trade union or staff association?

Tick one box only

Yes	No, but have been in the past	No, have never been a member
☐	☐	☐

D2 Ideally, who do you think would best represent you in dealing with managers here about the following?

Tick one box in each row

	Myself	Trade Union	Employee representative (non-union)	Line manager	Another employee
Getting increases in your pay	☐	☐	☐	☐	☐
If your employer wanted to reduce your hours or pay	☐	☐	☐	☐	☐
Getting training	☐	☐	☐	☐	☐
If you wanted to make a complaint about working here	☐	☐	☐	☐	☐
If a manager wanted to discipline you	☐	☐	☐	☐	☐

D3 How would you describe management's general attitude towards trade union membership among employees here?

Management is....

Tick one box only

In favour of trade union membership	☐
Not in favour of trade union membership	☐
Neutral about it	☐
Don't know	☐

D4 Is there a trade union or staff association at this workplace?

Tick one box only

Yes	☐ → Go to **D5**
No	☐
Don't know	☐ → Go to **E1**

D5 Do you agree or disagree with the following statements about unions or staff associations at this workplace?

Tick one box in each row

Unions/staff associations here...	Strongly agree	Agree	Neither agree nor disagree	Disagree	Strongly disagree	Don't know
...take notice of members' problems and complaints	☐	☐	☐	☐	☐	☐
...are taken seriously by management	☐	☐	☐	☐	☐	☐
...make a difference to what it is like to work here	☐	☐	☐	☐	☐	☐

E. FINALLY, ABOUT YOURSELF

E1 Are you male or female?

Male ☐   Female ☐

E2 How old are you?   *Tick one box only*

16-17 ☐   22-29 ☐   50-59 ☐

18-19 ☐   30-39 ☐   60-64 ☐

20-21 ☐   40-49 ☐   65 and above ☐

E3 Which of the following describes your current status?

Tick one box only

Single	Married or living with a partner	Divorced/separated	Widowed
☐	☐	☐	☐

E4 How many dependent children do you have, if any, in the following age groups?

Enter number of children   *Enter number of children*   *Tick if applies*

0 – 2 years ☐   8 – 11 years ☐   No dependent children ☐

3 – 4 years ☐   12 – 15 years ☐

5 – 7 years ☐   16 – 18 years ☐

E5 Do you look after or give help or support to any family members or friends who have a long-term physical or mental illness or disability, or who have problems related to old age?

Tick one box only

No	Yes, 0 – 4 hours a week	Yes, 5 – 9 hours a week	Yes, 10 – 19 hours a week	Yes, 20 – 34 hours a week	Yes, 35 or more hours a week
☐	☐	☐	☐	☐	☐

E6 Are your day-to-day activities limited because of a health problem or disability which has lasted, or is expected to last, at least 12 months? *Please include problems related to old age.*

Tick one box only

No	Yes, limited a little	Yes, limited a lot
☐	☐	☐

E7 Which, if any, of the following academic, vocational or professional qualifications have you obtained? *Tick all that apply*

GCSE grades D-G/CSE grades 2-5, SCE O grades D-E/SCE Standard grades 4-7 ☐

GCSE grades A-C, GCE 'O'-level passes, CSE grade 1, SCE O grades A-C, SCE Standard grades 1-3 ☐

1 GCE 'A'-level grades A-E, 1-2 SCE Higher grades A-C, AS levels ☐

2 or more GCE 'A'-levels grades A-E, 3 or more SCE Higher grades A-C ☐

First degree, eg BSc, BA, BEd, HND, HNC, MA at first degree level ☐

Higher degree, eg MSc, MA, MBA, PGCE, PhD ☐

Other academic qualifications ☐

No academic qualifications ☐

Level 1 NVQ or SVQ, Foundation GNVQ or GSVQ ☐

Level 2 NVQ or SVQ, Intermediate GNVQ or GSVQ, City and Guilds Craft, BTEC First/General Diploma, RSA Diploma ☐

Level 3 NVQ or SVQ, Advanced GNVQ or GSVQ, City and Guilds Advanced Craft, BTEC National, RSA Advanced Diploma ☐

Level 4 NVQ or SVQ, RSA Higher Diploma, BTEC Higher level ☐

Level 5 NVQ or SVQ ☐

Completion of trade apprenticeship ☐

Other vocational or pre-vocational qualifications, e.g. OCR ☐

Other professional qualifications, e.g. qualified teacher, accountant, nurse ☐

No vocational or professional qualifications ☐

E8 What is the full title of your main job?
e.g. Primary School Teacher, State Registered Nurse, Car Mechanic, Benefits Assistant. If you are a civil servant or local government officer, please give your job title, not your grade or pay band.

E9 Describe what you do in your main job. Please describe as fully as possible.

E10 Do you supervise any other employees? *A supervisor, foreman or line manager is responsible for overseeing the work of other employees on a day-to-day basis.*

Yes ☐   No ☐

E11 **How much do you get paid for your job here, before tax and other deductions are taken out?** *If your pay before tax changes from week to week because of overtime, or because you work different hours each week, think about what you earn on average.*

Tick one box only

£60 or less per week (£3,120 or less per year) ☐
£61 - £100 per week (£3,121 - £5,200 per year) ☐
£101 - £130 per week (£5,201 - £6,760 per year) ☐
£131 - £170 per week (£6,761 - £8,840 per year) ☐
£171 - £220 per week (£8,841 - £11,440 per year) ☐
£221 - £260 per week (£11,441 - £13,520 per year) ☐
£261 - £310 per week (£13,521 - £16,120 per year) ☐
£311 - £370 per week (£16,121 - £19,240 per year) ☐
£371 - £430 per week (£19,241 - £22,360 per year) ☐
£431 - £520 per week (£22,361 - £27,040 per year) ☐
£521 - £650 per week (£27,041 - £33,800 per year) ☐
£651 - £820 per week (£33,801 - £42,640 per year) ☐
£821 - £1,050 per week (£42,641 - £54,600 per year) ☐
£1,051 or more per week (£54,601 or more per year) ☐

E12 **Which of the following do you receive in your job here?**

Tick all that apply

Basic fixed salary/wage ☐
Payments based on your individual performance or output ☐
Payments based on the overall performance of a group or a team ☐
Payments based on the overall performance of your workplace or organisation (e.g. profit-sharing scheme) ☐
Extra payments for additional hours of work or overtime ☐
Contributions to a pension scheme ☐

E13 To which of these groups do you consider you belong?

Tick one box only

White

British ☐

Irish ☐

Any other white background ☐

Mixed

White and Black Caribbean ☐

White and Black African ☐

White and Asian ☐

Any other mixed background ☐

Asian or Asian British

Indian ☐

Pakistani ☐

Bangladeshi ☐

Chinese ☐

Any other Asian background ☐

Black or Black British

Caribbean ☐

African ☐

Any other Black background ☐

Other ethnic group

Arab ☐

Any other ethnic group ☐

E14 What is your religion?

Tick one box only

No religion ☐

Christian (including Church of England, Church of Scotland, Catholic, Protestant, and all other Christian denominations) ☐

Buddhist ☐

Hindu ☐

Jewish ☐

Muslim ☐

Sikh ☐

Another religion ☐

E15 Which of the following options best describes how you think of yourself? 2020

Tick one box only

Heterosexual or straight	Gay or lesbian	Bisexual	Other	Prefer not to say
☐	☐	☐	☐	☐

E16 Do you have any final comments you would like to make about your workplace, or about this questionnaire?

Thank you for taking the time to complete this questionnaire.

Please now return the questionnaire by using the freepost envelope provided.

References

Aguinis, H., & Branstetter, S. A. (2007). Teaching the concept of the sampling distribution of the mean. *Journal of Management Education, 31*(4), 467–483. https://doi.org/10.1177/1052562906290211

Allison, P. D. (1999). *Multiple regression: A primer*. Pine Forge Press.

Appelbaum, A., Bailey, T., Berg, P., & Kalleberg, A. L. (2000). *Manufacturing advantage: Why high performance work systems pay off*. ILR Press.

Babbie, E. R. (2020). *The practice of social research*. Cengage Learning.

Bakker, M., & Wicherts, J. M. (2014). Outlier removal, sum scores, and the inflation of the Type I error rate in independent samples *t* tests: The power of alternatives and recommendations. *Psychological Methods, 19*(3), 409–427. https://doi.org/10.1037/met0000014

Barnard, G. A. (1984). Comparing the means of two independent samples. *Journal of the Royal Statistical Society: Series C (Applied Statistics), 33*(3), 266–271. https://doi.org/10.2307/2347702

Berk, R. A. (2004). *Regression analysis: A constructive critique* (Vol. 11). Sage. https://doi.org/10.4135/9781483348834

Berkson, J. (1938). Some difficulties of interpretation encountered in the application of the chi-square test. *Journal of the American Statistical Association, 33*(203), 526–536. https://doi.org/10.1080/01621459.1938.10502329

Berry, W. D., Feldman, S., & Stanley Feldman, D. (1985). *Multiple regression in practice* (No. 50). Sage. https://doi.org/10.4135/9781412985208

Bollen, K. (1989). *Structural equations with latent variables*. John Wiley. https://doi.org/10.1002/9781118619179

Brown, T. A. (2015). Confirmatory factor analysis for applied research. Guilford Press.

Bryman, A. (2012). *Social research methods* (4th ed.). Oxford University Press.

Bryson, A., Cappellari, L., & Lucifora, C. (2004). Does union membership really reduce job satisfaction? *British Journal of Industrial Relations, 42*(3), 439–459. https://doi.org/10.1002/9781118619179

Budd, J. W., Lamare, J. R., & Timming, A. R. (2018). Learning about democracy at work: Cross-national evidence on the effects of employee participation in workplace decision-making on political participation in civil society. *Industrial and Labor Relations Review, 71*(4), 956–985. https://doi.org/10.1177/0019793917746619

Byrne, B. M. (2010). Structural equation modeling with AMOS: Basic concepts, applications, and programming (multivariate applications series). Taylor & Francis.

Cardinal, R. N., & Aitken, M. R. (2013). *ANOVA for the behavioral sciences researcher*. Psychology Press. https://doi.org/10.4324/9780203763933

Chatterjee, S., & Hadi, A. S. (2015). *Regression analysis by example*. John Wiley.

Coleman, J. S. (1994). *Foundations of social theory*. Harvard University Press.

Cortina, J. M., & Nouri, H. (2000). *Effect size for ANOVA designs* (No. 129). Sage. https://doi.org/10.4135/9781412984010

Costello, A. B., & Osborne, J. (2005). Best practices in exploratory factor analysis: Four recommendations for getting the most from your analysis. *Practical Assessment, Research, and Evaluation, 10*(1), Article 7, 1–9.

Cox, D. R. (2006). *Principles of statistical inference*. Cambridge University Press. https://doi.org/10.1017/CBO9780511813559

Cully, M., Woodland, S., O'Reilly, A., & Dix, G. (1999). *Britain at work*. Routledge. https://doi.org/10.4324/9780203165386

Daniel, W. W., & Millward, N. (1983). *Workplace industrial relations in Britain*. Heinemann.

Darlington, R. B., & Hayes, A. F. (2017). *Regression analysis and linear models*. Guilford Press.

Derrick, B. (2017). How to compare the means of two samples that include paired observations and independent observations: A companion to Derrick, Russ, Toher and White (2017). *Quantitative Methods for Psychology, 13*(2), 120–126. https://doi.org/10.20982/tqmp.13.2.p120

Dickerson, A. P., Gibson, H. B., & Tsakalotos, E. (1997). The impact of acquisitions on company performance: Evidence from a large panel of UK firms. *Oxford Economic Papers, 49*(3), 344–361. https://doi.org/10.1093/oxfordjournals.oep.a028613

Dillman, D. A., Smyth, J. D., & Christian, L. M. (2014). *Internet, phone, mail, and mixed-mode surveys: The tailored design method* (4th ed.). John Wiley.

Dinov, I. D., Christou, N., & Sanchez, J. (2008). Central limit theorem: New SOCR applet and demonstration activity. *Journal of Statistics Education, 16*(2), 1–15. https://doi.org/10.1080/10691898.2008.11889560

Fabrigar, L. R., & Wegener, D. T. (2011). *Exploratory factor analysis*. Oxford University Press. https://doi.org/10.1093/acprof:osobl/9780199734177.001.0001

Feldman, D. C., & Bolino, M. C. (1999). The impact of on-site mentoring on expatriate socialization: A structural equation modelling approach. *International Journal of Human Resource Management, 10*(1), 54–71. https://doi.org/10.1080/095851999340639

Field, A. (2018). Discovering statistics using IBM SPSS. Sage.

Fink, A (2003) *How to design survey studies*. Sage. https://doi.org/10.4135/9781412984447

Franke, T. M., Ho, T., & Christie, C. A. (2012). The chi-square test: Often used and more often misinterpreted. *American Journal of Evaluation, 33*(3), 448–458. https://doi.org/10.1177/1098214011426594

French, M. T., Popovici, I., & Timming, A. R. (2020). Analysing the effect of commuting time on earnings among young adults. *Applied Economics, 52*(48), 5282–5297. https://doi.org/10.1080/00036846.2020.1761537

George, D., & Mallery, P. (2019). *IBM SPSS statistics 26 step by step: A simple guide and reference*. Routledge. https://doi.org/10.4324/9780429056765

Gibbons, J. D., & Chakraborti, S. (1991). Comparisons of the Mann–Whitney, Student's *t*, and alternate *t* tests for means of normal distributions. *Journal of Experimental Education, 59*(3), 258–267. https://doi.org/10.1080/00220973.1991.10806565

Girden, E. R. (1992). *ANOVA: Repeated measures* (No. 84). Sage. https://doi.org/10.4135/9781412983419

Gosling, S. D., Rentfrow, P. J., & Swann, W. B., Jr. (2003). A very brief measure of the Big-Five personality domains. *Journal of Research in Personality, 37*(6), 504–528. https://doi.org/10.1016/S0092-6566(03)00046-1

Guest, D. E. (2011). Human resource management and performance: Still searching for some answers. *Human Resource Management Journal, 21*(1), 3–13. https://doi.org/10.1016/S0092-6566(03)00046-1

Hall, P. A., & Soskice, D. (Eds.). (2001). Varieties of capitalism: The institutional foundations of comparative advantage. Oxford University Press.

Hanna, D., & Dempster, M. (2013). *Psychology statistics for dummies*. John Wiley.

Hanneman, R. A., Kposowa, A. J., & Riddle, M. D. (2012). *Basic statistics for social research* (Vol. 38). John Wiley.

Harrington, D. (2009). *Confirmatory factor analysis*. Oxford University Press. https://doi.org/10.1093/acprof:oso/9780195339888.001.0001

Hayes, A. F. (2017). Introduction to mediation, moderation, and conditional process analysis: A regression-based approach. Guilford Press.

Healey, J. F. (1999). *Statistics: A tool for social research* (5th ed.). Wadsworth.

Heiman, G. (2013). Basic statistics for the behavioral sciences. Cengage Learning.

Henry, G. T. (1990). *Practical sampling* (Vol. 21). Sage. https://doi.org/10.4135/9781412985451

Hilbe, J. M. (2009). *Logistic regression models*. Chapman & Hall/CRC. https://doi.org/10.1201/9781420075779

Holcomb, Z. (2016). *Fundamentals of descriptive statistics*. Routledge. https://doi.org/10.4324/9781315266510

Holmes Finch, W., & French, B. F. (2015). Modeling of nonrecursive structural equation models with categorical indicators. *Structural Equation Modeling: A Multidisciplinary Journal, 22*(3), 416–428. https://doi.org/10.1080/10705511.2014.937380

Hosmer, D. W., Jr., Lemeshow, S., & Sturdivant, R. X. (2013). *Applied logistic regression* (Vol. *398*). John Wiley. https://doi.org/10.1002/9781118548387

Hu, L. T., & Bentler, P. M. (1999). Cutoff criteria for fit indexes in covariance structure analysis: Conventional criteria versus new alternatives. *Structural Equation Modeling: A Multidisciplinary Journal, 6*(1), 1–55.

Huck, S. W., Ren, B., & Yang, H. (2007). A new way to teach (or compute) Pearson's r without reliance on cross-products. *Teaching Statistics, 29*(1), 13–16. https://doi.org/10.1111/j.1467-9639.2007.00240.x

Hurley, A. E., Scandura, T. A., Schriesheim, C. A., Brannick, M. T., Seers, A., Vandenberg, R. J., & Williams, L. J. (1997). Exploratory and confirmatory factor analysis: Guidelines, issues, and alternatives. *Journal of Organizational Behavior, 18*(6), 667–683. https://doi.org/10.1002/(SICI)1099-1379(199711)18:6<667::AID-JOB874>3E3.0.CO;2-T

Jackson, J. J., Wood, D., Bogg, T., Walton, K. E., Harms, P. D., & Roberts, B. W. (2010). What do conscientious people do? Development and validation of the behavioral indicators of conscientiousness (BIC). *Journal of Research in Personality, 44*(4), 501–511. https://doi.org/10.1016/j.jrp.2010.06.005

Jick, T. D. (1979). Mixing qualitative and quantitative methods: Triangulation in action. *Administrative Science Quarterly, 24*(4), 602–611. https://doi.org/10.2307/2392366

Jolliffe, I. T., & Cadima, J. (2016). Principal component analysis: A review and recent developments. *Philosophical Transactions of the Royal Society A: Mathematical, Physical and Engineering Sciences, 374*(2065), Article 20150202. https://doi.org/10.1098/rsta.2015.0202

Kader, G., & Franklin, C. (2008). The evolution of Pearson's correlation coefficient. *The Mathematics Teacher, 102*(4), 292–299. https://doi.org/10.5951/MT.102.4.0292

Kersley, B., Alpin, C., Forth, J., Bryson, A., Bewley, H., Dix, G., & Oxenbridge, S. (2006). *Inside the workplace*. Routledge.

Kleinbaum, D. G., Dietz, K., Gail, M., Klein, M., & Klein, M. (2002). *Logistic regression*. Springer-Verlag.

Kline, R. B. (2015). Principles and practice of structural equation modeling. Guilford Press.

Knight, G. A., & Cavusgil, S. T. (2004). Innovation, organizational capabilities, and the born-global firm. *Journal of International Business Studies, 35*(2), 124–141. https://doi.org/10.1057/palgrave.jibs.8400071

Krosnick, J. A. (2018). Questionnaire design. In D. L. Vannette & J. A. Krosnick (Eds.), *The Palgrave handbook of survey research* (pp. 439–455). Palgrave Macmillan. https://doi.org/10.1007/978-3-319-54395-6_53

Kyburg, H. E., Jr. (2012). *The logical foundations of statistical inference* (Vol. *65*). Springer Science & Business Media.

Leech, N. L., Barrett, K. C., & Morgan, G. A. (2014). *IBM SPSS for intermediate statistics: Use and interpretation*. Routledge. https://doi.org/10.4324/9780203122778

Lewis, D., & Burke, C. J. (1949). The use and misuse of the chi-square test. *Psychological Bulletin, 46*(6), 433–489. https://doi.org/10.1037/h0059088

Lind, D. A., Marchal, W. G., & Wathen, S. A. (2019). *Basic statistics for business and economics*. McGraw-Hill.

Lu, J. W., & Beamish, P. W. (2001). The internationalization and performance of SMEs. *Strategic Management Journal, 22*(6–7), 565–586. https://doi.org/10.1002/smj.184

Mattila, A. S., & Wirtz, J. (2001). Congruency of scent and music as a driver of in-store evaluations and behavior. *Journal of Retailing, 77*(2), 273–289. https://doi.org/10.1016/S0022-4359(01)00042-2

Menard, S. (2002). *Applied logistic regression analysis* (Vol. *106*). Sage. https://doi.org/10.4135/9781412983433

Miller, R. G., Jr. (1997). *Beyond ANOVA: Basics of applied statistics*. Chapman & Hall/CRC Press. https://doi.org/10.1201/b15236

Millward, N., & Stevens, M. (1986) *British workplace industrial relations, 1980–1984*. Gower. https://doi.org/10.1111/j.1467-8543.1987.tb00713.x

Millward, N., Stevens, M., Smart, D., & Hawes, W. R. (1992). *Workplace industrial relations in transition*. Dartmouth.

Mood, C. (2010). Logistic regression: Why we cannot do what we think we can do, and what we can do about it. *European Sociological Review, 26*(1), 67–82. https://doi.org/10.1093/esr/jcp006

Pallant, J. (2020). SPSS survival manual: A step by step guide to data analysis using IBM SPSS. Routledge. https://doi.org/10.4324/9781003117445

Pampel, F. C. (2000). *Logistic regression: A primer* (Vol. *132*). Sage. https://doi.org/10.4135/9781412984805

Pett, M. A., Lackey, N. R., & Sullivan, J. J. (2003). Rotating the factors. In *Making sense of factor analysis* (pp. 131–166). Sage. https://www.doi.org/10.4135/9781412984898

Popper, K. (2005). *The logic of scientific discovery*. Routledge. https://doi.org/10.4324/9780203994627

Pugh, S. D. (2001). Service with a smile: Emotional contagion in the service encounter. *Academy of Management Journal, 44*(5), 1018–1027. https://doi.org/10.5465/3069445

Rasch, D., Teuscher, F., & Guiard, V. (2007). How robust are tests for two independent samples? *Journal of Statistical Planning and Inference, 137*(8), 2706–2720. https://doi.org/10.1016/j.jspi.2006.04.011

Rawlings, J. O., Pantula, S. G., & Dickey, D. A. (2001). *Applied regression analysis: A research tool*. Springer Science & Business Media.

Reid, N., & Cox, D. R. (2015). On some principles of statistical inference. *International Statistical Review, 83*(2), 293–308. https://doi.org/10.1111/insr.12067

Rietveld, T., & van Hout, R. (2015). The *t* test and beyond: Recommendations for testing the central tendencies of two independent samples in research on speech, language and hearing pathology. *Journal of Communication Disorders, 58*, 158–168. https://doi.org/10.1016/j.jcomdis.2015.08.002

Roberts, A., & Roberts, J. M., Jr. (2020). *Multiple regression: A practical introduction*. Sage.

Rochon, J., Gondan, M., & Kieser, M. (2012). To test or not to test: Preliminary assessment of normality when comparing two independent samples. *BMC Medical Research Methodology, 12*(1), 1–11. https://doi.org/10.1186/1471-2288-12-81

Rutherford, A. (2001). Introducing ANOVA and ANCOVA: A GLM approach. Sage.

Schmidt, F. L., & Hunter, J. (2004). General mental ability in the world of work: Occupational attainment and job performance. *Journal of Personality and Social Psychology, 86*(1), 162–173. https://doi.org/10.1037/0022-3514.86.1.162

Sharpe, D. (2015). Chi-square test is statistically significant: Now what? *Practical Assessment, Research, and Evaluation, 20*(1), Article *8*, 1–10.

Sivo, S. A., Fan, X., Witta, E. L., & Willse, J. T. (2006). The search for 'optimal' cutoff properties: Fit index criteria in structural equation modeling. *Journal of Experimental Education, 74*(3), 267–288. https://doi.org/10.3200/JEXE.74.3.267-288

Spector, P. E. (1997). Job satisfaction: Application, assessment, causes, and consequences. Sage. https://doi.org/10.4135/9781452231549

Stern, M. J., Bilgen, I., & Dillman, D. A. (2014). The state of survey methodology: Challenges, dilemmas, and new frontiers in the era of the tailored design. *Field Methods, 26*(3), 284–301. https://doi.org/10.1177/1525822X13519561

Sudman, S., & Bradburn, N. M. (1982). Asking questions: A practical guide to questionnaire design. Jossey-Bass.

Tabachnick, B. G., & Fidell, L. S. (2019). *Using multivariate statistics* (7th ed.). Pearson.

Thompson, S. K. (2012). *Sampling* (3rd ed.). John Wiley.https://doi.org/10.1002/9781118162934

Timming, A. R. (2009). WERS the validity? A critique of the 2004 Workplace Employment Relations survey of employees. *Work, Employment and Society, 23*(3), 561–570. https://doi.org/10.1177/0950017009337070

Timming, A. R. (2010a). Cross-national variations in the determinants of job satisfaction: How far do our results 'travel'? *International Journal of Organization Theory and Behavior, 13*(4), 525–545. https://doi.org/10.1108/IJOTB-13-04-2010-B004

Timming, A. R. (2010b). Dissonant cognitions in European works councils: A 'comparative ethnomethodological' approach. *Economic and Industrial Democracy, 31*(4), 521–535. https://doi.org/10.1177/0143831X10365928

Timming, A. R. (2012). Tracing the effects of employee involvement and participation on trust in managers: An analysis of covariance structures. *International Journal of Human Resource Management, 23*(15), 3243–3257. https://doi.org/10.1080/09585192.2011.637058

Timming, A. R. (2015). Visible tattoos in the service sector: A new challenge to recruitment and selection. *Work, Employment and Society, 29*(1), 60–78. https://doi.org/10.1177/0950017014528402

Timming, A. R. (2017a). Body art as branded labour: At the intersection of employee selection and relationship marketing. *Human Relations, 70*(9), 1041–1063. https://doi.org/10.1177/0018726716681654

Timming, A. R. (2017b). The effect of foreign accent on employability: A study of the aural dimensions of aesthetic labour in customer-facing and non-customer-facing jobs. *Work, Employment and Society, 31*(3), 409–428. https://doi.org/10.1177/0950017016630260

Timming, A. R. (2019). Human resource management and evolutionary psychology: Exploring the biological foundations of managing people at work. Edward Elgar. https://doi.org/10.4337/9781788977913

Timming, A. R., French, M. T., & Fan, D. (2019). Exploring the fluid boundary between 'legitimate performance management' and 'downward bullying': An experimental approach. *Industrial Relations Journal, 50*(4), 348–361. https://doi.org/10.1111/irj.12262

Timming, A. R., French, M. T., & Mortensen, K. (2021). Health anxiety versus economic anxiety surrounding COVID-19: An analysis of psychological distress in the early stages of the pandemic. *Journal of Affective Disorders Reports, 5*, Article 100152. https://doi.org/10.1016/j.jadr.2021.100152

Timming, A. R., Nickson, D., Re, D., & Perrett, D. (2017). What do you think of my ink? Assessing the effects of body art on employment chances. *Human Resource Management, 56*(1), 133–149. https://doi.org/10.1002/hrm.21770

Timming, A., & Summers, J. (2020). Is workplace democracy associated with wider pro-democracy affect? A structural equation model. *Economic and Industrial Democracy, 41*(3), 709–726. https://doi.org/10.1177/0143831X17744028

van Wanrooy, B., Bewley, H., Bryson, A., Forth, J., Freeth, S., Stokes, L., & Wood, S. (2013). *Employment relations in the shadow of recession.* Palgrave Macmillan. https://doi.org/10.1007/978-1-137-27578-3

Wagner, W. E., III. (2019). Using IBM SPSS statistics for research methods and social science statistics. Sage.

Yung, Y. F., & Bentler, P. M. (1996). Bootstrapping techniques in analysis of mean and covariance structures. In G. A. Marcoulides & R. E. Schumacker (Eds.), *Advanced structural equation modeling: Issues and techniques* (pp. 195–226). Psychology Press.

Index

Page numbers followed by *f, t* and *b* indicate figures, tables and boxes, respectively.

CPSIA information can be obtained
at www.ICGtesting.com
Printed in the USA
JSHW020901240822
29616JS00003B/77